PARENTING

CHALLENGES, PRACTICES AND CULTURAL INFLUENCES

FAMILY ISSUES IN THE 21ST CENTURY

Additional books in this series can be found on Nova's website
under the Series tab.

Additional e-books in this series can be found on Nova's website
under the e-book tab.

CHILDREN'S ISSUES, LAWS AND PROGRAMS

Additional books in this series can be found on Nova's website
under the Series tab.

Additional e-books in this series can be found on Nova's website
under the e-book tab.

PARENTING

CHALLENGES, PRACTICES AND CULTURAL INFLUENCES

PETER BARBERIS

AND

STELIOS PETRAKIS

EDITORS

nova publishers
New York

For permission to use material from this book please contact us:
Telephone 631-231-7269; Fax 631-231-8175
Web Site: http://www.novapublishers.com

NOTICE TO THE READER

he Publisher has taken reasonable care in the preparation of this book, but makes no expressed or implied warranty of any kind and assumes no responsibility for any errors or omissions. No liability is assumed for incidental or consequential damages in connection with or arising out of information contained in this book. The Publisher shall not be liable for any special, consequential, or exemplary damages resulting, in whole or in part, from the readers' use of, or reliance upon, this material. Any parts of this book based on government reports are so indicated and copyright is claimed for those parts to the extent applicable to compilations of such works.

Independent verification should be sought for any data, advice or recommendations contained in this book. In addition, no responsibility is assumed by the publisher for any injury and/or damage to persons or property arising from any methods, products, instructions, ideas or otherwise contained in this publication.

This publication is designed to provide accurate and authoritative information with regard to the subject matter covered herein. It is sold with the clear understanding that the Publisher is not engaged in rendering legal or any other professional services. If legal or any other expert assistance is required, the services of a competent person should be sought. FROM A DECLARATION OF PARTICIPANTS JOINTLY ADOPTED BY A COMMITTEE OF THE AMERICAN BAR ASSOCIATION AND A COMMITTEE OF PUBLISHERS.

Additional color graphics may be available in the e-book version of this book.

Library of Congress Cataloging-in-Publication Data

Parenting : challenges, practices and cultural influences / editors, Peter Barberis and Stelios Petrakis.
    p. cm.
  Includes index.
  ISBN 978-1-62257-881-8 (hbk.)
  1. Parenting. 2. Parenting--Cross-cultural studies. I. Barberis, Peter, 1948- II. Petrakis, Stelios, 1974-
  HQ755.8.P37912 2013
  649'.1--dc23
                        2012034751

Published by Nova Science Publishers, Inc. † New York

CONTENTS

PREFACE

In this book, the authors present current research on the challenges, practices and cultural influences of parenting. Topics discussed in this compilation include young maternal age along with preterm birth and the transition to motherhood; parents' perceptions of their child's mental health problems; Asian-American parenting; culture and parenting; parental influence on children's mate choice; gay and lesbian parenting; and parenting practices in a global world.

Chapter 1 – This chapter presents an overview of the research on preterm birth and adolescent parenting, highlighting the challenges faced during the transition to parenthood in these contexts. Also presented is current research investigating how these factors combine to influence the experience of parenting for young mothers of preterm infants. Parenting as an adolescent has been associated with a range of negative outcomes for both the young woman and her infant. Similarly, preterm birth is also associated with a number of acute and chronic difficulties that make parenting more challenging. It is well documented that maternal mental health influences the woman's ability to parent and, as such, factors that increase stress, anxiety and depression can have ongoing implications for their capacity to parent effectively. Both preterm birth and adolescent parenting are associated with an increased risk of distress and mental health issues. However, little research has investigated how these two factors combine to influence the parenting experience for young women who have preterm infants, despite a theoretical double risk. As such, the research presented in this chapter investigated the experience of parenting, both during the early or acute stages of a preterm birth, and longitudinally over the first year of the infant's life. Quantitative and qualitative longitudinal data from adult mothers of preterm infants, adolescent mothers of full term infants, and adolescent mothers of preterm infants is presented highlighting the specific challenges, as well as similarities, in experiences of parenting.

Results from the quantitative data suggest adult mothers of preterm infants reported higher levels of psychological distress pre-discharge than did adolescent mothers but this difference had dissipated post-discharge. Qualitative data findings supported this result, suggesting that parenting for young women was not unduly altered by having a preterm infant, with few overall differences in the parenting experience for young mothers of preterm and full term infants. Preterm birth compounded the everyday challenges of motherhood for young women, by emphasizing transportation difficulties and placing women in more frequent contact with people who they perceived negatively judged them. Conversely, adult mothers were better able to negotiate the hospital system, eliciting parenting support from staff and other parents. These findings help challenge prevailing assumptions about the transition to motherhood and have implications for service delivery and interventions.

Chapter 2 – Professionals have a fairly clear understanding about the cause, development and maintenance of children's mental health problems based on the developmental psychopathology literature. However, it is unclear whether parents share this complex understanding. Parents' perceptions of their child's mental health problems have been largely unstudied. Using a qualitative method, this chapter described how parents viewed the cause and development of their child's mental health problems. Parents (N=24) seeking help for their child's mental health problem were interviewed. The overarching themes of complexity, ownership and disbelief described parents' perceptions of their child's problems. Parents described a multitude of causes for their child's problems crossing multiple domains (e.g., child, family, community). Four patterns describing how parents integrated the presence of multiple causes were presented (e.g., sequential, equifinality, cumulative, and complex). Three themes revealed how parents viewed the development of their child's problem: precipitating events exacerbated the problem, developmental timeline, and shifts in perspective over time. This chapter highlighted: 1) the importance of implementing a theoretical framework to understand parent's perceptions of mental health, and 2) the importance of a patient-centred care approach to treating children's mental health.

Chapter 3 – Over the past few decades a significant amount of empirical and theoretical work has accumulated in the parenting literature. Even though research methods, instruments, analyses, and theoretical constructs have evolved to a great extent, researchers in this field are still debating on important issues in relation to parenting. What are the challenges that parents face in the twenty first century? How did parents' practices change over time and how do parents still choose to rare their children? Is there such a thing as "universal parenting" or do the authors always have to take into account culturally specific parenting practices and equally specific outcomes? These questions will be at the core of this chapter which aims to bring together current empirical studies and theoretical work utilizing a wide array of parenting literature: from parenting styles and the discussion of the classical authoritarian-authoritative divide, a summary of recent findings in parenting practices such as parental monitoring, behavioral and psychological control, the role of parental involvement, especially in the discussion of a child's adjustment in school, and finally the authors will analyze the issue of parental knowledge; that is, what parents try to know about their child's socialization choices and what they actually know. In theoretical terms, The authors will try to bind together the most important parenting constructs and outcomes in a transactional framework of interpretation, arguing that while parents still shape some of their children's development, children also shape their parents behaviour. Based on this framework the authors argue, in line with other researchers, that the term parenting – which implies a parent to child effects - should be replaced by the term parent-child interactions which allows for a more dynamic and bidirectional interpretation.

Chapter 4 – The present chapter is aimed at a) examining theoretical and empirical contributions on the influences of parental models on partners' relational competences; and b) presenting findings from some recent studies examining parent-adult child similarities on dyadic coping, stress communication, and dyadic forgiveness. In particular, it presents several theoretical approaches (i.e., intergenerational family systems theory, attachment theory, social learning theory, and socialization theory), in which the existence of intergenerational linkages from the family of origin to children's couple relationship has been considered as a key assumption, and some models of the effects of family of origin variables on the offspring's couple relationship that are grounded on such theoretical frameworks. Following this review of intergenerational theories and models, the authors will highlight the importance of taking into account the cultural background when studying parental influences on children's relational competences. Finally, some recent empirical studies will be presented in which parent-child similarities were analyzed with reference to couples' key relational competences: Dyadic coping, stress communication, and dyadic forgiveness. Results of these studies highlighted how parents play a key role of models for children's adult romantic relationship, though children in turn take an active role in discriminating between positive and negative parental models.

Chapter 5 – Because of the uproar arising from Amy Chua's memoir, *Battle Hymn of the Tiger Mother*, Asian American parenting has generated immense interest and controversy. This chapter focuses on the antecedents and consequences of Asian American parenting styles in relation to cultural influences. Specifically, the authors examine Western and Asian conceptualizations of parenting as well as the influence of enculturation and acculturation on Asian American parenting. The authors also explore the challenges associated with cultural gaps between Asian American parents and their children and their implications for parent-child relationships and child outcomes. Implications for future research and practice are discussed.

Chapter 6 – The study of the parenthood has generated a large number of works on the intercultural plan. The main reason of this craze is doubtless that the parenthood is considered as an important vector of the transmission of cultural models, values and practices across human beings within societies. The parents indeed have for universal mission the education of their children. And what is the purpose of the education if it is not to bring the children to become socially competent adults integrated into the cultural group in which they are brought to live? This way, the study of the parenthood in cross-cultural psychology participates in this idea according to which the behavior of both the parents and the children can only be understood in relation to the environment they belong to.

The first objective of the intercultural studies is to highlight what is common to all the human beings regardless of their cultural membership. The common elements are labeled "universals". Universals relative to parenthood are considered in the current paper from several scientific works among which those of LeVine (1977) as a major reference describing the universal purposes of the parental function. Also the works of Keller (2007) have been considered as particularly relevant since they focus on the existence of universal behavioral patterns in parents.

The second objective of the intercultural studies consists in gauging the magnitude of the influence arising from the culture. The present contribution approaches the question of the parenthood in the light of the cultural peculiarities through two important concepts: "developmental niche" and "parental ethnotheories". These theoretical underpinnings of these two concepts are explained and illustrated through recent empirical.

Beyond their main theoretical contribution, these cross-cultural studies on parenting have evident implications in our multicultural societies and in particular for immigrant families, for example in the way they adjust to their host culture, build their social network or find psychosocial support in their surroundings. Moreover, cross-cultural studies on parenting offer to social workers working with immigrant population an excellent means to take distance with regard to their own models or values and to protect themselves of an evident risk of ethnocentrism.

Chapter 7 – Parents and children are not genetically identical and this leads to conflict between the two. One area of disagreement is mate choice, with children choosing spouses who do not comply with the preferences of their parents. In turn, this gives the incentive to the latter to control the mating decisions of their daughters and sons. To facilitate this control, parents employ social institutions that have originally evolved to serve different functions. This chapter attempts to explore how two of these social structures namely, inheritance rights and marriage transactions such as the bridewealth, are used by parents to promote control over mating. In addition, the cross-cultural variability of these institutions is further explored. Finally, the implications of the use of these social structures on mate choice and on the workings of sexual selection under parental choice are also examined.

Chapter 8 – Controversy surrounds lesbian and gay parenting. Some believe gay and lesbian parenting to be detrimental to children's development. A child with gay or lesbian parents may be wrongly believed to have impairments in psychological, social, and gender functioning as a result of their parents' sexual orientation. Specifically, gay and lesbian parents are thought to influence their children's sexual orientation; that is, gay and lesbian parents raise children who also are gay and lesbian. These societal views influence public policy, court rulings, and adoption regulation. Discrimination in these settings acts as a major challenge to gay and lesbian individuals who want to be parents and also as a barrier to their children. Gay fathers are compared with their heterosexual counterparts, just as lesbian mothers are compared with theirs. Similarities and differences also are evaluated between gay and lesbian parent dyads and heterosexual parent dyads. Gay and lesbian parents often parent just as, if not more, effectively than heterosexual parents. Research shows no evidence that gay and lesbian parenting is associated with any additional negative characteristics when compared to heterosexual parenting. Following a discussion of gender differences and barriers, recommendations and future directions related to gay and lesbian parenting are considered.

Chapter 9 – Parenting frequently has been defined using a combination of demandingness and responsiveness. The most beneficial parenting style is authoritative parenting, which is high in demandingness and responsiveness. Other aspects of positive parenting that may influence child development include parental involvement, consistency, and non-punitive discipline practices. These effective parenting practices result in more adaptive skills and better adjustment in children. Although research has indicated parenting may have a positive influence on child development, not all types of parenting are beneficial and may result in negative effects such as disruptive behavior, depression, and anxiety in children. Authoritarian (i.e., high demandingness, low responsiveness), permissive (i.e., low demandingness, high responsiveness), and neglectful (i.e., low demandingness, low responsiveness) parenting styles are associated with more maladaptive outcomes in children. Specific maladaptive parenting practices associated with negative outcomes include low warmth, high amounts of control, inconsistent parenting, a lack of parental involvement, and harsh discipline practices. Parents should focus on reducing negative parenting practices and enhancing positive practices. Following a discussion of positive and negative parenting practices, recommendations for improving parenting and parent-child relationships are considered.

Chapter 10 – Antisocial behaviour in children is common and has attracted considerable interest in recent years, not least because of the significant negative psychological and economic consequences for affected families and communities. A considerable body of research indicates that parenting programmes, particularly those delivered in group settings and based on behavioural and social learning principles, can produce clinically significant improvements in childhood emotional and behavioural difficulties and in parental mental health. However, despite these encouraging results, several challenges require further exploration. These include: (1) a need for improvements in the overall quality of studies; (2) an analysis of group-based parenting interventions in relation to outcomes about which the authors know relatively little; (3) a need for improved retention and engagement among socially disadvantaged and culturally distinctive families; and (4) the appropriate and effective translation of evidence into policy and practice. This chapter will discuss these issues and highlight possible avenues for future research which may enhance the evidence-base for, and the wide-scale implementation of, parenting programmes.

Chapter 11 – An individual's culture plays an important role throughout life; culture's influence on parenting is no exception. It is clear that parents play a valuable role in transmitting the values, rules, and standards of society to children. Globally, a range of parenting practices has emerged. What is considered to be normative parenting for a child varies across cultures. Differing parenting styles may be found between individualist and collectivist cultures, with the latter showing a stronger preference for authoritarian parenting. Cultural norms for family roles may be thought to influence parenting practices. Individualist cultures tend to emphasize an individual's independence from others, while collectivist cultures emphasize an individual's interdependence with his or her family, community, and country. As individualist cultures encourage autonomy, assertiveness, and a need for privacy, parenting practices may be more relaxed than in a collectivist culture. Specific examples across cultures will be discussed. Given the sometimes conflicting viewpoints of individualist and collectivist parenting, researchers and clinicians working with parents should ensure that their programs are culturally sensitive and appropriate. Suggestions for working with culturally diverse groups are discussed.

Chapter 12 – Parenting experiences children have lived within their families can play an important role for adult children's couple relationship, not only in terms of the actual behaviors and practices parents have engaged in during childhood and adolescence, but also in terms of the heritage of values, norms, and models adult children perceive that have settled from those experiences. The present study was designed to investigate the interplay among perceived family heritage, partners' individual well-being, and their relationship satisfaction. Two hundred and twenty premarital couples completed self-report measures of family heritage, personal well-being and relationship satisfaction. Structural equation modeling was used to test the connections among these variables. Results indicated that perceiving a positive family heritage promoted partners' psychological well-being, which in turn sustained a satisfying couple relationship. Results were discussed also in terms of their implication for family prevention programs.

Chapter 13 – Much has been written about the challenges of pregnancy and parenthood; however, few studies exist that examine how mothers prepare to cope with the potential challenges they will face during this major life transition. While pregnancy is filled with excitement in anticipation of the baby's arrival, it is also a period of time marked with an increased risk of stress and worry. One way that expectant parents can minimize this stress is through the utilization of effective coping strategies. A plethora of literature examines the impact of stress, but prior literature has focused almost exclusively on how individuals deal reactively with taxing situations. More recently, the stress and coping literature has begun to include coping for events before they occur, referred to as proactive coping. The literature on proactive coping is relatively new and has never been examined during the transition to parenthood. Due to this void in the literature, the current study utilized a sample of 118 first-time expectant mothers to examine the potential correlates and predictors of utilizing proactive coping during the transition to parenthood. The current study found a mother's internal locus of control and optimism were concurrently related to more proactive coping during pregnancy and at 1-month postpartum, while rumination was not. These results suggest the importance of examining predictors of coping during the transition to parenthood.

Chapter 14 – As economic development has swept across the globe, cultural values and the role of the parenting in various societies have become casualties of the drive towards social change and progress. As many industrialized nations face the economic strains of changing dependency ratios, societies will have to create social programs to meet the needs of their new demographic and child rearing environment. The long-discussed notion of empowerment is a useful concept or goal in this new world, but one which requires a concrete framework for implementation – a framework which can cross national and cultural boundaries to be utilized in many different situations. This chapter examines Japanese experiences as one of the model for future.

In: Parenting
Editors: Peter Barberis and Stelios Petrakis

ISBN: 978-1-62257-881-8
© 2013 Nova Science Publishers, Inc.

Chapter 1

Young Maternal Age and Preterm Birth: Specific Challenges During the Transition to Motherhood

Nicola Sheeran[1], Liz Jones[1], Jen Rowe[2] and Melanie Zimmer-Gembeck[3]

[1]School of Applied Psychology and Griffith Health Institute, Behavioural Basis of Health, Mt. Gravatt Campus, Griffith University
[2]School of Nursing and Midwifery, University of the Sunshine Coast
[3]School of Applied Psychology and Griffith Health Institute, Behavioural Basis of Health, Gold Coast Campus, Griffith University
South Brisbane, QLD, Australia

Abstract

This chapter presents an overview of the research on preterm birth and adolescent parenting, highlighting the challenges faced during the transition to parenthood in these contexts. Also presented is current research investigating how these factors combine to influence the experience of parenting for young mothers of preterm infants. Parenting as an adolescent has been associated with a range of negative outcomes for both the young woman and her infant. Similarly, preterm birth is also associated with a number of acute and chronic difficulties that make parenting more challenging. It is well documented that maternal mental health influences the woman's ability to parent and, as such, factors that increase stress, anxiety and depression can have ongoing implications for their capacity to parent effectively. Both preterm birth and adolescent parenting are associated with an increased risk of distress and mental health issues. However, little research has investigated how these two factors combine to influence the parenting experience for young women who have preterm infants, despite a theoretical double risk. As such, the research presented in this chapter investigated the experience of parenting, both during the early or acute stages of a preterm birth, and longitudinally over the first year of the infant's life. Quantitative and qualitative longitudinal data from adult mothers of preterm infants, adolescent mothers of full term infants, and adolescent mothers of preterm infants is presented highlighting the specific challenges, as well as similarities, in experiences of parenting.

Results from the quantitative data suggest adult mothers of preterm infants reported higher levels of psychological distress pre-discharge than did adolescent mothers but this difference had dissipated post-discharge. Qualitative data findings supported this result, suggesting that parenting for young women was not unduly altered by having a preterm infant, with few overall differences in the parenting experience for young mothers of preterm and full term infants. Preterm birth compounded the everyday challenges of motherhood for young women, by emphasizing transportation difficulties and placing women in more frequent contact with people who they perceived negatively judged them. Conversely, adult mothers were better able to negotiate the hospital system, eliciting parenting support from staff and other parents. These findings help challenge prevailing assumptions about the transition to motherhood and have implications for service delivery and interventions.

INTRODUCTION

Rates of preterm birth in the developed world have been rising over time despite advances in knowledge and technology (Goldenberg, 2008). In the U.S. rates of preterm birth range from 12-13% while in Europe and other developed countries rates vary from 5-9% (Goldenberg, 2008; Slattery, 2002). Currently in Australia, 8.2% of all babies are born prematurely. This increases to 8.6% in Queensland with over 9800 infants admitted to special care nurseries each year (Laws, Li, & Sullivan, 2010). Estimates on the percentage of preterm or low birth weight (LBW) births to teenage mothers based on U.S. figures suggests a much higher risk compared to most adult mothers with figures ranging from 8.6% to 15% (Partington, Steber, Blair, & Cisler, 2009; Roth, Hendrickson, & Stowell, 1998). There is ongoing debate in the literature as to whether the higher risk of preterm birth for teen aged mothers is due to biological or ecological factors, as much of the increased risk disappears once socioeconomic status (SES) has been controlled for (da Silva et al., 2003; Ekwo & Moawad, 2000). Regardless, in Australia, women under 20 years and Indigenous women are overrepresented in low-birth weight admissions to Level II and Level III special care (SCN) and intensive care (NICU) nurseries (Laws, Grayson, & Sullivan, 2006; Mohsin, Wong, Bauman, & Bai, 2003). An increased risk of preterm birth is also more likely for young women who live rurally (Robson, Cameron, & Roberts, 2006). These figures suggest that teenage mothers who give birth to preterm or LBW infants are a small but potentially vulnerable group of mothers who have been overlooked in research to date.

Preterm birth has been associated with a range of negative outcomes for parents and infants. Parents face additional challenges during the acute stage of having a preterm infant (i.e. infant hospitalization), the transition home from hospital where parents become sole care givers to infants, and over the long term as parents manage their infants' increased risk of morbidity. Research has investigated how mothers adjust to a preterm birth, i.e., rates of depression or anxiety, stress responses, and factors that influence these. There is now a large body of research demonstrating that maternal adjustment is a vital factor in parenting generally, with poor maternal health outcomes associated with poor relationships between infant and mother (Cohn, Campbell, Matias, & Hopkins, 1990) and negative parenting behaviors (Kohl, Kagotho, & Dixon, 2011; Lovejoy, Graczyk, O'Hare, & Neuman, 2000).

Further, consistent, high quality, sensitive parenting has been shown to moderate the negative effects associated with premature birth (Frye, Malmberg, Swank, Smith, & Landry, 2010a; Poehlmann et al., 2011).

One limitation of the current body of literature on parenting following a preterm birth is that it has primarily been conducted with adult mothers (mean ages in the mid 30's), most of whom were educated, in stable relationships, and employed (Affleck, Tennen, & Rowe, 1991; Doering, Dracup, & Moser, 1999; Doucette & Pinelli, 2000; Jones, Rowe, & Becker, 2009; Miles, 1989; Pinelli, 2000). These factors have been found to assist in positive maternal adaptation to the situation (Cronin, Shapiro, Casiro, & Cheang, 1995; Davis, Edwards, Mohay, & Wollin, 2003; Holditch-Davies et al., 2009). The few studies that have recruited younger mothers have collapsed over age, making it difficult to know if there are aged based differences in the experience (Cleveland, 2008). As such, the question remains as to how young 'teen' aged mothers, who may be contending with a number of other challenges in addition to those associated with a 'normal' transition to motherhood, experience the transition to motherhood with a preterm infant. The purpose of the current chapter is to review what is known about parenting as a young woman, including both the challenges and the positive aspects. Further, we review what is known about parenting in the context of a preterm birth, including the challenges faced during the acute stages, the transition home, and the long term challenges. We next summarize the smaller research literature that has specifically focused on adolescent parenting of their preterm infants. Finally, we present the results of our research that has focused on describing the parenting experience for Australian adolescent mothers who gave birth prematurely. To begin, the following section outlines the literature on the transition to motherhood for young women.

BEING A YOUNG MOTHER

The Challenges of Young Motherhood

Childbearing in the teenage years has been linked to a range of negative outcomes for the young woman and her infant (Furstenberg, Brooks-Gunn, & Chase-Lansdale, 1989). These negative outcomes often link poor maternal health outcomes to poor infant outcomes highlighting the social disadvantage that occurs as a result of early childbearing. However, more recently there has been a shift in the literature, with researchers acknowledging that these negatives may have been overstated. There has also been growing acknowledgement of the positive role that pregnancy may play for some young women (Sisson, 2012). The psychological health of the young mother has been one area of concern for researchers. This literature has suggested that young women are more likely to become depressed, experience anxiety, experience more stress, and thus interact less with their infants than their older counterparts (Baldwin & Cain, 1980; Barth, Schinke, & Maxwell, 1983; Furstenberg, Brooks-Gunn, & Morgan, 1987; Reis, 1989; T. M. Williams et al., 1987). Of note, one study had to covary the participant's age due to the disproportionate number of young women who were randomly recruited in a study on postnatal depression (Field et al., 1988). Rates of depression in an American sample were as high as 48% for young African-American mothers (28% for White) compared to 25% in a sample of older African-American mothers (14% for White). In this sample adolescent mothers were more than twice as likely to develop depression following birth than adult mothers (Deal & Holt, 1998). More recent research investigating rates of depression in adolescent mothers compared to low and high resourced adult mothers found significant differences between groups, with adolescent mothers reporting higher rates of depression (Lanzi, Bert, Jacobs, & The Centers for the Prevention of Child Neglect, 2009). However, these studies can be criticized for not considering preexisting differences between the groups, with young women (often African American) from low SES backgrounds often compared to middle class white adult mothers.

Research also suggests that young mothers have poorer life chances and are economically disadvantaged compared to women who delay childbearing. Being a young mother has been associated with having less education, having less prestigious jobs, less stable marriages, larger families, and an increased reliance on government financial assistance (Card & Wise, 1978; Furstenberg, et al., 1989; Furstenberg, et al., 1987; Rudd, McKenry, & Nah, 1990). In addition, adolescent mothers have lower income, possibly due to dependence on government assistance, increased risk taking behaviors (including illegal activity and drug use), interruption to education, which has long-term implications for welfare dependence, lack of career options, and higher rates of poverty compared to adult mothers or peers who delay childbearing (Bunting & McAuley, 2004a, 2004b; Condon & Corkindale, 2002; Fergusson & Woodward, 2000; Furstenberg, et al., 1989; Hanna, 2001; Quinlivan, Tan, Steele, & Black, 2004; Rudd, et al., 1990). These factors have then been associated with a host of psychological problems, placing young women in a high risk category. Further, research with adolescent mothers has found that they are highly mobile, with instability in areas such as relationships, accommodation, and employment creating additional challenges, and these situational factors often interfere with tasks of daily living (Furstenberg, et al., 1989; Quinlivan, Box, & Evans, 2003; Quinlivan, Petersen, & Gurrin, 1999).

Being a young mother can also have a negative impact on the young mother's children. Researchers have shown that children of adolescent parents are more likely to be financially disadvantaged and are at an increased risk for developmental delays, intellectual difficulties, and abuse (Baldwin & Cain, 1980; Haskett, Johnson, & Miller, 1994; Levine, Emery, & Pollack, 2007). Further, children of adolescent mothers have been shown to have poorer health outcomes, more behavioral problems, higher rates of delinquent behavior, less interactive behaviors, and are more likely to become young parents themselves, suggesting a range of long term and intergenerational negative outcomes (Baldwin & Cain, 1980; Barnes & Morris, 2012; Seamark & Pereira Gray, 1997). The causal role of young maternal age in outcomes for infants of young mothers however has been questioned in research. For instance, Levine, Emery & Pollack (2007) found that there was no direct effect of parents' age on children's cognitive test scores and some behavioral measures (such as child's marijuana use as an adolescent) when background variables such as grandmother's education level, location of residence (i.e., urban/rural; south/north), family composition, race, birth order, and mothers armed forces qualification test (AFQT-R) scores were accounted for. Further, Blinn-Pike & Mingus (2000) have questioned the validity of measures being used with adolescent populations to assess abuse potential due to low internal consistency and lack of appropriate normative data. Similarly, the relationship between young maternal age and psychological health can be challenged when appropriate comparison groups are used rather than middle aged white women.

When young mothers are compared to a matched sample of same aged peers and compared pre- and post- pregnancy, a more detailed picture emerges. Research has found few differences in levels of emotional distress during the first two years of parenting (Milan, Ickovics, Kershaw, Lewis, & Meade, 2004), parenting young women reported less stress than same aged peers (Barratt & Roach, 1995) and similar rates of depression were noted (Troutman & Cutrona, 1990) when young mothers were compared to matched same age peers. Milan, et al. (2004) investigated emotional distress, as measured by the BSI (brief symptom inventory), in adolescent mothers and non-mothers and found a decrease in distress over time from the third trimester to 18 months postpartum for adolescent mothers. The same trend was seen for matched adolescent non-mothers, although the level of emotional distress experienced by the adolescent mothers following the birth of a baby was significantly lower than the non-mothers (Milan et al., 2004). The fact that four months after the birth of the baby adolescent mothers were experiencing less distress than comparable non-mothering teens suggests that giving birth may, instead, play a positive role in the adolescent mother's life (Barratt & Roach, 1995). Further, Mollborn and Morningstar (2009) found no significant difference between distress in adolescent mothers and all other mothers after controlling for factors including parental education, grade point average, family structure, and previous sexual experience. Finally, a study investigating the prevalence and correlates of psychopathology in adolescent mothers found that they exhibited less severe and lower rates of pathology than comparison groups of never pregnant, and clinically referred and non-referred female adolescents (Wiemann, Berenson, Wagner, & Landwehr, 1996). Hence, what may appear to be a strong relationship between age of parenting and psychological distress may be accounted for by preexisting differences in the samples. Similarly, the causal role of young maternal age in educational and financial outcomes for young women has been called into question. Research that controlled for preexisting background variables has found that much of the difference between mothers who delay childbearing until adulthood and younger mothers can be explained by pre-existing differences between the groups. For instance, longitudinal research with sister dyads found few differences in high school completion or employment rates for early or late child bearers, despite differences in welfare assistance, education, marital, and employment status when young mothers were compared to the overall sample (Geronimus, Korenman, & Hillemeier, 1994). Further, longitudinal research from New Zealand found that many of the women who became mothers had disengaged from education *prior* to falling pregnant and not as a result of becoming pregnant, suggesting that there may be mutual risk factors for school disengagement and early pregnancy (Fergusson & Woodward, 2000).

There is also evidence to suggest that young women now have more opportunities to re-engage in education over the course of their lives than previous generations may have had. An ethnographic study which followed up mothers three to eight years post birth found that the current educational system (such as tertiary colleges) compared to previous more inflexible models of secondary schooling, allowed women who parented as teens to return to study at a later date; of note, nearly all women in this study had completed high school equivalence (Carey, Ratliff, & Lyle, 1998). Further, several young women in Carey et al.'s study had gone on to complete or were completing diplomas at a tertiary college and university degrees via distance education and all placed high value on education attainment. Only one mother in the study had been unable to re-engage in education; she was the youngest mother in the sample, having first given birth at 14 and having the greatest number of children (three) at follow-up

(Carey et al., 1998). Consistent with Carey et al., Schultz (2001) found that of the women in her study, the adolescent mothers had more developed plans for the future than did non-parenting peers. The young women who had become parents reported that they had to take life more seriously because of their responsibilities (Schultz, 2001). This research suggests that the impact of adolescent parenting on education may not be as drastic as initially posited and that the negative effects of becoming a mother may be overstated for some young women.

Defining of motherhood as a social problem for young women has meant that there is stigma associated with being a young mother (Fessler, 2008). This stigma has resulted in negative attitudes towards young women who are mothers and they face high levels of criticism and few compliments. Hanna (2000), in reflecting on her research project with young women at risk of homelessness, noted her surprise at her participants' reports that no one complimented them on their parenting practices, despite her seeing much that was worthy of praise. This lack of praise was also reflected in the findings of her study (Hanna, 2001), which highlighted the negative judgment the young women faced as they accessed health services and more generally from the wider community. Similarly, in a grounded theory study of adolescent mothers in Uganda (Kay, 2008), adolescent mothers reported that one of the factors that reduced their satisfaction with motherhood was the rebuke by health workers, relatives and even strangers, who disapproved of the adolescent parent. Some felt that most people they interacted with considered them unfit parents by virtue of their age, and they experienced stigmatization (Kay, 2008). This theme was also echoed in Arai's (2003) study, where young mothers automatically expected that coordinators of teen programs would express condemnation and negative attitudes around their decision to become mothers. Young women manage this expectation of negative judgment in many ways. Arai (2003) found that because participants expected this negative judgment, they took an adversarial position towards the coordinators. Fessler (2008) also found that young women actively responded to others by projecting an attitude of defiance and self-reliance. Relatedly, Hanna (2001) found that young women avoided placing themselves in situations where they would be judged as 'bad mothers' and Fessler found that participants used friends and family members as buffers in situations where they were likely to experience stigma. Fessler also noted that some of her participants managed stigma through relatively extreme measures such as dropping out of school and refusing prenatal care. Unfortunately, these ways of managing may make things worse for pregnant and parenting young women as they represent those actions that are often associated with the stereotypical young mother.

Parenting and Positive Outcomes for Young Women

Some researchers have proposed that early parenting can have positive effects on young women. These studies have found that motherhood assisted in the development of identity and role formation (Hunt-Morse, 2002). Unger, Molina, and Teran (2000) found that motherhood provided an opportunity to secure love and fulfill an existential need. Similarly, becoming a mother was associated with increased self-esteem and sense of identity (Barrett et al., 1996). Spear and Lock (2003) reviewed 22 qualitative studies investigating adolescent pregnancy and found that most adolescent parents, across the studies, viewed parenting as a positive experience. Associated with the pregnancy was an often dramatic change in the young women's trajectories. For instance, Arenson (1994) found the adolescent mothers' lives improved by having a baby as they stopped taking drugs, stopped drinking alcohol, and their relationships with peers and family improved. Often the young women described developing a positive outlook on life, stating that pregnancy provided them with a second chance at life (Williams & Vines, 1999). Hanna (2001) found that parenting provided opportunities for change and transformation in their lives. Seamark and Ling's (2004) study also challenged the assumption that an adolescent pregnancy has only negative effects on young women's lives. They argued that alternatively, it can be the turning point to maturity and the development of a career. Adolescent mothers themselves recognized the importance of education (both formal and more general in life skills) to their successful adaptation to parenting and to meeting their goals (Seamark & Lings, 2004). Young women have also stated that they had a strong desire for independence and reported that they did not want to be dependent on welfare, government systems, or family for financial support (Scott Stiles, 2005). Young mothers were able to recognize their limitations as parents and knew what needed to be done to parent more effectively, demonstrating their developing maturity (Scott Stiles, 2005).

Motherhood has also been associated with increased maturity, whereby young women describe 'growing up' as a result of the pregnancy, with a reduction in the egocentric thinking typical of adolescence and a move toward thinking like a mother (Williams & Vines, 1999). Spear and Locks' (2003) review of the literature found that many participants across studies viewed early childbearing as a normative, positive event that transitioned them into adulthood. Paradoxically, the young mothers in Arenson's (1994) study documented that as they became more dependent on their families for financial support and shelter they were viewed by their parents as adults and were treated with more respect. These studies further emphasize the positive role that parenting can play in developing maturity and responsibility, and in transitioning the young women into adulthood. Another general theme present in many of the adolescent mothers' discourses across studies focused on their determination to raise their children better than they had been raised themselves, by talking to their infants, listening to them, and making sure they felt loved (Arenson, 1994; Seamark & Lings, 2004). In this way young women felt that they were able to provide the love that they had not received themselves. Similarly, a general theme across studies was that adolescent mothers viewed parenting as important to their lives and demonstrated a desire to meet their children's needs (Spear & Locke, 2004). The research provided an understanding of the motivations and priorities of the young women, which had often been lost in studies that focused on the young women's deficits in parenting. A further consideration is that women from disadvantaged backgrounds may see parenting as a positive life choice compared to alternative options. In a qualitative study that investigated two possible explanations for adolescent pregnancy in the UK, low expectations or poor knowledge about contraception, Arai (2003) highlighted that motherhood was often an advantageous choice - especially for working class young women. For some young women school and low paid employment were not regarded as viable options. Motherhood, by comparison, was viewed as a preferable career, providing positives in terms of receiving love and providing a meaningful vocation (Arai, 2003). As highlighted by SmithBattle (2005a), postponing parenthood would not enhance the life experiences for some young women unless the disadvantage that existed pre pregnancy was addressed. Arai argued that what needed to be questioned was the political and middle class view of adolescent pregnancy as wrong, not necessarily the women's decisions to become parents.

The Complexities of adjustment to Motherhood for Young Women

Rather than supporting the view that being a parent as a young woman is negatively influenced by their stage of psychosocial development, the qualitative studies reviewed above highlight the ways in which being a mother is perceived by the young mothers as aids for their positive psychosocial development (Arai, 2003; Arenson, 1994; Seamark & Lings, 2004). Nevertheless, the results of qualitative studies have also identified specific challenges associated with the experience, increasing the understanding of what factors help and hinder adjustment. Specifically, young mothers often acknowledged that parenting increased demands and responsibilities, and placed restrictions on their time (Hanna, 2001; Seamark & Lings, 2004; Spear & Lock, 2003). In addition, Spear (2004b) made clear both the positive and negative aspects of parenting for young women who were from poor backgrounds prior to their pregnancies (i.e., drug dealing, domestic violence, and extreme poverty). During pregnancy, the young women expressed the sentiment that early maternity would have little effect on their lives (Spear, 2004b). However, in follow up interviews 1½ years later, the young women maintained a sense of optimism and hope for the future, but this was tempered by feelings of regret, isolation, and mourning for a lost childhood due to the day-to day realities and restrictions of being a young single mother (Spear, 2004a, 2004b). In a 4-year prospective study of adolescent mothers, SmithBattle and Leonard (1998) highlighted the situated nature of identities and how the self was socially embedded. That is, while motherhood was a corrective experience for many of the young women, this was limited by the poverty, illness, violence, and social exclusion in some women's worlds (SmithBattle & Leonard, 1998). For these women, mothering did not provide a clear purpose or identity. Moreover, these mothers displayed a clear lack of agency in the mothering role that was also reflected in their other relationships with their own mothers and partners (SmithBattle, 2005b). In sum, these studies suggest that aspects of motherhood are challenging and that the experience of parenting is constrained by the social context in which the mothers are embedded. Early research on adolescent parenting began with the assumption that parenting would be overwhelming for the young woman, who simultaneously had to deal with the challenges associated with parenting as well as the developmental challenges of adolescence (Stevenson, Maton, & Teti, 1999). However, it is increasingly evident that not all young women struggle with the demands of parenting. Instead, young women differ significantly in their experience of being mothers demonstrating that they are a heterogeneous group. This understanding has generated a large body of research that has investigated factors related to poor adjustment.

Domains Associated with Positive Adjustment to Motherhood for Young Women

In our view, the research has identified three interacting domains that help explain the experience of parenting for young women, including 1) internal resources (i.e., characteristics within the individual such as cognitive ability), 2) system level or cultural factors (such as access to housing and neighborhoods), and 3) external resources (i.e., factors external to the individual such as social support) (Knaak, 2008; Schellenbach, Whitman, & Borowski, 1992). First, internal resources include accurate knowledge and appropriate attitudes or realistic expectations and beliefs (Ketterlinus, Lamb, & Nitz, 1991; Knaak, 2008), cognitive readiness or high IQ (Schellenbach, et al., 1992; Sommer et al., 1993; Trad, 1995; Whiteside-Mansell, Pope, & Bradley, 1996), maternal maturity (Hess, Papas, & Black, 2002), self-esteem (Hess, et al., 2002; Meyers & Battistoni, 2003), lack of substance abuse, domestic violence, victimization and history of physical and sexual abuse (Gavin, Lindhorst, & Lohr, 2011; Meyers & Battistoni, 2003) social competence and problem solving ability (Passino et al., 1993), self-confidence (Schiefelbein, Susman, & Dorn, 2005) or a sense of personal mastery and control (Turner, Sorenson, & Turner, 2000), low perceived stress during pregnancy and high parenting stress post birth (Holub et al., 2007), and lack of interpersonal conflict (Hess, et al., 2002). All of these internal resources have been found to promote or undermine maternal and infant outcomes among young mothers. Second, at a system level, factors associated with increased risk of poor adjustment include ethnicity of the mother (i.e., being African American), lower socio-economic status (Schellenbach, et al., 1992), neighborhood characteristics (such as a lack of affluent neighbors) (Brooks-Gunn, Duncan, Klebanov, & Sealand, 1993), housing, financial support, and availability of child care (Mollborn, 2007). Often these factors were also related (either positively or negatively) to external resources such as the social support available within the mother's sociocultural context.

Social support is the most researched external factor for a positive adjustment to motherhood for young women. Several review articles show that social support can promote successful adaptation to parenthood for adolescent mothers and their children (Bunting & McAuley, 2004a, 2004b; Clemmens, 2001; Letourneau, Stewart, & Barnfather, 2004). Similarly, social support tends to ameliorate many of the negative outcomes associated with adolescent parenthood (Barth, et al., 1983). For instance, Spear (2004a) employed a naturalistic, qualitative case study approach and highlighted that young women were able to adequately manage single motherhood with support from family. Moreover, social support has been found to moderate depressive symptomology for adolescent mothers (Turner, et al., 2000). Related research indicates that greater help with caregiving is positively associated with mental health and that support plays an important role in reducing stress (Barratt, Roach, Morgan, & Colbert, 1996; Logson & Koniak-Griffin, 2005). Most commonly, research has focused on the source of social support for adolescent mothers. Typical sources of support include families, partners and friends and, to a lesser extent, professionals (Letourneau, et al., 2004) though, for the most part, support is garnered from maternal mothers.

To illustrate, research from the US indicates that the majority of adolescent mothers live at home with their mothers following the birth of their child (Caldwell & Antonucci, 1997). Grandmothers were found to be a primary source of assistance (i.e., housing, financial, and child-care) and living at home was linked to increased educational attainment and stable employment for the teen mother, as well as better developmental outcomes for their children (Caldwell and Antonucci, 1997; Clemmens, 2001). However, in one study, although nearly all adolescent mothers reported their mothers as a source of support, over one-third also reported that their mother was a source of conflict for them (Bunting & McAuley, 2004a). An interesting contradiction is that high levels of support from grandparents may be related to poorer parenting experiences for the young mother, suggesting that while it may be better for the infant's development (Clemmens, 2001), support from grandparents may not be best for the adolescent mother (Voight, Hans, & Bernstein, 1996). These studies suggest that the relationship between mother and daughter is not straightforward, with conflict diminishing some of the benefits that family support provided, leading to less optimal parenting behaviors (Bunting & McAuley, 2004a). For some young mothers relationships with parents were strained, and the mothers tended to become socially isolated (Rogeness, Ritchey, Alex, Zueler, & Morris, 1981). In such cases, peer and partner support may become an important factor.

Peers are also an important source of support for the adolescent mother (Bunting & McAuley, 2004a; Richardson, Barbour, & Bubenzer, 1995). Although it has been suggested that peers were less able to provide support to a young woman once she became a mother, research has also suggested that peers were able to offer more emotional support and less interference than family (Richardson, et al., 1995). It was thought that friends offer positive feedback and advice for mothers without the conflict that was often present in familial relationships (Bunting & McAuley, 2004a). In addition, Richardson et al. (1995) found that parenting stress was buffered more effectively by support garnered from friends than family when the adolescent mothers' infants were around a year old. However, many young women reported a reduction in peer support, with social isolation a common result of early childbearing. This reduction in support can then have consequences for adjustment, including increased rates of depression (Birkeland, Thompson, & Phares, 2005; Quinlivan, et al., 1999). Overall, this body of research suggests that peers are an important source of support for young women that may not always be available.

Father involvement is another complicated issue, with repercussions for maternal adjustment. Although the father of the child has been found to be a valuable source of social support for the young mother, there can be variations in how involved the father is (Bunting & McAuley, 2004b). According to international research on adolescent parenting, most adolescent mothers give birth outside of marriage (Bunting & McAuley, 2004a; Coleman & Dennison, 1998) and have unstable relationships with the fathers of the baby (Unger & Wandersman, 1988). In one study approximately 30% of a large sample of welfare dependent adolescent mothers received child support from the baby's father and only 4% lived with the father (Aber, Brooks-Gunn, & Maynard, 1995). Other longitudinal research found that 3.5 years postpartum, 56% of fathers were providing no instrumental or economic support for their children and only 28% of fathers paid for some or most of their child's expenses (Larson, Hussey, Gillmore, & Gilchrist, 1996). Similarly, the number of adolescent mothers who gave birth within marriage has been steadily decreasing in Australia (Kenny, 1995; Slowinski & Hume, 2001). One study in Australia found that 47% of pregnant adolescents reported that the relationship with the father of the baby had ended and that the father would not be involved in the care of the infant (Quinlivan, et al., 1999). Fathers often cited conflictual relationships with the adolescent mother or maternal grandparents as barriers to their continued involvement with their children (Bunting & McAuley, 2004b). In addition, fathers were less likely to stay involved if the young mother had experienced a large number of stressful life events during the pregnancy or in the first 6 weeks after the delivery (Cutrona, Hessling, Bacon, & Russell, 1998). Overall, these findings suggest that there is variability in the involvement of the father, and that involvement is influenced by a number of factors. Further, given that a preterm birth may be a stressful event for mothers, there is a concern that this may lead to less support from the father of the baby.

Although social support is heralded as an important factor in adjustment, less well explored are the negative aspects of social support. However, as alluded to above, not all support is perceived as positive to young women and relationships are not straightforward. This is also true for adult mothers of preterm infants where too much support can have negative effects on wellbeing especially when it is perceived as not required or needed (Affleck, Tennen, Allen, & Gershman, 1986; Affleck, Tennen, Rowe, Roscher, & Walker, 1989; Coyne & DeLongis, 1986). In addition, for some young women, accessing support places them in a position where they are exposed to negative judgments of others and this can have negative effects on their adjustment.

IN SUMMARY, early quantitative research studies tended to compare and contrast adolescent mothers with adult mothers, with little consideration of pre-existing differences between the groups. However, more recent research has challenged the causal link between age and poor outcomes, while also highlighting the heterogeneity of the group of young mothers. A growing body of qualitative literature highlights that the experience of parenting for young women is both positive and challenging, often providing the young women with direction and meaning for the future. However, while much is now known about parenting as a young woman, little is known about how preterm birth interacts with the experience or whether this creates additional challenges in the same way it can for adult mothers.

PARENTING A PRETERM INFANT

Challenges in the Acute Stage

The birth of a preterm infant has been identified as a time of stress for mothers that affects their adjustment. Davis et al. (2003) found that higher stress in mothers of preterm infants was associated with increased depressive symptomology. Similarly, Meyer et al. (1995) found that psychological distress among mothers of preterm infants was common, with 28% of mothers reporting clinically significant psychological distress, as indicated by the SCL-R 90. In addition, younger maternal age was associated with greater levels of distress (Meyer, et al., 1995). In another study, stress was found to vary as a function of infant morbidity, with more distress experienced by parents whose infants were ill. However, the majority of parents whose children were classified as well still reported that the event was emotionally distressing (Pederson, Bento, Chance, Evans, & Fox, 1987). Mothers have reported that the experience of having a preterm infant was highly stressful, with many parents reporting that it was the worst major life event they have experienced (Doering, et al., 1999; Whitfield, 2003). The strain experienced by parents at the time of hospitalization has been reported as being significantly higher than for parents who delivered full term infants (Affleck et al., 1991; Carter et al., 2005; Taylor et al., 2001). Parents have also reported that the experience of birth was contrary to their expectations and that they felt unprepared for the birth (Whitfield, 2003). However, Spielman (2009) has suggested that preterm birth may also be a catalyst for growth, with parents of preterm infants reporting greater stress-related growth than parents of full term infants.

Particular stressors related to the context of a preterm birth include the uncertainty of the infant's outcome, worry, anxiety and fear over the health and wellbeing of their child, the foreign environment of the NICU, the infant's appearance, the sense of loss associated with the expectation of giving birth to a healthy infant and subsequent alteration to the parenting role, being separated from their infant, and relinquishing control for care of the infant to nursing staff (Affleck, et al., 1991; Franck, Cox, Allen, & Winter, 2005; Hughes, McCollum, Sheftel, & Sanchez, 1994; Miles, 1989; Miles & Holditch-Davis, 1997; Seideman et al., 1997).

During the acute stage of the experience parents have reported their role as one of remaining vigilant, watching over and protecting the infant (Cleveland, 2008). They desire accurate information, being included in the infant's care, and a good relationship with staff (Cleveland, 2008). During this time parents also report a need for physical contact with their infants, which is often restricted due to infants being in isolettes or unwell (Cleveland, 2008). Nurses serve a primary support role which may be either facilitative or hindering, influencing the mother's experience of parenting (Cleveland, 2008; Fenwick, Barclay, & Schmied, 2000; Jones, Woodhouse, & Rowe, 2007). Communication between nurses and parents is particularly important, especially informal chatting, influencing parents' perceptions of the experience and adjustment (Fenwick, et al., 2000). Partner support is also very important during this time, with virtually all mothers reporting that their partners were an extremely helpful source of support (Jones, et al., 2009). Other factors found to influence adjustment positively include appraisal of the situation as a challenge rather than as stressful and type of coping strategy used (Jones, et al., 2009).

Challenges during the Transition Home

The majority of research has focused on the acute phase of the experience, when the infant is hospitalized (Shields-Poe & Pinelli, 1997), with research only recently beginning to investigate later stages of the experience such as discharge and when the infant first goes home (Gray, Edwards, O'Callaghan, & Cuskelly, 2012). However, this is another challenging stage of the experience as parents assume care of their infants, who prior to discharge have received 24-hour care from hospital staff. In addition, infants may continue to require ongoing specialized care, may remain immature, and may have a high risk of hospital readmission (Affleck, et al., 1986; Bakewell-Sachs & Gennaro, 2004; Kenner & Lott, 1990; Miles & Holditch-Davis, 1997). As such, the transition home can be a time of adjustment for parents, who often experience high levels of anxiety, making the homecoming of an infant from the NICU both a joyous and stressful transition for families (Bakewell-Sachs & Gennaro, 2004; Griffin & Pickler, 2011). In one study (Singer et el., 1999) ten percent of adult mothers of premature infants experienced severe symptoms of psychological distress neonatally and one third experienced clinically meaningful levels of depression and anxiety one month after discharge from the NICU (Singer et al., 1999). However, overall it appears that most parents adjust well and do not experience significant distress in the months following discharge (Evans, Whittingham, & Boyd, 2012; Rowe & Jones, 2008; Rowe & Jones, 2010). Predictors of poor adjustment include having a sicker infant and lower maternal educational attainment (Holditch-Davies, et al., 2009).

Long-Term Challenges

The birth of a preterm or LBW infant is also associated with a number of ongoing or chronic stressors. Some of these include ongoing health problems, readmission to hospital, developmental delays for the infants, the increased burden of finding appropriate childcare, behavioral problems and difficult temperaments of the infants, and possible ongoing financial commitments (Able-Boone & Stevens, 1994; Cronin, et al., 1995; Frye, et al., 2010a; Gray, Woodward, Spencer, Inder, & Austin, 2006; Taylor, Klein, Minich, & Hack, 2001). Premature infants continue to have special needs and remain at increased risk of health problems throughout the first year of life (Bakewell-Sachs & Gennaro, 2004). Six months after discharge mothers still report a fear of what the future will bring and are concerned about how they are managing the present challenges of parenting their preterm infant (Holditch-Davis & Miles, 2000). Further, parents of preterm infants are more likely to experience irritable parenting during the first year of their infant's life compared to term parents (Westrupp, Mensah, Giallo, Cooklin, & Nicholson, 2012). Cronin et al. (1995) found that the birth and upbringing of a very LBW infant was associated with long-term stress for all parents. Stress was related to the educational level and income of the respondent, with disadvantaged groups, in terms of low income and lack of education, manifesting more financial, familial, and personal stress (Cronin, et al., 1995). More recent research acknowledges the variability in experience, proposing there are 4 sub-groups of mothers whose level of distress and perceptions of infant and parenting systematically vary and predict level of distress over the first 24 months (Miles, et al., 2009). These sub groups differed mainly on the type of distress experienced and included mothers with low distress, mothers with extreme distress, mothers with high depressive symptomology, and mothers with high stress (Miles, et al., 2009). However, overall most parents seem to have recovered well by the time the child has reached the age of two (Tommiska, Ostberg, & Fellman, 2002).

There is a growing body of research suggesting that parenting behaviors are important for predicting and ameliorating the negative effects of preterm birth for children. For example, recent research suggests an interaction between deficits in self-regulatory function and parenting (Poehlmann, et al., 2011). Poehlmann et al. found an interaction between parenting and infants' proneness to distress which explained internalizing and externalizing behaviors when preterm/LBW infants were 9 months old. That is, preterm infants who were prone to distress and who experienced angry and critical parenting demonstrated increased externalizing behaviors (Poehlmann, et al., 2011). Further, preterm infants who did not experience angry and critical parenting demonstrated the least amount of externalizing behavior. Similarly, preterm infants who were prone to distress and who were exposed to intrusive anxious parenting demonstrated increased internalizing behaviors and those not exposed to this parenting style reported the least internalizing behaviors. Further, maternal responsiveness has been found to mediate the differences in cortical thickness again highlighting the role that parenting may play in cognitive development of preterm children (Frye et al., 2010). These findings suggest that parenting style interacts with the preterm/LBW infant's temperament to influence infant behavioral problems.

YOUNG PARENTS OF PRETERM INFANTS

The research findings available to us demonstrate how preterm birth can increase the parenting challenges for adult mothers. However, the transition to motherhood for young women who have preterm infants has received little attention in the literature despite a theoretical double risk and identified need (Cleveland, 2008; Thurman & Gonsalves, 1993). The double risk alludes to the fact that parenting at a young age and preterm birth are both independent risk factors for poor maternal and infant outcomes. However, what little research there is suggests that differences between adolescent mothers of preterm infants and adolescent mothers of full term infants are minimal and short lasting. Bell (1997) investigated which aspects of the NICU environment were major sources of distress for young women. The most stressful aspects were the alterations to the parenting role and the infant's appearance and behavior. These findings were similar to those in adult populations (Miles, Carlson, & Funk, 1996). In contrast to adult mothers, the sights and sounds of the NICU and communicating with staff caused less stress (Bell, 1997). The lack of stress associated with communicating with staff is also surprising given the findings that intergenerational communication, particularly between adolescents and adults in authority, is difficult and a source of distress for adolescents (Drury, 2003; Drury, Catan, Dennison, & Brody, 1998). In an investigation of the posited double risk, Field, Widmayer, Stringer, and Ignatoff (1980) examined the transition to parenthood for low-income African American adults and adolescents of full term and preterm infants. The primary focus was on infant developmental outcomes, and they investigated the proposition that infants born preterm and to an adolescent mother were at the highest risk for developmental delays. The study found no major differences in infant developmental outcomes between adolescent mothers and adult mothers.

The researchers suggested that the expected developmental differences between infants of teens and adults may have been attenuated by family support systems, as most of the adolescent mothers lived in their parent's homes (Field, et al., 1980). However, the study did find developmental delays at the 8-month follow-up for preterm infants born to adolescent mothers when compared directly to adult mothers of preterm infants suggesting that the attenuating influence of the family support may not extend to adolescent mothers of preterm infants. The Field et al. study also included the State-Trait Anxiety inventory (STAI) as a measure of maternal adjustment. Surprisingly for the researchers, the study failed to find differences between any of the groups on the STAI at birth or at the 4-month or 8-month follow-ups. The failure to find differences between the groups was inconsistent with the majority of research on the effects of preterm birth, which suggested that mothers of preterm infants experience more distress than mothers of full term infants (Affleck, et al., 1991; Carter, Mulder, Bartram, & Darlow, 2005; Taylor, et al., 2001).

The lack of difference suggests that in the context of adolescent motherhood the added stress of a preterm birth may not be significant enough to cause increased anxiety. Stone (1998) similarly failed to find differences in a follow-up of young mothers of full term and preterm infants who had participated in early intervention programs (Stone, Bendell, & Field, 1988). Stone et al. investigated infant development using a number of standardized tests as well as maternal self-esteem, stress, and interactions with the infant when the infant was 5-8 years old. They reported no differences between the mothers of preterm infants and mother of full term infants (Stone, et al., 1988). Prior to our program of study we were only able to find one study that investigated the impact of having a preterm infant from the young woman's perspective.

Neu and Robinson (2008) used naturalistic inquiry to obtain subjective descriptions of the postpartum experience of 12 Hispanic adolescent mothers who gave birth to preterm infants in the US (Neu & Robinson, 2008). Neu and Robinson's study, which looked at mothers experience's in the months post-discharge and not during the acute hospital stage, found three key themes. These themes included devotion to the baby (by way of providing loving care), responsibilities (initially to the infant but then incorporating care of family members and responsibility for household duties), and relationships. Relationships included the sub themes of family support and its importance, and estrangement from family and friends that had a significant impact on the mothers' early adaptation (Neu & Robinson, 2008). Of note, the descriptive themes generated were not associated with stress or challenge relating to the preterm birth. Instead, the results of this study were similar to the results of qualitative studies investigating the experience of motherhood for young women of full term infants, in that the mothers displayed devotion to the infant and support was an important component of the experience. These results again suggest that there may be few differences between the experiences of parenting for young women of full term and preterm infants. However, research directly exploring the experience of young mothers experiences of preterm and full term infants and during the acute stage is needed.

IN SUMMARY, a small body of research exists on the experience of being a mother for adolescent mothers of preterm/LBW infants. This research is beginning to challenge the posited double risk for poor maternal outcomes, as few differences appear to exist between adolescent mothers of full term and preterm infants. Similarly, the narratives of young mothers of preterm infants seem consistent with research on young mothers of full term infants suggesting preterm birth does not alter the experience of parenting in a significant way. However, such conclusions are still preliminary because so few studies exist that have investigated parenting of preterm infants among young mothers. To address this research gap, we completed three studies (Farnell, Jones, Rowe, & Sheeran, in press; Sheeran, 2011; Sheeran, 2012; Sheeran, Jones, & Rowe, under review) to elucidate the differences between young mothers' (Mage 17.1 years) and older mothers' (Mage 31 years) experience of parenting in the context of a preterm birth. We summarize the findings below.

Effects of Age and the Preterm Birth of an Infant on Adolescent Mothers' Psychological Adjustment

In the first study, we focused on how younger compared to older mothers adjusted to parenting during the transition home (Farnell, et al., in press). Thirty-nine adult mothers of preterm infants (Mage= 31 years) were compared to 19 adolescent mothers of preterm infants (Mage= 17.05 years) and 19 adolescent mothers of full term infants (Mage= 17.65 years) at time of discharge from hospital and again 3-4 months post-discharge. The study was framed in a stress and coping tradition (Lazarus & Folkman, 1983), which is common in the preterm birth literature, and investigated factors such as cognitive appraisal (i.e. threat and challenge appraisals), social support, and psychological adjustment (distress and parental efficacy). Contrary to the hypotheses, the results suggested that adult mothers were experiencing more distress and appraising their situation as more threatening than were adolescent mothers of full term infants at the point of the infant's hospital discharge, but this difference had dissipated by the 3 month follow-up. Four adult mothers of preterm infants and two adolescent mothers of preterm infants reported significant psychological distress pre-discharge. Post-discharge two adult mothers of preterm infants, two adolescent mothers of preterm infants, and four adolescent mothers of full term infants reported significant psychological distress.

This study also found that for all mothers, parental self-efficacy increased over time and perceived social support decreased over time (Farnell, et al., in press). These results suggest that despite the posited double risk for adolescent mothers of preterm infants that at both the time of infant discharge from hospital and three months post-discharge adolescent mothers were adjusting well to the birth of a preterm infant and there were no differences between adolescent mothers of preterm and full term infants. Further, it was adult mothers who were reporting higher levels of perceived threat and psychological distress associated with parenting a preterm infant. Farnell and colleagues proposed that one explanation for their findings was that adolescent and adult mothers differed in their expectations of birth and motherhood. Adult mothers have reported that a preterm birth violates their expectations of motherhood, contributing to their ensuing distress (Affleck, et al., 1991). Conversely, adolescent mothers have been found to have less complex, undifferentiated expectations of parenting, viewing it more as an opportunity to find meaning and purpose in a context of social and educational disadvantage (Lee & Gramatnev, 2006; Unger, et al., 2000), while also giving the young women the chance to secure love and fulfill an existential need (Unger, et al., 2000). Farnell et al. therefore proposed that preterm birth did not violate the young women's expectations of having a child to love and provide love and thus, there was less likelihood of a threat appraisal and the attendant psychological distress (Farnell, et al., in press). In terms of contributing to the broader literature on preterm birth, Farnell et al.'s study supported previous research that suggested that for most mothers and fathers of preterm infants without significant chronicity issues related to VLBW stress dissipates post-discharge (Bissell & Long, 2003; Gray, et al., 2012; Rowe & Jones, 2010). At the same time, adolescent mothers of full term infants reported an increase in psychological distress post-discharge, which was consistent with the argument that they may have had overly positive perceptions of parenting pre-discharge (see Unger et al., 2000) and that the reality of parenting leads to increased distress for some young women. Of note was the lack of significant differences between the two groups of adolescent mothers with respect to psychological distress at either time point. This suggests that developmental considerations may exert more influence than the birth context; a proposition explored in the third study discussed below (Sheeran, 2011).

The Impact of Age Based Categorizations on Communication, Relationships with Staff and Outcomes for Mothers of Preterm Infants

This qualitative study analyzed interviews from 39 adult mothers of preterm infants and from 20 adolescent mothers of preterm infants at time of discharge from hospital (Sheeran, 2012; Sheeran, et al., under review). The aim of this study was to identify factors that influenced the parenting experience for mothers during the hospital experience and to explore similarities and differences between adolescent and adult mothers. In particular, this research focused on support and communication as factors that influenced perceptions of challenge and adjustment during the acute stage of having a preterm infant hospitalized. Content analysis of interview transcripts generated 3 themes: challenges of parenting in the neonatal nursery, supportive relationships, and growth from experience. Of particular importance for this chapter are the themes relating to challenges both in the nursery and in developing and maintaining relationships. Overall, the findings of the study confirmed that parenting a preterm infant presented unique challenges for mothers, with both adult and adolescent mothers reporting similar challenges. These included practical challenges such as travelling to and from the hospital, situational challenges such as negotiating care of their infant with staff, managing alterations to the parental role, dealing with stress associated with the experience, and managing their emotions. For the most part, adult and adolescent mothers experienced the challenges of parenting in the SCN similarly. However, notable differences were found in their narratives, with adult mothers explicitly stating that the experience had been stressful while adolescent mothers did not. Further, adolescent mothers were more likely to report that though unplanned, the preterm birth of their infant was not negative. They were still mothers and their infant would come home at some stage. In this way, preterm birth did not interrupt their perceptions of themselves as mothers. Conversely, adult mothers noted that having a preterm infant was not how they had expected motherhood to be. For these mothers the loss of a normal birth experience was highly stressful, even traumatic. Adult mothers lamented not having the 'big celebration' that was expected to accompany the birth of a baby and this was considered 'unnatural'. This perception was not evident in adolescent mothers' narratives.

The results of this study help to further explicate the findings from Farnell et al. (in press) by suggesting that a preterm birth was perceived as personally threatening to adult mothers, resulting in increased self-reported psychological distress. That is, a preterm birth impacted directly on the adult women's beliefs and expectations of motherhood. Despite reporting better support from staff and other parents, these adult mothers still discussed the event as being stressful and traumatic. In contrast, preterm birth for adolescent mothers was not personally threatening; it did not challenge their perceptions of themselves as mothers as drastically as adult mothers. In this way, youth can be seen as a protective factor against distress in the nursery context.

Sheeran et al.'s (under review) findings also help to dispute an alternative explanation for Farnell et al.'s (in press) finding that adult mothers experienced greater distress; that they may have been contending with more demands. Sheeran et al. found that although adult mothers were more likely to have other children, husbands, and households to manage, and were more likely to have had more demands outside of the hospital to contend with possibly adding to perception of burden, young mothers of preterm infants had to contend with challenges that were more common for young women than for older mothers by virtue of age and experience. These challenges included lack of stable housing, limited access to transport, and limited access to money. They reported struggling to find money for public transport to attend the hospital and some were unsure where they would live once the infant was discharged. Therefore, both groups were experiencing demands, albeit different demands, outside of the hospital which may have contributed to burden. This suggests that despite a similar burden of challenge and more support in the SCN, adult mothers were still more likely to experience more distress.

One notable challenge present in the young women's narratives was their perception that they had to contend with stereotypical and negative judgment from staff, a judgment based on their young maternal age. This made it difficult for them to negotiate the hospital system.

This challenge was further explicated in the second theme which outlined the role of supportive relationships while in the SCN. Both partners and nursing staff were reported as essential sources of support. In particular, all adult mothers reported that staff were supportive. They minimized any negative experiences with staff explaining them in terms of individual difference variables for example personality clashes. In contrast, adolescent mothers, while recognizing nursing staff as essential, described their interactions and relationships differently to adult mothers. The young mothers tended to categorize nurses as 'good' or 'bad'. This categorization was based on their perception of the quality of nurses' communication and they felt keenly aware that they were talked down to, watched, and treated differently due to their age. The young mothers also provided an explanation for the negative behaviors that they were subjected to, that is, they perceived that they were labeled and treated first as adolescents, rather than as mothers. At the same time, in discussing their results, Sheeran et al. drew on communication accommodation theory (see Drury, 2010; Gallois, Ogay, & Giles, 2005) to argue that communication between adult mothers and nursing staff could be classified as interpersonal, with members of both groups interacting with each other as individuals. In contrast, communication between adolescent mothers and nurses could be classified as intergroup, with members of both groups interacting with each other primarily as members of the out-group and their commensurate stereotypes influencing interactions. In this way, the young women felt stereotyped as 'teenage mothers' who did not know how to parent. Interactions or offers for assistance by staff were then perceived negatively and interpreted as being due to them not knowing how to parent.

Young mothers can be seen to have faced more social threat by virtue of being a stigmatized group. That is, being a young mother in the SCN meant that they perceived they were categorized in line with age based social identities such as 'adolescent mother' or 'teenage mother' rather than as 'mothers'. Previous research with people with HIV has found that ambiguous stimuli were attributed negatively based on their group membership rather than to other possible causes (i.e. person was having a bad day). This biased attribution, while often acknowledged by stigmatized group members as being biased, was felt to be necessary as it served a self-protective function preparing the person for possible attack from the dominant group (Rintamaki & Brashers, 2010). This is consistent with the current study where young mother's reports suggested that they perceived all negative, unfriendly, or annoying staff behavior (i.e. bathing baby when mother was not at hospital) as the result of nurses considering adolescent mothers to be unable to undertake the task themselves. Young mothers reported that they interpreted these cues as nurses regarding them as incompetent rather than interpreting those cues as being a result of the system. The young mothers' reports then suggested increased perceived conflict between themselves and staff, decreased perceptions of support from staff, and perceived stigmatization and discrimination. The perceived stigmatization and feelings of discrimination in the nursery may be similar to that experienced by adolescent mothers from the general community (Fessler, 2008; Hanna, 2001), making the experience of parenting similar for both groups of adolescent mothers. This may explain why, despite the reported negative judgment in the nursery by young mothers of preterm infants, Farnell et al. (in press) failed to find differences between the two groups of adolescent mothers. This proposition was examined in a study by Sheeran (2011) described below.

Young Women's Experiences of Being a Mother during the First Year: A Comparative Study of Parenting Preterm and Full Term Infants

The third study in our program of research reported here analyzed interview data from 10 adolescent mothers of preterm infants and 4 adolescent mothers of full term infants to explore how the experience of parenting over the first 12 months differed for the two groups of younger mothers (Sheeran, 2011). In depth guided interviews were conducted at the time of discharge from hospital, 3-4 months post-discharge, and 12 months post-discharge. Interpretative Phenomenological Analysis (IPA) generated 3 main themes relating to the experience of being a mother as a young woman and in the context of a preterm birth. These were the *Dual nature of parenthood, Actual/ideal incongruence,* and *Transforming the self.* Further, accessing social support was found to interact with the three main themes. Despite the study's focus on the experience of having a preterm birth, the findings highlighted many common experiences among the young women, regardless of whether their infant was born preterm or full term.

The theme Dual nature of parenthood highlighted how being a mother could be described in terms of polarities – good moments and challenging moments. Day-to-day life was experienced by young women as both full of pleasurable moments spent with their infants combined with challenging moments as they managed the sometimes chaotic worlds around them and the needs of the infant. The young women contended with instability and uncertainty about what was best and right for their infants as well as situational challenges related to housing and transport. However, there was considerable variability in the perception of the challenges faced by young women and this was influenced by whether the young women had had opportunities to develop internal resources prior to pregnancy. Some young women felt that the challenges were manageable whereas other young women found parenting to be very overwhelming with its constant demands. Those that tended to find it less challenging had held roles before their pregnancy where they had developed a sense of efficacy and this generalized to the parenting domain. Preterm birth compounded the everyday challenges of motherhood for young women. As described above young women with infants in the SCN were challenged by transportation difficulties finding it difficult to meet the implicit expectation of long hours at the bedside, another factor that they felt attracted negative judgment. This compounded their concerns about not being able to get on with mothering on their terms because they were separated from their babies. However, while preterm birth did lead to more challenges, it did not detract from the predominant focus of their stories that is, their enjoyment and knowledge that they were mothers, for them a point of distinction from their adolescent peers.

The findings suggested a process of idealization of being mothers, captured in the second theme, actual/ideal incongruence. This theme captured the tension of their experiences of being mothers; the reality of their everyday life did not match their idealized image. It was proposed that idealization served a self-protective role for some of the young women, to help them defend against fears of not being good enough or not being able to cope and/or idealization served as a coping strategy for other mothers as they wished for an easier future. This was particularly pertinent for young mothers of preterm infants who idealized home as the place where things would be easier. The greater the degree of discrepancy between the idealized image and the actual experience of being a mother, the more challenges the young women perceived with parenting.

Further, young women with large discrepancies between their ideal and actual images of self were less likely to ask for help for fear that others would label them as inadequate mothers and thus emphasize the discrepancy between their idealized and actual views of self. The transformative nature of becoming a mother, captured in the third theme transforming self, was evident in the young women's accounts of their lived experience. The young women's stories varied in details, all had different pre-pregnancy narratives. However, pregnancy and the birth of their infants, preterm, low birth weight or at full term and healthy, was transforming for them. Each identified primarily as now being a mother and devoted themselves to their infant. Their alternative self concepts as teenager, daughter, sister, student, employee etc, were initially less salient. They also described behavior changes, some quite drastic as the young women constructed a trajectory away from behavior they saw now as potentially negative and unsuitable toward this significant new understanding of who they were and what was needed of themselves to fulfill their maternal identity and role. Over 12 months, the young women's self concepts became more diffuse and they rediscovered other aspects of their adolescent self or devoted more time to developing other areas of self. Also important in this process was that, for most, motherhood provided the vehicle for the development of internal resources such as organization, patience, reduced egocentrism, confidence in self and competence in their ability to succeed.

The interrelationships between these themes also suggested important factors that contribute to a positive transition to motherhood. Those mothers who had previous opportunities to develop confidence, competence, and self-efficacy, perceived fewer internal challenges in the parenting experience. These women appeared to be able to generalize efficacy to parenting and had less self-doubt in their ability to parent. This meant they were less likely to idealize self or other as there was little need to defend against fear and uncertainty about whether they could parent. For others, motherhood was the vehicle for change. Being a mother resulted in behavioral changes as they reduced drug and alcohol use, cognitive changes as they thought more concretely about the future and less egocentrically, and changes to self as they developed internal resources and a positive self-image. Early in the parenting experience these women were more likely to idealize themselves and others in order to cope and to defend against fears that they would not be good enough mothers. Parenting was more likely to be perceived as challenging. However, over time the everyday experience and the meanings that the young women were assigning to the experiences transformed their idealized understanding of motherhood and themselves as mothers into real practice and confidence grounded in the practice of everyday mothering. They developed a congruent understanding of the self and what was required to put this into practice.

External support and family background factors also interacted with the core themes but were not central to the experience of being a mother. Young women differed in their willingness and capacity to access support. Those with discrepancies between their idealized and actual view of self as parent were less likely to access support or admit that they needed support for fear that this discrepancy would be emphasized and reinforced. Similarly, young women from chaotic family backgrounds were less able to access support, as others in their networks were often contending with multiple challenges and instability themselves. Some had few problems in accessing support and used support effectively to manage parenting. These young women were more likely to have stable family systems and were more likely to have confidence in their parenting ability. So while support was important, it was internal factors that influenced the young women's ability to access it.

Consistent with previous research, support that was intrusive or that undermined the young woman's ability to parent autonomously negatively influenced the young woman (Bunting & McAuley, 2004a; SmithBattle, 1997). In addition, support that emphasized the view of self as not living up to their ideal (i.e., not being good enough) was perceived negatively. The young women did not want people to take over and parent for them or to tell them what to do. Rather they wanted time out in the form of short breaks and help with the little things (i.e., washing, cooking). Time out was probably the most vital aspect of support that the young women discussed. Unfortunately, many of them felt unable to ask for time out for fear of being labeled as the 'stereotypical teenage mother' who dumped her baby. Early in the experience of being a parent this prevented the young women from accessing support. However, over time they overcame this resistance to seeking help, as their idealized view of themselves and fear of not being a 'good enough mother' decreased and their confidence in the parenting role increased. This suggests that people in support roles for young women need to consider the type of support they provide and should be aware that they may struggle to ask for help when they feel that they are performing poorly as mothers or that others may judge them.

CONCLUSION

Our program of research explored whether experiences of parenting in the context of a preterm birth differed for young mothers compared to adult mothers. Further, we were interested in whether young women's experiences of having a preterm infant fit with the posited double risk in the extant literature (Thurman & Gonsalves, 1993). These studies found little support for the proposition that young mothers of preterm infants were at double risk for poor adjustment. Further, the findings flesh out the challenges faced by young mothers of preterm infants and highlighted the need to re-orientate our understanding of what might be meaningful and significant to these young mothers as they transition into maternal identity. Preterm birth itself was not overly stressful for the adolescent mother and it did not detract from the fact that they were mothers. Despite facing similar challenges as adult mothers with infants hospitalized in special care nurseries, young women did not report the same degree of perceived stress or threat as adult mothers, suggesting that age is a protective factor against psychological distress in this context. One reason posited, and supported by the qualitative research studies by Sheeran et al. (under review), is that preterm birth is perceived as personally threatening to adult mothers, as it threatens their ideas and expectations of motherhood. This personal threat contributes to the experience of increased distress. Conversely, maternal identity development following the birth of their infants dominated young mothers' discourses, reducing the potentially stressful impact of the preterm birth. In this way preterm birth was not perceived as threatening to the young woman contributing to their lower reported distress. This program of research also highlights the many commonalities between the experiences of adult mothers of preterm infants and adolescent mothers of preterm infants while their infants are hospitalized. Consistent with the experience of preterm birth in the broader adult literature, the young women in the current research reported distress associated with the separation from their infant and the relinquishment of control for care of their infant to nursing staff (Affleck & Tennen, 1991; Miles, Burchinal, Holditch-Davis, Brunssen, & Wilson, 2002) and this suggests that there are universal difficulties inherent in having a preterm infant.

There also appeared to be few differences between adolescent mothers of preterm and full term infants. Preterm birth represented an exacerbation of challenges experienced by all young mothers rather than being a unique stressor. As such, preterm birth exacerbated difficulties with transport, money, and perceived negative judgment. All of the young women in the study were exposed to negative attitudes from others, including health professionals and general members of the community. This finding is consistent with other Australian research by Hanna (2001), which found that the young women were exposed to high levels of stigma and condemnation from the wider community. Stigma and negative judgment can also translate into discrimination and can have a major impact on the experience of parenting and the mother's willingness to engage in help seeking (Fessler, 2008). The challenge for service providers then becomes how to advocate for young mothers by increasing awareness of the inaccuracies of stereotypes and the negative ramifications of stigma.

The SCN context did appear to exacerbate feelings of negative judgment as young women struggled to manage parenting in the hospital environment. One important finding from this program of research was that the context of a preterm birth became an intergroup context for adolescent mothers whereby they perceived that the staff labeled them as 'adolescent' rather than 'mother'. The young mothers perceived that they faced ensuing stigmatization and perceived discrimination such as being watched, observed, and monitored. As with other stigmatized groups (Rintamaki & Brashers, 2010), ambiguous cues were perceived as differential treatment by staff and young women attributed this to their age. Consistent with this finding, Peterson, Sword, Charles, and DiCenso (2007) found that young women inpatients perceived nursing care as more positive when they were treated the same as adult patients. Alternatively, being treated differentially due to age often hindered the development of an effective nurse/patient relationship (Peterson et al., 2007). This has important implications for working with young mothers, particularly in the SCN context, as many may resist being labeled as a teenage mother and may expect to be treated primarily as a mother/woman with age a secondary consideration. Nursing staff may need to be aware that subtle differences in treatment between adult and adolescent mothers will be noted and interpreted by young mothers as being due to nurses perceiving them as incompetent. Communication between nurses and young mothers becomes more difficult, as each may relate to stereotypical group categorizations and make assumptions of the other person's motives and meanings. This also influences relationship development and perceptions of support.

The young women's narratives suggest that as adolescent mothers they were doing reasonably well in the first 12-months of being a mother. However, the fragility of the situation for most of the young mothers does need to be emphasized. Although most young women felt that they were managing well and were in stable situations by the time the infant was 12-months of age, there was a sense expressed by Sheeran (2011) that if anything should go wrong within the system in which mother and baby were embedded that stability could be shattered. This fragility has been further emphasized in other work relating to these same young mothers (Jones, Rowe, & Sheeran, 2010). Research on adolescent pregnancy has suggested that second pregnancies can be a risk factor for poorer outcomes for a mother and her infants (Kalmuss & Namerow, 1994). Further, the risk of relationship breakdown for young women remains high (Bunting & McAuley, 2004b; Quinlivan, et al., 2004). Infants can become increasingly demanding as they enter in to toddlerhood (Gross and Conrad, 1995) and cognitive delays for preterm infants may continue and become apparent over time and when schooling commences (Short et al., 2006). In addition, contextual factors such as the difficulty of finding affordable housing and increasing costs of living could create further challenges in maintaining stable housing. Most of the young women in the current study were susceptible to several of these risk factors and this could easily contribute to altering the current state of equilibrium. As such, in-depth longitudinal research with young women is warranted to investigate whether the experience of motherhood becomes more or less challenging over the longer term.

REFERENCES

Aber, J. L., Brooks-Gunn, J., & Maynard, R. A. (1995). Effects of welfare reform on teenage parents and their children. *The Future of Children, 5*(2), 53-71. Retrieved from http://www.jstor.org.stable/1602357.

Able-Boone, H., & Stevens, E. (1994). After the intensive care nursery experience: Families' perceptions of their well being. *Children's Health Care, 23*(2), 99-114.

Affleck, G., & Tennen, H. (1991). The effect of newborn intensive care on parents' psychological well-being. *Children's Health Care, 20*(1), 6-14. doi: 10.1207/s15326888chc2001_2.

Affleck, G., Tennen, H., Allen, D. A., & Gershman, K. (1986). Perceived social support and maternal adaptation during the transition from hospital to home care of high-risk infants. *Infant Mental Health Journal, 7*(1), 6-18. doi: 10.1002/1097-.

Affleck, G., Tennen, H., Rowe, J., Roscher, B., & Walker, L. (1989). Effects of formal support on mothers' adaptation to the hospital-to-home transition of high-risk infants: The benefits and costs of helping. *Child Development, 60*(2), 488-501. Retrieved from http://www.jstor.org/stable/1130993.

Affleck, G., Tennen, H., & Rowe, J. C. (1991). *Infants in crisis : how parents cope with newborn intensive care and its aftermath*. New York: Springer-Verlag.

Arai, L. (2003). Low expectations, sexual attitudes and knowledge: explaining teenage pregnancy and fertility in English communities. Insights from qualitative research. *The Sociological Review, 51*(2), 199-218. Retrieved from http://find.galegroup. com/itx/infomark.do?andcontentSet=IAC-Documentsandtype=retrieveandtabID= T002andprodId=EAIManddocId=A105480274andsource=galeandsrcprod=EAIManduser GroupName=griffithandversion=1.0.

Arenson, J. D. (1994). Strengths and self-perceptions of parenting in adolescent mothers. *Journal of Pediatric Nursing, 9*(4), 251-258. doi: 0882-5963/94/0904-000753.00/0.

Bakewell-Sachs, S., & Gennaro, S. (2004). Parenting the post-NICU premature infant. *The American Journal of Maternal Child Nursing, 29*(6), 398-403. doi: 10.1097/00005721-200411000-00011.

Baldwin, W., & Cain, V., S. (1980). The children of teenage parents. *Family Planning perspectives, 12*(1), 34-39 42-43. Retrieved from http://links.jstor.org/sici?sici=0014-7354%28198001%2F02%2912%3A1%3C34%3ATCOTP%3E2.0.CO%3B2-L.

Barnes, J. C., & Morris, R. G. (2012). Young Mothers, Delinquent Children. *Youth Violence and Juvenile Justice, 10*(2), 172-189. doi: 10.1177/1541204011423260.

Barratt, M. S., & Roach, M. A. (1995). Early interactive processes: Parenting by adolescent and adult single mothers. *Infant Behaviour and Development, 18*, 97-109. doi: 10.1016/0163-6383(95)90011-X

Barratt, M. S., Roach, M. A., Morgan, K. M., & Colbert, K. K. (1996). Adjustment to motherhood by single adolescents. *Family Relations, 45*, 209-215.

Barth, R. P., Schinke, S. P., & Maxwell, J. S. (1983). Psychological correlates of teenage motherhood. *Journal of Youth and Adolescence, 12*(6), 471-487. doi: 10.1007/BF02088665.

Bell, P. L. (1997). Adolescent mothers' perceptions of the neonatal intensive care unit environment. *Journal of Perinatal and Neonatal Nursing, 11*(1), 77-84.

Birkeland, R. W., Thompson, J. K., & Phares, V. (2005). Adolescent motherhood and postpartum depression. *Journal of Clinical Child and Adolescent Psychology, 34*(2), 292-300. doi: 10.1207/s15374424 jccp3402_8.

Bissell, G., & Long, T. (2003). From the neonatal unit to home: how do parents adapt to life at home with their baby? *Journal of Neonatal Nursing, 9*, 7-12.

Blinn-Pike, L., & Mingus, S. (2000). The internal consistency of the Child Abuse Potential Inventory with adolescent mothers. *Journal of Adolescence, 23*(1), 107-111. doi: 10.1006/jado.1999.0297.

Brooks-Gunn, J., Duncan, G. J., Klebanov, P. K., & Sealand, N. (1993). Do neighbourhoods influence child and adolescent development. *The American Journal of Sociology, 99*(2), 353-395.

Bunting, L., & McAuley, C. (2004a). Research review: Teenage pregnancy and motherhood: the contribution of support. *Child and Family Social Work, 9*, 207-215. doi: 10.1111/j.1365-2206.2004.00328.x.

Bunting, L., & McAuley, C. (2004b). Research review: Teenage pregnancy and parenthood: the role of fathers. *Child and Family Social Work, 9*, 295-303. doi: 10.1111/j.1365-2206.2004.00335.x.

Caldwell, C. H., & Antonucci, T. C. (1997). Childbearing during adolescence: mental health risks and opportunities. In J. Schulenberg, J. Maggs and K. Hurrelmann (Eds.), *Health Risks and Developmental Transitions During Adolescence* (pp. 220-245). Cambridge; New York: Cambridge University Press.

Card, J. J., & Wise, L. L. (1978). Teenage mothers and teenage fathers: The impact of early childbearing on the parents' personal and professional lives. *Family Planning Perspectives, 10*(4), 199-205. Retrieved from http://www.jstor.org/stable/2134267.

Carey, G., Ratliff, D. A. N., & Lyle, R. R. (1998). Resilient adolescent mothers: Ethnographic interviews. *Families, Systems and Health, 16*(4), 347(341). doi: 10.1037/h0089861.

Carter, J. D., Mulder, R. T., Bartram, A. F., & Darlow, B. A. (2005). Infants in a neonatal intensive care unit: parental response. *Archives of Disease in Childhood - Fetal and neonatal edition, 90*, F109-F113. doi: 10.1136/adc.2003.031641.

Clemmens, D. (2001). The relationship between social support and adolescent mothers' interactions with their infants: A meta-analysis. *Journal of Obstetric, Gynecologic and Neonatal Nursing, 30*(4), 410-420. doi: 10.1111/j.1552-6909.2001.tb01560.x.

Cleveland, L. M. (2008). Parenting in the Neonatal Intensive Care Unit. *Journal of Obstetric Gynecologic and Neonatal Nursing, 37*(6), 666-691. doi: 10.1111/j.1552-6909.2008.00288.x.

Cohn, J. F., Campbell, S. B., Matias, R., & Hopkins, J. (1990). Face-to-face interactions of postpartum depressed and nondepressed mother-infant pairs at 2 months. *Developmental Psychology, 26*(1), 15-23.

Coleman, J., & Dennison, C. (1998). Teenage parenthood. *Children and Society, 12*(4), 306-314. doi: doi:10.1111/j.1099-0860.1998.tb00084.x.

Condon, J. T., & Corkindale, C. J. (2002). Teenage pregnancy: Trends and consequences. *Current Therapeutics, 43*(3), 25-31. Retrieved from http://search.informit.com.au. libraryproxy.griffith.edu.au/documentSummary;dn=526835297158502;res=IELHEA.

Coyne, J. C., & DeLongis, A. (1986). Going beyond social support: The role of social relationships in adaptation. *Journal of Consulting and Clinical Psychology, 54*(4), 454-460. doi: 10.1037/0022-006x.54.4.454.

Cronin, C. M. G., Shapiro, C. R., Casiro, O. G., & Cheang, M. S. (1995). The impact of very low-birthweight infants on the family is long lasting: A matched control study. *Archive of Pediatric and Adolescent Medicine, 149*, 151-158. doi: 10.1001/archpedi.1995.02170140033005.

Cutrona, C. E., Hessling, R. M., Bacon, P. L., & Russell, D. W. (1998). Predictors and correlates of continuing involvement with the baby's father among adolescent mothers. *Journal of Family Psychology, 12*(3), 369-387. doi: 10.1037/0893-3200.12.3.369.

da Silva, A. A., Simoes, V. M., Barbieri, M. A., Bettiol, H., Lamy-Filho, F., Coimbra, L. C., & Alves, M. T. (2003). Young maternal age and preterm birth. *Paediatric and Perinatal Epidemiology, 18*, 332-339.

Davis, L., Edwards, H., Mohay, H., & Wollin, J. (2003). The impact of very premature birth on the psychological health of mothers. *Early Human Development, 73*, 61-70. doi: 10.1016/S0378-3782(03)00073-2.

Deal, L. W., & Holt, V. L. (1998). Young maternal age and depressive symptoms: Results from the 1988 national maternal and infant health survey. *American Journal of Public Health, 88*(2), 266-266-270. doi: 10.2105/AJPH.88.2.266.

Doering, L. V., Dracup, K., & Moser, D. (1999). Comparison of psychosocial adjustment of mothers and fathers of high-risk infants in the neonatal intensive care unit. *Journal of Perinatology, 19*(2), 132-137.

Doucette, J., & Pinelli, J. (2000). The effects of family resources, coping, and strains on family adjustment 18 to 24 months after the NICU experience. *Advances in Neonatal Care, 4*(2), 92-104. doi: 10.1016/j.adnc.2004.01.005.

Drury, J. (2003). Adolescent communication with adults in authority. *Journal of Language and Social Psychology, 22*(1), 66-73. doi: 10.1177/0261927X02250057.

Drury, J. (2010). Identity development in Adolescent-Adult communication. In H. Giles, S. Reid and J. Harwood (Eds.), *The Dynamics of Intergroup Communication*. New York: Peter Lang.

Drury, J., Catan, L., Dennison, C., & Brody, R. (1998). Exploring teenagers' accounts of bad communication: a new basis for intervention. *Journal of Adolescence, 21*(2), 177-196.

Ekwo, E. E., & Moawad, A. (2000). Maternal age and preterm births in a black population. *Paediatric and Perinatal Epidemiology, 14*, 144-151.

Evans, T., Whittingham, K., & Boyd, R. (2012). What helps the mother of a preterm infant become securely attached, responsive and well-adjusted? *Infant Behavior and Development, 35*, 1-11. doi: 10.1016/j.infbeh.2011.10.002.

Farnell, L., Jones, L., Rowe, J., & Sheeran, N. (in press). Effects of age and the preterm birth of an infant on adolescent mothers' psychological adjustment. *Child Health Care.*

Fenwick, J., Barclay, L., & Schmied, V. (2000). 'Chatting': an important clinical tool in facilitating mothering in neonatal nurseries. *Journal of Advanced Nursing, 33*(5), 583-593. doi: 10.1046/j.1365-2648.2001.01694.x.

Fergusson, D. M., & Woodward, L. J. (2000). Teenage pregnancy and female education underachievement: A prospective study of a New Zealand birth cohort. *Journal of Marriage and the Family, 62*, 147-161. doi: 10.1111/j.1741-3737.2000.00147.x.

Fessler, K. B. (2008). *Reclaiming a spoiled maternal identity: Young mothers' experiences and rejection of stigma.* Ph.D., University of Michigan, Michigan. Retrieved from http://search.proquest.com.libraryproxy. griffith.edu.au/docview/304575273?accountid=14543.

Field, T., Morrow, C., Goldstein, S., Perry, D., Bendell, D., Schanberg, S., & Kuhn, C. (1988). Infants of depressed mothers show "depressed" behaviour even with nondepressed adults. *Child Development, 59*(6), 1569-1579.

Field, T., Widmayer, S. M., Stringer, S., & Ignatoff, E. (1980). Teenage, lower-class, black mothers and their preterm infants: An intervention and developmental follow-up. *Child Development, 51*(2), 426-436. doi: 10.1111/j.1467-8624.1980.tb02563.x.

Franck, L. S., Cox, S., Allen, A., & Winter, I. (2005). Measuring neonatal intensive care unit-related parental stress. *Journal of Advanced Nursing, 49*(6), 608-615. doi: 10.1111/j.1365-2648.2004.03336.x.

Frye, R. E., Malmberg, B., Swank, P., Smith, K., & Landry, S. (2010). Preterm birth and maternal responsiveness during childhood are associated with brain morphology in adolescence. *Journal of the International Neuropsychological Society, 16*(5), 784-784-794. doi: 10.1017/ s1355617710000585.

Furstenberg, F. F., Brooks-Gunn, J., & Chase-Lansdale, L. (1989). Teenaged pregnancy and childbearing. *American Psychologist, 44*(2), 313-320. doi: 10.1037/0003-066X.44.2.313.

Furstenberg, F. F., Brooks-Gunn, S., & Morgan, P. (1987). Adolescent mothers and their children in later life. *Family Planning Perspectives, 19*(4), 142-151. Retrieved from http://www.jstor.org.libraryproxy.griffith .edu.au/stable/2135159.

Gallois, C., Ogay, T., & Giles, H. (2005). Communication accomodation theory: A look back and a look ahead. In W. B. Gudykunst (Ed.), *Theorizing About Intercultural Communication* (pp. 121-148). Thousand Oaks, CA: Sage.

Gavin, A., Lindhorst, T., & Lohr, M. J. (2011). The prevalence and correlates of depressive symptoms among adolescent mothers: Results from a 17-year longitudinal study. *Women and Health, 51*(6), 525-545.

Geronimus, A. T., Korenman, S., & Hillemeier, M. M. (1994). Does young maternal age adversely affect child development? Evidence from cousin comparisons in the United States. *Population and Development Review, 20*(3), 585-609.

Goldenberg, R. L., Culhane, J.F., Iams, J.D., & Romero, R. (2008). Epidemiology and causes of preterm birth. *Lancet, 371*(9606), 75-84.

Gray, D., Woodward, L. J., Spencer, C., Inder, T. E., & Austin, N. C. (2006). Health service utilisation of a regional cohort of very preterm infants over the first 2 years of life. *Journal of Paediatrics and Child Health, 42*, 377-383. doi: 10.1111/j.1440-1754.2006.00876.x.

Gray, P. H., Edwards, D. M., O'Callaghan, M. J., & Cuskelly, M. (2012). Parenting stress in mothers of preterm infants during early infancy. *Early Human Development, 88*, 45-49. doi: 10.1016/j.earlhumdev.2011.06.014.

Griffin, J. B., & Pickler, R. H. (2011). Hospital-to-home transition of mothers of preterm infants. *MCN, 36*(4), 252-257. doi: 10.1097/NMC. 0b013e31821770b8.

Gross, D., & Conrad, B. (1995). Temperament in toddlerhood. *Journal of Pediatric Nursing, 10*(3), 146-151.

Hanna, B. (2000). Getting on the inside: A researcher's journey into the world of teenage motherhood. *The Australian Journal of Holistic Nursing 7*(2), 4-11.

Hanna, B. (2001). Negotiating motherhood: the struggles of teenage mothers. *Journal of Advanced Nursing, 34*(4), 456-464. doi: 10.1046/j.1365-2648.2001.01774.x.

Haskett, M.E., Johnson, C. A., & Miller, J. W. (1994). Individual differences in risk of child abuse by adolescent mothers: Assessment in the perinatal period. *Journal of Child Psychology and Psychiatry, 35*(3), 461-476.

Hess, C. R., Papas, M. A., & Black, M. M. (2002). Resilience among African American adolescent mothers: Predictors of positive parenting in early infancy. *Journal of Pediatric Psychology, 27*(7), 619-629. doi: 10.1093/jpepsy/27.7.619.

Holditch-Davies, D., Miles, M. S., Weaver, M. A., Black, B., Beeber, L., Thoyre, S., & Engelke, S. (2009). Patterns of distress in African-American mothers of preterm infants. *Journal of Developmental and Behavioural Pediatrics, 30*(3), 193-206.

Holditch-Davis, D., & Miles, M. (2000). Mothers' stories about their experiences in the neonatal intensive care unit. *Neonatal Network, 19*(1), 13-21.

Holub, C. K., Kershaw, T. S., Ethier, K. A., Lewis, J. B., Milan, S., & Ickovics, J. R. (2007). Prenatal and parenting stress on adolescent maternal adjustment: Identifying a high-risk subgroup. *Maternal and Child Health Journal, 11*, 153-159.

Hughes, M., McCollum, J., Sheftel, D., & Sanchez, G. (1994). How parents cope with the experience of neonatal intensive care. *Children's Health Care, 23*(1), 1-14. doi: 10.1207/s15326888chc2301_1.

Hunt-Morse, M. C. (2002). *Adolescent mothers' psychosocial development: Implications for parenting.* Doctor of Philosophy, University of Oregon, Oregon. Retrieved from http://search.proquest.com.libraryproxy. griffith.edu.au/docview/251764186?accountid=14543.

Jones, L., Rowe, J., & Becker, T. (2009). Appraisal, coping and social support as predictors of psychological distress and parenting efficacy in parents of premature infants. *Children's Health Care, 38*(4), 245-262. doi: 10.1080/02739610903235976.

Jones, L., Rowe, J., & Sheeran, N. (2010). Teenage maternal adjustment during the transition from hospital to home with a pre-term or low birth weight infant: One year post discharge. Brisbane: Griffith University and Department of Communities.

Jones, L., Woodhouse, D., & Rowe, J. (2007). Effective nurse parent communication: A study of parents' perceptions in the NICU environment. *Patient Education and Counselling, 69*, 206-212.

Kalmuss, D. S., & Namerow, P. B. (1994). Subsequent childbearing among teenage mothers: The determinants of a closely spaced second birth. *Family Planning Perspectives, 26*(4), 149-153.

Kay, D. K. (2008). Negotiating the transition from adolescence to motherhood: Coping with prenatal and parenting stress in teenage mothers in Mulago hospital, Uganda. *BMC Public Health, 8*(83). doi: 10.1186/1471-2458-8-83.

Kenner, C., & Lott, J. W. (1990). Parent transition after discharge from the NICU. *Neonatal Network, 9*(2), 31-37.

Kenny, D. T. (1995). Adolescent pregnancy in Australia. In D. T. Kenny and R. F. Soames Job (Eds.), *Australia's Adolescents: A health psychology perspective* (pp. 239-245). Armidale: University of New England.

Ketterlinus, R. D., Lamb, M. E., & Nitz, K. (1991). Developmental and ecological sources of stress among adolescent parents. *Family Relations, 40*(4), 435-441. Retrieved from http://www.jstor.org.libraryproxy.griffith .edu.au/stable/584901.

Knaak, S. J. (2008). *The process of postpartum adjustment.* Ph.D., University of Alberta Canada. Retrieved from http://search.proquest.com.libraryproxy.griffith.edu.au/docview /304409913?accountid=14543.

Kohl, P. L., Kagotho, J. N., & Dixon, D. (2011). Parenting practices among depressed mothers in the child welfare system. *Social Work Research, 35*(4), 215-225. doi: 10.1016/s0272-7358(98)00100-7.

Lanzi, R. G., Bert, S. C., Jacobs, B. K., & The Centers for the Prevention of Child Neglect. (2009). Depression among a sample of first-time adolescent and adult mothers. *Journal of Child and Adolescent Psychiatric Nursing, 22*(4), 194-202. doi: 10.1111/j.1744-6171.2009.00199.x.

Larson, N. C., Hussey, J. M., Gillmore, M. R., & Gilchrist, L. D. (1996). What about dad? Fathers of children born to school-aged mothers. *Families in Society, 77*(5), 279-289.

Laws, P., Grayson, N., & Sullivan, E. A. (2006). Australian mothers and babies 2004 *Perinatal Statistics series*. Sydney: AIHW National Perinational Statistics Unit.

Laws, P., Li, Z., & Sullivan, E. A. (2010). *Australia's mothers and babies 2008*. Canberra:: AIHW.

Lee, C., & Gramatnev, H. (2006). Predictors and outcomes of early motherhood in the Australian longitudinal study on women's health. *Psychology, Health, and Medicine, 11*(1), 29-47.

Letourneau, N. L., Stewart, M., J., and Barnfather, A. K. (2004). Adolescent mothers: Support needs, resources, and support-education interventions. *Journal of Adolescent Health, 35*, 509-525. doi: 10.1016/j.jadohealth.2004.01.007.

Levine, J. A., Emery, C. R., & Pollack, H. (2007). The wellbeing of children born to teenage mothers. *Journal of Marriage and Family, 69*, 105-122.

Logson, M. C., & Koniak-Griffin, D. (2005). Social support in postpartum adolescents: Guidelines for nursing assessments and interventions. *Journal of Obstetric, Gynecologic and Neonatal Nursing, 34*(6), 761-768.

Lovejoy, M. C., Graczyk, P. A., O'Hare, E., & Neuman, G. (2000). Maternal depression and parenting behavior: A meta-analytic review. *Clinical Psychology Review, 20*(5), 561-592. doi: 10.1016/s0272-7358(98)00100-7.

Meyer, E. C., Garcia Coll, C. T., Seifer, R., Ramos, A., Kilis, E., & Oh, W. (1995). Psychological distress in mothers of preterm infants. *Journal of Developmental and Behavioral Pediatrics, 16*(6), 412-417. doi: 10.1097/00004703-199512000-00004.

Meyers, S. A., & Battistoni, J. (2003). Proximal and distal correlates of adolescent mothers' parenting attitudes. *Journal of Applied Developmental Psychology, 24*(1), 33-49. doi: 10.1016/s0193-3973(03)00023-6.

Milan, S., Ickovics, J. R., Kershaw, T. S., Lewis, J. B., & Meade, C. (2004). Prevalence, course, and predictors of emotional distress in pregnant and parenting adolescents. *Journal of Consulting and Clinical Psychology, 77*(2), 328-340. doi: 10.1037/0022-006X.72.2.328.

Miles, M. S. (1989). Parents of critically ill premature infants: Sources of stress. *Critical Care Nursing Quarterly, 12*(3), 69-74.

Miles, M. S., Burchinal, P., Holditch-Davis, D., Brunssen, S., & Wilson, S. M. (2002). Perceptions of stress, worry, and support in black and white mothers of hosptialised, medically fragile infants. *Journal of Pediatric Nursing, 17*(2), 82-88. doi: 10.1053/jpdn.2002.124125.

Miles, M. S., Carlson, J., & Funk, S. G. (1996). Sources of support reported by mothers and fathers of infants hospitalised in a neonatal intensive care unit. *Neonatal Network, 15*(3), 45-52.

Miles, M. S., & Holditch-Davis, D. (1997). Parenting the prematurely born child: Pathways of influence. *Seminars in Perinatology, 21*(3), 254-266.

Mohsin, M., Wong, F., Bauman, A., & Bai, J.U.N. (2003). Maternal and neonatal factors influencing premature birth and low birth weight in Australia. *Journal of Biosocial Science, 35*(2), 161-174.

Mollborn, S. (2007). Making the best of a bad situation: Material resources and teenage parenthood. *Journal of Marriage and Family, 69*(1), 92-107. doi: 10.1111/j.1741-3737.2006.00347.x.

Neu, M., & Robinson, J. (2008). Early weeks after premature birth as experienced by Latina adolescent mothers. *The American Journal of Maternal/Child Nursing, 33*(3), 32-38.

Partington, S. N., Steber, D. L., Blair, K. A., & Cisler, R. A. (2009). Second births to teenage mothers: Risk factors for low birth weight and preterm birth. *Perspectives on Sexual and Reproductive Health, 41*(2), 101-109. doi: 10.1363/41 10109.

Passino, A. W., Whitman, T. L., Borkowski, J. G., Schellenbach, C. J., Maxwell, S. E., Keogh, D., & Rellinger, E. (1993). Personal adjustment during pregnancy and adolescent parenting. *Adolescence, 28*(109), 97-122.

Pederson, D. R., Bento, S., Chance, G. W., Evans, B., & Fox, m. (1987). Maternal emotional responses to preterm birth. *American Journal of Orthopsychiatry, 57*(1), 15-21.

Petersen, W. E., Sword, W., Charles, C., & DiCenso, A. (2007). Adolescents' perceptions of inpatient postpartum nursing care. *Qualitative Health Research, 17*, 201-212. doi: 10.1177/1049732306297414.

Pinelli, J. (2000). Effects of family coping and resources on family adjustment and parental stress in the acute phase of the NICU experience. *Neonatal Network, 19*, 27-37.

Poehlmann, J., Schwichtenberg, A. J. M., Shlafer, R. J., Hahn, E., Bianchi, J.P., & Warner, R. (2011). Emerging self-regulation in toddlers born preterm or low birth weight: Differential susceptibility to parenting? *Development and Psychopathology, 23*(1), 177-193. doi:10.1111/j.1467-8624.2007.01019.x.

Quinlivan, J. A., Box, H., & Evans, S. F. (2003). Postnatal home visits in teenage mothers: a randomised controlled trial. *The Lancet, 361*, 893-900. Retrieved from EBSCOhost.

Quinlivan, J. A., Petersen, R. W., & Gurrin, L. C. (1999). Adolescent pregnancy: psychopathology missed. *Australian and New Zealand Journal of Psychiatry, 33*, 864-868.

Quinlivan, J. A., Tan, L. H., Steele, A., & Black, K. (2004). Impact of demographic factors, early family relationships and depressive symptomology in teenage pregnancy. *Australian and New Zealand Journal of Psychiatry, 38*, 197-203. doi: 10.1111/j.1440-1614.2004.01336.x.

Reis, J. (1989). A comparison of young teenage, older teenage, and adult mothers on determinants of parenting. *Journal of Psychology, 123*(3), 141-151. Retrieved from EBSCOhost.

Richardson, R. A., Barbour, N. E., & Bubenzer, D. L. (1995). Peer relationships as a source of support for adolescent mothers. *Journal of Adolescent Research, 10*(2), 278-290. doi: 10.1177/0743554895102005.

Rintamaki, L. S., & Brashers, D. E. (2010). Stigma and intergroup communication. In H. Giles, S. Reid and J. Harwood (Eds.), *The Dynamics of Intergroup Communication* (pp. 155-169). New York: Peter Lang.

Robson, S., Cameron, C. A., & Roberts, C. L. (2006). Birth outcomes for teenage women in New South Wales, 1998-2003. *Australian and New Zealand Journal of Obsetrics and Gynecology, 46*, 305-310. doi: 10.1111/j.1479-828X.2006.00597.x.

Rogeness, G. A., Ritchey, S., Alex, P. L., Zueler, M., & Morris, R. (1981). Family patterns and parenting attitudes in teenage parents. *Journal of Community Psychology, 9*, 239-345.

Roth, J. R., Hendrickson, J., & Stowell, D. W. (1998). The risk of teen mothers having low birth weight babies: Implications of recent medical research for school health personnel. *The Journal of School Health, 68*(7), 271-275.

Rowe, J., & Jones, L. (2008). Stress and adjustment in parents of preterm infants during the transition home from hospital. *Journal of Advanced Nursing, 17*(6), 782-789. doi: 10.1111/j.1365-2702.2007.02118.x.

Rowe, J., & Jones, L. (2010). Discharge and beyond: A longitudinal study comparing stress and coping in parents of preterm infants. *Journal of Neonatal Nursing, 16*, 258-266. doi: 10.1016/j.jnn.2010.07.018.

Rudd, N. M., McKenry, P. C., & Nah, M. (1990). Welfare receipt among black and white adolescent mothers. *Journal of Family Issues, 11*(3), 334-352. doi: 10.1177/019251390011003006.

Schellenbach, C. J., Whitman, T. L., & Borowski, J. G. (1992). Towards an integrative model of adolescent parenting. *Human Development, 35*, 81-99. Retrieved from <Go to ISI>://A1992HY90800003.

Schiefelbein, V. L., Susman, E. J., & Dorn, L. D. (2005). Self-competence mediates earlier and later anxiety in adolescent mothers: A 3-year longitudinal perspective. *Journal of Research on Adolescence, 15*(4), 625-655. doi: 10.1111/j.1532-7795.2005.00114.x.

Schultz, K. (2001). Constructing failure, narrating success: Rethinking the "problem" of teen pregnancy. *Teachers College Record, 103*(4), 582-607. doi: 10.1111/0161-4681.00128.

Scott Stiles, A. (2005). Parenting needs, goals, and strategies of adolescent mothers. *MCN, 30*(5), 327-333. doi: 10.1097/00005721-200509000-00011.

Seamark, C. J., & Lings, P. (2004). Positive experiences of teenage motherhood: a qualitative study. *British Journal of General Practice, 54*, 813-818. Retrieved from http://www.ingentaconnect.com/content/rcgp/ bjgp/2004/00000054/00000508/art00004.

Seamark, C. J., & Pereira Gray, D. J. (1997). Like mother, like daughter: a general practice study of maternal influences on pregnancy. *British Journal of General Practice, 47*(416), 175-176.

Seideman, R. Y., Watson, M. A., Corff, K. E., Odle, P., Haase, J., & Bowerman, J. L. (1997). Parent stress and coping in NICU and PICU. *Journal of Pediatric Nursing, 12*(3), 169-177. doi: 10.1016/S0882-5963(97)80074-7.

Sheeran, N. (2011). *Young women's experiences of being a mother to preterm infants: An interpretative phenomenological analysis (IPA) approach*. Doctor of Philosophy (Clinical Psychology), Griffith University, Brisbane, Australia.

Sheeran, N. (2012, June). *The impact of age based categorisations on communication, relationships with staff and outcomes for mothers of preterm infants*. Paper presented at the International Conference for Language and Social Psychology (ICLASP), Leeuwardin, The Netherlands.

Sheeran, N., Jones, L., & Rowe, J. (under review). The impact of age based categorisations on communication, relationships with staff and outcomes for mothers of preterm infants. *Patient Education and Counselling*.

Shields-Poe, D., & Pinelli, J. (1997). Variables associated with parental stress in neonatal intensive care units. *Neonatal Network, 16*(1), 29-37.

Short, E. J., Klein, N. K., Lewis, B. A., Fulton, S., Eisengart, S., Kercsmar, C., & Singer, L. T. (2006). Cognitive and academic consequences of broncopulmonary dysplasia and very low birth weight: 8 year-old outcomes. *Pediatrics, 112*(5), 359-E366. doi: 10.1542/peds.112.5.e359.

Singer, L. T., Salvator, A., Guo, S., Collin, M., Lilien, L., & Baley, J. (1999). Maternal psychological distress and parenting stress after the birth of a very low-birth-weight infant. *Journal of the American Medical Association, 281*(9), 799-805. Retrieved from http://search.proquest.com. libraryproxy.griffith.edu.au/docview/61491322?accountid=14543.

Sisson, G. (2012). Finding a way to offer something more: Reframing teen pregnancy prevention. *Sexuality Research and Social Policy: A Journal of the NSRC, 9*(1), 57-69. doi: 10.1007/s13178-011-0050-5.

Slattery, M. M. J. J. (2002). Preterm delivery. *Lancet, 360*(9344), 1489.

Slowinski, K., and Hume, A. (2001). *Unplanned teenage pregnancy and the support needs of young mothers part c: Statistics*. South Australia: Retrieved from http://www.dcsi.sa .gov.au/Pub/Portals/7/unplanned-teenage-pregnancy-part-c-statistics.pdf.

SmithBattle, L. (1997). Change and continuity in family caregiving practices with young mothers and their children. *Journal of Nursing Scholarship, 29*(2), 145-150. Retrieved from http://find.galegroup.com.libraryproxy.griffith.edu.au/itx/start.do?prodId=HRCA.

SmithBattle, L. (2005a). Examining assumptions about teen mothers. *American Journal of Nursing, 105*(4), 13. Retrieved from http://find.galegroup.com/itx/infomark.do? andcontentSet=IAC-Documentsandtype=retrieveandtabID=T002andprodId=EAIM anddocId=A155895676andsource=galeandsrcprod=EAIManduserGroupName=griffithan dversion=1.0.

SmithBattle, L. (2005b). Teenage mothers at Age 30. *Western Journal of Nursing Research, 27*, 831-852. doi: 10.1177/0193945905278190.

SmithBattle, L., & Leonard, W. (1998). Adolescent mothers four years later: Narratives of the self and visions for the future. *Development and Aging, 20*(3), 36-49.

Sommer, K., Whitman, T. L., Borkowski, J. G., Schellenbach, C., Maxwell, S., & Keogh, D. (1993). Cognitive readiness and adolescent parenting. *Developmental Psychology, 29*(2), 389-398.

Spear, H. J. (2004a). A follow-up case study on teenage pregnancy:"Havin a baby isn't a nightmare, but it's really hard". *Pediatric Nursing, 30*(2), 120-125. doi: 10.1111/j.0737-1209.2004.021208.x.

Spear, H. J. (2004b). Personal narratives of adolescent mothers-to-be: Contraception, decision making, and future expectations. *Public Health Nursing, 21*(4), 338-346. doi: 10.1111/j.0737-1209.2004.21407.x.

Spear, H. J., & Lock, S. (2003). Qualitative research on adolescent pregnancy: a descriptive review and analysis. *Journal of Pediatric Nursing, 18*(6), 397-408. doi: 10.1016/S0882-5963(03)00160-X.

Spielman, V., & Taubman-Ben-Ari, O. (2009). Parental self-efficacy and stress-related growth in the transition to parenthood: A comparison between parents of pre- and full-term babies. *Health and Social Work, 34*(3), 201-212. doi: 10.1037/0012-1649.25.5.729.

Stevenson, W., Maton, K. I., & Teti, D. M. (1999). Social support, relationship quality, and well-being among pregnant adolescents. *Journal of Adolescence, 22*, 109-121. doi: 10.1006/jado.1998.0204.

Stone, W. L., Bendell, D., & Field, T. M. (1988). The impact of socioeconomic status on teenage mothers and children who received early intervention. *Journal of Applied Developmental Psychology, 9*, 391-408. doi: 10.1016/0193-3973(88)90008-1.

Taylor, H. G., Klein, N., Minich, N. M., & Hack, M. (2001). Long-term outcomes for children with very low birth weights. *Archives of Pediatric Medicine, 155*, 155-161. doi: 10.1001/archpedi.155.2.155.

Thurman, S. K., & Gonsalves, S. V. (1993). Adolescent mothers and their premature infants: Responding to double risk. *Infants and Young Children, 5*(4), 44-51. Retrieved from http://journals.lww.com/iycjournal/ Fulltext/1993/04000/Adolescent_mothers_and_their_premature_infants_.7.aspx.

Tommiska, V., Ostberg, M., & Fellman, V. (2002). Parental stress in families of 2 year old extremely low birth weight infants. *Archives of Disability Child Fetal Neaonatal Education, 86*, F161-F164. doi: 10.1136/fn.86.3.F161.

Trad, P. V. (1995). Mental health of adolescent mothers. *Journal of the Academy of Child and Adolescent Psychiatry, 34*(2), 130-142. doi: 10.1097/00004583-199502000-00008.

Troutman, B. R., & Cutrona, C. (1990). Nonpsychotic postpartum depression among adolescent mothers. *Journal of Abnormal Psychology, 99*(1), 69-78. doi: 10.1037/0021-843X.99.1.69.

Turner, R. J., Sorenson, A. M., and Turner, J. B. (2000). Social contingencies in mental health: A seven-year follow-up of teenage mothers. *Journal of Marriage and the Family, 62*, 777-791. doi: 10.1111/j.1741-3737.2000.00777.x.

Unger, D. G., Molina, G. B., & Teran, L. T. (2000). Perceived consequences of teenage childbearing among adolescent girls in an urban sample. *Journal of Adolescent Health, 26*, 205-212. doi: 10.1016/S1054-139X(99)00067-1.

Unger, D. G., & Wandersman, L. P. (1988). The relation of family and partner support to the adjustment of adolescent mothers. *Child Development, 59*, 1056-1060. doi: 10.1111/j.1467-8624.1988.tb03257.x.

Voight, J. D., Hans, S. L., & Bernstein, V. J. (1996). Support networks of adolescent mothers: Effects on parenting experience and behavior. *Infant Mental Health Journal, 17*(1), 58-73. doi: 10.1002/1097-0355(199621)17:1.

Westrupp, E. M., Mensah, F. K., Giallo, R., Cooklin, A., & Nicholson, J. M. (2012). Mental health in low-to moderate risk preterm, low birthweight, and small for gestational age children 4 to 5 years: The role of early maternal parenting. *Journal of the American Academy of Child and Adolescent Psychiatry, 51*(3), 313-323. doi: 10.1016/j.jaac.2011.12.004.

Whiteside-Mansell, L., Pope, S. K., & Bradley, R. H. (1996). Patterns of parenting behavior in young mothers. *Family Relations, 45*(3), 273-281.

Whitfield, M. F. (2003). Psychosocial effects of intensive care on infants and families after discharge. *Seminars in Neonatology, 8*, 183-193. doi: 10.1016/S1084-2756(02)00218-X.

Wiemann, C. M., Berenson, A. B., Wagner, K. D., & Landwehr, B. M. (1996). Prevalence and correlates of psychopathology in pregnant adolescents. *Journal of Adolescent Health, 18*(1), 35-43. doi: 10.1016/1054-139X(95)00099-E.

Williams, C., and Vines, S. W. (1999). Broken past, fragile future: Personal stories of high-risk adolescent mothers. *Journal of the Society of Pediatric Nurses, 4*(1), 15-23. Retrieved from http://search.proquest.com.libraryproxy.griffith.edu.au/docview/195762482?accountid=14543.

Williams, T. M., Joy, L. A., Travis, L., Gotowiec, A., Blum-Steele, M., Aiken, L. S., & al., e. (1987). Transition to motherhood: A longitudinal study. *Infant Mental Health Journal, 8*, 251-265.

In: Parenting
Editors: Peter Barberis and Stelios Petrakis

ISBN: 978-1-62257-881-8
© 2013 Nova Science Publishers, Inc.

Chapter 2

PARENTS' PERCEPTIONS OF THEIR CHILD'S MENTAL HEALTH PROBLEMS

Dianne C. Shanley, Graham J. Reid,
Judith Belle Brown and Jann Paquette-Warren

[1]The School of Applied Psychology, Griffith University, Gold Coast Campus,
Queensland Australia, The Behavioural Basis of Health Research Centre, Griffith Health
Institute, Griffith University, Queensland, Australia
[2]Department of Psychology, The University of Western Ontario, London, Ontario,
Canada, Department of Family Medicine, The University of Western Ontario, London,
Ontario, Canada
[3]School of Social Work, Kings' University College,
London, Ontario, Canada
[4]Department of Psychology, The University of Western Ontario,
London, Ontario, Canada

ABSTRACT

Professionals have a fairly clear understanding about the cause, development and maintenance of children's mental health problems based on the developmental psychopathology literature. However, it is unclear whether parents share this complex understanding. Parents' perceptions of their child's mental health problems have been largely unstudied. Using a qualitative method, this chapter described how parents viewed the cause and development of their child's mental health problems. Parents (N=24) seeking help for their child's mental health problem were interviewed. The overarching themes of complexity, ownership and disbelief described parents' perceptions of their child's problems. Parents described a multitude of causes for their child's problems crossing multiple domains (e.g., child, family, community). Four patterns describing how parents integrated the presence of multiple causes were presented (e.g., sequential, equifinality, cumulative, and complex). Three themes revealed how parents viewed the development of their child's problem: precipitating events exacerbated the problem, developmental timeline, and shifts in perspective over time. This chapter highlighted: 1) the importance of implementing a theoretical framework to understand parent's perceptions of mental health, and 2) the importance of a patient-centred care approach to treating children's mental health.

INTRODUCTION

One out of every five children and adolescents has a significant mental health problem (Children's Mental Health Ontario, 2001; Offord, 1998; Offord, Boyle, Fleming, Blum, and Grant, 1989; Pavuluri, Luk, and McGee, 1996). While researchers might seek to answer the question, 'How did so many children develop these problems?', parents who cope with the problem on a daily basis would likely have a more personal question, such as 'Why did *my* child develop this problem?'. To answer their question, researchers would likely explore the literature on adaptive and maladaptive functioning over the life-span, otherwise known as the developmental psychopathology literature (Kazdin, Kraemer, Kessler, Kupfer, and Offord, 1997; Lewis, 2000). However, the parent, who has personal experience with the problem, might be more likely to observe their child's behaviour and draw their own conclusions about how the problem developed. Do parents and researchers draw similar conclusions?

Developmental Psychopathology:
How Child Mental Health Problems Develop

The fundamental principle underlying developmental psychopathology asserts that pathology is a process that develops over time. This principle is in contrast to how medicine has historically viewed the development of pathology. The disease model, which first originated in medicine, described maladaptive functioning as a syndrome that was either present or absent. This all or none simplicity has helped the disease model to retain its influence over other models for the development of many forms of pathology (Shirk, Talmi, and Olds, 2000; Sroufe, 1997). Evidence of this influence can be seen in manuals such as the Diagnostic and Statistical Manual of Mental Disorders (DSM-IV-TR) where diagnostic categories place emphasis the categorical presence or absence of the pathology (American Psychiatric Association, 2000). In contrast to the disease model, developmental psychopathology views maladaptation as "evolving through the successive adaptations of persons in their environments. It is not something a person "has" or an ineluctable expression of an endogenous pathogen. It is the complex result of a myriad of risk and protective factors operating over time" (Sroufe, 1997, p. 251).

The principle that psychopathology develops as a process can be conceptualized according to the dynamic systems process, the longitudinal process, and the transactional process.

Dynamic Systems Process. Early models of etiology asserted that a specific factor or pathogen could account for a specific psychopathology (Kazdin, et al., 1997; Shirk, et al., 2000). In other words, it assumed that there was a linear relationship between one causal factor and a maladaptive outcome. While simple causal models can be accurate in domains such as medicine (e.g., bacteria causes infection), they do not adequately explain more complex phenomenon that have multiple influences at different levels, operating at different points in time (e.g., weather, economic patterns, psychopathology; Kazdin, et al., 1997). The dynamic systems process arose to complement this single factor causal model of dysfunction because the more simplistic causal model was not providing a comprehensive understanding of etiology. For example, it is unlikely that one single causal factor (such as victim of childhood bullying) would exclusively account for the development of childhood depression (Waslick, Kakouros, and Kandel, 2002). The dynamic systems process holds that "most dysfunction results from the complex interplay of multiple psychological, social, and biological processes" (Shirk, et al., 2000, p. 836). A child's behaviour is therefore a result of the dynamic system surrounding the child. This system involves the child's biology (e.g., genetics, neurochemistry), psychology (e.g., cognitions and emotions), immediate social environment (e.g., family and peer influences) and surrounding social environment (external influences such as the school or community; Bronfenbrenner, 1989).

The biological, psychological, and social processes that lead to or prevent the development of psychopathology are referred to as risk and protective factors. Risk and protective factors can act in a variety of ways to affect the development of psychopathology. Two concepts that exemplify how risk and protective factors operate are multifinality and equifinality (Cicchetti and Rogosch, 1996; Shirk, et al., 2000). These concepts are direct implications of the dynamic systems view. Multifinality suggests that "a particular adverse event or risk factor may not lead to the same pathological outcome across individuals, in part because pathogens or risk factors typically do not operate in isolation" (p. 837) (Cicchetti and Rogosch, 1996; Shirk, et al., 2000). In other words, an isolated risk factor does not necessarily produce the same outcome in different individuals. For example, maternal depression is a risk factor for the development of externalizing problems in children; however, not all children who have a mother with depression will have externalizing problems (Munson, McMahon, and Spieker, 2001). Equifinality suggests that the same pathology can develop from a variety of different risk factors or through dissimilar processes (Shirk, et al., 2000). For example, while one child may develop anxiety problems primarily because of the social interactions they experienced outside the family, another child may develop anxiety by modeling a parents' anxious behaviour (Hudson, Kendall, Coles, Robin, and Webb, 2002). Multifinality and equifinality emphasize how there is a dynamic interplay between multiple risk and protective factors during the development of psychopathology (Shirk, et al., 2000).

Longitudinal Process. The longitudinal process highlights how the accumulation of risk and protective factors over time leads to the development of psychopathology (Shirk, et al., 2000). A developmental trajectory is the pathway that a child's development follows throughout his/her life-span. There are a multitude of pathways that a child may follow and each pathway continuously branches into different developmental options. While biological and psychological factors predispose a child to a particular developmental trajectory, environmental factors such as life events, risk factors and protective factors dictate whether a child will remain on the same developmental trajectory. An example of the importance of environmental factors can be seen in research on maltreatment, where early childhood abuse is a risk factor for the future development of a variety of psychopathologies (Chandy, Blum, and Resnick, 1996; Hooper, 1990; Roberts, 1996). When a positive environment remains positive, or a negative environment remains negative, developmental trajectories are relatively simple to predict. The cumulative protective factors operating for the child in a positive environment will likely prevent future psychopathology. The cumulative risk factors operating for the child in a negative environment will increase the likelihood of future psychopathology.

Difficulty predicting developmental trajectories arises when a negative environment changes to a positive environment, or vice versa. Sameroff, Lewis and Miller (2000) stated that "the degree to which the environment remains consistent, and in [this] case, psychopathogenic, is the degree to which psychopathology will be consistently found within the subject" (p. 11). Critical periods in childhood are an example of when a child may be more susceptible to environmental influences (Lewis, 2000). Critical periods are specific periods of time when environmental influences will have a stronger effect on later childhood adjustment (Lewis, 2000). A series of positive influences during a critical period will act as a buffer for later negative experiences. Furthermore, one negative risk factor experienced during a critical period will be more detrimental than a negative risk factor encountered in a non-critical period, and will take more protective factors or positive environmental influences to neutralize this impact later in life.

Transactional Process. The transactional process model suggests that risk and protective factors are non-linear, bi-directional or reciprocal (Kazdin, et al., 1997; Shirk, et al., 2000). The transactions that occur between the environment, the caregiver and the child impact each future transaction in a spiral so that "the child alters his environment and in turn is altered by the changed world he has created" (Sameroff, 1975, p. 234). In other words, the child and his environment are in a constant state of fluctuation whereby each interaction impacts and changes both entities. The transactional process conceptualizes the development of maladjustment using the goodness-of-fit model and the transformational model (Lewis, 2000).

The goodness-of-fit model suggests that psychopathology occurs when the child's characteristics do not complement the surrounding environment. "Maladjustment is the consequence of the mismatch. It is not located in either the nature of the child's characteristic or in the environmental demand" (Lewis, 2000, p. 13). If a temperamentally active child is raised in an environment where active behaviour and noise are not valued, but inhibition and self-control are valued, maladjustment may be more likely to ensue (Lewis, 2000). Parents who have an understanding of this concept may be less likely to find their child's behaviour unacceptable and more likely to work towards creating a suitable environment to match the behaviour before maladjustment develops. For example, the inhibited family may decide to enroll their child in particularly active extra-curricular activities.

While mismatched noise levels in a household will not likely lead to psychopathology, an example of the goodness-of-fit model whereby psychopathology is more likely to develop would be the case of a child with a number of risk factors (Lewis, 2000). In a supportive environment, this child may appear well adjusted. However, in a non-supportive environment, this child may appear maladjusted because of the combined impact of the child's risk factors and the non-supportive environment. In either situation, the risk factors remained present and independent of the environment. However, the changing environment affected whether the child was seen as adjusted or maladjusted. Therefore, the interaction between the environment and the child depended on how well the child's characteristics 'fit' the surrounding environment (Lewis, 2000).

The second transactional model is known as the transformational model. The transformational model suggests that the child and his environment are never independent of each other (Lewis, 2000). Similar to the essential feature of the transactional process, the relationship between the child and his/her environment is not linear. Using parent and child behaviour as an example, "the parent's behaviour affects the child's behaviour; however, the parent's behaviour was affected by the child's earlier behaviour" (Lewis, 2000, p. 15). A more concrete example would be that of an irritable child. It is possible for the temperament of an irritable child to be shifted early in life if raised in a supportive, secure environment. However, the irritable child also interacts with the environment (in this case, the caregivers) and can transform this positive environment into a negative environment that subsequently reinforces the irritable child's behavior (Lewis, 2000). Therefore, it is the interplay between the child and the risk and protective factors in the environment that maintain or redirect the child towards their personalized developmental trajectory (Shirk, et al., 2000).

In summary, the developmental psychopathology perspective provides an alternative to the disease model, which emphasizes either the presence or absence of pathology, and to the simple causal model, which emphasizes a single factor as the cause of pathology. Focusing attention on the *process* of how normal development can progress into psychopathology underscores a number of key principles that can help parents, practitioners and researchers to understand the dynamic nature of the development of psychopathology: 1) children's mental health problems result from the interaction between multiple biological, psychological and social processes that act as risk and protective factors (Shirk, et al., 2000); 2) "There are multiple pathways to one disorder (equifinality) and one pathway may have multiple outcomes (multifinality)" (Hudson, et al., 2002, p. 821); 3) The accumulation of risk and protective factors *over time* leads to the development of psychopathology; and 4) Risk and protective factors can be nonlinear, bi-directional, or reciprocal. The child and his/her environment are not mutually exclusive; they are constantly interacting and altering each other based on previous exchanges (Kazdin, et al., 1997; Shirk, et al., 2000).

Parents' Perceptions of Child Mental Health Problems

It is unclear whether parents share this complex understanding of the cause, development and maintenance of children's mental health problems. Parents may be more likely to endorse either a disease model or a simple causal model when conceptualizing child mental health problems. Johnston and Freeman (1997) provide an example of parents who likely endorse the disease model. In a sample of 52 parents of children with Attention Deficit Hyperactivity Disorder (ADHD), the majority described an incident of their child's behavior as the symptom of an underlying neurological disorder.

No known studies have directly examined whether parents endorsed a simple causal model for their child's mental health problems, however research on attributions suggests that parents are more likely than professionals to believe there is a primary cause for their child's problematic behavior (Baden and Howe, 1992; Bradley and Peters, 1991; Compas, Adelman, Freundl, Nelson, and Taylor, 1982; Morrissey-Kane and Prinz, 1999). Studies examining parents of children with oppositional defiant (ODD) or conduct disorder found that when recalling an incident of their child's misbehavior, parents placed the onus of the child's problem on dispositional factors within the child and minimized their role in the development of the disorder (Baden and Howe, 1992; Bradley and Peters, 1991; Compas, et al., 1982; Morrissey-Kane and Prinz, 1999). Yeh et al. (2004) examined ethnic differences in how parents explain their child's mental health problems. Parents in their study tended to endorse three global causal categories: biopsychosocial (e.g., personality, family issues), sociological (e.g., friends, culture) and spiritual/nature disharmony (e.g., possession, disruption of energy). However, the percentage of parents who endorsed single or multiple causes was not reported.

Parents' perceptions about the cause and development of child mental health problems have not been directly compared to developmental psychopathology. However, the concept that lay opinions differ from expert opinions is not new. The difference between layperson theories and scientific theories has been recognized in a number of fields (Furnham, 1988). Aside from psychology, people create their own theories in domains such as psychiatry, medicine, economics, statistics, law and education. People are curious about their surroundings and they tend to act as mini-scientists, collecting information and drawing inferences about the people around them and the experiences they have (Furnham, 1988). However, the type of information a lay person collects from their environment has been shown to differ greatly from the type of information scientists collect. Lay people tend to a) create theories that are more implicit rather than explicit, b) formulate ideas that are more ambiguous and inconsistent instead of coherent and consistent, c) look for information that will verify rather than falsify their data collected (confirmatory bias), d) infer causal relationships from variables that are at best correlated, e) underestimate external or situational factors when examining others behaviour, and f) create theories based on specific situations that are do not reliably reoccur (Furnham, 1988). Not every lay theory will exhibit each of the above criteria, nor will every scientific theory possess all forms of scientific rigor. Nevertheless, even when a few of these differences are considered, it is understandable that lay and expert theories would differ dramatically.

If a parents' understanding of the development of psychopathology does not agree with the theoretical framework and empirical evidence proposed by the developmental psychopathology literature, what impact will this have? Many prevention and intervention treatment programs for child psychopathology are based on the prevailing developmental psychopathology view. If parents do not share developmental psychopathology's view on the etiology of maladjustment, they may be less likely to comply with the treatment requirements of programs based on those premises. Resistance in help-seeking, poor engagement in treatment, and drop-out poses large problems for positive treatment outcomes in children with psychopathology. Therefore, in order to maximize treatment engagement and outcome, it is important to understand parents' views and how they develop so that professionals may either match the treatment regimen to parents' expectations or alter parents' expectations to match the requirements of the treatment.

One approach to understanding parents' views of how psychopathology develops is to look at what they believe caused their child's problem. In other words, to examine their attributions about how the problem developed.

Attribution Theory. Attribution theory could be useful for guiding research on parents' perceptions. From our everyday observations, we are aware that people spend a certain amount of time understanding and evaluating others actions, as well as justifying their own actions. Most of others' behavior is either unnoticed or processed relatively automatically; however, when a behavior is unexpected or different from the typical or anticipated behavior, people attempt to create explanations about 'why' a person acted in such a way (Antaki and Brewin, 1982; Forsterling, 1988; Hewstone, 1989; Weiner, 1979). These explanations take the form of attributions. An attribution is an explanation, understanding or prediction of an event or behavior based upon beliefs or cognitive perceptions (Antaki and Brewin, 1982; Forsterling, 1988; Hewstone, 1989). In other words, attributions represent our own beliefs about the cause of a person's behavior or why a person has reacted in a particular way. When a person behaves "normally", we rarely invest much thought into explaining why they behaved as they did. However, when faced with aberrant or unexpected behavior (positive or negative), a person creates an attribution, which may be accurate or inaccurate, to help them make sense of the behavior (Antaki and Brewin, 1982; Forsterling, 1988). For this reason, attributions can be of particular importance to mental health, in that many mental health problems involve behaviors that are thought of as atypical or that are different from what society classifies as normal.

Three core dimensions of attributions were proposed by Weiner (1972; 1979), based on Heider's (1944; 1958) research: locus of causality [internal (e.g., ability or effort) and external (e.g., circumstances or luck) causes of behaviour], stability (e.g., behaviours that remain the same or become variable over time), and controllability (e.g., the amount of volition involved in the behaviour).

While the attribution literature may be helpful for guiding research on parents' perceptions, attributions about behavior are unique from perceptions of mental health problems. An attribution is an explanation of a *single event or behavior* based upon cognitive perception (Antaki and Brewin, 1982; Forsterling, 1988; Hewstone, 1989). It is quite possible for a single, isolated behavior (e.g., refusing to do homework) to have only one cause; however psychopathology often results from multiple causes. If parents were asked about a syndrome of related behaviors (such as a mental health problem), rather than a specific behavior, they might be more likely to report multiple causal factors. Alternative theoretical models may need to be explored to help guide research on perceptions of mental health problems.

Illness Perception Theory. Illness perception theory, which originated in health psychology, may provide an additional guide for researching parents' perceptions of mental health problems. When individuals are diagnosed with an illness, such as diabetes or cancer, they strive to make sense of the illness (i.e., where it came from, how long it will last, how it will affect their life). An individual's perception about this illness can often influence coping styles, reactions to treatments and speed of recovery (Frostholm et al., 2005; Frostholm et al., 2007; Hagger, 2003; Petrie and Weinman, 2006; Petrie, Weinman, Sharpe, and Buckley, 1996). A number of illness perception theories have emerged over the decades (Janz and Becker, 1984; Seeman and Seeman, 1983; Wallston, Wallston, and DeVellis, 1978). The Self-Regulation Model (SRM), proposed by Leventhal and colleagues (1998; 1980; 1984) has the largest scope and is the most widely applied theory evaluating an individual's perception of their illness. The basic premise of the SRM is that, when faced with a health threat, an individual creates a cognitive representation to evaluate their health status and to develop strategies for how they intend to cope with the health threat. This "Illness Representation" is an individual's unique way of integrating information about their illness, which provides them with a 'lay' view of the illness and a cognitive map to guide coping behaviors (Hagger, 2003). It is created from previous knowledge and social communication, external sources of information from authoritative sources (e.g., doctor or parent), and personal experience with the illness (Hagger, 2003). It can also be influenced by the individual's personality style and culture. It is the individuals' interpretation of this information that sets the stage for help-seeking, coping with and managing the illness (Hagger, 2003).

Based from nearly 30 years of research on Leventhal et al.'s (1998; 1980; 1984) theory, Weinman et al. (1996) and Moss-Morris et al. (2002) collaboratively proposed seven theoretically defined and factor analysed domains to describe the content of illness representations: identity (i.e., illness diagnosis and the associated symptoms), timeline (i.e., beliefs about the duration of the illness), causes (i.e., beliefs about the origins of the illness), consequences (i.e., expected physical, social and psychological effects), controllability (i.e., beliefs about the extent that the illness can be managed or resolved through treatment), illness coherence (i.e., the amount that the illness made sense to the individual), and emotional representations (i.e., emotional reactions to the illness). Illness representations have been applied to diseases such as diabetes, rheumatic diseases, cancers, chronic fatigue syndrome, and cardiovascular disease, among others (Hagger, 2003). Just as an individual develops an illness representation of their medical disease, parents likely develop representations of their child's mental health problems. However, there has been very little research applying the SRM to mental health, and no research applying the SRM to parents' perceptions of their child's mental health problems.

A Qualitative Study Exploring Parent Perceptions

This chapter presents data that explores whether parents' perceptions about the cause and development of their child's mental health problems are aligned with developmental psychopathology literature. Do parents endorse a disease or simple causal model when describing their child's problem, or do they have a complex view of mental health similar to the developmental psychopathology literature? Given the lack of research and theoretical guidance on this topic, the exploratory and descriptive strengths of a qualitative description research design can describe parent perceptions with the breadth, depth, and clarity that is necessary at this preliminary stage of research (Sandelowski, 2000). This chapter presents the qualitative results from interviews that ask parents of children who have diagnosed mental health problems about their perceptions of their child's mental health problems. It concludes by presenting the practical and theoretical implications resulting from the qualitative findings.

METHODS

Recruitment and Procedures

The study was approved by The University of Western Ontario's Institutional Review Board. Parents of 6- to 12-year-old children seeking help for their child's behavioral or emotional problems were recruited from three Children's Mental Health Centres in Southwestern Ontario, Canada. Two procedures for recruitment were used: (a) Intake workers asked parents if they were willing to be contacted about the study by research staff, and (b)

Receptionists at each agency provided a handout detailing the study to parents arriving for an appointment; interested parents provided contact information on the handout to the receptionist, which was forwarded to research staff. Research staff mailed a letter of information to parents and obtained informed consent from interested parents. Interviews were held in a private room at the agency from which parents sought help or, for parents who could not arrange an in-person interview, a telephone interview was completed (n = 14). Parents received a $20 gift certificate for completing the interview.

The semistructured interview administered to parents consisted of open-ended questions asking parents to describe: the type of problems their child experienced; what caused the problems; how they developed over time; what maintained the problems; and what would make the problems better. All interviews were recorded and transcribed verbatim. Data analyses were conducted concurrently as interviews were completed. Interviews continued until theme saturation occurred (Patton, 2002).

Given that parents seek help for an average of two different child problems (ranging from one to six problems; Shanley, Reid, and Evans, 2008), interviews intentionally chose to ask about parents' perceptions of all their child's problems. The comorbidity in children's mental health better reflects reality for these families and this comorbidity could shift parents' perceptions. The results presented below aimed to capture this complexity, to gain a broad understanding of potential perceptions across mental health problems and to understand how parents integrate the presence of multiple causes for their child's problems. Future studies intend to target specific problems (i.e., Anxiety, Oppositional Defiance) to identify distinct perceptions specific to a problem area.

Data Analyses

Two researchers independently reviewed the transcripts to identify key concepts and emerging themes. Researchers then met to compare and corroborate findings. Discrepancies between the two researchers were discussed and resolved by a third researcher who corroborated the key concepts and themes. Analyses were supported by the use of NVivo (Q. S. R. International, 2007).

Crystallization and immersion (Crabtree and Miller, 1999) were used to identify the overarching themes presented in sections 1, 2, and 4 of the findings. In section 3, patterns that emerged across participants were presented. These patterns originated from diagrams created independently by two researchers documenting the multiple causes that parents suggested and how these causes interacted over time. The diagrams were compared for consistency; discrepancies were resolved by discussion with a third researcher. Researchers then attempted to disconfirm the diagram by re-reading the transcript. Once a diagram was agreed upon for each parent, they were categorized into the four patterns discussed in Section 3.

Trustworthiness and Credibility

Trustworthiness and credibility were maximized by conducting independent and team analyses, providing investigator triangulation (Guion, 2007). Researchers were from multiple disciplines (social work, family medicine and psychology), providing theory triangulation

(Guion, 2007). Researchers also searched for negative cases that would disconfirm emerging themes.

Final Sample

Forty-eight parents agreed to forward their contact information to the research team. Of these parents, 24 agreed to participate, eight declined, and 16 could not be contacted despite multiple attempts. The 24 participating parents reflected maximum variation based on child and parent age, child and parent sex, rural/urban living situations, and child problem type and severity. Parents were an average of 35-years-old, ranging from age 25 to 46; there were 21 mothers, one father and two legal guardian grandmothers. Children of participating parents were an average of 9-years-old ranging from age 6 to 12; 18 were boys. Eight families lived in a rural location. All families were actively seeking help from a children's mental health agency. Children presented with a range of both externalizing and internalizing problems. Externalizing problems included ADHD, Oppositional Defiant Disorder, Tourettes Disorder, anger and aggression. Internalizing problems included Depression, Bipolar Disorder and Anxiety (generalized worry, phobias, separation anxiety and Obsessive Compulsive Disorder).

RESULTS

The findings are organized into four sections. The first section presents overarching themes. The second section outlines the causes parents perceived as responsible for their child's problems. The third section presents patterns that describe parents' understanding of single or multiple causes. These patterns represented perceptions of cause at the time the interview was administered, and did not portray the fluidity of many parents' perceptions. The fourth section describes how parents' viewed the development of their child's problems (i.e., how the problems progressed over time).

Section 1: Over-Arching Themes about Parents' Perceptions

Complexity. The complexity of perceptions about the cause of child mental health problems varied. Some parents had a straightforward, and sometimes inflexible view of the problems. For example, when asked about what caused her child's anger problems to continue, one parent stated, "I think it has to do with his Tourette's. I think it's as plain and simple as that. Once the Tourette's has vanished, he'll be fine."

Some parents were in the process of conceptualizing their child's problems; hence their perception about what caused the problems was poorly defined. When asked about what caused her child's problems to continue, one parent stated, "I really don't know, to be quite honest, I really don't know whether it's how we say things to him, what we say to him; whether it's our approach to parenting or whether it's the way he internalizes the dialogue."

Some parents demonstrated a complex, multifaceted understanding of the cause and development of their child's mental health problems. One parent stated,

> "I think that the genetics and the negative life experiences have fuelled both [her bi-polar and her ADHD]. Any emotional distress would have a negative impact on either disorder ... I think that the diagnostics are correct. It has to be a combination of we haven't quite hit the right medication or the correct dose and also my inability or lack of knowledge of how to deal with a child that's bi-polar."

Ownership. Parents' perceptions about their role in the cause and resolution of their child's problems differed. Some parents acknowledged their responsibility in both areas. When discussing what caused her child's social anxiety, one mother stated, "In hindsight, I would have him be more social with children ... that's where I've failed him most." When asked what would help to make the problems better, she stated, "I think that if we could get into some sort of program to help myself as well as him." Other parents did not feel they were responsible for any part of the cause or solution for their child's problems.

> "He seems to have developed this almost hatred for me ... I always encouraged him ... I'm not an awesome Mom but I'm damned close. Seriously, he's my life, my children are my life, so I can't see where he's getting this ... so we found someone [to speak with him] one on one."

Some parents accepted responsibility for the onset of problems, but did not see themselves as part of the solution. Many of these parents adopted a 'fix my child' approach to treatment, where they recognized themselves as part of the cause, but they wanted the school or another professional solve the problems. This often resulted from frustration and exhaustion attempting to manage their child's problems. The mother of an 8-year-old boy with separation anxiety and sleep problems stated,

> "I guess it's partly my fault that I didn't force him to stay in his bed, but honestly the only way I could get any sleep at all would be for him to sleep with me ... he never liked to be alone from the time he was a baby. I'm probably partly to blame for that too because when my ex-husband left it was just the two of us alone so I would take him into bed with me, for comfort for him, and also for comfort for me and security in knowing that he's safe with me."

When asked what might make the problems better, this mother stated, "Cognitive behavior therapy [for my child], definitely, he needs to learn how to deal with his fears at night."

Lastly, there were parents who did not perceive themselves as part of the cause, but were willing to be part of a solution. A grandmother stated that it was her grandson's prior home environment that caused his defiance; however, she viewed herself as part of the solution, "I have tried numerous things at home ... I'm willing to try almost anything ... but, [after] another visit [from his mom], the behavior is right back again." Often guardians who had obtained custody of the child held these views, however, guardians were not exclusive to this category.

Disbelief. Parents often expressed disbelief that their child's problems continued and they appeared puzzled about why their child could not learn from previous experiences. As one parent stated,

> "She's had a lot of little things going on in her life, but that's life. You know, we can't fall down and say 'okay I'm going to surrender because life sucks'. I've tried to teach her that no matter what happens you've got to get up and go, don't let them defeat you. … it just doesn't seem to have any effect on her."

Another parent appeared frustrated because her child would not implement strategies that she learned during treatment. "[The skills to prevent bullying] are being presented, but they're not being learned. It's like she just does not get it." The frustration of another parent was expressed by the following,

> "My child already knows…how to calm down, apologize, to think before he speaks or reacts, how to come up with an idea of how he can get out of the situation he's in … he's in [a mentor] program, he's got a behavior counselor, he sees a social worker at school … he knows it all. He's been hearing it long enough… but how do you get him to use it…[it seems] to work for a day, or a couple days, and I just start to think that he's doing better and then the next thing you know I get a phone call [from the school about his bad behavior]."

Section 2: The Multitude of Causes Perceived by Parents

Parents reported a variety of causes for their child's problems crossing multiple domains. The breadth of causes described across parents was summarized in themes (See Table 1). These themes were organised under broad domains based on Bronfenbrenner's Ecological Systems model (See Table 1; Bronfenbrenner, 1989).

Examples of themes in Table 1 are presented using representative quotes. Within the child domain, one parent described her child's problems as being caused by an internal state within the child. She stated that the problems "seemed to be caused by boredom." Another parent felt that her child's problems were the result of a skills deficit: the inability to cope with stressors in his environment. This parent stated, "as adults we know what [stress] feels like … and we have learned to cope. His problems [are that] he has no coping mechanisms."

Table 1. Causes of Child Mental Health Problems: Parents' Perceptions

Child	Family	Community
Child Characteristics Characteristics internal to the child *Examples:* feelings (e.g., guilt, anger, boredom); personality traits (e.g., stubborn, manipulative, overly sensitive); physiological states (e.g., tiredness); self-esteem (too high or low)	**Adjustment Difficulty in Family** Difficulty adjusting to family change *Examples:* moving / placed in foster care; change in caregiver; change in daily routine; birth/death of family members; parental separation or divorce	**Adjustment Difficulty in School** Difficulty adjusting to school changes *Examples:* starting school; changing grades or schools; disliking school or teacher

Child	Family	Community
Child Skill Deficits Deficits in daily living skills *Examples:* lack of coping skills; lack of emotion regulation; lack of problem solving skills; lack of self-control; lack of social skills	**Parent** Something internal to the parent *Examples:* mental or physical illness of the parent; stress in the parents' life, including financial or job related stress	**Teacher / Staff** Teacher, principal or other school staff *Examples:* teacher gives too much attention to bad behaviour; teacher lacks knowledge on how to deal with the problems; school not working with parent
Learning/Comprehension Difficulty learning new information or age appropriate school curriculum *Examples:* difficulty understanding specific subjects; difficulty completing homework	**Parenting** Parenting skills, deficits, or conflicting parenting styles *Examples:* discipline style (too strict, too passive); lack of support of child	**Peers** *Examples:* bullying; negative influence from peers; child does not fit in with peers
Genetics/Hereditary Biological predisposition *Examples:* chemical imbalance; genetics; personality trait clearly identified as inherited from a family member	**Sibling** *Examples:* learned behavior from the sibling; sibling rivalry; a lack of siblings (only child)	**Neighbourhood** The surrounding community *Examples:* lack of extra-curricular activities; lack of good role models; living in a bad neighbourhood; discrimination
Disease/Disability The presence of a disease or disability *Examples:* physical disease or disability; learning disability; one mental health problem causes another (ADHD caused depression)	**Trauma** Some form of abuse *Examples:* physical, emotional, or sexual; witnessing family violence; experiencing a traumatic event (custody court proceedings); neglect	
Prenatal Issues occurring during pregnancy *Examples:* prenatal stress; drug use; car accident		
Early Childhood Attachment A significant separation from the primary caregiver at an early age *Examples:* separation from mother negatively affected bond or attachment		
Development A developmental delay or stage *Examples:* speech, language, or motor delay; puberty		

Within the family domain, one parent felt that changing primary caregivers caused the problems.

"A baby-sitter looked after her [while I was in school]. Then she lived with her grandparents for a while because I couldn't find anyone to baby-sit during the evenings. Then she was back [with me], so she's been juggled around a bit and … I started noticing some emotional behavior after she came back from her grandparents."

Another parent felt that her own mental health issues and discipline patterns caused her child's problems. "I used to be a lot meaner to [him] ... he's getting better now that I have had time to go to counseling."

Within the community domain, one parent felt that her child's problems were a result of starting school. She stated that her son's problems were caused by "the stress of being in grade one... going every single day, instead of every other day like in senior kindergarten." Another parent felt that the children in her neighborhood were part of the cause. "The kids [in our neighborhood] aren't good ... no one ever asks him to play. So he always ends up playing with the littler kids because they will play with him."

Section 3: How Parents Described and Integrated the Presence of Multiple Causes

Four patterns described how parents integrated the presence of multiple causes. These patterns represented a 'snap-shot' of parents' perceptions at the time of the interview (See Figure 1). Patterns are described with exemplar quotes from one parent for each pattern.

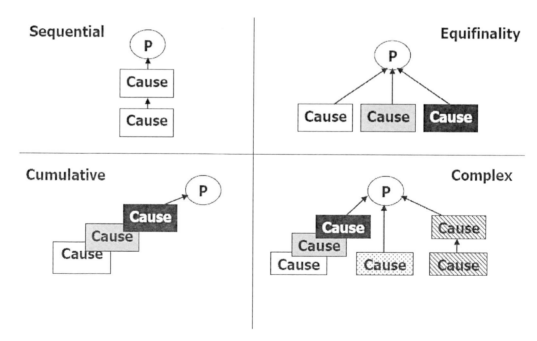

P = Problems

Parents integrated the presence of multiple causes according to four models. Shaded boxes represent unique, unrelated causes. Causes in like shaded boxes represent sequential (or related) causes. Overlapping boxes represent the collective impact of multiple causes.

Figure 1. Causal Models for Parents' Perceptions.

Sequential Pattern. Some parents identified one cause as the origin of their child's problems. This cause either led directly to the problems, or it was the origin of a sequential pathway that caused the problems. Each cause was directly related to the previous cause.

The mother of a 12-year-old boy diagnosed with ADHD and ODD stated that his behavior "had been consistent since he was very young, even with the teachers." When asked what had caused his problems, she said, "In my husband's family there has been bi-polar, severe depression, and eating disorders. There seems to be a lot of brain imbalances from his family and unfortunately [my child] inherited something from that family." After being prompted for other causes she said, "If you were grasping you might [come up with something], but at the end of the day, I don't think I could say anything else [caused his problems]." This parent viewed genetics as causing her child's ADHD and ODD. The ADHD and ODD then caused him to misbehave at home and at school.

Equifinality Pattern. Some parents viewed their child's problems as resulting from many different causes, where each cause was unrelated to the other causes, and the causes had no chronological significance. In other words, each cause independently contributed to the presentation of the problem; when that cause occurred was irrelevant.

For example, when asked what caused her child's problems, the mother of a 6-year-old girl, who "lacked social and emotional skills," was defiant, and had lengthy temper tantrums, explained that her child was in control of her misbehavior. "The easiest way to outline it is: if she's not getting her own way, then she goes into a fit ... I think she's just trying to get our attention. And she doesn't ever seem to get enough attention." The mother discussed a number of other causes including general personality traits, such as her child's perfectionism and difficulty adjusting to change, switching daycares between the ages of two and four, being bullied, the birth of her brother. Further, she wondered whether an underlying disease or her own parenting techniques caused the problems. Despite not being confident about the exact combination of factors that caused her child's problems, this parent had a clear idea that multiple factors had independently contributed to her daughter's problems. She did not indicate that these causes were related to each other or that the cumulative impact of the causes was relevant.

Cumulative Pattern. Some parents described their child's problems as being caused by multiple factors, where each cause was unrelated to other causes, but the causes followed a chronological sequence, whereby over time each cause added to the previous cause, progressively making the problems worse. The cumulative model was different from sequential model in that each progressive cause was not a direct result of the previous cause. This model was different from the equifinality model in that each new cause multiplied the effect of previous causes. One parent used the word "snowballing" to describe how causes accumulated over time.

For example, the mother of a 9-year-old boy who was defiant and aggressive at school described her child's problems as starting because he didn't have

"any other siblings around. He never went to preschool or daycare ... All a sudden he went to school and there's 27 kids in his class and 300 kids out in the playground and he just didn't know what to do ... he didn't really know how to deal with socializing with a group of kids."

She continued to explain how she had separated from his father, shortly after school had started, and how, since the separation, there had been "two sets of parenting rules." She was clear that the parents' separation had added to the stress of attending school, "the problems at school have escalated since [my separation]." Also, she added that after her separation his great-grandmother, aunt, neighbor, dog, and two rabbits died, which exacerbated the problems. The mother perceived the chain of events that caused her child's problems as cumulative, where each event added to or "snowballed" on previous events. Unlike the sequential pattern, starting school was unrelated to parents' separation, which was unrelated to deaths in the family, and so forth.

Complex Pattern. A complex pattern was defined as a combination of the patterns described above. In this pattern, multiple factors following multiple pathways were related to the child's problems. These parents did not perceive one cause or one progression of causes, rather they perceived multiple isolated causes as well as sequential and cumulative pathways that had converged to result in their child's problems.

For example, the mother of a 7-year-old boy, who lied, stole, and was violent towards property and people described the cause of her child's problems by stating, "There was a whole host of things". She described a sequence of feeling extremely stressed while pregnant, followed by family illnesses, deaths and financial difficulties that caused further stress. Following her child's birth, the mother was diagnosed with postpartum depression and with a physical illness that caused her to be hospitalized.

> "[My child] was [an infant] when I got sick, and so we didn't bond. [As a result,] there were attachment issues … So I think, between being away from him and having postpartum depression, I'm not sure which of the two [caused the problem more]."

After returning from the hospital, she and her husband separated and she intermittently relied on social services to help care for her child, which she felt exacerbated his attachment problems. "I was just at the point where emotionally, mentally and physically I had nothing more to give to [my child]. And I think from that, stemmed his behavior."

In addition to this cumulative pathway, she listed independent causes such as his "strong willed" personality, and her lack of knowledge about parenting skills. She also noted a sequential pathway whereby his speech problems caused other children and teachers to misunderstand him; this led to frustration, which resulted in anger and aggression in the classroom. Thus for this mother, it was not any one cause, or pathway, that resulted in her child's problems but rather a complex interplay of different pathways and different causes.

Section 4: Parents' Perceptions about the Development of their Child's Mental Health Problems

Parents were able to clearly articulate a viewpoint about how their child's problems had progressed over time. This was captured in three key themes: precipitating events exacerbated the problems, developmental timeline, and shifts in perspective over time.

Precipitating Events. Parents often described an event in life, or a trigger, that appeared to exacerbate their child's problems. This precipitating event was different from the cause, in that it represented a moment in time when the existing problems were triggered or became significantly worse. For example, one parent stated, "it all ended up coming back on July sixteenth." She described how a parental dispute witnessed by the child on that date caused the existing problems to become worse.

Developmental Timeline. Parents' views about the amount of time that it took for their child's problems to develop differed. Some parents viewed their child as having acute problems that had developed very quickly. "[He was out of school] for about a week, he came back from my Mom's ... then all of a sudden [he became aggressive]." Others viewed their child's problems as chronic, or life-long. "[His behavior] has been consistent since he was very young ... finally he was diagnosed with ADHD and ODD." Still other parents viewed their child's problems as episodic. One parent stated, "just when I think [the problems] are not an issue [any longer], they become an issue again." Another parent reported, "The problems he was having at that time had been resolved ... [but now] they're coming back and they're coming back worse."

Shifts in Perspective. Some parents shifted their perspective over time about what caused their child's problems. For some, their view shifted because the problems had changed with time. For example, when asked what caused her child's aggression this mother replied,

> "In the beginning, it was the ADHD. I think now it's because of a lot of stress going on in his life. Four days after we received court papers, [a close family member] passed away, and that was all really hard [on him]."

For others, their view shifted because they had tried different approaches to resolving the problems. When the problems did not improve, their view of the cause shifted. As one parent stated, "I had wondered if it was diet related. I've tried to change his food but I did not find better results." When asked, "Do you still see food as a cause?," the parent replied, "I don't think so."

Shifts in perspective also became apparent when asking parents about their perceptions of cause versus maintenance. Some parents were quite clear that there was no distinction between what caused and what maintained the problems, demonstrating no shift in perspective over time. Other parents viewed the cause of problems to be quite distinct from what maintained the problems. In addition, parents spoke about how their child's problem had changed over time. Although some commented on how it had improved, many felt that the problem had deteriorated. "When he first started school it was just the odd thing, and then as the years have gone on he's gotten worse."

CONCLUSION

The complexity of parents' perceptions about their child's mental health problems varied widely. While some parents endorsed simple causal models, others perceived the cause of their child's mental health problems in a manner consistent with the developmental psychopathology literature. For example, developmental psychopathology has outlined that multiple causes from different areas within the child's life cause mental health problems; this was consistent with the equifinality pattern. Similarly, developmental psychopathology has outlined that the interaction of different causes *over time* lead to mental health problems; this was consistent with the cumulative pattern. Developmental psychopathology has outlined how exposure to risk factors during critical periods increases the likelihood of developing psychopathology. Parents demonstrated knowledge that there are specific times when children are more sensitive to developing a problem, and that "precipitating events" in life contribute to problem development. Overall the results highlighted how parents' perceptions were diverse. Generalisations across parents are difficult to make and parents' perspectives should be considered individually when conceptualising cases and developing treatment plans.

Practical Implications

Findings provide further rational for incorporating a patient-centered approach to treating child mental health problems and incorporating parent preferences into the treatment process. In practise, considering parents' perceptions of the problem could help shape how we deliver treatment in a manner that is most acceptable to parents, which has the potential for improving treatment engagement and decreasing dropout. A parent endorsing a single cause for their child's mental health problems might be less flexible when treatment options are presented. For example, the parent who views her child's hyperactivity as resulting from diet alone might have difficulty perceiving a parenting program as a viable treatment option. A similar case could be made for parents' ownership of the child's problems, whereby parents who do not view themselves as part of the solution to their child's problem would likely have difficulty engaging in a parenting class, but might be more open to child individual therapy. Furthermore, disbelief could make parents less likely to continue seeking treatment if they felt the treatment was no longer working (i.e., their child was not implementing the strategies learned previously). When perceptions do not match the treatment approach, the treatment is less likely to be implemented by the parent, and there is more risk of dropout. Keeping parents engaged in the treatment process is key for ongoing attendance or participation. Understanding the flexibility of parental perceptions could help clinicians decide whether it would be more beneficial to adapt the treatment approach to match the parents' views or work towards adapting the parents' view of the problem to match the treatment approach. An error in judgement about parents' engagement with a particular treatment approach can be costly to the health care system and to the therapeutic alliance, which is paramount for a successful treatment outcome (Al-Darmaki and Kivilghan, 1993).

Understanding parents' perceptions provides clinically useful data to guide therapists' understanding of child problems and assist therapists who are seeking to generate new treatment ideas or directions for a particular child. For example, parents' perceptions about what makes the problem worse, how quickly it is progressing, how it has changed over time, or how it is currently in the process of changing can be useful therapeutic information and can guide therapists in targeting and addressing specific goals. Furthermore, the results suggested that parents' perceptions can shift over time, supporting previous research on this topic (Kaimal and Beardslee, 2010) and indicating that therapists should inquire about how perceptions have shifted prior to treatment as well as how they shift throughout the course of treatment. This could provide an indication of how flexible the parent might be toward different treatment options. Ultimately, taking the above points into consideration during clinical practice provides clinically useful data and can be beneficial to child treatment outcomes.

One interesting finding related to parents' perceptions of cause was that although disorders such as ADHD and ODD are typically viewed as a grouping of symptoms, parents often viewed the disorder (i.e., ADHD) as one of the causes of misbehaviour. However, this resulted in a circular argument whereby parents would recognize that symptoms combine to create the disorder, but they would then describe the disorder as creating the symptoms. For example, parents sometimes viewed a diagnostic label (such as ADHD) as causing the symptoms of the mental health problem (i.e., my child's inability to pay attention in class is caused by his ADHD), when in fact the symptom (e.g., inability to pay attention) was described as part of the problem. Therefore, it would appear that some parents had difficulty viewing mental health problems as a collection of symptoms.

Theoretical Implications

Parents perceived a variety of causes as responsible for the onset of their children's problems. Causes presented by parents aligned roughly with Bronfennbrenner's Ecological System's Theory of etiology (Bronfenbrenner, 1986, 1989), which emphasized the importance of, not only the child, but the interactions of the child directly with the people and institutions surrounding the child (e.g., family, school, peers), as well as indirectly with the wider array of social and cultural institutions (e.g. religious institutions, neighborhood). This highlights how parents can be perceptive of the entire system of inter-related influences surrounding the child, and how treatments should reflect these multiple influences, targeting not only the child, but the family and the surrounding community (e.g., schools, peer influences, role models).

The four patterns presented in Figure 1 highlighted the importance of understanding that parents not only perceive multiple causes, but they can have complex views about how these causes interact to lead to mental health problems. Parents' perceptions of how mental health problems develop have not been discussed in previous literature. These results highlighted the need to apply a theoretical framework to understanding perceptions about the cause and development of mental health problems. Attribution theory alone does not capture the complexity of how parents perceived the cause, development and maintenance of child mental health problems, nor should we expect that it would capture this complexity. Attribution theory focuses on explanations for single incidents of behaviour whereas mental health problems involve multiple co-occurring behaviours.

Illness perception theory might provide a suitable alternate theoretical guide because parents in this study demonstrated views about each of the seven dimensions discussed in illness perception theory [i.e., identity, cause, timeline (acute, chronic, episodic), control (ownership), consequences, illness coherence (disbelief), and emotional representations]. To date, this theory has not been widely applied to mental health and while this study provided some preliminary validity for the broad domains of the theory within mental health, measuring each domain within mental health will require further validation. For example, the

Illness Perception Questionnaire – Revised (IPQ-R) is one widely used measure that evaluates the domains of illness perception theory (Moss-Morris, 2002). When measuring perceptions of cause, the IPQ-R only included items relevant to causes of health problems. The causes of health problems likely differ from causes of mental health problems. The content of parents' perceptions of causes in Table 1 could be used to adapt future measures assessing causes of mental health problems. Furthermore, the patterns described in section three could provide an additional theoretical framework for understanding how parents perceive and integrate the presence of multiple causes.

Future Research

There was far more diversity in parents' knowledge and perceptions of cause than the current literature would suggest. Current questionnaires evaluating perceptions of cause do not include items from each of the content areas outlined in this chapter (Table 1) (Angold, Costello, Burns, Erkanli, and Farmer, 2000; Yeh, et al., 2004), suggesting that current measures do not adequately reflect the diversity of parents' perceptions. Given the breadth of potential causes that parents perceive, a more comprehensive measure of this topic would be beneficial.

Some parents felt that there was a precipitating event that made their child's problem worse. This was related to a study on help-seeking (Shanley, et al., 2008), which demonstrated that precipitating events often trigger parent's initiative to seek help. It is possible that parents' perception about precipitating events in this study triggered their help-seeking episode, as all parents were currently seeking help for their child's problem. Future research could benefit from further examining how other perceptions that parents have, such as perceptions about the cause and development of mental health problems, influence the help-seeking process.

It would be interesting to examine how subgroups of parents differ with respect to their perception of causes. Furthermore, the endorsement of the four models presented in this article varied across parents. A variety of factors could influence perceptions of cause and model endorsement including the severity of child problems, different child problems, multiple comorbid problems, a longer history of problems, or parents' own history of mental health problems. In addition, endorsement of one model over another might affect the acceptability of and engagement in certain treatments. In a larger sample, future research could explore these issues and identify the percentage of parents endorsing each model.

What makes some parents more likely than others to view problems in a complex manner? Again, parents with a history of mental health problems might be more likely to have complex views because of they have experienced a similar disorder. Likewise, parents who have been accessing treatments for longer might be more likely to think complexly about the problems. Future research could explore the correlates of complexity and the corresponding impact on treatment acceptability and engagement.

Limitations

Member checking was not completed as part of the qualitative methodology. Given the emotional nature of the interview, the team refrained from having parents review transcripts. Member checking is also questioned in the literature as it relies on the assumption that a fixed truth exists, that can be accounted for by a researcher and confirmed by a respondent (Angen, 2000; Cohen and Crabtree, 2006; Sandelowski, 1993). The majority of interviews were with mothers. However, this would be expected because mothers are more often the primary caregivers. Furthermore, by recruiting the parent/caregiver who was seeking help, this sample captured the parents most likely to be engaged in the treatment process. More families with boys were interviewed than girls. This likely reflected the over-representation of boys and externalizing problems in treatment.

Summary

In conclusion, the findings from this study contribute to our practical knowledge, theoretical knowledge, and provide new avenues for future research. This chapter demonstrated that parents differ widely in their perceptions about child mental health problems. While some are capable of articulating the complexities in developmental psychopathology, others view their child's problem according to a simple causal model. Attempting to create generalizations that apply across all parents would not accurately reflect parent perceptions, as there is substantial diversity in the content and complexity of how parents perceive their child's problems. Future research would benefit from adapting and applying illness perception theory to parents' perceptions of child mental health problems. The results from this study would assist in adapting this theory to be applicable to mental health.

REFERENCES

Al-Darmaki, F., and Kivilghan, D. M. (1993). Congruence in client-counselor expectaions for relationship and the working alliance. *Journal of Counseling Psychology, 40,* 379-384.

American Psychiatric Association. (2000). *DSM-IV-TR: Diagnositic and statistical manual of mental disorders - Text Revision* (Vol. 4). Washington, DC: American Psychiatric Association.

Angen, M. J. (2000). Evaluating Interpretive Inquiry: Reviewing the validity debate and opening the dialogue. *Qualitative Health Research, 10*(3), 378-395.

Angold, A., Costello, E. J., Burns, B. J., Erkanli, A., and Farmer, E. M. (2000). Effectiveness of nonresidential specialty mental health services for children and adolescents in the "real world". *Journal of the American Academy of Child and Adolescent Psychiatry, 39*(2), 154-160.

Antaki, C., and Brewin, C. (1982). *Attributions and psychological change: Application of attributional theories to clinical and education practice.* New York Academic Press.

Baden, A. D., and Howe, G. W. (1992). Mothers' attributions and expectancies regarding their conduct-disordered children. *Journal of Abnormal Child Psychology, 20*(5), 467-485.

Bradley, E. J., and Peters, R. D. (1991). Physically abusive and nonabusive mothers' perceptions of parenting and child behavior. *American Journal of Orthopsychiatry, 61*(3), 455-460.

Bronfenbrenner, U. (1986). Ecology of the family as a context for human development: Research perspectives. *Developmental Psychology, 22*, 723-742.

Bronfenbrenner, U. (1989). Ecological systems theory. *Annals of Child Development, 6*, 187-249.

Chandy, J. M., Blum, R. W., and Resnick, M. D. (1996). Gender-specific outcomes for sexually abused adolescents. *Child Abuse and Neglect, 20*(12), 1219-1231.

Children's Mental Health Ontario. (2001). Overview / Issues and Information. from http://www.cmho.org/Overview.html.

Cicchetti, D., and Rogosch, F. A. (1996). Equifinality and multifinality in developmental psychopathology. *Development and Psychopathology, 8*(4), 597-600.

Cohen, D., and Crabtree, B. F. (2006). Qualitative research guidelines project.

Compas, B. E., Adelman, H. S., Freundl, P. C., Nelson, P., and Taylor, L. (1982). Parent and child causal attributions during clinical interviews. *Journal of Abnormal Child Psychology, 10*(1), 77-84.

Crabtree, B. F., and Miller, W. L. (1999). *Doing qualitative research* (Vol. 2). Thousand Oaks: Sage Publications.

Forsterling, F. (1988). *Attribution theory in clinical psychology*. Chichester: Wiley.

Frostholm, L., Fink, P., Christensen, K. S., Toft, T., Oernboel, E., Olesen, F., et al. (2005). The patients' illness perceptions and the use of primary health care. *Psychosomatic Medicine, 67*(6), 997-1005.

Frostholm, L., Oernboel, E., Christensen, K. S., Toft, T., Olesen, F., Weinman, J., et al. (2007). Do illness perceptions predict health outcomes in primary care patients? A 2-year follow-up study. *Journal of Psychosomatic Research, 62*(2), 129-138.

Furnham, A. (1988). *Lay theories: Everyday understanding of problems in the social sciences*. Oxford Oxfordshire: Pergamon Press.

Guion, L. A. (2007). Triangulation: Establishing the validity of qualitative studies. In J. Uddin (Ed.), *Triangulation Research: An overview*. New Delhi, India: Sage.

Hagger, M. S., and Orbell, S. (2003). A meta-analytic review of the common-sense model of illness representations. *Psychology and Health, 18*, 141-184.

Hewstone, M. (1989). *Causal attribution: From cognitive processes to collective beliefs*. Oxford: B. Blackwell.

Hooper, P. D. (1990). Psychological sequelae of sexual abuse in childhood. *British Journal of General Practice, 40*(330), 29-31.

Hudson, J. L., Kendall, P. C., Coles, M. E., Robin, J. A., and Webb, A. (2002). The other side of the coin: using intervention research in child anxiety disorders to inform developmental psychopathology. *Developmental Psychopathology, 14*(4), 819-841.

Janz, N. K., and Becker, M. H. (1984). The health belief model: A decade later. *Health Education Quarterly, 11*(1), 1-47.

Johnston, C., and Freeman, W. (1997). Attributions for child behavior in parents of children without behavior disorders and children with attention deficit-hyperactivity disorder. *Journal of Consulting and Clinical Psychology, 65*(4), 636-645.

Kaimal, G., and Beardslee, W. R. (2010). Emerging adulthood and the perception of parental depression. *Qualitative health research, 20*(9), 1213-1228.

Kazdin, A. E., Kraemer, H. C., Kessler, R. C., Kupfer, D. J., and Offord, D. R. (1997). Contributions of risk-factor research to developmental psychopathology. *Clinical Psychology Review, 17*(4), 375-406.

Leventhal, H., Leventhal, E., and Contrada, R. J. (1998). Self-regulation, health and behaviour: a perceptional cognitive approach. *Psychology and Health, 13,* 717-734.

Leventhal, H., Meyer, D., and Nerenz, D. (1980). The common sense model of illness danger. In S. Rachman (Ed.), *Medical Psychology*. New York: Pergamon.

Leventhal, H., Nerenz, D. R., and Steele, D. J. (1984). Illness representations and coping with health threats. In J. Baum. (Ed.), *Handbook of psychology and health*. Hilldale, NJ: Lawrence Erlbaum Associates.

Lewis, M. (2000). Toward a Development of Psychopathology. In A. J. Sameroff, M. Lewis and S. M. Miller (Eds.), *Handbook of Developmental Psychopathology*. New York: Kluwer Academic/Plenum Publishers.

Morrissey-Kane, E., and Prinz, R. J. (1999). Engagement in child and adolescent treatment: the role of parental cognitions and attributions. *Clinical Child and Family Psychology Review, 2*(3), 183-198.

Moss-Morris, R., Weinman, J., Petrie, K., Horne, R., Cameron, L., and Buick, D. (2002). The revised illness perception questionnaire (IPQ-R). *Psychology and Health, 17*(1-16).

Munson, J. A., McMahon, R. J., and Spieker, S. J. (2001). Structure and variability in the developmental trajectory of children's externalizing problems: impact of infant attachment, maternal depressive symptomatology, and child sex. *Developmental Psychopathology, 13*(2), 277-296.

Offord, D. (1998). *Charting the mental health status and service needs of children: Report from the UNOCCAP oversight board to the national advisory mental health council.* Rockville,MD: National Institute of Mental Health.

Offord, D. R., Boyle, M. H., Fleming, J. E., Blum, H. M., and Grant, N. I. (1989). Ontario Child Health Study. Summary of selected results. *Canadian Journal of Psychiatry, 34*(6), 483-491.

Patton, M. Q. (2002). *Qualitative Research and Evaluation Methods*. Thousand Oaks, California: Sage.

Pavuluri, M. N., Luk, S. L., and McGee, R. (1996). Help-seeking for behavior problems by parents of preschool children: A community study. *Journal of the American Academy of Child and Adolescent Psychiatry, 35*, 215-222.

Petrie, K. J., and Weinman, J. (2006). Why Illness Perceptions Matter. *Clinical Medicine, 6,* 536-539.

Petrie, K. J., Weinman, J., Sharpe, N., and Buckley, J. (1996). Role of patients' view of their illness in predicting return to work and functioning after myocardial infarction: Longitudinal study. *British Medical Journal, 312*, 1191-1194.

Q. S. R. International. (2007). NVivo. Cambridge, MA QSR Internationat Pty. Ltd.

Roberts, S. J. (1996). The sequelae of childhood sexual abuse: a primary care focus for adult female survivors. *Nurse Practitioner, 21*(12), 42-52.

Sameroff, A. J., Lewis, M., and Miller, S. M. (2000). *Handbook of Developmental Psychopathology* (2nd ed.). New York: Springer.

Sandelowski, M. (1993). Rigor or rigor mortis:The problem of rigor in qualitative research revisited. *Advances in Nursing Science, 16* (2), 1-8.

Sandelowski, M. (2000). Whatever happened to qualitative description? *Research in Nursing and Health, 23*(4), 334-340.

Seeman, M., and Seeman, T. E. (1983). Health behavior and personal autonomy: a longitudinal study of the sense of control in illness. *Journal of Health and Social Behaviour, 24*(2), 144-160.

Shanley, D. C., Reid, G. J., and Evans, B. (2008). How Parents Seek Help for Children with Mental Health Problems. *Administration and Policy in Mental Health and Mental Health Services Research, 35*(3), 135-146.

Shirk, S., Talmi, A., and Olds, D. (2000). A developmental psychopathology perspective on child and adolescent treatment policy. *Developmental Psychopathology, 12*(4), 835-855.

Sroufe, L. A. (1997). Psychopathology as an outcome of development. *Development and Psychopathology, 9*(2), 251-268.

Wallston, K. A., Wallston, B. S., and DeVellis, R. (1978). Development of the Multidimensional Health Locus of Control (MHLC) Scales. *Health Education Monographs, 6*(2), 160-170.

Waslick, B. D., Kakouros, A., and Kandel, R. (2002). Depression in children and adolescents: An overview. In D. Schaffer and B. D. Waslick (Eds.), *The many faces of depression in children and adolescents* (pp. 1-36). Washington, D.C.: American Psychiatric Publishing.

Weiner, B. (1979). A theory of motivation for some classroom experiences. *Journal of Educational Psychology, 71*(1), 3-25.

Weinman, J., Petrie, K. J., Moss-Morris, R., and Horne, R. (1996). The illness perception questionnaire: A new method for assessing the cognitive representation of illness. *Psychology and Health, 11*, 431-445.

Yeh, M., Hough, R. L., McCabe, K., Lau, A., and Garland, A. (2004). Parental beliefs about the causes of child problems: exploring racial/ethnic patterns. *Journal of the American Acadamy of Child and Adolescent Psychiatry, 43*(5), 605-612.

In: Parenting
Editors: Peter Barberis and Stelios Petrakis

ISBN: 978-1-62257-881-8
© 2013 Nova Science Publishers, Inc.

Chapter 3

PARENTING: CHALLENGES, PRACTICES AND CULTURAL INFLUENCES

Panayiotis Stavrinides and Militsa Nikiforou

Department of Psychology, University of Cyprus, Cyprus

ABSTRACT

Over the past few decades a significant amount of empirical and theoretical work has accumulated in the parenting literature. Even though research methods, instruments, analyses, and theoretical constructs have evolved to a great extent, researchers in this field are still debating on important issues in relation to parenting. What are the challenges that parents face in the twenty first century? How did parents' practices change over time and how do parents still choose to rare their children? Is there such a thing as "universal parenting" or do we always have to take into account culturally specific parenting practices and equally specific outcomes? These questions will be at the core of this chapter which aims to bring together current empirical studies and theoretical work utilizing a wide array of parenting literature: from parenting styles and the discussion of the classical authoritarian-authoritative divide, a summary of recent findings in parenting practices such as parental monitoring, behavioral and psychological control, the role of parental involvement, especially in the discussion of a child's adjustment in school, and finally we will analyze the issue of parental knowledge; that is, what parents try to know about their child's socialization choices and what they actually know. In theoretical terms, we will try to bind together the most important parenting constructs and outcomes in a transactional framework of interpretation, arguing that while parents still shape some of their children's development, children also shape their parents behaviour. Based on this framework we argue, in line with other researchers, that the term parenting – which implies a parent to child effects - should be replaced by the term parent-child interactions which allows for a more dynamic and bidirectional interpretation.

1. PARENTING

1.1. Theoretical Framework of Parental Style

Parental style according to Baumrind (1991) describes parental behaviors and practices the way they are perceived by children. It is composed by two main dimensions, demandingness and responsiveness. Demandingness describes parental expectations that are related to children's behavior and socialization while responsiveness refers to parents' general tendency of providing warmth, support and a positive attitude towards their child's needs. Based on these dimensions four parental styles emerge. Authoritative style for example, encompasses high scores in both demandingness and responsiveness while low scores in both dimensions describe the neglectful style. Additionally, in this taxonomical approach, we find authoritarian style which places extreme emphasis in high demandingness while parental responsiveness is rather low. And finally, high responsiveness and low demandingness describe a tendency towards the permissive style.

There is a large body of research in the relevant literature showing an association between parental style and children's adjustment. Authoritative parenting, which allows children to view their parents behavior as responsive while adequately controlling, seems that facilitates the development of child competent behavior (Baumrind, 1991). Evidence for that argument comes from a number of studies that consistently show that children of authoritative parents do better at school and have less adjustment problems (Georgiou, 2008a; Kaufmann et al., 2000; Radziszewska, Richardosn, Dent, & Flay, 1996; Spera, 2005; Strage and Swanson, 1999). Also, other studies have shown that authoritative style is positively associated with indices of social and school competence and negatively associated with adjustment problems (Chen, Dong, & Zhou, 1997; Lamborn, Mounts, Steinberg, & Dornbusch, 1991). To sum up, most empirical studies provided evidence that authoritative parental style is associated with better outcomes in children and adolescents.

In contrast, authoritarian parents are controlling and rather non-responsive in their children's needs. They tend to use prohibitive and punitive strategies and emphasize in child obedience. A study conducted by Pereira, Canavarro, Cardoso, and Mendonca (2009) showed that children of authoritarian parents have higher levels of behavioral problems and specifically externalizing problems. Also, a number of studies have found that authoritarian parenting is positively associated with childhood aggression and bullying behavior (Baldry & Farrington 2000; Chen, Dong and Zhou, 1997; Kaufmann et al., 2000). Furhermore, children of authoritarian parents tend to have low self-esteem and negative attitudes (Lempers, Clark-Lempers, & Simons, 1989; Weiss, Dodge, Bates, & Pettit, 1992), which, in turn, may contribute to the development of deviant behaviors and adjustment problems (Eisenberg & Murphy, 1995; Hart, DeWolf, Wozniak, & Burt, 1992; Lamborn, Mounts, Steinberg, & Dornbusch, 1991). In support of these claims, Heaven, Newbury, and Mak (2004) reported that adolescents with authoritarian parents tend to exhibit high levels of depression and delinquency. Some researchers have also suggested that children involved in bullying experiences are more likely to come from families where parents use authoritarian, harsh, and punitive child-rearing practices (Espelage, Bosworth, & Simon, 2000). In sum, the line of evidence seems to support Olweus (1980) earlier argument "that a young boy who gets too little love and interest from his mother and too much freedom and lack of clear limits with regard to aggressive behavior is particularly likely to develop into an aggressive adolescent" (p. 657).

Permissive parents on the other hand tend to be more responsive towards the child than demanding. They do not set restrictions to their children for appropriate behavior. Children who have permissive parents tend to feel there are no limits or parental control in their lives. Rather worryingly, recent findings have shown that permissive parental style might be related with victimization experiences in school (e.g. Georgiou, 2008b). According to Georgiou, permissive parents are more likely to become overprotective and as a result, they create psychological barriers in their children effort to develop initiative and social skills. In this way, children become socially and psychologically dependent on their parents resulting in lack of the capacity to overcome aggressive behaviours from their peers. Apart from victimization however, children with permissive parents tend to exhibit difficulties in inhibiting impulsive aggression (Miller, Diiorio, & Dudley, 2002) providing further evidence to earlier claims that permissiveness for aggression is linked to bullying experiences (Olweus, 1980).

Neglectful parental style refers to parents that exhibit little or no responsiveness to their children and show little or no effort to control their child's behavior. Children who have neglectful parents tend to feel no support from their parents while they also feel that their parents do not care about them. A neglectful parent is disengaged with an exaggerated and developmentally inconsistent view of autonomy boundaries of their children (Karavasilis, Doyle, & Markiewicz, 2003). Relevant studies have indicated that this particular style is linked to maladaptive children's adjustment. Specifically, children from neglectful families usually have lower levels of psychosocial development, lower school achievement, and higher levels of internalized distress and behavior problems (Lamborn, Mounts, Steinberg, & Dornbusch, 1991; Steinberg, Lamborn, Darling, Mounts, Dornbusch, 1994).

In conclusion, parents tend to choose to rare their children in the way that themselves consider 'right' for them and their children's healthy development. Nevertheless, we cannot ignore that there is a large body in the relevant parenting literature that shows that the combination of high levels of parental warmth (responsiveness) and demandingness (strictness) represent a rather positive parenting strategy (Georgiou, 2005; Maccoby & Martin, 1983). In this environment, children usually have less adjustment difficulties including emotional and psychosocial problems combined with higher school achievement.

Although, most of the studies have traditionally examined how parent's behavior influence children's behavior, there are recent studies that examine the opposite effect – child effect as well (e.g. Stattin & Kerr, 2000). This transactional approach (parent to child and child to parent effects) will be discussed later in this chapter.

1.2. Parental Characteristics

Numerous studies have shown that parental characteristics and attitudes such as parental depression, overprotection, and anxiety are linked to children's adjustment problems (Aguilar, Sroufe, Egeland, & Carlson, 2000; Connell and Goodman, 2002; Perren and Hornung, 2005). More specifically, some studies emphasized in examining family parameters of children's maladjustment and they focus on a variety of indices of maternal characteristics such as emotional and behavioural tendencies. Placing mothers in the center of many of empirical studies has long been a standard form of research practice acknowledging that mothers are still influential in family dynamics and child development. While we also acknowledge the significant role of fathers, in this section we will discuss the relationship between maternal characteristics and children's adjustment.

Maternal Depression

Maternal depression is a significant risk factor for children effort to grow in a socially and psychologically healthy environment. Some authors claim that maternal depression can be a significant predictor of numerous behavioral and emotional difficulties in children (Connell and Goodman, 2002; Downey & Coyne, 1990; Goodman, 2007). More specifically, in some empirical studies it was found that when mothers suffer from chronic depression their children are more likely to involve themselves in bullying behavior (Connolly & O'Moore, 2003; Nigg & Hinshaw, 1998).

What are the causal processes, however, that explain the link between a mother suffering from depressive symptoms (or a clinical form of depression) and her child's difficulties to adjust both at home and school? Some researchers have proposed that there is a variety of reasons that can explain the dynamics of this association (Campbell, Pierce, Moore, Marakovitz, & Newby, 1996; Cummings & Davies, 1994; Goodman & Gotlib, 1999; Patterson, 1980). For example, a study conducted by Burke (2003) found that maternal depression can be a causal factor in children's social, emotional, and cognitive difficulties. Burke also argued that children of depressed mothers have significantly greater chances to be diagnosed with conduct disorder. In the same line, earlier studies have demonstrated that maternal the quality of parenting practices can moderate the relationship between maternal depression and children's externalizing problems. That is, when mothers who already suffer from depressive symptoms choose rather maladaptive parenting practices then the combination of the two may lead to significantly worse outcomes in children (see for example Harnish, Dodge, & Valente, 1995). In general, it appears that mothers who suffer from depression frequently find themselves in a situation where they cannot see their child's emotional needs while trying to overcome their own emotional difficulties and as a result they are less likely to provide positive psychological care to their children. The results of these processes are often that depressive mothers may lose their consistency in the way they respond to their children's needs (Downey & Coyne, 1990; Goodman, 2007). Consequently, a depressed parent is likely to use rather maladaptive discipline practices and at times extreme punishment, both of which are linked to child aggressive behavior (Craig, Peters, & Konarski, 1998; Loeber & Stouthamer-Loeber, 1986). As a result they are less effective in dealing with conflict with their youths when disagreement between them their children emerges or when parents and children try to fulfill different priorities (Dumas, Gibson, & Albin, 1989; McLoyd, Jayaratne, Ceballo, & Borquez, 1994). Following these dysfunctional processes, as Patterson argues, a depressive mother may also be unable to control effectively her children's aggressive behavior, and that may turn her in becoming a victim of bullying by her own child. Generally, depressive mothers tend to be the "unacknowledged victims" where children are often both the victims of their mother's inappropriate behavior and the active participants of a coercive family system (Patterson, 1980).

Maternal Overprotection

Overprotective parents tend to adopt and exhibit a set of behaviours beyond what most parents would in similar circumstances (Levy, 1980). They tend to over-manage situations for their child, restrict child behaviours, discourage child independence, and direct child activities (Coplan, Mila, & Rowan, 2009). Maternal overprotective behaviours are defined as either maternal domination and overregulation or inability to set limits and excessive absence of control of a child's behaviour. Examples of overprotecting behaviour include routine assistance with daily activities despite the child's ability to perform such tasks independently, delaying school entry, and allowing the child to play and socialize only within a parent's sight (Samra & McGrath, 2009). In sum, overprotective behaviours are restrictive and controlling, and overprotective parenting is highly controlling, supervising, vigilant, and difficult with separation.

A large body of research in the literature shows consistently the association between maternal overprotection and children's developmental difficulties. For example, Perren and Hornung (2005) found that parental overprotection, may block children's initiative and limit their ability to defend themselves or deal effectively with aggressive attacks by other children. Accordingly, Rubin, Burgess, and Hastings (2002) claim that overprotective parenting is associated with children's shyness and internalizing problems. Moreover, empirical evidence clearly show that while parental overprotection may lead to children's victimization, the negative consequences may continue later on in a child's pathway since earlier victimization is often correlated with later anxiety and depression (Brockenbrough, Cornell, & Loper, 2002; Kaltiana-Heino, Rimpela, & Rimbela 2000). Furthermore, overprotective parenting cuts away children from natural life challenges and opportunities to develop skills for managing difficulties. Such parents often use include intrusion, reinforcement of child's dependence on parents, and exclusion of outside influences (Parker, 1983). Consequently, these parenting practices may lead children to develop aversive cognitions about themselves and the world while they may also develop a negative set of beliefs constantly informing themselves that primary relationships do not provide support and safety.

Maternal Stress or Anxiety

Parenting stress is created by a mismatch between the perceived demands of parenting and the resources available to meet those demands (Abidin, 1995). It is defined as a negative mental response attributed to the self and/or the child and it is reinforced by "a series of appraisals made by each parent in the context of his or her level of commitment to the parent role" (Abidin, 1992, p. 410). Also, stress from external events or challenges in daily living may erode women's perceived capabilities as mothers (Walker, 1989) and their internal resources. Consequently, maternal stress may spill over to caregiving and eventually place children at risk for problem behaviours (Aguilar, Sroufe, Egeland, & Carlson, 2000).

Empirical studies have documented that parenting stress is strongly associated with children's psychological adjustment. Daily events that cause stress and anxiety upon parents are also related to children's adjustment, and in fact, such event may be more related with children's outcomes than other variables, such as maternal employment (e.g. Pett, Vaughan-Cole, & Wampold, 1994). Further, daily difficulties negatively affect the quality of parents interactions with their children, and consequently, mothers who report higher levels of parenting stress also report more externalizing behaviours in their children (Feldman, Hancock, Rielly, Minnes, & Cairns, 2000; Qi & Kaiser, 2003). Moreover, significant maternal stressors, such as change in, loss of, or conflict with a partner, are also related to greater symptomatology in children (Najman et al., 1997). Walker and Cheng (2007) found that maternal stress was directly related to behaviour problems in young children, an important indicator of early socio-emotional development. Further, there is convincing evidence linking stress experiences related to parenting, daily life, and major life events, to reports of child behavioural problems, adjustment difficulties, and internalizing or externalizing problems during the early childhood period (Conger, McCarty, Yang, Lahey, & Kropp, 1984; Coplan, Bowker, & Cooper, 2003; Creasey & Reese, 1996; Crnic & Greenberg, 1990; Deater-Deckard & Scarr, 1996; Holahan & Moos, 1987; Kliewer & Kung, 1998; Peterson & Hawley, 1998; Weinraub & Wolf, 1983).

Conclusion

Identifying maternal characteristics that put a child at risk for experiencing future psychological adjustment difficulties is very important for all agents of socialization in a child's life. These characteristics could be useful knowledge for addressing parental difficulties, training programs for parents, and for intervention programs for parents and children. Facilitating parents to achieve a positive and functional relationship with their children is important for both immediate and long-term healthy development.

2. PARENTAL INVOLVEMENT

2.1. Definition of this Concept

Parental involvement is a multidimensional construct that includes both direct school involvement such as attending parent–teacher association meetings or volunteering in classrooms, and indirect involvement such as conveying educational expectations and monitoring extracurricular behavior (Epstein & Sanders, 2002). While traditionally the view was that the *more* parental involvement, the better a child does, more recently a number of authors have shown that it's the *quality* of parental involvement that appears to be a key factor in improving children's academic outcomes and adjustment (Georgiou, 1996; Georgiou, 1997; Pomerantz, Moorman, & Litwack, 2007).

2.2. Types of Parental Involvement

Empirical studies have demonstrated that there are numerous facets of parental involvement (Eccles & Harold, 1996; Georgiou 1996, 1997; Shumow & Miller, 2001; Sui-Chu & Willms, 1996). While some researchers distinguish between parental involvement "at home" and "at school", other experts adopted a more analytical approach describing a series of different forms of parental involvement such as: a. supervision of school behavior, b. control of extracurricular behavior, c. assisting and monitoring school homework, d. developing children's talents and interests, e. communication with school and attending parent–teacher association meetings and school events (e.g. Georgiou, 1996, 1997, 1999).

Parents often engage in their children's school life by using a combination of parental involvement practices. But what kind of involvement is the most beneficial for children? A long series of empirical data have established that there are numerous types of parental involvement associated with positive school-related academic and social competencies. For example, Keith et al. (1993) found that parental participation in school-related activities such as monitoring homework and attending parent–teacher association meetings is the most beneficial for children academic achievement. Further, other studies have found that involvement at home, especially parents discussing school activities, has the strongest effect on academic achievement (Sui-Chu & Willms, 1996; VanVoorhis, 2003). Some other researchers have suggested that the frequent communication between parents and teachers and parent's involvement in school activities is linked to children's high school achievement (Fan, 2001; Georgiou, 1997; Keith et al., 1998; Kim, 2002; Hong & Ho, 2005). Summing up, it appears that the most effective types of parental involvement seem to be communication of parents with teachers and supervision of child's school behavior.

2.3. Factors that Influence Parental Involvement (Parents, Children, School-teachers)

When examining factors that influence parental involvement, several studies have relied on Bronfenbrenner's 1989 ecological systems' approach because it takes into account the multiple systems that potentially influence children.

Dauber and Epstein (1993) examined the characteristics of parents, children, and school, in order to determine the most important factors that influence school and home involvement using a large sample of elementary and middle school students with achievement difficulties. Their results revealed that parents with higher education were more involved at school and at home. In line to this result, Baker and Stevenson (1986) reported that educated mothers were more involved in children's educational experiences than less educated mothers. Adding to the effects of educational level, family socio-economic status also tends to be an important factor that is related parental involvement. Studies have shown that low socioeconomic status causes practical and psychological barriers to parents who are otherwise willing to involve in their children's lives (e.g. Calsyn, 1980).

Children's age and gender are the most predominant individual differences that are related with parental involvement. Parents' involvement generally tends to decline between elementary and high school years (Eccles & Harold 1996; Shumow & Miller, 2001). As far as children's' gender is concerned, some researchers have argued that parents with male children tend to involve in educational processes more since boys generally exhibit more behavioral and academic problems than girls (Stevenson & Baker, 1987). Moreover, another factor that influences parental involvement is children's school achievement. Parents who consider that their child is doing well at school, they are more likely to reduce their school involvement because they realize that their child does not need their supervision or their assistance.

Finally, school characteristics seem to influence parental involvement. Perhaps of most importance, the strongest predictors of school and home involvement are school practices and programs that encourage parental involvement. It is important to note that school context (e.g. administration and staff) is considered to play a significant role in determining whether parents would become involved in their children's school life.

Maintaining a healthy and close relationship between parents and school is essential for better school outcomes. Epstein (1987, 1991) suggested that home-school cooperation can optimize children's development by promoting consistency and mutual reinforcement of learning-related practices in the two contexts. At a more practical level, teachers and other school experts have long argued that at the intervention level is always critical to implement parent-teacher interventions that target an increase in parental involvement and parental communication with school. Such programs however, have to allow children and adolescents to continue to have a sense of independence and initiative.

2.4. Outcomes of Parental Involvement

Numerous studies have suggested that the close relationship that parents develop with the school system and specifically with the school personnel is linked to children's adjustment and school achievement (Fan, 2001; Georgiou, 1997; Keith et al., 1998; Kim, 2002; Hong & Ho, 2005). Epstein (1992) wrote that "students at all grade levels do better academic work and have more positive school attitudes, higher aspirations, and other positive behaviors if they have parents who are aware, knowledgeable, encouraging and involved" (p. 1141).

Some studies have found that parental involvement is associated with multiple positive consequences. According to Georgiou and Christou (2000) parental involvement is associated with children's development of positive self-esteem. Furthermore, earlier studies have shown that children whose parents are more involved in their schooling usually get higher grades (Sewell & Hauser, 1980; Stevenson & Baker, 1987). Additionally, these children have better and more frequent school attendance (Epstein & Sheldon, 2002), and have fewer discipline problems than their peers whose parents are less involved (Deslandes & Royer, 1997; Lee, 1994).

2.5. Constraints of Parental Involvement

Definitely, children whose parents are more involved in their educational lives, have better adaptive development. Thus, it is important to note that parental involvement should be seen as a series of parental practices that nurture child's acceptance and encouragement. At the same time, parents should reinforce their children's initiative, gradually allowing them to develop their own sense of responsibility in relation to their school life. Accordingly, the way children experience parental involvement is also crucial for having positive outcomes. Children that see their parents' involvement as supportive to their schooling are more likely to benefit from their parents' actions rather than children who see involvement as a barrier to their effort for independence and autonomy. Another issue that is also important for the effectiveness of parental involvement is whether teachers see involvement as an intrusion to their professional boundaries. Teachers with such attitude are more likely to try and keep distance from communicating with parents. If teachers and generally the school system do not promote and encourage parental involvement, parents generally feel less welcome in their children's school and academic life. Home and school partnerships seem to need significant amount of effort from both parents and teachers in order to promote an equal and healthy relationship between the two parties.

2.6. Parental Attributions

Attribution style describes how people tend to explain the causes of their own as well as other people's behavior (Aronson, Wilson, & Akert, 2002). Parental attributions on the other hand refer to the explanation that parents give about the causes of their children's behaviour or, more specifically, for their children's school achievement. Weiner (1985) proposed a three-dimensional taxonomy of attributions, according to which attributions can be classified on the basis of three criteria: a. locus (internal or external causes), b. stability (stable over time or unstable causes), and c. controllability (controllable or uncontrollable causes). Typically, children with low grades or school failure are more likely to have parents explaining their children's failure to a stable and uncontrollable cause (e.g. intelligence). In contrast, when children achieve well at school, parents tend to explain their children's excellence to their own effort (Georgiou, 1999).

Research on parental attributions has shown that when parents consider themselves as capable and when they view their role as that of the teacher, they are more likely to get involved in their children's schooling (Grolnick, Benjet, Kurowski, & Apostoleris, 1997). Also, Hoover- Dempsey, Bassler, and Brissie (1992) found that parents who believe that they are able to "make a difference" are more likely to plan activities and to participate in events that require their active involvement. Another study found that attributing a child's achievement to internal and controllable factors such as the parent's own effort increased the strength of the "getting involved" *belief* (Georgiou & Tourva, 2007) and this in turn seems to have a strong effect on transforming the belief into an actual parental involvement activity. In sum, parents' beliefs and thoughts about their parental role and their beliefs concerning this role in their children's learning processes are essential for understanding the amount and the quality of parental involvement in children's schooling.

3. PARENTAL MONITORING AS KNOWLEDGE AND AS ACTION

3.1. What Parents Do and What they Know?

Parents often assume that the more they know about their children whereabouts, particularly during the adolescent years, their children will have healthier development. Still, there are many questions that have to be answered. In what ways do parents consciously try to gain knowledge about their children's whereabouts? What they know about their children's whereabouts and what kind of developmental outcomes do these different sources of knowledge produce? A number of studies have focus on a variety of indices of this knowledge gaining process (Crouter & Head, 2002; Laird, Pettit, Bates, & Dodge, 2003; Stattin & Kerr, 2000).

Parents try to gain knowledge about their children's socialization through two main sources: monitoring and child disclosure. Parental monitoring describes parents' active effort to know how their children behave, with whom they socialize, and what activities they engage. More importantly, they try to gain this knowledge directly and through their own observation (Stattin & Kerr, 2000; Stavrinides, Georgiou, & Demetriou, 2010; Stavrinides, 2011). According to Dishion and McMahon (1998, p. 66) parental monitoring is defined as "a set of correlated parenting behaviors involving attention to and tracking of the child's whereabouts, activities and adaptation". Parental monitoring consists of two dimensions: parental control and parental solicitation. Parental control refers to parent's efforts to limit their children's behaviour within the boundaries and norms they set while parental solicitation describes parent's efforts to gain information about their children's whereabouts and activities through their friends or other people closed to their children.

Both cross-sectional and longitudinal studies have indicated that inadequate monitored adolescents tend to be antisocial, delinquent, or criminal (Patterson & Stouthamer-Loeber, 1984; Cernkovich & Giordano, 1987; Crouter, MacDermid, McHale, & Perry-Jenkins, 1990; Weintraub & Gold, 1991). Further, Laird, Pettit, Bates, and Dodge (2003) found that lower levels of parental monitoring predicted greater delinquent behavior the following year and that lower levels of delinquent behavior predicted higher levels of monitoring. Additionally, poorly monitored youths are more likely to use illegal substances (Flannery, Vazsonyi, Torquati, & Fridrich, 1994). Evidence also suggests that poorly monitored youths have deviant friends (Dishion, Capaldi, Spracklen, & Li, 1995) and do worse in school (Crouter, MacDermid, McHale, & Perry-Jenkins, 1990; White & Kaufman, 1997). Contrary however, some recent studies have failed to confirm significant relations between parenting practices (such as solicitation and control) and adolescent problem behaviour (Soenens, Vansteenkiste, Luyckx, & Goossens, 2006; Stattin & Kerr, 2000; Stavrinides, Georgiou, & Demetriou, 2010; Waizenhofer, Buchanan, & Jackson-Newsom, 2004).

Moreover, although most studies have reported negative correlations between parental monitoring and children's negative outcomes, some studies have claimed the opposite. For example some researchers argue in favor of the autonomy–granting perspective (Steinberg & Silverberg, 1986). These authors propose that reductions in monitoring are followed by reductions in delinquent behavior as parents grant more autonomy to well-adjusted adolescents. Furthermore, a number of studies have shown that perceived maternal monitoring is linked to an increase in adolescent alcohol use (Webb, Bray, Getz, & Admas, 2002). Thus, the relationship between active parental monitoring and children's problem behavior is still a matter of some debate.

On the other hand, child disclosure is the children's free, willing information providing to their parents about where they are during their free time, how they do in school, whether they keep secrets from them, who they socialize with, and what they do when they go out at night. It's important to note that voluntary disclosure toward parents becomes an increasingly important facet in parent–adolescent relationships. To show how important child disclosure is in building a healthy relationship between parents and children, Kerr, Stattin, and Trost (1999) showed that knowledge of daily activities that came from the child's spontaneous disclosure was most closely linked to parental trust. To build on that, another study has indicated that parental knowledge came mainly from child disclosure, and child disclosure was the source of knowledge that was most closely linked to broad and narrow measures of delinquency (Stattin & Kerr, 2000). In line with this study, Stavrinides (2011) has found that child disclosure at Time 1 predicted a decrease in both major and minor delinquency at Time 2. Interestingly, parental monitoring at Time 1 did not significantly predict a decrease in delinquency at Time 2. Other studies have concluded that adolescents who are involved in deviant behavior are more likely to withhold information to avoid negative parental reactions such as low trust, sarcasm, or criticism (Darling, Cumsille, Caldwell, & Dowdy, 2006; Engels, Finkenauer, & van Kooten, 2006; Kerr, Stattin, & Trost, 1999; Marshall, Tilton-Weaver, & Bosdet, 2005; Tilton-Weaver & Galambos, 2003).

Leisure time that adolescents spend with their parents and their peers has recently been identified as an important factor in the link between adolescent disclosure and delinquency. Parents who spend time with adolescents may prevent delinquency by facilitating adolescent disclosure, and by being physically present they may keep adolescents away from potential deviant activities within peer groups. Kerr and Stattin (2000) suggested that adolescents who refrain from disclosure, because they are not in a warm relationship with their parents, tend to spend relatively less leisure time with their parents and are relatively more attracted by peer contexts (Kerr, Stattin, Biesecker, & Ferrer-Wreder, 2003).

In conclusion, most studies have indicated that the most significant source of knowledge is the child herself. Parents should not expect active control to be as a protective mechanism against problem behavior as previously thought. Especially when their children are at the stage of adolescence when parental authority is likely to be questioned or resisted. In contrast, parents should try in creating and maintaining a warm, trusting, and non-judgmental family environment. As a result, children will be encouraged to talk to them when they find themselves involved in any form of problem behavior.

4. TRANSACTIONAL MODELS OF PARENT-CHILD RELATIONSHIP

4.1. Theoretical Framework

Many authors suggest a dynamic view of family systems in which parents and children influence each other in a reciprocal way. In this manner, parental actions become agents of change in their child's development and at the same time the child's actions are agents of change in parenting practices (Caldwell, Beutler, Ross, & Silver, 2005; Crouter, MacDermid, McHale, & Perry-Jenkins, 1990; Stavrinides, Georgiou, & Demetriou, 2010; Waizenhofer, Buchanan, & Jackson-Newsom, 2004). Sameroff and Chandler (1975) were among the first who strongly supported this idea when they claimed that researchers must engage in bidirectional data analysis as the model's theoretical base is that "children affect their environments and environments affect children. Environments change and are affected by each other" (p. 19). Rather recently Sameroff (2010) added that unidirectional analysis is no longer efficient when trying to study, understand, and predict human behavior, suggesting that the transactional model is "at the forefront of the developmental research" (p. 115).

About a decade or so ago transactionally oriented studies have showed initial evidence of reciprocal associations between externalizing problems and parenting variables in childhood and adolescence (Buist, Dekovic, Meeus, & Van Aken, 2004; Burt, McGue, Krueger, &

Iacono, 2005; Eisenberg et al., 1999; Eisenberg et al., 2005; Jang & Smith, 1997; Laird, Pettit, Bates, & Dodge, 2003; Vuchinich, Bank, & Patterson, 1992).

Empirical research on parental monitoring has shown that the relationship between parental monitoring and children's rule breaking behaviour should be reinterpreted as a two-way rather than a one-way (parent to child) process (Kerr & Stattin, 2000; Stattin & Kerr, 2000). Specifically, Stavrinides, Georgiou, and Demetriou (2010) found that parental monitoring did not predict reductions in subsequent adolescent alcohol use. However, child disclosure at Time 1 did predict a reduction in adolescent alcohol use at Time 2. In this line of research, other studies have found that lower levels of parental monitoring predicted greater delinquent behavior the following year and that lower levels of delinquent behavior predicted higher levels of monitoring (Laird, Pettit, Bates, & Dodge, 2003; Stavrinides, 2011). On one hand, from a parent-effects perspective, adolescent delinquent behavior tends to decrease in response to parental efforts. On the other hand, however, from a child-effects perspective, high levels of delinquent behavior can cause a decrease in parental monitoring (Crouter, MacDermid, McHale, & Perry-Jenkins, 1990; Laird, Pettit, Bates, & Dodge, 2003).

Moreover, research on parenting has shown that transactional models are corroborated by research studies that use multiple research and statistical methods in order to estimate bidirectional parent–child relations. For example, Pesonen et al. (2007) suggested that higher negative emotionality and lower positive affectivity in the infants contribute to an increase in maternal stress over a five-year period, beginning in infancy. Further, higher maternal stress contribute to an increase in child negative affectivity and a decrease in positive affectivity and self-regulation over the same period. Accordingly, VanderValk, deGoede, Spruijt, and Meeus (2007) found that marital distress and adolescent emotional adjustment were reciprocally related in a transactional model. In line with that, a longitudinal study conducted by Jaffee and Poulton (2006) spanning across middle childhood to early adolescence provided evidence for a strong reciprocal relationship between maternal depression and antisocial behaviour in middle childhood. Moreover, Gross, Shaw, and Moilanen (2008) demonstrated a transactional relationship between maternal depression and boy's externalizing behaviour problems. Similarly, Nicholson, Deboeck, Farris, Boker, and Borkowski (2011) found that as maternal depressive symptoms became more severe, children's behaviour problems increased while the opposite was also found to be true: an increase in children's behaviour problems predicted maternal depressive symptoms. This finding provided further evidence toward a reciprocal relationship between parents' emotional state and children's outcomes supporting even more the transactional interpretation of parent-child interactions. Also recently, Fanti, Henrich, Brookmeyer, and Kuperminc (2008) revealed a longitudinal, reciprocal association between the quality of adolescent relationships with their mothers and internalizing problems. Previously Buist, Dekovic, Meeus, and Van Aken (2004) also showed a transactional association between adolescent internalizing problems and the quality of relationships with their parents.

Research on bullying that investigates transactional relationship between bullying and parental variables has provided support to the hypothesis that parental and child behavior influence reciprocally each other. Georgiou and Fanti (2010) found that maternal involvement, including monitoring, predicts negatively both the initial value of bullying and its degree of change over time. More specifically, the more a parent is involved, and the closer her supervision is, the less possible it is for her child to participate in bullying. On the other hand, an increase in bullying behavior causes a reduction in maternal involvement and monitoring over time. Also, as far as victimized children are concerned, anxiety and depression in victimized children may influence parent's behaviour. In other words, parents may be more protective and less demanding toward their children to compensate for their child's social deficiencies (Smokowski & Kopasz, 2005). Eventually, as a line of data suggest, parents may react to their child's behaviour rather than shaping it with their own actions (Bell & Harper, 1977). Therefore, it is important to emphasize the potential role of the child's behavior in shaping parent's behavior. Although, most research studies have tested unidirectional models, in which either parents affect their children's behaviour or the opposite, evidence continues to build in support of a transactional perspective. A number of studies have consistently confirmed that children and their parents are intertwined in a cycle of reciprocal associations (Lollis & Kuczynski, 1997; Sameroff, 1975; Sameroff & MacKenzie, 2003).

4.2. Criticism of Unidirectional Design-Model

Research in social sciences tends to investigate relationships in a unidirectional manner. Research designs and data collection techniques reflect this inclination, typically addressing questions such as the effect of particular interventions on student outcomes, or causal parent-child relationship. However, those studies are using cross-sectional designs to answer their hypotheses and as a result they are quite likely to ignore the processes involved in an ongoing reciprocal interchange (parent-child relationship). Consequently, linear designs limit the research to linear conclusions which may be inaccurate and incomplete.

On the other hand, transactional design describes development as a product of the ongoing interaction between the child and the experiences provided by the environment (Sameroff, 1975). The main hypothesis in a transactional design is that the child's developmental outcome at any point in time is the product of the interrelationship between the child and the environment (i.e. family, peers, social context) over time.

5. CULTURAL INFLUENCES

Why should we emphasize to the significance of the cultural context in understanding parenting related to children's outcomes? Is there such a thing as a "universal parenting"? A number of studies conducted in several countries (e.g. United Kingdom, Israel, Spain, USA, Finland, Cyprus) related to parenting and children outcomes have shown similar results in this field (Aunóla, Stattin, & Nurmi, 2000; Garcia & Gracia, 2009; Georgiou, 2008a; Knafo & Schwartz, 2003; Rodrilguez, Donovick, & Crowley, 2009; Shucksmith, Hendry, & Glendinning, 1995), suggesting that authoritative parental style corresponds with children's better psychosocial adjustment in compared to neglectful parental style whereas authoritarian and permissive parental style occupy an intermediate position. In addition, despite the different cultural differences, Rohner and Britner (2002) provided evidence for a universal relationship between parental style and mental health problems.

Against this argument however, a number of studies conducted in the USA with ethnic minority groups (e.g. African-Americans, Chinese-Americans, Hispanic-Americans, multi-ethnic Americans) have shown different results in different culture contexts (Deater-Deckard & Dodge, 1997; Wang & Phinney, 1998; Zayas & Solari, 1994; Steinberg, Dornbusch, & Brown, 1992). For example, Chao, (1994) found that Chinese children who have authoritarian parents do better at school than children of authoritative parents. Further, Steinberg, Dornbusch, and Brown, (1992) found that authoritative parenting in African American adolescents had no relationship with adolescent achievement and engagement in school. Interestingly, they also found that authoritarian parenting in Hispanic adolescents was highly related to adolescent school engagement. Additionally, studies that examine parental styles in poor families with low-educated parents in the United States and Australia have found that authoritarian parenting was positively linked to academic achievement (Leung, Lau, & Lam, 1998). Finally, Dwairy, Achoui, Ahouserie, and Farah (2006) found that authoritarian parenting in Arab societies was an adequate parenting strategy leading to positive developmental outcomes in children and adolescents.

Research on parental involvement has also suggested that parental involvement in different ethnic groups can lead to different results. For example, Jeynes (2003) argued that little is known about the effects of parental involvement on academic outcomes among children from different ethnic groups. Effects of parental involvement in school achievement appear to differ among racial-ethnic groups (Desimone, 1999). Also, the nature and quality of academic parental involvement may be very different among parents from different ethnic groups. Therefore, it is important for future research studies to examine these differences because many teachers and administrators in schools may not understand the kind of involvement of parents from different ethnic background. This lack of understanding could prevent school personnel from working with parents on issues and problems these children may face. In this line, Steinberg, Dornbusch, and Brown (1992) concluded that on average, parental involvement in schooling enhanced adolescents' academic performance. But when these data were analyzed by ethnic group, parental involvement was not a significant predictor of school performance for African American students.

In sum, the findings from numerous studies suggest that we should take into account culturally specific parenting practices and equally specific outcomes in children. Also, results from multi-ethnic studies propose that certain relations between parents and children may apply only to families who belong to a specific cultural context. Therefore, prevention programs and intervention strategies based on theories of "universal parenting" may be inadequate in some populations than others, or more beneficial for western countries than others. To our understanding, cultural context is essential in the dynamic relationship between parents and children.

CONCLUSION

Parents often feel the pressure to avoid as many actions as possible that may lead to maladaptive outcomes for their children. Even though this is an easily understandable behaviour, at the same time, educators and other specialists can convey a somewhat different message. First, is that parents should acknowledge that absolute control over their child's development is neither something that can be achieved, nor something that should be pursuit. Instead, as we tried to discuss in this chapter, parents can recognize their child's developmental needs, be flexible and adapt their behaviour according to their child's developmental stage, the family structure, and the environmental pressures. Moreover, it is equally important to understand that children do shape parents' behaviour. Their day to day implicit and sometimes explicit signals about how well they adjust, how much they need their parents' involvement, what kind of involvement and at what frequency and intensity they need, which parenting style may be more adaptive at a certain period of a child's development, all these are issues that parents can recognize and allow their behaviour to be expressed accordingly.

Are there things that parents can avoid? Probably yes, especially when referring to extremes such as extremely harsh parental style or extremely indifferent parenting, are both "choices" that can easily place a child's development at-risk. Other than that however, it is not as much about "good" or "bad" parenting but it is more about choices that bring better outcomes. Sometimes a child may need her parents monitoring in a more intense way, other times however the same child may need a completely different parental approach. And this is why we argue in favour of parents that recognize their children's adaptive and maladaptive periods, and within each period, the children's adaptive and less adaptive behaviours.

Finally, there is the issue of culture, either in its micro-cultural expressions such as the particular differences that make each family unique, or the macro-cultural characteristics that we find common within families of certain ethnic and/or socio-geographical areas. Both cultural specificities are important in family functioning and in parent-child relationships. Therefore, parents face another challenge, and that is to adjust their parenting practices according to the culture of their own family and at the same time as active agents to shape that family culture to the extent they can. Accordingly, at a more macro-systemic level, the discussion is about parenting in context. Social, historical, even economic influences do have an impact on how parents choose to rare their youths, and within a dynamic and transactional framework, how their youths impact their parents and their relationship with them.

REFERENCES

Abidin, R. R. (1995). *Manual for the Parenting Stress Index*. Odessa, FL: Psychological Assessment Resources.

Abidin, R. R. (1992). The determinants of parenting behavior. *Journal of Clinical Child Psychology, 21*(4), 407–412.

Aguilar, B., Sroufe, L. A., Egeland, B., & Carlson, E. (2000). Distinguishing the early-onset/persistent and adolescence-onset antisocial behavior types: From birth to 16 years. *Development and Psychopathology, 12*, 109–132.

Aronson, E., Wilson, T. D. and Akert, R. M. (2002) *Social Psychology,* 4th edn. Upper Saddle River, NJ: Prentice Hall.

Aunóla, K, Stattin, H., & Nurmi, J. E. (2000). Parenting styles and adolescents' achievement strategies. *Journal of Adolescence, 23,* 205-222.

Baldry, A. C., & Farrington, D. P. (2000). Bullies and delinquents: Personal characteristics and parental styles. *Journal of Community & Applied Social Psychology, 10*, 17–31.

Baker, D., & Stevenson, D. (1986). Mothers' strategies for school achievement: Managing the transition to high school. *Sociology of Education, 59,* 156-167.

Baumrind, D. (1991). Parenting styles and adolescent development. In J. Brooks-Gunn, R. Lerner, & A. Petersen (Eds.), *The encyclopedia of adolescence* (pp. 746–758). New York: Garland.

Bell, R., & Harper, L. (1977). *Child effects on adults.* Hillsdale, NJ: Erlbaum.

Brockenbrough, K. K., Cornell, D. G., & Loper, A. B. (2002). Agreessive attitudes among victims of violence at school. *Education and Treatment of Children, 25,* No. 3, 273-287.

Bronfenhrenner, U. (1989). Ecological systems theory. *Annals of Child Development, 6,* 187-249.

Buist, K. L., Dekovic, M., Meeus, W., & Van Aken, M. A. G. (2004). The reciprocal relationship between early adolescent attachment and internalizing and externalizing problem behaviour. *Journal of Adolescence, 27,* 251-266.

Burke, L. (2003). The impact of maternal depression on familial relationships. *International Review of Psychiatry, 15,* 243–255.

Burt, A. S., McGue, M., Krueger, R. F., & Iacono,W. G. (2005). How are parent-child conflict and childhood externalizing symptoms related over time? Results from a genetically informative cross-lagged study. *Development and Psychopathology, 17,* 145-165.

Calsyn, R. (1980). A community psychologist's view of community education. *Community Education Journal, (October),* 10-13.

Caldwell, R. S., Beutler, L. E., Ross, S. A., & Silver, N. C. (2005). Brief report: An examination of the relationships between parental monitoring, self-esteem and delinquency among Mexican American male adolescents. *Journal of Adolescence, 3,* 461–483.

Campbell, S. B., Pierce, E. W., Moore, G., Marakovitz, S., & Newby, K. (1996). Boys' externalizing problems at elementary school age: Pathways from early behaviour problems, maternal control, and family stress. *Development and Psychopathology, 8,* 701-719.

Cernkovich, S. A., & Giordano, P. C. (1987). Family relationships and delinquency. *Criminology, 24,* 295–321.

Chao, R. K. (1994). Beyond parental control and authoritarian parenting style: Understanding Chinese parenting through the cultural notion of training. *Child Development, 65,* 1111-1119.

Chen, X., Dong, Q., & Zhou, H. (1997). Authoritative and authoritarian parenting practices and social and school performance in Chinese children. *International Journal of Behavioral Development, 21,* 855–873.

Conger, R. D., McCarty, J. A., Yang, R. K., Lahey, B. B., & Kropp, J. P. (1984). Perceptions of child, child-rearing values and emotional distress as mediating links between environmental stressors and observed maternal behavior. *Child Development, 55,* 2234–2247.

Connell, A.M., Goodman, S.H., 2002. The association between psychopathology in fathers versus mothers and children's internalizing and externalizing behavior problems: a meta-analysis. *Psychol. Bull., 128,* 746–773.

Connolly, I., & O'Moore, M. (2003). Personality and family relations of children who bully. *Personality and Individual Differences, 35,* 559–567.

Coplan, R. J., Mila, R. & Rowan, K. (2009). Exploring the associations between maternal personality, child temperament, and parenting: A focus on emotions. *Personality and Individual Differences, 46,* 241-246.

Coplan, R. J., Bowker, A., & Cooper, S. M. (2003). Parenting daily hassles, child temperament, and social adjustment in preschool. *Early Childhood Research Quarterly, 18,* 376– 395.

Craig,W., Peters, R., & Konarski, R. (1998). *Bullying and victimization among Canadian school children.* Quebec, Canada: Applied Research Branch, Human Resources Development.

Creasey, G., & Reese, M. (1996). Mothers' and fathers' perception of parenting hassles: Associations with psychological symptoms, nonparenting hassels, and child behavior problems. *Journal of Applied Developmental Psychology, 17,* 393–406.

Crnic, K. A., & Greenberg, M. T. (1990). Parenting stresses with young children. *Child Development, 61,* 1628–1637.

Crouter, A. C., & Head, M. R. (2002). *Parental monitoring and knowledge of children.* In M. Bornstein (Ed.), Handbook on parenting (2nd ed.). Mahwah, NJ: Erlbaum.

Crouter, A. C., MacDermid, S. M., McHale, S. M., & Perry-Jenkins, M. (1990). Parental monitoring and perceptions of children's school performance and conduct in dual- and single-earner families. *Developmental Psychology, 26,* 649–657.

Cummings, E. M., & Davies, P. T. (1994). Maternal depression and child development. *Journal of Child Psychology and Psychiatry, 35,* 73‾112.

Darling, N., Cumsille, P., Caldwell, L. L., & Dowdy, B. (2006). Predictors of adolescents' disclosure to parents and perceived parental knowledge: Between- and within-person differences. *Journal of Youth and Adolescence, 35,* 667–678.

Dauher, S. L., & Epstein, J. L. (1993). Parents' attitudes and practices of involvement in inner city elementary and middle school. In N. Chavkin (Ed.), *Families and schools in a pluralistic society* (pp. 53-71). Albany, NY: SUNY Press.

Deater-Deckard, K., & Dodge, K. A. (1997). Externalizing behavior problems and discipline revisited: Nonlinear effects and variation by culture, context, and gender. *Psychological Inquiry, 8,* 161-175.

Deater-Deckard, K., & Scarr, S. (1996). Parenting stress among dual-earner mothers and fathers: Are there gender differences? *Journal of Family Psychology, 10,* 45–59.

Desimone, L. (1999). Linking parent involvement with student achievement: Do race and income matter? *Journal of Educational Research, 93,* 11-30

Deslandes, R., & Royer, E. (1997). Family-related variables and school disciplinary events at the secondary level. *Behavioral Disorders, 23,* 18–28.

Dishion, T. J., & McMahon, R. J. (1998). Parental monitoring and the prevention of child and adolescent problem behaviour: A conceptual and empirical formulation. *Clinical Child and Family Psychology Review, 1,* 61–75.

Dishion, T. J., Capaldi, D., Spracklen, K. M., & Li, F. (1995). Peer ecology of male adolescent drug use: Developmental processes in peer relations and psychopathology [Special issue]. *Development and Psychopathology, 7,* 803–824.

Downey, G., & Coyne, J. C. (1990). Children of depressed parents: An integrative review. *Psychological Bulletin, 108,* 50–76.

Dumas, J.E., Gibson, J.A., & Albin, J.B. (1989). Behavioral correlates of maternal depressive symptomatology in conduct-disorder children. *Journal of Consulting and Clinical Psychology, 57,* 516–521.

Dwaiiy, M., Achoui, M., Abouserie, R., & Farah, A. (2006). Adolescent-family connectedness among Arabs: A second cross-regional research study. *Journal of Cross-Cultural Psychology, 37,* 248-261.

Eccles, J. S., & Harold, R. D. (1996). Family involvement in children and adolescents' schooling. In A. Booth & J. F. Dunn (Eds.), *Family-School Links: How do they affect educational outcomes?* (pp. 3-34). Hillsdale, NJ: Lawrence Erlbaum Assoc. Inc.

Eisenberg, N., Fabes, R. A., Shepard, S. A., Guthrie, I. K., Murphy, B. C., & Reiser, M. (1999). Parental reactions to children's negative emotions: Longitudinal relations to quality of children's social functioning. *Child Development, 70*(2), 513-534.

Eisenberg, N., Zhou, Q., Spinrad, T. L.,Valienet, C., Fabes, R. A., & Liew, J. (2005). Relations among positive parenting, children's effortful control, and externalizing problems: A threewave longitudinal study. *Child Development, 76*(5), 1055-1071.

Eisenberg, N., & Murphy, B. (1995). Parenting and children's moral development. In M.H. Bornstein (Ed.), *Handbook of parenting: Vol. 4. Applied and practical parenting* (pp. 227–258). Mahwah, NJ: Lawrence Erlbaum Associates Inc.

Engels, R. C. M. E., Finkenauer, C., & van Kooten, D. C. (2006). Lying behavior, family functioning and adjustment in early adolescence. *Journal of Youth and Adolescence, 35,* 949–958.

Epstein, J. L., & Sheldon, S. B. (2002). Present and accounted for: Improving student attendance through family and community involvement. *The Journal of Educational Research, 95,* 308–318.

Epstein, J. (1992). *School and family partnerships.* In M. Alkin (Ed.), Encyclopedia of Educational Research (6th ed.), (pp. 1139–1151). New York: MacMillan.

Epstein, J. L. (1987). Toward a theory of family-school connections: Teacher practices and parent involvement. In K. Hurrelmann, F. Kaufmann, & F. Losel (Eds.), *Social intervention: Potential and constraints.* (pp. 121–136). Berlin, Germany: Walter de Gruyter.

Epstein, J. L. (1991) Effects on student achievement of teachers' practices of parent involvement. In S. Silvern (Ed.), *Advances in reading/language research: Literacy through family, community, and school interaction.* (Vol. 5, pp. 261–276). Greenwich, CT: Jai Press.

Epstein, J. L., & Sanders, M. C. (2002). Family, school, community partnerships. In M. H. Bornstein (Ed.), *Handbook of parenting, Vol. 5: Practical issues in parenting* (pp. 407-437). Mahwah, NJ: Erlbaum

Espelage, D. L., Bosworth, K., & Simon, T. R. (2000). Examining the social context of bullying behaviors in early adolescence. *Journal of Counselling and Development, 78,* 326–333.

Fan, X. (2001). Parental involvement and students' academic achievement: A growth modeling analysis. *Journal of Experimental Education, 70,* 27–61.

Fanti, K. A. Henrich, C. C., Brookmeyer, K. A., & Kuperminc, G. P. (2008). Toward a Transactional Model of Parent-Adolescent Relationship Quality and Adolescent Psychological Adjustment. *The Journal of Early Adolescence, 28,* (2), 252-276.

Feldman, M. A., Hancock, C. L., Rielly, N., Minnes, P., Cairns, C. (2000). Behavior problems in young children with or at risk for developmental delay. *J Child Fam Stud* 9, 247-261.

Flannery, D. J., Vazsonyi, A. T., Torquati, J., & Fridrich, A. (1994). Ethnic and gender differences in risk for early adolescent substance use. *Journal of Youth and Adolescence, 23*, 195–213.

Garcia, F., & Gracia, E. (2009). Is always authoritative the optimum parenting style? Evidence from Spanish Families. *Adolescence, Vol. 44, No. 173,* 101-131.

Georgiou, St. (1996). Parental involvement in Cyprus. *International Journal of Educational Research, 25(1)*, 33-43.

Georgiou, St. (1997). Parental involvement: Definition and outcomes. *Social Psychology of Education, 1*(3), 189–209.

Georgiou, St. (1999). Parental attributions as predictors of involvement and influences of achievement. *British Journal of Educational Psychology, 69(3),* 409-429.

Georgiou, St. (2005). Growing and learning in the Greek Cypriot family context. Advances in Psychology, *Nova Science Publications, 35,* 121-141.

Georgiou, S. N. (2008a). Parental style and child bullying and victimization experiences at school. *Soc Psychol Educ, 11,* 213 – 227.

Georgiou, S. (2008b). Bullying and victimization at school: The role of mothers. *British Journal of Educational Psychology, 78,* 109–125.

Georgiou, St., & Christou, C. (2000). Family parameters of achievement: a structural equation model. *European Journal of Psychology of Education, 15(2),* 297-311.

Georgiou, St., & Tourva, A. (2007). Parental attributions and parental involvement. *Soc Psychol Educ, 10,* 473–482.

Georgiou, St., & Fanti, K. (2010). A transactional model of bullying and victimization. *Soc Psychol Educ, 13,* 295–311.

Goodman, S. H. (2007). Depression in mothers. *Annual Review of Clinical Psychology, 3,* 107–135.

Goodman, S., & Gotlib, I. H. (1999). Risk for psychopathology in the children of depressed mothers: A developmental model for understanding mechanisms of transmission. *Psychological Review, 106,* 458–490.

Grolnick,W., Benjet, C., Kurowski, C., & Apostoleris, N. (1997). Predictors of parent involvement in children's schooling. *Journal of Educational Psychology, 89*(3), 538–548.

Gross, H. E., Shaw, D. S., & Moilanen, K. L. (2008). Reciprocal associations between boys' externalizing problems and mothers' depressive symptoms. *Journal of Abnormal Psychology, 36,* 693–709.

Harnish, J. D., Dodge, K. A., & Valente, E. (1995). Mother-child interaction quality as a partial mediator of the roles of maternal depressive symptomatology and socioeconomic status in the development of child behavior problems. *Child Development, 66,* 739–753.

Hart, C.H., DeWolf, D.M., Wozniak, P., & Burts, D.C. (1992). Maternal and paternal disciplinary styles: Relations with preschoolers' playground behavioral orientations and peer status. *Child Development, 63,* 879–892.

Heaven, P., Newbury, K., & Mak, A. (2004). The impact of adolescent and parental characteristics on adolescent levels of delinquency and depression. *Personality and Individual Differences, 36*(1), 173–185.

Holahan, C. J., & Moos, R. H. (1987). Risk, resistance, and psychological distress: A longitudinal analysis with adults and children. *Journal of Abnormal Psychology, 96*, 3–13.

Hong, S., & Ho, H. Z. (2005). Direct and indirect longitudinal effects of parental involvement on student achievement: Second-order latent growth modeling across ethnic groups. *Journal of Educational Psychology, 97*(1), 32–42.

Hoover-Dempsey, K., Bassler, O., & Brissie, J. (1992). Explorations in parent-school relations. *Journal of Educational Research, 85*, 287–294.

Jang, S. J., & Smith, C. A. (1997). A test of reciprocal causal relationships among parental supervision, affective ties, and delinquency. *Journal of Research in Crime and Delinquency, 34*, 307-336.

Jaffee, S. R., & Poulton, R. (2006). Reciprocal effects of mothers' depression and children's problem behaviors from middle childhood to early adolescence. In M. N. Ripke & A. C. Huston (Eds.), *Developmental contexts in middle childhood: Bridges to adolescence and adulthood* (pp. 107–129). New York, NY: Cambridge University Press.

Jeynes,W. H. (2003). A meta-analysis: The effects of parental involvement on minority children's academic achievement. *Education and Urban Society, 35*, 202-218.

Karavasilis, L., Doyle, A.B., & Markiewicz, D. (2003). Associations between parenting style and attachment to mothers in middle childhood and adolescence. International Journal of Behavioral Development, 27, 153–175.

Kaltiana-Heino, R., Rimpela, M., Rantanen, P., & Rimpela A. (2000). Bullying at school – an indicator of adolescents at risk for mental disorders. *Journal of Adolescence, 23*, 661-674.

Kaufmann, D., Gesten, E., Santa Lucia, R. C., Salcedo, O., Rendina-Gobioff, G., and Gadd, R. (2000). The Relationship Between Parenting Style and Children's Adjustment: The Parents' Perspective. *Journal of Child and Family Studies, Vol. 9, No. 2, pp. 231–245.*

Keith, T., Keith, P. B., Quirk, K. J., Sperduto, J., Santillo, S., & Killings, S. (1998). Longitudinal effects of parent involvement on high school grades: Similarities and differences across gender and ethnic groups. *Journal of School Psychology, 35*, 335–363.

Keith, T. Z., Keith, P. B., Troutman, G. C., Bickley, P. G., Trivette, P. S., & Singh, K. (1993). Does parental involvement affect eighth-grade student achievement? Structural analysis of national data. *School Psychology Review, 22*, 474–496.

Kerr, M., & Stattin, H. (2000). What parents know, how they know it, and several forms of adolescent adjustment: Further support for a reinterpretation of monitoring. *Developmental Psychology, 36*, 366 – 380.

Kerr, M., Stattin, H., Biesecker, G., & Ferrer-Wreder, L. (2003). Relationships with parents and peers in adolescence. In R. M. Lerner, M. A. Easterbrooks, & J. Mistry (Eds.), *Handbook of psychology: Developmental psychology* (Vol. 6, pp. 395–419). New York: John Wiley & Sons.

Kerr, M., Stattin, H., & Trost, K. (1999). To know you is to trust you: Parents' trust is rooted in child disclosure of information. *Journal of Adolescence, 22*, 737–752.

Kim, E. (2002). The relationship between parental involvement and children's educational achievement in the Korean Immigrant Family. *Journal of Comparative Family Studies, 33*(4), 529–543.

Kliewer, W., & Kung, E. (1998). Family moderators of the relations between hassles and behavior problems in inner city youth. *Journal of Clinical Child Psychology, 27*, 278–292.

Knafo, A., & Schwartz, S. H. (2003). Parenting and adolescents' accuracy in perceiving parental values. *Child Development, 74*, 595-611.

Laird, R. D., Pettit, G. S., Bates, J. E., & Dodge, K. A. (2003). Parents' monitoring-relevant knowledge and adolescents' delinquent behaviour: Evidence of correlated developmental changes in reciprocal influences. *Child Development, 74*, 752–768.

Lamborn, S. D., Mounts, N. S., Steinberg, L. D., & Dornbusch, S. M. (1991). Patterns of competence and adjustment among adolescents from authoritative, authoritarian, indulgent, and neglectful families. *Child Development, 62*, 1049–1065.

Lee, S. (1994). *Family-school connections and student's education: Continuity and change of family involvement from the middle grades to high school.* Ann Arbor, MI: ProQuest Information & Learning.

Lempers, J.D., Clark-Lempers, D., & Simons, R.L. (1989). Economic hardship, parenting, and distress in adolescence. *Child Development, 60*, 138–151.

Leung, K., Lau, S., & Lam, W. L. (1998). Parenting styles and academic achievement: A cross-cultural study. *Merrill-Palmer Quarterly-Journal of Developmental Psychology, 44*, 157-172.

Levy J. (1980). Vulnerable children: parents' perspectives and the use of medical care. *Pediatric, 65*, 956-963.

Loeber, R., & Stouthamer-Loeber, M. (1986). Family factors as correlates and predictors of juvenile conduct problems and delinquency. In M. Tonry & N. Morris (Eds), *Crime and justice: An annual review of research* (pp. 29–149). Chicago: University of Chicago.

Lollis, S., & Kuczynski, L. (1997). Beyond one hand clapping: Seeing bidirectionality in parent–child relations. *Journal of Social and Personal Relationships, 14*(4), 441-461.

Maccoby, E., & Martin, J. (1983). Socialization in the context of the family: Parent-child interaction. In E. M. Hetherington (Ed.), P. H. Mussen (Series Ed.), *Handbook of child psychology: Vol. 4. Socialization, personality, and social development* (pp. 1-101). New York: Wiley.

Marshall, S. K., Tilton-Weaver, L. C., & Bosdet, L. (2005). Information management: Considering adolescents' regulation of parental knowledge. *Journal of Adolescence, 28*, 633–647.

McLoyd, V. C., Jayaratne, T. E., Ceballo, R., & Borquez (1994). Unemployment and work interruption among African American single mothers: Effects on parenting and adolescent socioemotional functioning. *Child Development, 65*, 562–589.

Miller, J.M., Diiorio, C., & Dudley,W. (2002). Parenting style and adolescent's reaction to conflict: Is there a relationship? *Journal of Adolescent Health, 31*(6), 463–468.

Najman, J. M., Behrens, B. C., Andersen, M., Bor, W., O'Callaghan, M., Williams, G. M. (1997). Impact of family type and family quality on child behaviour problems: a longitudinal study. J *Am Acad Child Adolesc Psychiatry, 36*, 1357-1365.

Nicholson, J. S., Deboeck, P.R., Farris, J. R., Boker, S. M., & Borkowski, J. G. (2011). Maternal depressive symptomatology and child behavior: Transactional relationship with simultaneous bidirectional coupling. *Developmental Psychology, Vol 47(5),*1312-1323.

Nigg, J. T., & Hinshaw, S. P. (1998). Parent personality traits and psychopathology associated with antisocial behaviors in childhood attention deficit hyperactivity disorder. *Journal of Child Psychology and Psychiatry and Allied Disciplines, 39*, 145–159.

Olweus, D. (1980). Familial and temperamental determinants of aggressive behavior in adolescent boys: A causal analysis. *Developmental Psychology, 16*, 644–660.

Parker G. (1983). *Parental overprotection: a risk factor in psychosocial development.* New York: Grune & Straton, Inc.

Patterson, G. R. (1980). *Mothers: The unacknowledged victims.* Monographs of the Society for Research in Child Development, 45 (Serial No. 186).

Patterson, G. R., & Stouthamer-Loeber, M. (1984). The correlation of family management practices and delinquency. *Child Development, 55,* 1299–1307.

Pereira, A., Canavarro, C., Cardoso, M., & Mendonca, D. (2009). Patterns of Parental Rearing Styles and Child Behaviour Problems among Portuguese School-Aged Children. *J Child Fam Stud, 18,* 454–464.

Perren, S., & Hornung, R. (2005). Bulling and delinquency in adolescence: Victim's and perpetrators' family and peer relations. *Swiss Journal of Psychology, 64*(1), 51–64.

Pesonen, A., Räikkönen, K., Heinonen, K., Komsi, N., Järvenpää, A., &, Strandberg, T. (2007). A Transactional Model of Temperamental Development: Evidence of a Relationship between Child Temperament and Maternal Stress over Five Years. *Social Development, 17,* 2, 326-340.

Peterson, J., & Hawley, D. R. (1998). Effects of stressors on parenting attitudes and family functioning in a primary prevention program. *Family Relations, 47,* 221.

Pett, M. A., Vaughan-Cole, B., Wampold, B. E. (1994). Maternal employment and perceived stress: their impact on children's adjustment and mother-child interaction in young divorced and married families. *Fam Relat Interdisciplinary J Appl Fam Stud, 43,* 151-158.

Pomerantz, E. M.. Moorman, E. A., & Litwack, S. D. (2007).The how, whom, and why of parents' involvement in children's academic lives: More is not always better. *Review of Educational Research, 77,* 373-410.

Qi, C. H., & Kaiser, A. P. (2003). Behavior problems of preschool children from low-income families: review of the literature. *Top Early Child Special Educ, 23,* 188-216.

Radziszewska, B., Richardosn, J. L., Dent, C. W., & Flay, B. R. (1996). Parenting style and adolescent depressive symptoms, smoking and academic achievement: Ethnic, gender, and SES differences. *Journal of Behavioral Medicine, 19*(3), 289–305.

Rodrilguez, M. D., Donovick, M. R., & Crowley, S. L. (2009). Parenting Styles in a Cultural Context: Observations of "Protective Parenting" in First-Generation Latinos. *Family Process, Vol. 48, No. 2,* 195-210.

Rohner, R. P., & Britner, P. A. (2002). Worldwide mental health correlates of parental acceptance-rejection: Review of crosscultural and intracultural evidence. Cross-Cultural Research. *The Journal of Comparative Social Science, 36,* 16–47.

Rubin, K. H., Burgess, K. B., & Hastings, P. D. (2002). Stability and Social- Behavioral Consequences of Toddlers' Inhibited Temperament and Parenting Behaviors. *Child Development, 73* (2), 483-495.

Sameroff, A. J. (1975). Transactional models in early social relations. *Human Development, 18,* 65-79.

Sameroff, A. (2010). The transactional model of development: how children and contexts shape each other. *Infant Mental Health Journal, Vol. 31(1),* 115–117.

Sameroff, A.J., & Chandler, M.J. (1975). Reproductive risk and the continuum of caretaking casualty. In F.D. Horowitz, M. Hetherington, S. Scarr-Salapatek, and G. Siegel (Eds.), *Review of child development research* (Vol. 4, pp. 187.244). Chicago: University of Chicago.

Sameroff, A. J., & MacKenzie, M. J. (2003). Research strategies for capturing transactional models of development: The limits of the possible. *Development & Psychopathology, 15*(3), 613-640.

Samra, H., & McGrath, J. M. (2009). Infant Vulnerability and Parent Overprotection: Recommendations for Health Professionals. *Family Dynamics, 9* (3), 136-138.

Sewell, W. H., & Hauser, R. M. (1980). The Wisconsin longitudinal study of social and psychological factors in aspirations and achievements. *Research in Sociology and Education and Socialization, 1*, 59–99.

Shucksmith, J., Hendry, L. B., & Glendinning, A. (1995). Models of parenting: Implications for adolescent well-being within different types of family contexts. *Journal of Adolescence, 18,* 253-270.

Shumow, L., & Miller, J. D. (2001). Parents' at-home and at-school academic involvement with young adolescents. *Journal of Early Adolescence, 21,* 68-91.

Smokowski, P. R., & Kopasz, K. H. (2005). Bullying in school: An overview of types, effects, family characteristics, and intervention strategies. *Children & Schools, 27*(2), 101–110.

Soenens, B., Vansteenkiste, M., Luyckx, K., & Goossens, L. (2006). Parenting and adolescent problem behavior: An integrated model with adolescent self-disclosure and perceived parental knowledge as intervening variables. *Developmental Psychology, 42,* 305–318.

Spera, C. (2005). A review of relationships among parenting practices, parenting styles and adolescent school achievement. *Educational Psychology Review, 17*(2), 125–146.

Stattin, H., & Kerr, M. (2000). Parental monitoring: A reinterpretation. *Child Development, 71,* 1072–1085.

Stavrinides, P. (2011). The Relationship Between Parental Knowledge and Adolescent Delinquency: a Longitudinal Study. *International Journal about Parents in Education, Vol. 5, No. 1,* 46-55.

Stavrinides, P., Georgiou, S., & Demetriou, A. (2010). Longitudinal associations between adolescent alcohol use and parents' sources of knowledge. *Journal of Developmental Psychology, 28,* 643-655.

Steinberg, L., Lamborn, S. D., Darling, N., Mounts, N. S., & Dornbusch, S. M. (1994). Over-time changes in adjustment and competence among adolescents from authoritative, authoritarian, indugent and neglectful families. *Child Development, 65,* 754– 770.

Steinberg, L., Dombusch, S. M., & Brown, B. B. (1992). Ethnic-differences in adolescent achievement: An ecological perspective. *American Psychologist, 47,* 723-729.

Steinberg, L., & Silverberg, S. (1986). The vicissitudes of autonomy in early adolescence. *Child Development, 57,* 841–851.

Stevenson, D. L., & Baker, D. P. (1987). The family-school relation and the child's school performance. *Child Development, 58,* 1348–1357.

Strage, A., & Swanson, T. (1999). Authoritative parenting and college students' academic adjustment and success. *Journal of Educational Psychology, 91,* 146–156.

Sui-Ghu, E. H., & Willms, J. D. (1996). Effects of parental involvement on eighth-grade achievement. *The Sociological Quarterly, 69,* 126-141.

Tilton-Weaver, L. C., & Galambos, N. L. (2003). Adolescents' characteristics and parents' beliefs as predictors of parents' peer management behaviors. *Journal of Research on Adolescence, 13,* 269–300.

VanderValk, I., deGoede, M., Spruijt, E., & Meeus, W. (2007). A longitudinal study on transactional relations between parental marital distress and adolescent emotional adjustment. *Adolescence, Vol. 42, No. 165*, 116-136.

VanVoorhis, F. L. (2003). Interactive homework in middle school: Effects on family involvement and science achievement. *Journal of Educational Research, 96,* 323-339.

Vuchinich, S., Bank, L., & Patterson, G. R. (1992). Parenting, peers, and the stability of antisocial behavior in preadolescent boys. *Developmental Psychology, 28*(3), 510-521.

Walker, L. O. (1989). Stress process among mothers of infants: Preliminary model testing. *Nursing Research, 38,* 10–16.

Walker, L. O. & Cheng, C. (2007). Maternal Empathy, Self-Confidence, and Stress as Antecedents of Preschool Children's Behavior Problems. *Journal of Personality and Social Psychology,12* (2), 93-104.

Waizenhofer, R. N., Buchanan, C. M., & Jackson-Newsom, J. (2004). Mothers' and fathers' knowledge of adolescents' daily activities: Its sources and its links with adolescent adjustment. *Journal of Family Psychology, 18,* 348–360.

Wang, C. H. C, & Phinney, J. S. (1998). Differences in child-rearing attitudes between immigrant Chinese mothers and Anglo-American mothers. *Early Development and Parenting, 7,* 181-189.

Webb, J. A., Bray, J. H., Getz, J. G., & Adams, G. (2002). Gender, perceived parental monitoring, and behavioural adjustment: Influences on adolescent alcohol use. *American Journal of Orthopsychiatry, 72*(3), 392–400.

Weiner, B. (1985). An attributional theory of achievement motivation and emotion. *Psychological Review, 92,* 548–573.

Weinraub, M., & Wolf, B. (1983). Effects of stress and social supports on mother–child interactions in single and two-parent families. *Child Development, 54,* 1297–1311.

Weintraub, K. J., & Gold, M. (1991). Monitoring and delinquency. *Criminal Behaviour and Mental Health, 1,* 268–281.

Weiss, B., Dodge, K.A., Bates, J.E., & Pettit, G.S. (1992). Some consequences of early harsh discipline: Child aggression and maladaptive social information processing style. *Child Development, 63,* 1321–1335.

White, M. J., & Kaufman, G. (1997). Language usage, social capital, and school completion among immigrants and native-born ethnic groups. *Social Science Quarterly, 78,* 385–398.

Zayas, L. H., & Solari, F. (1994). Early-childhood sociaUzation in Hispanic families: Context, culture, and practice implications. *Professional Psychology- Research and Practice, 25,* 200-206.

In: Parenting
Editors: Peter Barberis and Stelios Petrakis

ISBN: 978-1-62257-881-8
© 2013 Nova Science Publishers, Inc.

Chapter 4

PARENTS AS MODELS FOR PARTNERS' RELATIONAL COMPETENCES: THEORETICAL BASES AND EMPIRICAL FINDINGS

Silvia Donato, Raffaella Iafrate and Daniela Barni
Catholic University of Milan, Italy

ABSTRACT

The present chapter is aimed at a) examining theoretical and empirical contributions on the influences of parental models on partners' relational competences; and b) presenting findings from some recent studies examining parent-adult child similarities on dyadic coping, stress communication, and dyadic forgiveness. In particular, it presents several theoretical approaches (i.e., intergenerational family systems theory, attachment theory, social learning theory, and socialization theory), in which the existence of intergenerational linkages from the family of origin to children's couple relationship has been considered as a key assumption, and some models of the effects of family of origin variables on the offspring's couple relationship that are grounded on such theoretical frameworks. Following this review of intergenerational theories and models, we will highlight the importance of taking into account the cultural background when studying parental influences on children's relational competences. Finally, some recent empirical studies will be presented in which parent-child similarities were analyzed with reference to couples' key relational competences: Dyadic coping, stress communication, and dyadic forgiveness. Results of these studies highlighted how parents play a key role of models for children's adult romantic relationship, though children in turn take an active role in discriminating between positive and negative parental models.

Keywords: Intergenerational influences; parent-child similarities; relational competence

INTRODUCTION

The individual's development is a lifelong process in which prior and present experiences interact to result in an outcome that is, at the same time, in continuity with the past and a new emergent entity. This chapter is going to examine the literature and research on the influences of the experiences occurred within the family of origin on partners' relational competences (e.g., partners' conflict resolution styles, communication modes, forgiveness, and dyadic coping tendencies). In particular, this chapter will review several theoretical approaches (intergenerational family systems theory, attachment theory, social learning theory, and socialization theory), in which the existence of intergenerational linkages from the family of origin to children's couple relationship has been considered as a key assumption, and some recent models of the effects of family of origin variables on the offspring's couple relationship that are grounded on such theoretical frameworks. Following this review of intergenerational theories and models, we are going to highlight the importance of taking into account the cultural background when studying parental influences on children's relational competences. Finally, we are going to present findings from some recent studies we run to analyze parent-adult child similarities on dyadic coping, stress communication, and dyadic forgiveness.

INTERGENERATIONAL INFLUENCES ON ADULT ROMANTIC RELATIONSHIPS

Partners' relational competences may be, at least in part, shaped by the experiences they have lived in their families of origin and particularly by the parental models of that competence they have been exposed to. Several theoretical approaches have provided knowledge on how some family of origin characteristics may shape the way partners enter their adult romantic relationships. Since a comprehensive account of intergenerational theories is beyond the scope of this chapter, we selected here those perspectives that formed the theoretical bases for some models explicitly designed to investigate how family of origin variables may influence adult children's romantic relationships (e.g., Bryant & Conger, 2002; Busby, Gardner, & Taniguchi, 2005; Mallinckrodt, 2000; Sabatelli & Bartle-Haring, 2003; Tallman, Gray, Kullberg, & Henderson, 1999). In the following paragraphs we are going to present these theories and the models that derived from them.

Family Systems Theory: Self-Differentiation over the Generations

Bowen's (1978) theory posits that the individual's development occurs within and is influenced by the multigenerational family system. In particular, according to this theoretical approach the family of origin is the first and most important theatre in which children develop their level of self-differentiation. Differentiation of self, a core construct within this perspective, is defined at both the individual and the system level: At the individual level, it refers to the individual's ability to maintain cognitive functioning despite emotional arousal; and, at the system level, it refers to the individual's ability to sustain a separate sense of self within relationship pressures, thus tolerating both closeness and distance from others. Differentiation of self is considered necessary in order to establish healthy intimate relationships both within and outside the family of origin. Although Bowen's conceptualization of differentiation of self encompasses a balance between intimacy and individuality, he devoted greater attention to the development of individuality, therefore Williamson (1981, 1991) further refined the concept of differentiation (or individuation) by clarifying that it doesn't refer to a form of detachment from other family members, but to a mutual sense of respect that allows for both intimacy and separateness. Williamson also identified a more advanced form of differentiation, normally reached when individuals are in their thirties (Harvey & Bray, 1991; Lawson, Gaushell, & Karst, 1993), that he named Personal Authority in the Family System (PASF) and refers to the ability of individuals to experience a peerlike intimacy with parents and to maintain an individuated position. In general, theorists of intergenerational family functioning assume that relational patterns tend to be reproduced from one generation to the next, from the relationship with parents to the relationship with intimate partners, and invoke two possible transmission processes: On the one hand, parents' level of differentiation influences their children's level of differentiation through social learning with parents and grand-parents (Williamson & Bray, 1988), and, on the other hand, through the maintenance of loyalty to the previous generations by fulfilling parents' perceived expectations and mandates (Boszormenyi-Nagi & Ulrich, 1981).

This intergenerational transmission of self-differentiation across generations results in a certain degree of parent-child similarity in self-differentiation, but it does not imply a static intergenerational continuity, in which parents and children are bound to repeat deterministically the same pattern of differentiation: The degrees of freedom given to each new relationship (between parent and child as well as between partners), in fact, allow for a dynamic process of either progression or regression in self-differentiation over the generations, in which the level of differentiation can gradually decrease or increase.

Although the intergenerational transmission hypothesis is one of the key assumptions of Bowen's theory and the models derived from it, most empirical studies conducted beneath this theoretical framework have explored the link between differentiation (within the family of origin or the new nuclear family) and the individual or the couple's functioning, while only a handful of studies has been devoted to directly test the intergenerational transmission of differentiation (Harvey, Curry, & Bray, 1991; Klever 2005; Lawson & Brossart, 2001; Rosen, Bartle-Haring, & Stith, 2001; Sabatelli & Bartle-haring, 2003; Tuason & Friedlander, 2000).

Drawing from the intergenerational family systems theory, Sabatelli and Bartle-Haring (2003) proposed a model that examines how spouses' perceptions of the level of differentiation in their family of origin influence their ability to experience intimacy and satisfaction within their marital relationships. Important features in this model are the crossover effects that are hypothesized between each spouse's experience in his/her own family of origin (in terms of relationship with both parents and the parental couple relationship) and the other's marital adjustment (in terms of intimacy and levels of complaints within the marriage): This model suggests that each partner's family history, once they enter into the marital relationship, needs to deal with the one of the other and that both partners' marital well-being is linked to the other's capacity to balance relatedness and autonomy with respect to his/her own family of origin. Research supports these crossover effects, in particular women's experiences in their family of origin are proven to be linked to both their own and their spouse's marital adjustment (Sabatelli & Bartle-Haring, 2003; Wambolt & Reiss, 1989).

Attachment Theory: The Role of the Parent-child Bond

Attachment theory has shed light on the impact that early experiences in the family of origin may have on adults' romantic relationships through the examination of the importance of the parent-child bond. Bowlby (1969, 1973, 1980) described the emotional bond linking children and caregivers in terms of its evolutionary functions (i.e., responding to the universal need for security and comfort). He argued that secure attachment bonds play a key role in sustaining children's social and emotional development and that such bonds derive primarily from responsive parenting. Responsiveness and emotional availability of caregivers, in fact, are crucial in forming children's beliefs about the self and the social world; in particular, cognitive representations (i.e., internal working models) of self as worthy of care and of the attachment figure as supportive and caring result from children's internalization of experiences with caregivers who consistently responded to their needs.

A key concept within this conceptual framework is that working models are carried forward to form the basis for adult beliefs of self and others (Bowlby, 1973; Main, Kaplan, & Cassidy, 1985) and that (in)secure attachment patterns developed in childhood are associated with security (or lack of it) in adults' intimate relationships (Collins & Read, 1990; Feeney & Noller, 1990; Hazan & Shaver, 1987). Furthermore, Bowlby (1988) posited that attachment models are relatively stable across time, but they can also be revised and altered by the individual's new relational experiences, especially the one with the spouse or partner. A vast body of research has examined the correlates and consequences of parent-child attachment security and considerable attention has been devoted to the intergenerational transmission of attachment patterns (e.g., van IJzendoorn, 1995). Moreover, research on changes in attachment models has confirmed Bowlby's contentment that attachment is a moderately stable pattern that, nonetheless, can be subject to change over time. Research, in fact, has consistently found that attachment representations are moderately to highly stable, but still a percentage of adults (ranging from 30% to 40% of research participants) report changes in attachment models (see, for a review, Scharfe, 2003). One line of thought, generally referred to as the "contextual model" (cfr. Davila, Karney, & Bradbury, 1999), maintains that attachment changes result from changes in people's life circumstances (e.g., beginning a new relationship or going through a life transition) in line with Bowlby's (1973) reasoning that new relational experiences may question prior models and require them to adapt to the new context (see Scharfe & Cole, 2006).

Rooted in attachment theory (Ainsworth, Blehar, Waters, & Wall, 1978; Bowlby, 1969, 1973, 1980) and its advances in the study of adult relationships (Bartholomew, 1990; Bartholomew & Horowitz, 1991; Hazan & Shaver, 1987) Mallinckrodt's (2000) Social Competencies and Interpersonal Processes (SCIP) model assumes that a possible mechanism of the intergenerational transmission of attachment patterns is the impact that childhood attachment may exert on partners' social competencies.

Drawing from these theoretical premises, Mallinckrodt (1992, 2000, 2001) argued that the parent-child relationship can foster (or undermine) the individual's capacity to develop and maintain close and supportive relationships in adulthood. According to Mallinckrodt often individuals who lack a secure childhood attachment also lack social skills, such as social self-efficacy, the ability to elicit social support or to resolve interpersonal conflicts. In the SCIP model the author considered that "insecure childhood attachment leads to attachment avoidance or anxiety in adults and also to deficits in social competencies" (Mallinckrodt & Wei, 2005, p. 358).

From Social Learning Theory toIntegrative Approaches: Learning in a Developmental and Contextual Framework

Social learning theory has influenced most of the models addressing the intergenerational predictors of the couple functioning. Recent models, however, have integrated this theory with other approaches, especially in order to overcome some limitations of traditional social learning theory as, for example, its lack of a developmental perspective.

Social learning theory considers the family as the training ground for the adult offspring's relational competences. Direct experience, observation and modeling are the mechanisms invoked to explain this intergenerational process (Bandura, 1977). According to this theoretical framework, behaviors that individuals express in their couple relationship are learned, in part, through direct interactions with parents and siblings, in which children learn how to behave in other social contexts. Moreover, thanks to the observation of their parents' interactions with each other and with other siblings, children develop their so-called marital paradigm, that is "the picture, the set of images we have formed about how marriage practice might be or seems to be done, for better or worse" (Marks, 1986, p. 13) and contains the guidelines for relationship functioning that constitute the basis for subsequent relationships.

Drawing from social learning theory, Busby and colleagues (2005) developed an integrative model aimed at describing how family of origin variables can predict marital satisfaction and stability. The Family of Origin Parachute Model is part of a broader theoretical model of premarital factors leading to marital outcomes (see Busby, Holman, & Taniguchi, 2001). The overall model was based on a comprehensive review of premarital predictors of marital quality (Gottman, 1994; Karney & Bradbury, 1995; Larson & Holamn, 1994) and grounded its assumptions on three theoretical perspectives: The social learning perspective, the developmental approach, and the bioecological perspective (cfr. Busby, Holman, & Walker, 2008).

The authors added to the premises of social learning theory a developmental perspective by arguing that early experiences may have enduring effects on adults' relationships, but they are also subject to modification over time through the occurrence of new experiences. According to this perspective, the developing human being transacts with the changing environment in such a way that a new complexity emerges, which is neither directed by earlier experiences nor by the new challenges, but rather is a product of the interplay between both prior functioning and new conditions. In addition, the bioecological perspective (Bronfenbrenner, 2005) posits that relationships begin and are maintained within a series of contexts or subsystems and that such contexts interact with one another: For example, individuals can inherit traits and tendencies through biology (their biological context), and these attributes may be strengthened or weakened by their experiences in their family of origin (the family context), in their social environment (the cultural context), and in their couple relationships (the couple context). Moreover, the bioecological perspective suggests that contexts can be ordered in terms of the more proximal or distal influence they can exert on the outcome of interest.

Within the broader model (Busby et al., 2001), designed to tap the interplay among four contexts (individual, family of origin, couple and culture), the "Family of Origin Parachute Model" refers in particular to the influence of the family of origin to the individuals' self-esteem and couple variables[1]. The metaphor of the parachute refers to the idea that the function of the family of origin is to help individuals to land safely in adult life with the equipment they need to develop successful adult relationships. Parachutes can be more or less strong: Whereas strong cords provide individuals with strengths and resiliency for their landing, weak cords set up chances for potential difficulties, especially when several cords are frayed.

Seven aspects of the family of origin experience were taken into account: family structure (years spent in intact two-parent family); family stressors (e.g., job loss, illness, legal problems), quality of the relationship with father and with mother, quality of the parents' marriage, and experiences of physical or sexual abuse in the home. A crucial feature of this model is that the impact of family of origin experiences is filtered by the individual's evaluation of the influence that such experiences had on his/her adult relationships. Embedded in this model is the idea of children's resiliency: Children can overcome problems arisen from their family of origin experience. Moreover, the model poses emphasis on the influence that positive family experiences, not only negative ones, may have on the individual's adjustment and later relationships.

Another model derived from social learning theory, while integrating other theoretical perspectives, is the Development of Early Adult Romantic Relationship (DEARR) model by Bryant and Conger (2002). The model describes how interactional processes in the family of origin predict young adults' interpersonal skills, which are in turn related to their couple relationship quality. In delineating the features of their model the authors referred to different theoretical perspectives (social learning theory, attachment theory, and socialization theory) as well as to the empirical evidence available within the research on the intergenerational transmission of interpersonal violence and divorce (e.g., Amato & Booth, 1997; Amato & Keith, 1991; O'Leary & Cascardi, 1998; Sanders, Halford, & Beherens, 1999). The DEARR model proposes that some characteristics of the family of origin influence early adults' competences in romantic relationships (in terms of cognitions, behaviors, and emotions) both directly and through their impact on a) the offspring's social and economic circumstances and b) their individual characteristics. In turn, young adults' relational competences are linked to the success or failure of their relationship (in terms of commitment and satisfaction). Three mechanisms were hypothesized in order to explain the influence of family of origin experiences on early adults' interpersonal skills: 1. According to the *observational learning hypothesis*, children may observe and then emulate parents and siblings' behaviors; 2. according to the *sibling or parent socialization hypothesis*, children may learn such behavioral patterns through direct interaction with siblings or parents[2]; 3. according to the *behavioral continuity hypothesis*, children's characteristics may, in part, elicit certain

---

[1] The latter path of influence of family of origin variables on couple variables is explicitly assumed by the authors (see also Busby et al., 2001), but not shown in this part of the model (Busby et al., 2005).
[2] This conception refers to a definition of parent socialization in terms of direct parent-target interactions, whereas more comprehensive definitions emphasize several pathways of socialization, which include observational learning and parent-child bidirectional processes as well (see Grusec & Hastings, 2007; and the next paragraph).

behaviors from the family members and the interactions with family members may in turn reinforce these characteristics that will then be transferred to their adult romantic relationships.

Socialization Theory: From the Primacy of Parents to Children's Agency

Socialization theory has emphasized the role of the experiences in the family of origin, and particularly the parent-child relationship, on children's social behavior in other settings and at later times (see, for a review, Maccoby, 1992; 2007). Despite the broad array of socialization agents that the individual encounters throughout his/her life-cycle (siblings, peers, teachers, employers, religious figures, etc.), parents have been considered as primary agents of children's socialization (Grusec & Davidov, 2007), and not exclusively at the earliest stages of it (Arnett, 2007).

Socialization has been defined in many different ways, but at the broadest level it refers to "the way in which individuals are assisted in becoming members of one or more social groups" (Grusec & Hastings, 2007, p. 1) and in functioning adequately within the standards of such groups (Maccoby, 1992). According to Maccoby (1992) the meaning of *adequate* can vary greatly, but its common core refers to acquiring the habits, skills, values and motives that will enable an adult to a) refrain from deviant behavior; b) contribute economically to the support of self and family; c) initiate and maintain close relationships with others; and d) be able to raise children in turn. More specifically, Grusec (2002) proposed that socialization involves three goals: 1) the development of self-regulation of emotion, thinking, and behavior, 2) the acquisition of cultural standards, attitudes, and values, and 3) the development of role-taking skills, strategies for resolving conflicts, and ways of viewing relationships. It is clear in these definitions that forming and maintaining a couple relationship, along with the relevant processes and skills it requires, pertain to the core objectives of socialization.

Research has explored the variety of outcomes that socialization can involve (e.g., from the acquisition of rules and values to the one of behavioral patterns and routines) as well as the numerous paths through which it can occur (e.g., discipline, modeling, direct training, rituals) ranging from more explicit and deliberate actions of the socialization agents to more implicit and indirect practices (see Grusec & Hastings, 2007).

Despite the numerous mechanisms invoked to explain the socialization process, a key concept in socialization theory is the one of internalization, a process whereby parental and societal values and behaviors, once accurately perceived and accepted by children (Grusec & Goodnow, 1994), are gradually integrated into the child's self system. Integration of parental models in turn should lead to a certain degree of parent-child similarity.

Socialization theory has gradually moved away from a deterministic idea of the socialization process and started to conceptualize parents and children as both *agents* in initiating and accepting (or resisting) influence (Barni, Ranieri, Scabini, & Rosnati, 2011; Kuczynski & Parkin, 2007; Maccoby, 2007). Moreover, socialization theorists have traditionally argued that socialization is a lifelong process (see Grusec & Hastings, 2007) that can be accomplished by a variety of socialization agents, whose role and importance may vary during the individual's life cycle (Arnett, 2007). Most research, however, is devoted to the socialization in childhood and adolescence and little is known about socialization in later life. In particular, socialization theory considers the partner as an important socialization agent, especially when children enter emerging and young adulthood (Arnett, 2007), but the specific role of partners as a source of socialization has rarely been defined theoretically and explored empirically (see, for exceptions, Collins & van Dulmen, 2006; Tallman et al., 1999).

Tallman and colleagues (1999) proposed a process model of the intergenerational transmission of divorce and marital conflict derived from socialization theory. The model is aimed at expanding the traditional individual model (e.g., Caspi & Elder, 1988) according to which the intergenerational transmission of marital relationship patterns occurs through the mediating role of children's individual personality characteristics. Tallman and colleagues argued that such a model needs to be expanded in order to take into account also the individual's potential for learning, especially through his/her new relationships.

In order to extend the individual model, the authors developed and tested a *couple process model* describing the intergenerational transmission of divorce and marital conflict. The model is composed of five phases: In line with socialization theory the authors posited that conflicting parents are likely to engage in harsh, inconsistent parenting (phase 1), which in turn can influence the child's developing self-image, that is the evaluation of his/her own competences and psychological well-being (phase 2). A positive self-image is considered a basis for individuals' proneness to trust the partner; both partners' self-images as well as attachment to each other affect partners' mutual trust (phase 3). The level of trust that characterized the couple relationship is then linked to the relevance that partners attach to the couple's disagreements (phase 4). Finally, the more partners value their disagreements as serious for their relationship, the higher their likelihood of incurring in marital conflict (phase 5). Both mutual trust and disagreement are couple-level factors, requiring both partners contribution and integrating both partners' points of view.

The novelty of this model with respect to the individual one is the emphasis given to the fact that when individual histories finally encounter in a new relationship they have to face different, unanticipated conditions that can alter each partner's individual trajectory. Intergenerational continuity of behaviors and representations only occurs as long as partners' individual experiences and representations mesh and no other event in the larger community affects their situation.

The model was tested in a five-year three-wave longitudinal study involving newlywed couples (Tallman et al., 1999); support was found for the mediating effects hypothesized[3] and for the importance of couple level variables, especially over time, while individual factors instead decreased their influence over the course of the five years.

Intergenerational Theories and Models: Different Perspectives and Common Ideas

These different theoretical perspectives and empirical models share several key ideas: a) they highlight the importance of the experiences lived in the family of origin for partners' future relationships; b) they show how some attributes can pass from one generation to the next, thus leading in a certain degree of intergenerational similarity in that attribute; c) they

---

[3] It is worth noting, however, that parents' marital conflict was only inferred from parents' divorced status and not directly measured.

refer to the process leading to such a similarity, more or less explicitly, as a form of *internalization* (even though with different connotations); d) they hypothesize several mechanisms through which some parents' attributes can pass on to the children (ranging from direct influence to different mediating paths); and finally, e) they assume that intergenerational influences are not deterministic and static, but new relationships (and particularly the couple relationship) may set the conditions to either perpetuate or alter the heritage received from previous generations.

For the purpose of the present chapter the literature reviewed above also provides some insights on the potential influence of family of origin experiences on partners' relational competences. In line with this literature, in fact, these competences may be transmitted across generations, not only because of their potential heritable component, but also because of the internalization of parental models of them.

As we remarked above, intergenerational theories have described the transmission of parental attributes and behavioral patterns across generations in terms of internalization. Internalization is the process through which children transform the attitudes and behaviors expressed by their parents into their own attitudes and behaviors, endorsed not because of external pressure but because of internal motivation; such an integration produces a certain degree of parent-child similarity, so that children result similar to their parents in the attitudes, values and behaviors they have internalized. Recent conceptualization of internalization have highlighted the agency of the child in such a process (Kuczynski & Parkin, 2007), especially his/her active participation in understanding and accepting/rejecting parental models (Grusec & Goodnow, 1994; Zentner & Renaud, 2007), and therefore cautioned researchers against simply equating parent-child similarity with internalization. Nevertheless, verifying the existence of such a similarity is undoubtedly the first step to examine whether internalization actually occurs across generations, as studies on intergenerational influences have shown (e.g., Bengtson, 1975; Cashmore & Goodnow, 1985; Glass, Bengtson, & Dunham, 1986; Zentner & Renaud, 2007). Extant research provides evidence that parents and children are similar across a wide range of domains, including attitudes (e.g., Cashmore & Goodnow, 1985), values (Barni, 2009; Knafo & Schwartz, 2008), ideal selves (Zentner & Renaud, 2007), perfectionism (Soenens, Elliot, Goossens, Vansteenkiste, Luyten, & Duriez, 2005) and empathy (Soenens, Duriez, Vansteenkiste, & Goossens, 2007). Research based on married offspring also indicates that parents and children are similar in their risk of marital instability (e.g., Amato & DeBoer, 2001), in their level of marital conflict, intimacy, and individuation (Harvey, Curry, & Bray, 1991; Lawson & Brossart, 2001; Story, Karney, Lawrence, & Bradbury, 2004).

THE CULTURAL BACKGROUND: INFLUENCES ON PARENT-CHILD SIMILARITY

Up to know we have explored reasons for parent-child similarity in partners' relational competences, but what exactly might be internalized and reciprocated? Socialization theory claims that socialization occurs within a cultural context (Keller, 2003; Super & Harkness, 1986) and comprises those processes through which culture is transmitted from one generation to the next (Rogoff, Moore, Najafi, Dexter, Correa-Chavez, & Solis, 2007). The aim of socialization, in fact, is to raise children to become competent adults in their cultural context.

Since the family and the couple are important social agents, communities have interest in coordinating family and societal standards. Beliefs and views of how partners should behave in a couple relationship are widely available: Family interactions, school experiences, exchanges with peers, and media portrayals, all contribute to this shared background. Evidence shows that a number of cross-cultural variations exist in relationship rules (Argyle, Henderson, Bond, Iizuka, & Contarello, 1986), indicating that rules regarding how to behave in specific relationships are affected by the cultural context in which they are applied. Therefore, parental models may convey both what is idiosyncratic and unique of one parent as well as what that parent endorses as a more or less normative way of behaving, as defined within his/her cultural context.

Influences of the Cultural Background on Similarity

In particular, the cultural background people share about the couple relationship is likely to affect parent-child similarity on couple competences and therefore needs to be considered when evaluating the association between parents and children's attitudes and behaviors (see Kenny, Kashy, & Cook, 2006). Members of a dyad might appear to be similar not only because they are similar *to each other,* but also because they respond *stereotypically*, matching the profile of responses of other people in the same cultural group (e.g., Cronbach, 1955; Kenny & Acitelli, 1994). This phenomenon has been referred to as *stereotype effect* (Kenny & Acitelli, 1994), where stereotype means the "typical or normative responses persons tend to give for a set of variables (rather than the more common definition of an oversimplified shared view of a group)" (Kenny et al., 2006; p. 331). In other words, because both members of a dyad are part of a larger group, in which some responses of the partner are more typical or normative than others, as a result of shared cultural values, social desirability, and social biases (e.g., Klohnen & Mendelsohn, 1998), their responses are expected to be similar not only because of their own relationship, but also because of this stereotype effect.

Both stereotypical responding and matching specific parent responses are mechanisms responsible for parent-child similarity (Kenny & Acitelly, 1994; Kenny et al., 2006), but it is important to distinguish between these two types of similarity: Stereotypical and unique. Stereotypical similarity stems from parents and children sharing the same cultural background and means that, for example, a woman may be similar to her father in the same way she may be similar to any other father in the sample, simply because they share the same view on way things are done in a couple. While unique similarity is the one that is specific of one dyad. In the case of stereotypical similarity parents and offspring are similar to each other because they share a similar background on partners' relational competences, while in the case of unique similarity they are similar in their specific and unique relational responses. It is important to note that we do not consider stereotype as merely an error to eliminate, but as a meaningful source of similarity in itself. In particular, the absence of a unique similarity might not mean the absence of internalization, but a different mechanism through which this process may take place, namely through parents and children's endorsement of the general cultural background on the behaviors that are culturally expected within a couple. Parental models that children might internalized may comprise both idiosyncratic as well as culturally shared aspects. Both types of similarities are meaningful, though need to be theoretically and empirically distinguished.

PARENTS AS MODELS: FINDINGS ABOUT DYADIC COPING, STRESS COMMUNICATION, AND FORGIVENESS

Illustrative examples of how parents represent key models for their children are findings related to parent-child similarity in dyadic coping (see also Donato, Iafrate, Bradbury, & Scabini, 2011), stress communication (cfr. Donato, 2009), and dyadic forgiveness (see also Paleari, Donato, Iafrate, & Regalia, 2009). Dyadic coping refers to the way partners manage their everyday stress as a couple and is defined as the cyclical sequence in which the stress signals of one partner activate the coping reactions of the other partner (e.g., Bodenmann, 2005; Iafrate & Donato, in press), which can be positive as well as negative. In this sequence stress communication is a crucial step and refers to the way partners express to the other their stressful situation and their emotional reactions to this situation. Dyadic forgiveness, instead, can be defined as a general propensity to overcome avoidant, resentful or revengeful reactions (i.e., thoughts, feelings, intentions, and behaviors), and to develop benevolent and conciliatory ones, when facing the partner's offences (e.g., Fincham, Hall, & Beach, 2005). In measuring the tendency of partners to engage in dyadic forgiveness two dimensions are considered particularly relevant: Benevolence, which refers to a benevolent and forgiving attitude toward the partner and unforgiveness, which refers to a resentful and avoidant attitude.

We specifically chose these competences for two reasons: On the one hand, they are key factors in predicting children's relationship success and failure (e.g., Bodenmann, Pihet, & Kayser, 2006; Donato & Parise, in press; Paleari, Regalia & Fincham, 2005; Tsang, McCullough, & Fincham, 2006) and, on the other hand, they are dyadic constructs referring to relationship-specific processes. Evidence of intergenerational similarities in these constructs would then be particularly relevant for both couple relationship studies and intergenerational research.

Despite the growing evidence about the importance of dyadic coping, stress communication and forgiveness in promoting and maintaining partners' well-being and relationship quality (see Bodenmann et al., 2006; Donato & Parise, in press; Paleari et al., 2005; Tsang et al., 2006), still research has not fully tapped the antecedents of such critical competences. We therefore run a series of studies (cfr. Donato, 2009; Donato et al., 2011; Paleari et al., 2009) examining how young adults' relational competences they express in their couple relationship may be significantly related to the ones of their parents. Specifically, we assessed the extent to which partners were similar to their parents with respect to dyadic coping, stress communication, and dyadic forgiveness, using a dyad-centered approach in order to appropriately analyze the similarity within each dyad and to separate stereotypical and unique similarity. Moreover, potential moderators of parent-child similarities were considered. Parent-child similarities in fact may be modulated by the domain in which they are displayed (dyadic coping, stress communication, dyadic forgiveness) as well as by the circumstances in which they develop, in terms of whether they are expressed by different children (sons or daughters), that may have been socialized in different ways, by different parents (mothers or fathers), that may play specific roles in the socialization process, and in the context of different perceptions of the kind of models parents represented for their children's lives.

In addition, these studies have highlighted the importance of taking into account both stereotype and uniqueness effects when studying similarities. Stereotype adjustment, in fact, allowed to highlight the existence of a shared cultural background about partners' relational competences and to reveal the impact it exerts on parent-child similarities. At this regard controlling for stereotype significantly lowered the level of similarities, proving the existence among participants of a stereotypical way of responding about partners' relational competences. Moreover, correlations among stereotypes revealed a substantial overlap between gender and generational stereotypes, suggesting that mothers, fathers, sons and daughters in the sample share a highly similar view of dyadic coping, stress communication and forgiveness in couples.

In general, our studies revealed that a significant level of similarity in the tendency to engage in dyadic coping, stress communication, and forgiveness exists between children and their parents. This similarity, although modest on average, is especially noteworthy in light of the fact that several factors that could reduce similarities are present: a) children and parents are referring to different targets of their competences (i.e., their partners); b) data are collected directly from parents and children (multiple informant) and therefore common method variance should not have inflated these similarities; c) parents and children are measured in different moments of their life cycle, when they may have different priorities and different perceptions (cfr. the generational stake hypothesis in Bengtson & Troll, 1978; and a similar argument in Cairns, Cairns, Xie, Leung, & Hearne, 1998; Patterson, 1998); and finally, d) in some cases parents and children show both a stereotypical and a unique degree of similarity. Moreover, from a conceptual point of view, this modest level of parent-child similarity is also in line with the idea that similarity and internalization are not the ultimate outcomes of socialization, but are "steps in an ongoing process that sets the stage for further change" (Kuczynski & Parkin, 2007; p. 276). Modest levels of similarity may stand for children's possibility of change and renovation of their family heritage.

In any case, the present findings suggest that the internalization of parental models of dyadic coping may actually occur. Nevertheless, it appears to follow different paths depending on the specific process we focus on. Before summarizing the findings related to each specific competence, we note that a consistent finding of our investigation was that children were equally similar to their mothers and fathers regardless of the specific competence we considered. A possible interpretation of this result is that, since the relational competences we considered here are relational constructs in which both parents are equally involved (though with their own skills and styles), they may necessitate of both parental models to be socialized. Compared to other variables so far investigated in research on internalization of parental attributes (e.g., ideals, attitudes, and feelings), in fact, the tendency to engage in dyadic coping, stress communication, and forgiveness are more interpersonal in nature and have a greater likelihood of being manifested during interactions with the partner. Accordingly, parents' supportive or unsupportive responses to each other's stress, openness to stress communication, as well as their forgiving or unforgiving attitudes are more likely to be exhibited (and accurately perceived by children) during their mutual interactions, thereby resulting in a more equal involvement of fathers and mothers in their children's socialization of relational competences.

Dyadic Coping

In studying parent-child similarities in dyadic coping we distinguished between positive (i.e., supportive, understanding) and negative (i.e., hostile, superficial) dyadic coping responses. Findings showed evidence for internalization of parental models, though differences were found for positive and negative dyadic coping: In positive dyadic coping only stereotypical parent–child similarities were significant. At this regard, children seem to internalize socially acceptable ways of interacting with their partners in times of stress, rather than their parents' specific ways. It seems here at work the oblique cultural transmission posited by Cavalli-Sforza and Feldman (1981), in which parents are co-responsible with the other members of the older generation of the message that is conveyed to the younger generations. As the authors pointed out, in fact, a cultural group can transmit its attributes across subsequent generations through three forms of cultural transmission: Vertical, horizontal and oblique. While vertical transmission refers to parents conveying cultural values, beliefs and skills to their offspring, and horizontal transmission to children learning from their peers in day-to-day interactions, in the oblique transmission children learn from adults and institutions in general. In line with this conception of cultural transmission, parents may play as socialization agents in both the vertical and oblique transmission, being co-responsible with the other adults of what is conveyed to the younger generations. Parents may contribute to the individual's acquisition of values, beliefs, and skills not only through their own specific attributes but also, as part of the older adult generation, through the cultural models they embody and manifest.

With negative dyadic coping, however, children internalized their parents' specific responses; stereotypical and unique similarities were in fact significant. Furthermore, similarities in negative dyadic coping were higher than those on positive dyadic coping, and daughters in particular were more similar to their parents in negative dyadic coping than were sons. A possible explanation could lie in the fact that negative behaviors may be more salient to children (particularly when contradicting the positive stereotypes shared by participants): Research shows in fact that children have strong emotional and physiological reactions to parental anger and conflict (Davies & Cummings, 1994).

Nonetheless, children's ability to discriminate between parental models influenced these processes. Daughters, in fact, were more similar to their parents the less parents engaged in negative dyadic coping. Sons, instead, did not show the same association with unique similarities. These findings suggest that daughters may be more sensitive to the parental models than sons and more prone to reproduce them as long as they are less negative and more socially acceptable.

Stress Communication

As for stress communication, the results of our studies reveal that in general daughters are not similar to their parents in the way they communicate their stress and ask for support to the partner, whereas men are similar to both their parents, but this similarity is due to a stereotypical effect. Son-parent similarities in stress communication, in fact, are no more significant once stereotype is removed. It may be that, since women report having more intimate friendships than men (Antonucci, 1990) and value communication as a central feature in their friendships (Gouldner & Strong, 1987; Walker ,1994), they may also have more occasions to use such a competence in other relationships outside the family and to be exposed to models other than their parental ones.

Young men instead seem to share with their parents the same stereotypical view of stress communication. However, son-mother unadjusted similarity in stress communication is stronger the less mothers communicate their stress. Given that generally young men communicate their stress less than their partners, mother-son similarity may be higher the less mothers embody a model of stress communication that departs from sons' typical responses. Interestingly, the reverse pattern is found for daughter-father similarities, in which daughter are more similar to their fathers the more fathers communicate their stress to their partners. These findings may be another sign of children's ability to discriminate the model parents embody and suggests that children may also be more prone to internalize this model the more it is compatible with their views.

Dyadic Forgiveness

A significant level of similarity between children and their parents was also found in the tendency to forgive the partner, even after adjusting for stereotype. In particular, daughters were found to be similar to their parents in both forgiveness dimensions (benevolence and unforgiveness), whereas sons were similar to their fathers only in the unforgiveness dimension.

As for child gender, results showed that, consistent with previous studies on the intergenerational transmission of individual and relationship variables (e.g., ideals, relational outcomes), daughters were more similar to their parents in their willingness to forgive the partner than sons (e.g., Caspi & Elder, 1998; Zentner & Renaud, 2007). Moreover, the actual level of forgiveness reported by parents was associated with parent –child similarities, in that children were more similar to their parents, especially mothers, the more their parents showed benevolent and the less they showed unforgiving attitudes toward the partner, suggesting that children may be sensitive to the fact that parents embody a socially desirable model of forgiveness.

Even though the use of convenience samples (all studies were conducted using data from premarital partners and their parents) and the correlational nature of the analyses limit generalizability and scope of the findings presented here, it is nonetheless relevant to acknowledge the presence of such an intergenerational continuity in couple relational competences. At this regard, although the present findings are in line with the assumption of intergenerational transmission of relational competences, establishing the existence of parent-child similarities is only a first step to come to this conclusion. Therefore, future research should aim at investigating internalization more closely - especially by verifying the role of children's accuracy in perceiving their parents' models as well as their acceptance of such models (Grusec & Goodnow, 1994). On the other hand, similarity doesn't necessarily mean a parent-to-child transmission, but can also stand for a bidirectional process: By engaging in dyadic coping, stress communication, and forgiveness toward the partner, children can also influence parents' ongoing socialization (Kuczynski & Parkin, 2007).

REFERENCES

Ainsworth, M. D. S., Blehar, M. C., Waters, E., & Wall, S. (1978). *Patterns of attachment: A psychological study of the Strange Situation*. Hillsdale: Erlbaum.

Amato, P. R., & Booth, A. (1997). *A generation at risk: Growing up in an era of family upheaval*. Cambridge: Harvard University Press.

Amato, P. R., & DeBoer, D. D. (2001). The transmission of marital instability across generations: Relationship skills or commitment to marriage? *Journal of Marriage and Family, 63*, 1038-1051.

Amato, P. R., & Keith, B. (1991). Consequences of parental divorce for children's well-being; A meta-analysis. *Psychological Bulletin, 110*, 26-46.

Antonucci, T. A. (1990). Social support and social relationships. In R. H. Binstock & L. K. George (Eds.), *Handbook of aging and the social sciences* (3rd ed., pp. 205–226). San Diego: Academic Press.

Argyle, M., Henderson, M., Bond, M., Iizuka, Y., & Contarello, A. (1986). Cross-cultural variation in relationship rules. *International Journal of Psychology, 21*, 287-315.

Arnett, J. J. (2007). Socialization in emerging adulthood: From the family to the wider world, from socialization to self-socialization. In J.E. Grusec & Hastings, P.D. (Eds.), *Handbook of socialization: Theory and research* (pp. 208-231). New York,: Guilford Press.

Bandura, A. (1977). Self-efficacy: Toward a unifying theory of behavior change. *Psychological Review, 84*, 191-215.

Barni, D. (2009). *Trasmettere valori: Tre generazioni familiari a confronto* [Transmitting values: A comparison among three family generations]. Milano: Unicopli.

Barni, D., Ranieri, S., Scabini, E., & Rosnati, R. (2011). Value transmission in the family: Do adolescents accept the values their parents want to transmit? *Journal of Moral Education, 40*, 105-121.

Bartholomew, K. (1990). Avoidance of intimacy: An attachment perspective. *Journal of Social and Personal Relationships, 7* , 147-178.

Bartholomew, K., & Horowitz, L. M. (1991). Attachment styles among young adults: A test of a four-category model. *Journal of Personality and Social Psychology, 61*, 226-244.

Bengtson, V. L. (1975). Generation and family effects in value socialization. *American Sociological Review, 40*, 358-371.

Bengtson, V. L., & Troll, L. (1978). Youth and their parents: Feedback and intergenerational influence in socialization. In R. M. Lerner & G. B. Spanier (Eds.), *Children's influences on marital and family interaction: A lifespan perspective* (pp. 106–130). New York: Academic Press.

Bodenmann, G. (2005). Dyadic coping and its significance for marital functioning. In T. Revenson, K. Kayser, & G. Bodenmann (Eds.), *Couples coping with stress: Emerging perspectives on dyadic coping* (pp. 33-50). Washington: American Psychological Association.

Bodenmann, G., Pihet, S., & Kayser, K. (2006). The relationship between dyadic coping, marital quality and well-being: A two-year longitudinal study. *Journal of Family Psychology, 20,* 485-493.

Boszormenyi-Nagy, I., & Ulrich, D. (1981). Contextual family therapy. In A. Gurman & D. Kniskern (Eds.), *Handbook of family therapy* (pp. 159-186). New York: Brunner/Mazel.

Bowen, M. (1978). *Family therapy in clinical practice*. New York: Jason Aaroson.

Bowlby, J. (1969). *Attachment and loss: Vol. 1. Attachment*. New York: Basic Books.

Bowlby, J. (1973). *Attachment and loss: Vol. 2. Separation: Anxiety and anger*. New York: Basic Books.

Bowlby, J. (1980). *Attachment and loss: Vol. 3. Loss*. New York: Basic Books.

Bowlby, J. (1988). *A secure base: Parent-child attachment and healthy human development*. New York: Basic Books.

Bronfenbrenner, U. (Ed.). (2005). *Making human beings human: Bioecological perspectives on human development*. Thousand Oaks: Sage Publications.

Bryant, C. M., & Conger, R. D. (2002). An intergenerational model of romantic relationship development. In A. L. Vangelisti, H. T. Reis, & M. A. Fitzpatrick (Eds.), *Stability and change in relationships* (pp. 57–82). New York: Cambridge University Press.

Busby, D. M., Gardner, B. C., & Taniguchi, N. (2005). The family of origin parachute model: Landing safely in adult romantic relationships. *Family Relations, 54*, 254-264.

Busby, D. M., Holman, T. B., & Taniguchi, N. (2001). RELATE: Relationship evaluation of the individual, family, cultural, and couple contexts. *Family Relations, 50*, 308-316.

Busby, D. M., Holman, T. B., & Walker, E. (2008). Pathways to relationship aggression between adult partners. *Family Relations, 57*, 72-83.

Cairns, R. B., Cairns, B. D., Xie, H., Leung, M., & Hearne, S. (1998). Paths across generations: Academic competence and aggressive behaviours in young mothers and their children. *Developmental Psychology, 34*, 1162-1174.

Cashmore, J. A., & Goodnow, J. J. (1985). Agreement between generations: A two-process approach. *Child Development, 56*, 493-501.

Caspi, A., & Elder, G. H. (1988) Childhood precursors of the life course: Early personality and life disorganization. In E. M. Hetherington, R. M. Lerner, & M. Perlmutter (Eds.). *Child development in life-span perspective* (pp. 115-142). Hillsdale: Lawrence Erlbaum Associates.

Cavalli-Sforza, L. L., & Feldman, M. (1981). *Cultural transmission and evolution*. Princeton: Princeton University Press.

Collins, N. L., & Read, S. J. (1990). Adult attachment,working models, and relationship quality in dating couples. *Journal of Personality and Social Psychology, 58*, 644-663.

Collins, W. A., & van Dulmen, M. (2006). Friendship and romance in emerging adulthood: Assessing distinctiveness in close relationships. In J. J. Arnett & J. L. Tanner (Eds.), *Coming of age in the 21st century: The lives and context of emerging adults* (pp. 219-234). Washington: American Psychological Association.

Cronbach, L. J. (1955). Processes affecting scores on "understanding of others" and "assumed similarity". *Psychological Bulletin, 52,* 177-193.

Davies, P. T., & Cummings, E. M. (1994). Marital conflict and child adjustment: An emotional security hypothesis. *Psychological Bulletin, 116*, 387-411.

Davila, J., Karney, B. R., & Bradbury, T. N. (1999). Attachment change processes in the early years of marriage. *Journal of Personality and Social Psychology, 76*, 783-802.

Donato, S. (2009). *Dyadic coping within the couple and across generations*. Unpublished doctoral dissertation, Catholic University of Milan, Milan, Italy.

Donato, S., Iafrate, R., Bradbury, T., & Scabini, E. (2012). Acquiring dyadic coping: partners and parents as models. *Personal Relationships, 19,* 386-400.

Donato, S., & Parise, M. (2012). The role of enacted and perceived dyadic coping for young couples' satisfaction. In B. Molinelli & V. Grimaldo (Eds.), *Handbook of the Psychology of Coping: New research*, Hauppauge: Nova Science Publishers.

Feeney, J. A., & Noller, P. (1990). Attachment style as a predictor of adult romantic relationships. *Journal of Personality and Social Psychology, 58*, 281-291.

Fincham, F. D., Hall, J. H., & Beach, S. R. H. (2005). "'Til lack of forgiveness doth us part": Forgiveness in marriage. In E. L. Worthington, Jr. (Ed.), *Handbook offForgiveness* (pp.207-226). New York: Brunner-Routledge.

Glass, J., Bengtson, V. L., & Dunham, C. C. (1986). Attitude similarity in three generation families: Socialization, status inheritance or reciprocal influence? *American Sociological Review, 51*, 685-698.

Gottman, J. M. (1994). *What predicts divorce? The relationship between marital processes and marital outcomes*. Hillsdale: Lawrence Erlbaum Associates.

Gouldner, H., & Strong, M. S. (1987). *Speaking of friendship: Middle-class women and their friends*. New York: Greenwood Press.

Grusec, J. (2002). Parental socialization and children's acquisition of values. In M. Bornstein (Ed.), *Handbook of parenting* (pp. 142-168). Mahwah: Lawrence Erlbaum Associates.

Grusec, J. E., & Davidov, M. (2007). Socialization in the family: The roles of parents. In J. E. Grusec & P. D. Hastings (Eds.), *Handbook of socialization: Theory and research* (pp. 284-308). New York: Guilford Press.

Grusec, J. E., & Goodnow, J. J. (1994). Impact of parental discipline methods on the child's internalization of values: A reconceptualization of current points of view. *Developmental Psychology, 30*, 4-19.

Grusec, J. E., & Hastings, P. D. (2007). *Handbook of socialization: Theory and research*. New York: Guilford Press.

Harvey, D. M., & Bray, J. H. (1991). Evaluation of an intergenerational theory of personal development: Family process determinants of psychological and health distress. *Journal of Family Psychology, 4*, 298-325.

Harvey, D. M., Curry, C. J., & Bray, J. H. (1991). Individuation and intimacy in intergenerational relationships and health: Patterns across two generations. *Journal of Family Psychology 5*, 204-236.

Hazan, C., & Shaver, P. R. (1987). Romantic love conceptualized as an attachment process. *Journal of Personality and Social Psychology, 52*, 511- 524.

Iafrate, R., & Donato, S. (2012). Coping in a relational context: The case of dyadic coping. In B. Molinelli & V. Grimaldo (Eds.), *Handbook of the Psychology of Coping: New research*, Hauppauge: Nova Science Publishers.

Karney, B. R., & Bradbury, T. N. (1995). The longitudinal course of marita quality and stability: A review of theory, method and research. *Psychological Bulletin, 118*, 3-34.

Keller, H. (2003). Socialization for competence: Cultural models of infancy. *Human Development, 46*, 288-311.

Kenny, D.A., & Acitelli, L. (1994). Measuring similarity in couples. *Journal of Family Psychology, 8*, 417-431.

Kenny, D. A., Kashy, D. A., & Cook, W. L. (2006). *Dyadic data analysis*. New York: Guilford Press.

Klever, P. (2005). The multigenerational transmission of family unit functioning. *The American Journal of Family Therapy, 33*, 253-264.

Klohnen, E. C., & Mendelsohn, G. A. (1998). Partner selection for personality characteristics: A couple-centered approach. *Personality and Social Psychology Bulletin, 24,* 268-278.

Knafo, A., & Schwartz, S. H. (2008). Accounting for parent-child value congruence: Theoretical considerations and empirical evidence. In U. Schönpflug (Ed.), *Cultural transmission: Developmental, psychological, social and methodological aspects* (pp. 240-268). Oxford: Oxford University Press.

Kuczynski, L., & Parkin, C. M. (2007). Agency and bidirectionality in socialization: Interactions, transactions, and relational dialectics. In J. E. Grusec & P. D. Hastings (Eds.), *Handbook of socialization: Theory and research* (pp. 259-283). New York: Guilford Press.

Larson, J. H., & Holman, T. B. (1994). Premarital predictors of marital quality and stability. *Family Relations, 43,* 228-237.

Lawson, D. M., & Brossart, D. F. (2001). Intergenerationa transmission: Individuation and intimacy across three generations. *Family Process, 40,* 429-442.

Lawson, D., Gaushell, H. & Karst, R. (1993). The age onset of personal authority in the family system. *Journal of Marital and Family Therapy, 19,* 287-292.

Maccoby, E. E. (1992). The role of parents in the socialization of children: An historical overview. *Developmental Psychology, 28,* 1006-1017.

Maccoby, E. E. (2007). Historical overview of socialization theory and research. In J. E. Grusec & P. D. Hastings (Eds.), *Handbook of socialization: Theory and research.* New York: Guilford Press.

Main, M., Kaplan, N., & Cassidy, J. (1985). Security in infancy, childhood and adulthood: A move to the level of representation. *Monographs of the Society for Research in Child Development, 50* (1-2, Serial No. 209).

Mallinckrodt, B. (1992). Childhood emotional bonds with parents, development of adult social competencies, and the availability of social support. *Journal of Counseling Psychology, 39,* 453-461.

Mallinckrodt, B. (2000). Attachment, social competencies, social support and interpersonal process in psychotherapy. *Psychotherapy Research, 10,* 239-266.

Mallinckrodt, B. (2001). Interpersonal processes, attachment, and development of social competencies in individual and group psychotherapy. In B. Sarason & S. Duck (Eds.), *Personal relationships: Implications for clinical and community psychology* (pp. 69-118). New York: Wiley.

Mallinckrodt, B., & Wei, M. (2005). Attachment, social competencies, social support, and psychological distress. *Journal of Counseling Psychology, 52,* 358-367.

Marks, S. R. (1986). *Three corners: Exploring marriage and the self.* Lexington: Lexington Books.

O'Leary, K. D., & Cascardi, M. (1998). Physical aggression in marriage: A developmental analysis. In T. N. Bradbury (Ed.), *The developmental course of marital dysfunction* (pp. 343-374). New York: Cambridge University Press.

Paleari, G., Regalia, C., & Fincham, F. D. (2005). Marital quality, forgiveness, empathy, and rumination: A longitudinal analysis. *Personality and Social Psychology Bulletin, 31,* 368-378.

Paleari, G., Donato, S., Iafrate, R., & Regalia, C. (2009). The tendency to forgive in premarital couples: Reciprocating the partner or reproducing parental dispositions? In E.

Cuyler & M. Ackhart (Eds.), *Psychology of Relationships (pp. 191-211)*. New York: Nova Science Publishers.

Patterson, G. R. (1998). Continuities-A search for causal mechanisms [Comment on the special section]. *Developmental Psychology, 34*, 1263-1268.

Rogoff, B., Moore, L., Najafi, B., Dexter, A., Correa-Chavez, M., & Solìs, J. (2007). Children development of cultural repertoires through participation in everyday routines and practices. In J. E. Grusec & P. D. Hastings (Eds.), *Handbook of socialization: Theory and research* (pp. 490-515). New York: Guilford Press.

Rosen, K. H., Bartle-Haring, S., & Stith, S. M. (2001). Using Bowen theory to enhance understanding of the intergenerational transmission of dating violence. *Journal of Family Issues, 22*, 124-142.

Sabatelli, R. M., & Bartle-Haring, S. (2003). Family-of-origin experiences and adjustment in married couples. *Journal of Marriage and Family, 65*, 159-169.

Sanders, M. R., Halford, W. K, & Beherens, B. C. (1999). Parental divorce and premarital couple communication. *Journal of Family Psychology, 13*, 60-74.

Scharfe, E. (2003). Stability and change of attachment representations from cradle to grave. In S. M. Johnson & V. E. Whiffen (Eds.), *Attachment processes in couple and family therapy* (pp. 64-84). New York: Guilford Press.

Scharfe, E., & Cole, V. (2006). Stability and change of attachment representations during emerging adulthood: An examination of mediators and moderators of change. *Personal Relationships, 13*, 363-374.

Soenens, B., Duriez, B., Vansteenkiste, M., & Goossens, L. (2007). The intergenerational transmission of empathy-related responding in adolescence: The role of maternal support. *Personality and Social Psychology Bulletin, 33*, 299-311.

Soenens, B., Elliot, A. J., Goossens, L., Vansteenkiste, M., Luyten, P., & Duriez, B. (2005). The intergenerational transmission of perfectionism: Parents' psychological control as intervening variable. *Journal of Family Psychology, 19*, 358-366.

Story, L. B., Karney, B. R., Lawrence, E., & Bradbury, T. N. (2004). Interpersonal mediators in the intergenerational transmission of marital dysfunction. *Journal of Family Psychology, 18*, 519-529.

Super, C. M., & Harkness, S. (1986). The developmental niche: A conceptualization at the interface of child and culture. *International Journal of Behavioral Development, 9*, 545-569.

Tallman, I., Gray, L. N., Kullberg, V., & Henderson, D. (1999). Intergenerational transmission of marital conflict: Testing a process model. *Social Psychology Quarterly, 62*, 219-239.

Tsang, J., McCullough, M. E., & Fincham, F. D. (2006). The longitudinal association between forgiveness and relationship closeness and commitment. *Journal of Social and Clinical Psychology, 25*, 448-472.

Tuason, M. T., & Friedlander, M. L. (2000). Do parents' differentiation levels predict those of their adult children? And other tests of Bowen theory in a Philippine sample. *Journal of Counseling Psychology 47*, 27-35.

van IJzendoorn, M. H. (1995). Adult attachment representations, parental responsiveness, and infant attachment: A meta-analysis on the predictive validity of the Adult Attachment Interview. *Psychological Bulletin, 117*, 387-403.

Walker, K. (1994). Men, women, and friendship: What they say, what they do. *Gender and Society, 8*, 246-265.

Wamboldt, F. S., & Reiss, D. (1989). Defining a family heritage and a new relationship identity: Two central tasks in making of a marriage. *Family Process, 28*, 317-335.

Williamson, D. S. (1981). Personal authority via termination of the intergenerational hierarchical boundary: A new stage in the family life cycle. *Journal of Marital and Family Therapy, 7*, 441-452.

Williamson, D. S. (1991). *The intimacy paradox: Personal authority in the family system.* New York: Guilford Press.

Williamson, D. S., & Bray, J. H. (1988). Family development and change across the generations: An intergenerational perspective. In C. J. Falicov (Ed.), *Family transitions: Continuity and change over the life cycle* (pp. 357-384). New York: Guilford Press.

Zentner, M., & Renaud, O. (2007). Origins of adolescents' ideal self: An intergenerational perspective. *Journal of Personality and Social Psychology, 92*, 557-574.

In: Parenting
Editors: Peter Barberis and Stelios Petrakis

ISBN: 978-1-62257-881-8
© 2013 Nova Science Publishers, Inc.

Chapter 5

BEYOND THE TIGER MOM: ASIAN AMERICAN PARENTING AND PARENT-CHILD RELATIONSHIPS

Minkyeong Shin and Y. Joel Wong
Indiana University Bloomington, Bloomington, IN, US

ABSTRACT

Because of the uproar arising from Amy Chua's memoir, *Battle Hymn of the Tiger Mother*, Asian American parenting has generated immense interest and controversy. This chapter focuses on the antecedents and consequences of Asian American parenting styles in relation to cultural influences. Specifically, the authors examine Western and Asian conceptualizations of parenting as well as the influence of enculturation and acculturation on Asian American parenting. The authors also explore the challenges associated with cultural gaps between Asian American parents and their children and their implications for parent-child relationships and child outcomes. Implications for future research and practice are discussed.

BEYOND THE TIGER MOM: ASIAN AMERICAN PARENTING AND PARENT-CHILD RELATIONSHIPS

Because of the uproar arising from Amy Chua's memoir, *Battle Hymn of the Tiger Mother*, Asian American parenting has generated immense interest and controversy. In a 2011Wall Street Journal article, *Why Chinese Mothers Are Superior*, Chua (2011) included excerpts from her book which describes her strict "Chinese" child rearing beliefs and parenting practices, such as having high academic expectations and restricting her children from having play dates, watching TV, or choosing their own extracurricular activities. Chua's article generated strong negative reactions, particularly toward her argument that Chinese mothers are "superior" to Western parents because they can help their children be more successful through their strict parenting style.

However, in reality, raising children in the United States is often a struggle for Asian American parents. Many Asian American parents -- especially those who recently immigrated to the United States -- face difficulties understanding their "Americanized children" and finding a balance between their parental expectations and their children's expectations toward them. In an ABC Good Morning America interview (2011), Chua revealed similar challenges she encountered. She describes her memoir as a journey of a Chinese American mother who transformed from a "tiger" to a "crying little rabbit" mom. The goal of this chapter is to provide a critical review of the literature on Asian American parenting and parent-child relationships. In particular, we focus on challenges that Asian American parents and children may face due to living in a multicultural context. We first examine Asian Americans' parenting styles as well as cultural influences on their parenting styles. Then we explore the challenges associated with cultural gaps between Asian American parents and their children and their implications for parent-child relationships and child outcomes. Finally, we discuss the research and practical implications of these findings.

ASIAN AMERICAN PARENTING STYLES

Arguably the most well-known theoretical model on parenting in the United States is Baumrind's (1973) typology of parenting styles. Baumrind suggested that most parenting styles can be categorized as authoritarian, authoritative, or permissive based on different combinations of parental warmth and control. Maccoby and Martin (1983) further suggested a fourth category -- disengaged parenting. Authoritative parenting is characterized by the parent being consistently warm and responsive to the child while also setting expectations and providing discipline that are appropriate to the child's developmental level (Baumrind, 1973). Research has found that authoritative parenting was correlated with positive child outcomes, (Dornbusch, Ritter, Leiderman, Roberts, & Fraleigh, 1987; Steinberg, Lamborn, Darling, Mounts, & Dornbusch, 1994). In contrast, authoritarian (high in parental control, low in warmth), permissive (low in parental control, high in warmth), and disengaged parenting (low in both parental control and warmth) have been shown to be associated with negative outcomes in child development (Steinberg et al., 1994).

Asian American parents are often perceived as authoritarian in their parenting style due to their highly controlling parenting practices combined with a relative lack of warmth. Comparison studies on the parenting practices of Asian Americans and other ethnic groups (e.g., African American, Caucasian American, and Hispanic American) have found that Asian American parents tended to exhibit more control over their children (Chiu, 1987; Julian, McKenry, & McKelvey, 1994). For example, Kwak and Berry (2001) found that Asian Canadian parents paid greater attention to parental authority and children's obligations and less on children's rights than Anglo-Celtic Canadian families. Another study revealed that Vietnamese American parents placed more emphasis on their children's obligations toward the family than Armenian, Mexican, and European American families (Phinney, Ong, & Madden, 2000). Studies have also shown that Asian American parents emphasized their children's education more than other ethnic groups (Fuligni, 1997; Steinberg, Dornbusch, & Brown, 1992), which could lead to higher parental expectations and demands. In contrast, expressions of love and warmth were observed less in Asian Americans than European

Americans (Chiu, 1987; Herz & Gullone, 1999). Specifically, research findings revealed that Asian American parents were less likely to express their love toward their children verbally (e.g., saying "I love you" to their children) and physically (e.g., hugging and kissing their children) than Caucasian American parents (Chao & Tseng, 2002). For this reason, some Asian American parents may be perceived by their children as cold and uncaring from a Western viewpoint (Pyke, 2000).

Based upon these research findings, one might suspect that Asian American parenting practices would be associated with negative child outcomes. However, interestingly, the research findings on Asian American parenting styles and child outcomes (e.g., school performance, parent satisfaction) are somewhat inconsistent with those on European Americans (Chao & Tseng, 2002). For Asian Americans, studies have indicated that the relationship between authoritative parenting and adolescents' academic achievement was either weaker or not significant as compared to European Americans (Dornbusch et al., 1987; S. Kim, 1996; Steinberg et al., 1994; Steinberg, Mounts, Lamborn, & Dornbusch, 1991). With regard to mental health outcomes, P. V. Nguyen (2008) found that Vietnamese American adolescents with fathers who were authoritarian reported lower levels of self-esteem and higher levels of depression than those with fathers who were authoritative. However, another study showed that parental harshness (e.g., parents' disapproval when talking to children and getting annoyed with children for their disobedience) was positively associated with children's aggression in European Canadian families but negatively associated for their South Asian Canadian counterparts (C. Ho, Bluestein, & Jenkins, 2008).

One possible explanation for this inconsistency is the different cultural meanings associated with parenting behavior (Chao & Tseng, 2002). Chao (1994) proposed that parental control for Chinese American mothers involves *chiao shun* (i.e., training or educating the child to exhibit appropriate behaviors), a concept not included in Western parenting practices. A comparison of Chinese and European American mothers' parenting styles revealed that Chinese American mothers scored significantly higher on *chiao shun* than their European counterparts, even after controlling for their education and authoritarian/authoritative scores (Chao, 1994). Chao further argued that Chinese American parenting includes the indigenous concept of *guan*, which has a positive connotation because it can mean "to govern" as well as "to love or care for." Several studies on Asian adolescents provide some evidence of positive relationships between parental control and parental warmth (Rohner & Pettengill, 1985; Stewart, Bond, Kennard, Ho, & Zaman, 2002). Hence, Western conceptualizations of parenting styles (Baumrind,1973) may not be culturally sensitive enough to capture the characteristics of Asian American parenting (Chao, 1994).

CULTURAL INFLUENCES ON ASIAN AMERICAN PARENTING

In contrast to parents living in Asian countries, Asian American parenting takes place in an environment in which children are exposed to multiple cultural contexts (i.e., their Asian culture and mainstream European American culture). Within this environment, Asian American parents tend to invest time and effort to preserve their culture of origin (Zhou, 1997). On the other hand, their children often struggle to find a balance between their culture of origin and mainstream European American culture (Dublin, 1996). This cultural learning of mainstream European American culture (i.e., acculturation) as well as the learning and maintenance of one's indigenous culture (i.e., enculturation) among Asian American parents and children is critical to an understanding of Asian American families (Berry, 1998; Redfield, Linton, & Herskovits, 1936; B. S. K. Kim, 2007). In the following sections, we discuss the enculturation and acculturation of Asian American families with a focus on Asian cultural values and practices related to parenting.

Enculturation of Asian American Families

Scholars have identified several Asian values that are especially salient to Asian American parenting and family life. Specifically, collectivism, filial piety, emotional self-control, family recognition through achievement, and respect for hierarchy have been proposed as important cultural values that highly enculturated Asian Americans adhere to (Berg & Jaya, 1993; J. M. Kim, 2003; B. S. K. Kim, Atkinson, & Umemoto, 2001; Mercado, 2000; Suzuki, 1982).

An emphasis on collectivism and interdependence cultivates a sense of self as embedded within one's relationships, especially familial relationships (Tang, 1992; Yu, 1982). Striving to meet the expectations of parents and bringing honor to the family can be understood in the same vein (Berg & Jaya, 1993; Mercado, 2000; Zane & Mak, 2003). Asian American parents teach their children to avoid behaving in a manner that would result in loss of face to one's family and/or cultural group (G. C. N. Hall & Eap, 2007). Consistent with these collectivistic values, research findings indicate that many parents in Asian countries teach their children at an early age to think of other's perspectives toward themselves through the examples of other children (e.g., "Don't behave like that promiscuous girl -- everyone looks down on her!") (Fung, 1999).

The manner in which Asian American parents express love to their children is also influenced by enculturation. Asian American parents tend to express their love through instrumental support, such as helping their children with their homework, providing them with food and clothing, and paying for their educational expenses (Xiong, Eliason, Detzner, & Cleveland, 2005). To illustrate, Asian American parents were found to have greater involvement in helping their children with reading and homework than Hispanic American parents (Julian, et al., 1994). Another way Asian American parents express love is by sacrificing their own needs and desires to provide their child with opportunities and resources (e.g., Asian American parents may move to live in a specific neighborhood so that their children can attend a good public school, although the location might be far from their workplace; Chao & Kaeochinda, 2010). Due to this difference in the meaning of parental love and care, Asian American parents may not be accustomed to expressing their love verbally or physically (e.g., hugs and kisses; E. Kim & Hong, 2007; Y. J. Wong et al., 2011). For example, in one study (E. Kim & Hong, 2007), Korean American parents perceived that expressing love physically and verbally to their children was difficult for them and therefore, tended to require effort to incorporate in their parenting practice.

In addition to different modes of expressing love, enculturation also influences the nature and level of hierarchy in Asian American families (Drachman, Kwon-Ahn, & Paulino,1996; Ying, Coombs, & Lee, 1999). The hierarchy of the family is often expressed in terms of specific roles within the family (E. Lee, 1982). In Asian cultures, the father is often the disciplinarian and breadwinner, whereas the mother is the caregiver of the family (Jankowiak, 1992; Mercado, 2000). This distinction between Asian paternal and maternal roles is captured in the following Korean phrase based upon Confucian values, *umbu jamo,* which means, *"strict father, benevolent mother"* (Rohner & Pettengill, 1985). The hierarchy of the Asian American family structure is also expressed through expectations that older siblings would take care of younger siblings and that children would show respect and be unquestionably obedient to their parents and grandparents (Xiong, Detzner, & Cleveland, 2004; N. A. Nguyen & Williams, 1989).

Acculturation of Asian American Families

Whereas enculturation of Asian Americans has been studied in relation to Asian values and behaviors, acculturation studies focus on the level of adherence to European American values and behaviors. Compared to Asian cultures, European American culture places more emphasis on individualism, independence, and expression of one's thoughts and feelings (Berg & Jaya, 1993). Asian American parents' levels of acculturation may influence their parenting style. Cheung and Nguyen (2007) examined a sample of 30 Vietnamese American parents who generally endorsed the verbal expression of affection to their children. The researchers suggested that the parents' length of residency in the US (average = 16.9 years) may have resulted in higher acculturation, which, in turn, influenced their attitudes toward parenting. Another study on Vietnamese American adolescents and their parents showed that Vietnamese American parents endorsed both traditional Vietnamese values (e.g., obedience to parental authority) and some European American values (e.g., child's freedom to make decisions), possibly because of parents' increased acculturation levels (N. A. Nguyen & Williams, 1989). A more direct connection between acculturation and parenting style was found in Farver, Xu, Bhadha, Narang, and Lieber (2007)'s study where Asian Indian American parents who were highly acculturated scored higher in authoritative parenting style than parents who were less acculturated. Ying and Han (2008) also showed that parental behavioral acculturation (i.e., English proficiency) was related to increased parental involvement in home-educational and social contexts among Southeast Asian Americans. Further, parental involvement in these two contexts was found to mediate the relationship between parent's English ability and family conflict (Ying & Han, 2008).

PARENT-CHILD CULTURAL GAPS

Given that Asian American parents and children may each adhere to varying levels of acculturation and enculturation, Asian American children may hold different parenting expectations and values from their parents, resulting in mutual misunderstanding between parents and children. The rate in which Asian American parents and children change in their levels of acculturation and enculturation depends on factors such as length of residency in the US and generation status (Szapocznik & Kurtines, 1993). N. A. Nguyen and Williams (1989) found that Vietnamese American adolescents tend to endorse less traditional Vietnamese values with increase in their length of time in the US, whereas Vietnamese American parents' adherence to cultural values did not change significantly over time. Research has also revealed that Asian American parents tend to endorse stronger Asian values than their children (e.g., Ahn, Kim, & Park, 2008; Phinney et al., 2000), whereas children tend to endorse stronger Western values than their parents (e.g., Crane, Ngai, Larson, & Hafen, 2005). For example, J. Ho (2010) found that first generation Vietnamese American adolescents tended to identify themselves with mainstream European American culture, engage in European American activities, and speak English more so than their parents. Their parents, on the other hand, tended to be more enculturated than their children, resulting in cultural gaps between parents and children.

Parent-child gaps in acculturation and enculturation may also result in different views toward parenting. A study on Vietnamese, Hmong, Cambodian, and Lao Americans showed that parents and adolescents disagreed on the qualities that constitute "good parenting" (Xiong et al., 2005). In particular, parents viewed providing instrumental support to their children (e.g., food, clothes, shelter), spending time with them, and monitoring their children as characteristics of good parenting (Xiong et al., 2005).However, adolescents perceived that good parenting constitutes parental understanding and verbal expression of affection (Xiong et al., 2005). This cultural gap between Asian American parents and children could lead to Asian American children misunderstanding the intentions of their parents (Herz & Gullone, 1999). Pyke (2000) discovered that highly acculturated children of Korean and Vietnamese immigrants perceived European American parents as less strict, more liberal and open-minded, and more communicative and affectionate than their parents.Moreover, their definition of "the normal American" family and life included having parents who were highly acculturated, which led to evaluating their parents as "deficient." In another study, Southeast Asian American adolescents viewed their parents as overly controlling and lacking warmth based upon their Westernized viewpoint of an ideal parent (Xiong, et al., 2004).

OUTCOMES OF PARENT-CHILD CULTURAL GAPS

To summarize, many Asian American families may be characterized by parent-child cultural gaps resulting in differing views of appropriate parenting. What follows is a discussion of the outcomes associated with these cultural gaps, focusing in particular parent-child relationships, children's mental health, and children's problematic behaviors.

Parent-Child Relationships

Studies have reported that there is a significant relationship between parent-child cultural gaps and family functioning (e.g., Chung, 2001; Dinh & Nguyen, 2006; Tardif & Geva, 2006; Ying & Han, 2007). One study demonstrated that Asian Americans' parenting difficulties, such as communication difficulties and uncertainty of appropriate parenting increased when there was greater discrepancy between the acculturation levels of children and parents (Buki, Ma, Strom, & Strom, 2003). Discrepancies between Asian American college students and their parents in their adherence to European American values and behavior were significantly correlated with the likelihood of family conflict (R. Lee, Choe, Kim, & Ngo, 2000). Further, the least amount of family conflict could be found in Asian American parents and children who were both highly acculturated (R. Lee et al., 2000). Another study explored the interaction effects of Vietnamese American adolescents'and their parents' Vietnamese identities on family cohesion and satisfaction of the parent-child relationship (J. Ho, 2010). Findings indicated that family cohesion and satisfaction with the parents decreased when parents' stronger endorsement of Vietnamese identity was combined with adolescents' low endorsement of Vietnamese identity (J. Ho, 2010). The opposite was observed in adolescents who reported high Vietnamese identity (J. Ho, 2010).

Several studies on Asian American families have also found that children and adolescents reported less emotional support from and less emotional bond with their parents, as the acculturation gap with their parents increased (e.g., Dinh & Nguyen, 2006; Leong, 2005; Lorenzo, Forst, & Reinherz, 2000). For example, one study demonstrated that the depth of the mother-child relationship, maternal support, and satisfaction in the mother-child relationship was negatively correlated with children's perceptions of the acculturation gap (Dinh & Nguyen, 2006). For father-child relationships, the satisfaction of the father-child relationship was also negatively associated with children's perceptions of the acculturation gap.

Research findings have identified several cultural domains that provide more insight about the relationship between cultural gaps and Asian American parent-child relationships. Tsai-Chae and Nagata (2008)'s investigation of the association between Korean American parent-child Asian values gap and family conflicts indicated three critical family conflict domains -- conformity to traditional Asian values endorsed within the family, education and career issues, and respect for elders.Consistent with these findings, studies have found that the values enculturation gap (e.g., filial piety, modesty, bringing pride to one's family, controlling one's emotions) between Korean American college students and their parents was positively associated with family conflict, particularly in family expectations (e.g., using one's Asian language and conforming to cultural traditions), education and career issues, and dating and marriage (Ahn, et al., 2008; B. S. K. Kim, Ahn, & Lam, 2009). Similarly, acculturation gaps in the values dimension have been found to be related to family conflict (Tsai-Chae & Nagata, 2008).

In addition to the values dimension of culture, some research findings also provided evidence that the behavioral dimension of acculturation and enculturation gaps is also essential to understanding Asian American parent-child relationships. A study on Latino, East Asian, and Filipino American adolescents and their parents found that adolescents who spoke different languages from their parents reported less family cohesion (i.e., feeling emotionally closer to their parents) and less discussion with their parents than their peers who spoke the same language with their parents (Tseng & Fuligni, 2000). Hwang (2006a) explained that cultural differences in language usage among Asian American family members can restrict indepth discussion about problems and needs.Furthermore, Hwang proposed that Asian American parent-child dissonance in body movements, facial expressions, and communication styles could hinder effective communication by causing misunderstandings. For instance, Asian Americans who are highly enculturated may communicate their thoughts and emotions implicitly through nonverbal means rather than use direct and explicit communication (E. T. Hall, 1976; Uba, 1994).

Children's Mental Health

Studies have also shown that parent-child cultural gaps were associated with children's mental health (e.g., Dinh, 2000; Crane, et al., 2005; Kitano, 1989). Asian Indian American adolescents and parents were who were similar in their acculturation and enculturation levels reported higher self-esteem and less anxiety than those with different levels (Farver, Narang, & Bhadha, 2002). Research findings also suggest that greater Asian American parent-child acculturation gaps were correlated with increased depression and psychological distress (Crane, et al., 2005; Hwang & Wood, 2009; E. Kim & Cain, 2008; R. M. Lee, Jung, Su, Tran, & Bahrassa, 2009; Wu & Chao, 2005). Longitudinal studies also indicate that perceived parent-child acculturation gaps in early adolescents significantly predicted depression in later adolescence (S. Y. Kim, 2003; Ying & Han, 2007).

Several studies have attempted to identify the mechanisms through which parent-child cultural gaps influence children's psychological adjustment. Two studies found that cultural conflict between Asian American parents and children mediated the relationship between parent-child cultural gaps and children's depression and psychological distress (Hwang & Wood, 2009; Ying & Han, 2007). Another study found that parenting behaviors (e.g., monitoring, inductive reasoning, and warmth) mediated the relationship between father–child acculturation gap and Chinese American adolescents' depressive symptoms (S. Y. Kim, 2003).

Children's Problematic Behaviors

Cultural gap research has also been conducted in relation to youth's problematic behaviors. R. M. Lee and colleagues (2009) found that cultural conflicts between Hmong American parents and college students were positively correlated with substance use. Acculturation gaps of Cambodian, Vietnamese, and Chinese American adolescents and their parents were a significant predictor of youth violence (e.g., robbing, having ideas of hurting someone, or being involved in gang fights) (Le & Stockdale, 2008). Acculturation gaps were also positively related to Asian American adolescents' delinquent behavior (Crane, et al., 2005; S. K. Wong, 1997). Wu and Chao (2005) investigated Chinese and Caucasian American adolescents' perceptions of parental warmth and its relation to children's problematic behaviors. Delinquent behaviors of Chinese American adolescents increased when adolescents perceived their parents to be less warm than their expected parental warmth, whereas no significant relationship between delinquent behaviors and discrepancy in warmth expectations existed for Caucasian American adolescents (Wu & Chao, 2005, 2011).

CLINICAL IMPLICATIONS

Findings across studies in parenting, cultural gaps and family conflict highlight the complexity of Asian American parenting and parent-children relationships. For mental health professionals (e.g., school counselors, social workers, and therapists) who work with Asian

American families, the above literature review suggests the importance of gaining knowledge of Asian Americans' cultural orientation.

Studies have suggested that some clinicians may misperceive families with traditional Asian values as maladjusted (Berg & Jaya, 1993). For example, a clinician might mistakenly perceive the hierarchical relationships and strong family bonds between Asian American family members as evidence that the family structure is rigid and enmeshed (K. K. Kim, 2002). Asian American parents who exhibit high levels of emotional self-control might also be perceived by their clinicians as uncaring toward their children, whereas such parents might demonstrate their love for their children in other ways (e.g., through instrumental support). Accordingly, gaining knowledge of Asian cultural values associated with parenting practices is important for conceptualizing the presenting concerns of Asian American families and finding ways to intervene successfully.

Nonetheless, Okazaki, Lee, and Sue (2007) cautioned against naively assuming that all Asian American families adopt traditional Asian values, since this does not take into account the diversity within the Asian American population. Therefore, knowledge of Asian cultures is insufficient. It is also important to assess each family member's level of acculturation and enculturation (B. S. K. Kim, et al., 2009). What follows is a discussion of the assessment of Asian American families' cultural characteristics.

Assessment of Cultural Characteristics

The assessment of the cultural characteristics of Asian American families is imperative at the beginning of therapy since there is no single family that has the same acculturation and enculturation levels. This not only requires the clinician to be culturally competent but also to use the appropriate assessment tools (Hwang, 2006b). The components of such assessment include immigration history, generation status, individuals' and family members' acculturation and enculturation levels, and communication styles (E. Y.-K. Kim, Bean, & Harper, 2004; Huang, 1994; Hwang, 2006a). In particular, it would be useful for clinicians to identify the specific types of cultural gaps that might exist among family members (e.g., differences in behavioral enculturation).

Several theoretical models and measures have been proposed for the clinical assessment of Asian American families. Huang (1994) proposed an integrative approach to the clinical assessment of Asian American children and their social systems (i.e., family, school, and peers). This multilevel and multidimensional model is composed of standard and ethnocultural assessments. The individual is assessed in relation to different systems (i.e., individual, family, school, and peers) and different dimensions in each system (e.g., individual level: generation status, sexuality, acculturation level, etc.). The clinician is encouraged to gather cultural information about family members, including migration history, the acculturation level of parents, children, and peers, acculturation gaps, and generation status. Hwang (2006a) proposed another theoretical framework based on the construct of acculturative family distancing; he suggested that therapists should assess immigrant families' cultural values and communication styles to identify parent-child cultural gaps. E. Y.-K. Kim et al. (2004) suggested that the assessment of support systems is also necessary to help Asian American families have access to educational, social, and community services. Additionally, A. Wong, Wong, and Obeng (2011) emphasized the identification and exploration of family strengths from the perspectives of both Asian American parents and their children. Despite possible limitations due to criterion and construct validity (e.g., Hasui, Kishida, & Kitamura, 2004), widely used clinical assessments such as the Family Adaptability and Cohesion Evaluation Scales (FACES-IV; Olson, Gorall, & Tiesel, 2004) could also yield some insight into the functioning of Asian American families.

Promoting Bicultural Competence

In addition to assessing the cultural characteristics of Asian American families, scholars have suggested that promoting bicultural competence could help decrease parent-child conflicts in Asian American families (e.g., B. S. K. Kim et al., 2009; Phinney & Divich-Navarro, 1997). Researchers have defined bicultural competence using different terms. Berry (1990, 2003, 2007) proposed that people use an *integration strategy* when they maintain their indigenous culture while adopting the values and behaviors of the mainstream culture. Benet-Martinez, Leu, Lee, and Morris (2002) used the term, *bicultural identity integration (BII)*. They argued that individuals with high BII have internalized two cultures and can flexibly change their perceptions, behaviors, and identities according to the cultural context (e.g., a Japanese American speaks Japanese with her/his parents but speaks English with European, Hispanic, and African American friends). Accordingly, an individual with high levels of bicultural competence is one who successfully integrates and navigates two different cultural values, norms, and behaviors through maintaining some aspects of the indigenous culture while adopting some aspects of the dominant culture. B. S. K. Kim and colleagues (2009) suggested that cognitive flexibility could foster bicultural competence within individuals. Cognitive flexibility is the awareness that a situation can be interpreted in multiple ways, and the ability to flexibly adapt one's behavior, thoughts, and attitudes to a situation to cope with possible conflicts (B. S. K. Kim & Omizo, 2005, 2006). According to B. S. K. Kim and colleagues (2009), cognitive flexibility can help family members generate alternative interpretations of a family conflict caused by an acculturation gap. Ahn et al. (2008) demonstrated that the seriousness of family conflicts decreased with the increase of cognitive flexibility among Korean American college students. Considering that Asian American parents and children may have difficulty shifting between two cultures (Fang & Wark, 1998; Uba, 1994), possess different cultural perspectives in interpreting behavior (Hwang, 2006a), and often use different communication styles (Buki, et al., 2003; E. T. Hall, 1976; L. Lee, 1997; Uba, 1994), promoting bicultural competence through teaching family members to attain cognitive flexibility might help reduce family conflict. Our review of the literature on interventions for Asian American families identified three main strategies to promote biculturalism – (a) psychoeducation on different cultural values and behavior, (b) reframing, and (c) practical skills (e.g., communication and parenting skills) to help parents develop more flexible parenting styles.

Psychoeducation is often used at the initial stage of family therapy. Providing information about Asian and Western cultures helps bring the cultural differences between parents and children to their awareness. This foundation becomes the starting point for change. For example, the Intergenerational/Intercultural Ties in Immigrant Families (SITIF; Ying, 1999), a community-based educational intervention for strengthening the relationship between Chinese American immigrant parents and their children, enabled parents to experience the cultural conflict their children face in daily life, and learn about cultural differences through two books, *The Monkey King* and *Hensel and Gretel*. Study findings showed an increase in the quality of parent-child relationships and a sense of parental control over the child (i.e., paternal efficacy and paternal responsibility) after the intervention (Ying, 1999). In another study, Vietnamese immigrant parents observed a group of Vietnamese American adolescents discuss their experiences of cultural conflict with their parents, followed by small group discussions about their parenting styles and their reactions to the adolescents (Y. J. Wong, et al., 2011). After the intervention, these parents reported increased parental empathy and intention to show expressive love to their children.

Additionally, reframing is a useful family intervention to reduce parent-child conflict in Asian American families (e.g., Hwang, 2006a; S. C. Kim, 1985; J. M. Kim, 2003; Mercado, 2000; Spiegel, 1983; Szapocznik, Santisteban, Kurtines, Perez-Vidal, & Hervis, 1984). Reframing involves reattributing the cause of family conflict from a specific family member to cultural gaps. Szapocznik, and colleagues (1984) suggested that reframing helps establish empathy and understanding between the parent and the child. A similar concept is "cultural brokering" in which the therapist presents cultural differences between the child and the parent to help them view their family problems as problems with acculturation (Spiegel, 1983). For example, a highly acculturated child's behavior of disagreeing with his mother can be interpreted by the therapist as an attempt to communicate about the situation based on European American cultural norms rather than being disrespectful (J. M. Kim, 2003).

In addition to gaining awareness about parent-child cultural gaps, Asian American parents need to have the skills to successfully navigate two different cultures to become more biculturally competent. Hwang (2006a) raised the importance of improving parent-child communication skills to reduce family conflict. Parent-child communication skills can be improved through role-playing exercises (Hwang, 2006a). For instance, clinicians and parents can take turns playing the roles of parents and children engaged in a conversation to enable Asian American parents to practice providing a rationale for their instructions to their children (e.g., "I want you to come home early because I get worried if you come home late"). It may also be useful to help highly enculturated Asian American parents learn and practice parenting skills based upon European American culture (e.g., setting structure and limits, and rewarding the child) (Ying, 1999). This does not mean that Asian American parents have to abandon their traditional Asian parenting style. Rather, clinicians can help Asian American parents broaden their repertoire of parenting styles so that they can combine elements of parenting styles from both Asian and European American cultures to strengthen their relationships with their children. In sum, we encourage clinicians who work with Asian American parents and their children to assess the cultural orientations of family members, examine the possible cultural factors relevant to their presenting concerns (e.g., cultural gaps, conflict domains), and provide interventions to promote bicultural competence.

LIMITATIONS AND FUTURE DIRECTIONS FOR RESEARCH

In this section, we discuss several limitations in the extant empirical literature on Asian American parenting and parent-child relationship which researchers can address in the future. First, although studies have examined how parental behaviors or parent-child cultural gaps correlate with parent-child relationships and child outcomes, investigations of mediators and moderators of these correlations have only recently emerged (e.g., Chao & Aque, 2009; Wu & Chao, 2011). is One example is Wu and Chao (2011)'s study which showed that a positive correlation between parent-adolescent cultural gaps (i.e., discrepancy between adolescents' expectation of parental warmth and perceived parental warmth) and Chinese American adolescents' internalizing problems was weaker when adolescents perceived their parents had high levels of parental devotion and sacrifice. However, perception of parental devotion and sacrifice was not a significant moderator for European American adolescents. The researchers suggested that perceived parental devotion and sacrifice may be a protective factor for Chinese American adolescents who experience cultural gaps in parental warmth. Therefore, research on mediators and moderators provide a more nuanced account of why and when parent-child cultural gaps are problematic for Asian American families.

Second, more research is needed on cultural variations among Asian American ethnic subgroups. Although some cultural values and behaviors are shared across Asian American ethnic subgroups (e.g., family interdependency), the level of emphasis on certain values and behaviors, such as parental authority, may differ across ethnic subgroups (Chao & Tseng, 2002). For example, the relationship between Filipino American parents and children may be slightly more egalitarian than that between East Asian and Vietnamese parents and children because of less emphasis on a hierarchical family structure based on age and gender (Chao & Tseng, 2002). Several studies demonstrated differences between Asian American ethnic subgroups in parenting behaviors, child outcomes of parenting, and domains of cultural conflict between parents and children (Ang, 2006; Chung, 2001; Kwak & Berry, 2001). To illustrate, comparisons of Chinese, Filipino, Korean, and Southeast Asian American college students' domains of family conflict revealed that Korean and Southeast Asian college students reported more family conflict associated with cultural gaps in family expectations than their Japanese American counterparts (Chung, 2001). Future research can address whether the correlates of parent-child cultural gaps differ across Asian American ethnic subgroups (e.g., Chinese versus Filipino Americans).

Third, research on parent-child cultural gaps tend to be based on an assumption that such cultural gaps are related to negative outcomes, whereas a lack of parent-child cultural gaps is associated with positive outcomes (Birman, 2006). However, Birman argued for the use of interaction effects to test different combinations of parent-child cultural orientations rather than a sole focus on cultural discrepancies. The strength of this approach can be found in Shin and Wong (2010)'s study which examined interaction effects between the cultural orientations of Asian American college students and their parents. The authors found that Asian American children's psychological distress was high when mothers' and children's value acculturation levels were both low (i.e., no parent-child cultural gap). This finding suggests that parent-child congruence in cultural orientation is not necessarily associated with positive outcomes. Hence, future studies need to examine the correlates of different combinations of parent-child cultural orientations.

Fourth, more research on indigenous cultural meanings associated with Asian American parenting and parent-child relationships is essential. Although several quantitative studies have examined cultural notions of Asian American parenting and parent-child relationships (e.g., Chao, 1994; Stewart, et al., 2002; Stewart et al., 1998; Wu & Chao, 2011), most studies on Asian American parenting continue to rely on the constructs of parental control and warmth as articulated by Baumrind (1973). Qualitative studies on Asian American parenting and parent-child relationships can be useful in identifying cultural characteristics unique to parenting in Asian American ethnic subgroups (e.g., Hmong Americans). Qualitative research findings can, in turn, facilitate the development of culturally-sensitive measures of Asian American parenting. Such measures are important because parenting measures based on the constructs of parental control and warmth may have different cultural meanings for Asian American and European American adolescents (Crockett, Veed, & Russell, 2010). Therefore, we encourage the development of Asian American parenting measures based on indigenous cultural meanings of parenting.

Fifth, another limitation of the extant research is the lack of empirical studies on culturally sensitive interventions for Asian American parents and their children. Through a literature review of therapy and interventions for Asian American families, Shin (2010) found few studies that evaluated interventions tailored for Asian American families. The only exceptions were Ying (1999)'s empirical study on SITIF program and Y. J. Wong and colleagues' (2011) study on an intervention for Vietnamese American parents. Empirical research on culturally sensitive interventions for Asian American families is important since it can serve as a foundation for more effective work with Asian American families. Therefore, future studies should further investigate the effectiveness of interventions for Asian American parents and children (e.g., culturally informed psychoeducation) as well as clinicians' characteristics (e.g., cultural competency) associated with positive client outcomes.

CONCLUSIONS

In this chapter, we explored the cultural characteristics of Asian American parenting and parent-child relationships in relation to parenting styles, acculturation and enculturation of parents and children, and the influence of cultural orientation on parent-child relationships and child outcomes. We also discussed practical implications for mental health professionals in relation to assessing the cultural characteristics of Asian American families and promoting bicultural competence. Finally, we identified several limitations of current research which warrant further study. Overall, this chapter highlights the importance of considering the cultural orientations of parents and children when understanding and intervening with Asian American families.

REFERENCES

ABC Good Morning America. (2011, January 26). *Interview with Amy Chua*. Retrieved from http://www.youtube.com/watch?v=GAel_qRfKx8

Ahn, A. J., Kim, B. S. K., & Park, Y. S. (2008). Asian cultural values gap, cognitive flexibility, coping strategies, and parent-child conflicts among Korean Americans. *Cultural Diversity and Ethnic Minority Psychology, 14*, 353-363.

Ang, R. P. (2006). Effects of parenting style on personal and social variables for Asian adolescents. *American Journal of Orthopsychiatry, 76*, 503-511.

Baumrind, D. (1973). The development of instrumental competence through socialization. In A. D. Pick (Ed.), *Minnesota Symposia on Child Psychology* (vol. 7, pp. 3-46). Minneapolis, MN: University of Minnesota Press.

Benet-Martínez, V., Leu, J., Lee, F., & Morris, M. (2002). Negotiating biculturalism: Cultural frame-switching in biculturals with "oppositional" vs. "compatible" cultural identities. *Journal of Cross-Cultural Psychology, 33*, 492-516.

Berg, I. K., & Jaya, A. (1993). Different and same: Family therapy with Asian American families. *Journal of Marital and Family Therapy, 19*, 31-38.

Berry, J. W. (1990). Psychology of acculturation. In J. Berman (Ed.), *Cross-cultural perspectives: Nebraska symposium on motivation* (pp.201-234). Lincoln, NE: University of Nebraska Press.

Berry, J. W. (1998). Acculturation and health: Theory and research. In S. S. Kazarian & D. R. Evans (Eds.), *Cultural clinical psychology: Theory, research, and practice* (pp. 39-57). New York: Oxford University Press.

Berry, J. W. (2003). Conceptual approaches to acculturation. In K. M. Chun, P. B. Organista, & G. Marin (Eds.), *Acculturation: Advances in theory, measurement, and applied research* (pp. 17-37). Washington, DC: American Psychological Association.

Berry, J. W. (2007). Acculturation strategies and adaptation. In J. E. Landsford, K. Deater-Deckard, & M. H. Bornstein (Eds.), *Immigrant families in contemporary society* (pp.69-82). New York: Guilford Press.

Birman, D. (2006). Measurement of the "Acculturation Gap" in immigrant families and implications for parent-child relationships. In M. Bornstein & L. Cotes (Eds.), *Acculturation and parent child relationships: Measurement and development* (pp. 113-134). Mahwah, NJ: Lawrence Erlbaum Associates.

Buki, L. P., Ma, T., Strom, R. D., & Strom, S. K. (2003). Chinese immigrant mothers of adolescents: Self-perceptions of acculturation effects on parenting. *Cultural Diversity and Ethnic Minority Psychology, 9*, 127-140.

Chao, R. K. (1994). Beyond parental control and authoritarian parenting style: Understanding Chinese parenting through the cultural notion of training. *Child Development, 65*, 1111-1119.

Chao, R. K., & Aque, C. (2009). Interpretations of parental control by Asian immigrant and European American youth. *Journal of Family Psychology, 23*, 342-354.

Chao, R. K., & Kaeochinda, K. F. (2010). Parental sacrifice and acceptance as distinct dimensions of parental support among Chinese and Filipino American adolescents. In S. T. Russell, L. J. Crockett, & R. K. Chao (Eds.), *Asian American Parenting and Parent-Adolescent Relationships* (pp. 61-77). New York: Springer.

Chao, R. K., & Tseng, V. (2002). Parenting of Asians. In M. H. Bornstein (Series Ed.), *Handbook of Parenting: Social Conditions and Applied Parenting* (2nd ed., Vol. 4, pp. 59-93). Hillsdale, NJ: Lawrence Erlbaum Associates.

Cheung, M., & Nguyen, M. S. (2007). Pilot testing the Vietnamese parental attitude scale: Three major factors. *International Social Work, 50*, 213-227.

Chiu, L. H. (1987). Child-rearing attitudes of Chinese, Chinese-American, and Anglo-American mothers. *International Journal of Psychology, 22*, 409–419.

Chua, A. (2011, January 8). Why Chinese Mothers Are Superior. *The Wall Street Journal.* Retrieved from http://online.wsj.com/article/SB10001424052748704111504576059713 528698754.html

Chung, R. H. G. (2001). Gender, ethnicity, and acculturation in intergenerational conflict of Asian American college students. *Cultural Diversity and Ethnic Minority Psychology, 7*, 376-386.

Crane, D. R., Ngai, S. W., Larson, J. H., & Hafen, M., Jr. (2005). The influence of family functioning and parent-adolescent acculturation on North American Chinese adolescent outcomes. *Family Relations, 54*, 400-410.

Crockett, L. J., Veed, G. J., & Russell, S. T. (2010). Do measures of parenting have the same meaning for European, Chinese, and Filipino American adolescents? Tests of measurement equivalence. In S. T. Russell, L. J. Crockett, & R. K. Chao (Eds.), *Asian American Parenting and Parent-Adolescent Relationships* (pp.17-35). New York: Springer.

Dinh, K. T. (2000). Predictors of psychosocial well-being in an Asian-American sample: Acculturation, intergenerational conflict, and parent-child relationships. *Dissertation Abstracts International: Section B. Sciences and Engineering, 60* (08), 4216.

Dinh, K. T., & Nguyen, H. H. (2006). The effects of acculturative variables on Asian American parent-child relationships. *Journal of Social and Personal Relationships, 23*, 407-426.

Dornbusch, S. M., Ritter, P. L., Leiderman, P., Roberts, D. F., & Fraleigh, M. J. (1987). The relation of parenting style to adolescent school performance. *Child Development, 58*, 1244-1257.

Drachman, D., Kwon-Ahn, Y., & Paulino, A. (1996). Migration and resettlement experiences of Dominican and Korean families. *Families in Society, 77*, 626-638.

Dublin, T. (1996). *Becoming American, becoming ethnic: College students explore their roots*. Philadelphia, PA: Temple University Press.

Fang, S. R. S., & Wark, L. (1998). Developing cross-cultural competence with traditional Chinese Americans in family therapy: Background information and the initial therapeutic contact. *Contemporary Family Therapy, 20*, 59–75.

Farver, J. M., Narang, S., & Bhadha, B. R. (2002). East meets West: Acculturation and conflict in Asian Indian families. *Journal of Family Psychology, 16*, 338–350.

Farver, J. M., Xu, Y., Bhadha, B. R., Narang, S., & Lieber, E. (2007). Ethnic identity, acculturation, parenting beliefs, and adolescent adjustment. *Merrill-Palmer Quarterly, 53*, 184-215.

Fuligni, A. J. (1997). The academic achievement of adolescents from immigrant families: The roles of family background, attitudes, and behavior. *Child Development, 68*, 351-363.

Fung, H. (1999). Becoming a moral child: The socialization of shame among young Chinese children. *Ethos, 27*, 180–209.

Hall, E. T. (1976). *Beyond culture*. New York: Anchor Press.

Hall, G. C. N., & Eap, S. (2007). Empirically supported therapies for Asian Americans. In F. T. L. Leong, A. Ebreo, L. Kinoshita, A. G. Inman, L. H. Yang, & M. Fu (Eds.), *Handbook of Asian American Psychology* (2nd ed., pp. 449-467). Thousand Oaks, CA: Sage Publications, Inc.

Hasui, C., Kishida, Y., & Kitamura, T. (2004). Factor Structure of the FACES-III in Japanese University Students. *Family Process, 43*, 133-140.

Herz, L., & Gullone, E. (1999). The relationship between self-esteem and parenting style: A cross-cultural comparison of Australian and Vietnamese Australian adolescents. *Journal of Cross-Cultural Psychology, 30*, 742-761.

Ho, C., Bluestein, D. N., & Jenkins, J. M. (2008). Cultural differences in the relationship between parenting and children's behavior. *Developmental Psychology, 44*, 507-522.

Ho, J. (2010). Acculturation gaps in Vietnamese immigrant families: Impact on family relationships. *International Journal of Intercultural relations, 34*, 22-33.

Huang, L. N. (1994). An integrative approach to clinical assessment and intervention with Asian-American adolescents. *Journal of Clinical Child Psychology, 23*, 21-31.

Hwang, W.-C. (2006a). Acculturative family distancing: Theory, research, and clinical practice. *Psychotherapy: Theory, Research, Practice, Training, 43*, 397-409.

Hwang, W.-C. (2006b). The psychotherapy adaptation and modification framework: Application to Asian Americans. *American Psychologist, 61*, 702-715.

Hwang, W.-C., & Wood, J. (2009). Acculturative family distancing: Links with self-reported symptomatology among Asian Americans and Latinos. *Child Psychiatry Human Development, 40*, 123-138.

Jankowiak, W. (1992). Father-child relations in urban China. In B. S. Hewlett (Ed.), *Father-child relations: Cultural and biosocial contexts* (pp.345-363). New York: De Gruyter.

Julian, T. W., McKenry, P. C., & McKelvey, M. W. (1994). Cultural variations in parenting: Perceptions of Caucasian, African-American, Hispanic, and Asian-American parents. *Family Relations, 43*, 30-37.

Kim, B. S. K. (2007). Acculturation and enculturation. In F. T. L. Leong, A. Ebreo, L. Kinoshita, A. G. Inman, L. H. Yang, & M. Fu (Eds.), *Handbook of Asian American Psychology* (2nd ed., pp. 141-158). Thousand Oaks, CA: Sage Publications, Inc.

Kim, B. S. K., Ahn, A. J., & Lam, N. A. (2009). Theories and research on acculturation and enculturation experiences among Asian American families. In N. Trinh, Y. C. Rho, F. G. Lu, & K. M. Sanders (Eds.), *Handbook of mental health and acculturation in Asian American families* (pp. 25-43). Totowa, NJ: Humana Press.

Kim, B. S. K., Atkinson, D. R., & Umemoto, D. (2001). Asian cultural values and the counseling process: Current knowledge and directions for future research. *The Counseling Psychologist, 29*, 570-603.

Kim, B. S. K., & Omizo, M. M. (2005). Asian and European American cultural values, collective self-esteem, acculturative stress, cognitive flexibility, and general self-efficacy among Asian American college students. *Journal of Counseling Psychology, 52*, 412-419.

Kim, B. S. K., & Omizo, M. M. (2006). Behavioral acculturation and enculturation and psychological functioning among Asian American college students. *Cultural Diversity and Ethnic Minority Psychology, 12*, 245-258.

Kim, E., & Cain, K. C. (2008). Korean American adolescent depression and parenting. *Journal of Child and Adolescent Psychiatric Nursing, 21*, 105-115.

Kim, E., & Hong, S. (2007). First-generation Korean-American parents' perceptions of discipline. *Journal of Professional Nursing, 23*, 60-68.

Kim, E. Y.-K., Bean, R. A., & Harper, J. M. (2004). Do general treatment guidelines for Asian American families have applications to specific ethnic groups? The case of culturally-competent therapy with Korean Americans. *Journal of Marital and Family Therapy, 30*, 359-372.

Kim, J. M. (2003). Structural family therapy and its implications for the Asian American families. *The Family Journal, 11*, 388-392.

Kim, K. K. (2002). Family functioning, intergenerational conflict, and psychological symptomology of Asian American collge students. *Dissertation Abstracts International: Section B. Sciences and Engineering, 63* (05), 2589.

Kim, S. (1996). The effects of parenting style, cultural conflict, and peer relations on academic achievement and psychosocial adjustment among Korean immigrant adolescents. *Dissertation Abstracts International: Section A. Humanities and Social Sciences. 57*(2), 578.

Kim, S. C. (1985). Family therapy for Asian Americans: A strategic-structural framework. *Psychotherapy: Theory, Research, Practice, Training, 22*, 342-348.

Kim, S. Y. (2003). Generational consonance and dissonance: Acculturation, parent-child relationships, and adolescent adjustment in Chinese American families. *Dissertation Abstracts International: Section B. Sciences and Engineering, 64*(03), 1523.

Kitano, H. H. L. (1989). A model for counseling Asian Americans. In P. B. Pedersen, J. G. Draguns, W. J. Lonner, & J. E. Trimble (Eds.), *Counseling across cultures* (3rd ed., pp. 139-151). Honolulu, HI: University of Hawaii Press.

Kwak, K., & Berry, J. W. (2001). Generational differences in acculturation among Asian families in Canada: A comparison of Vietnamese, Korean, and East-Indian groups. *International Journal of Psychology, 36*, 152-162.

Le, T. N., & Stockdale, G. (2008). Acculturative dissonance, ethnic identity, and youth violence. *Cultural Diversity and Ethnic Minority Psychology, 14*, 1-9.

Lee, E. (1982). A social systems approach to assessment and treatment for Chinese American Families. In M. McGoldrick, J. Pearce, & J. Giordano (Eds.), *Ethnicity and family therapy* (pp. 527-551). New York: Guilford.

Lee, L. (1997). Chinese American families. In E. Lee (Ed.), *Working with Asian Americans: A guide for clinicians* (pp. 46–78). New York: Guilford Press.

Lee, R. M., Choe, J., Kim, G., & Ngo, V. (2000). Construction of the Asian American family conflicts scale. *Journal of Counseling Psychology, 47*, 211–222.

Lee, R. M., Jung, K. R., Su, J. C., Tran, A. G. T. T., & Bahrassa, N. F. (2009). The family life and adjustment of Hmong American sons and daughters. *Sex Roles, 60*, 549-558.

Leong, C. (2005). Asian American parent-teen conflicts. *Dissertation Abstracts International: Section B. Sciences and Engineering, 66* (06), 3443.

Lorenzo, M. K., Forst, A. K., & Reinherz, H. Z. (2000). Social and emotional functioning of older Asian American adolescents. *Child and Adolescent Social Work Journal, 17*, 289-304.

Maccoby, E. E., & Martin, J. A. (1983). Socialization in the context of the family: Parent–child interaction. In P. H. Mussen & E. M. Hetherington (Eds.), *Handbook of child psychology: Socialization, personality, and social development* (4th ed., Vol. 4, pp. 1-101). New York: Wiley.

Mercado, M. M. (2000). The invisible family: Counseling Asian American substance abusers and their families. *The Family Journal, 8*, 267-272.

Nguyen, N. A., & Williams, H. L. (1989). Transition from East to West: Vietnamese American adolescents and their parents. *Journal of American Academy of Child and Adolescent Psychiatry, 28*, 505-515.

Nguyen, P. V. (2008). Perceptions of Vietnamese fathers' acculturation levels, parenting styles, and mental health outcomes of Vietnamese American adolescent immigrants. *Social Work, 53*, 337-346.

Okazaki, S., Lee, R. M., & Sue, S. (2007). Theoretical and conceptual models: Toward Asian Americanist psychology. In F. T. L. Leong, A. Ebreo, L. Kinoshita, A. G. Inman, L. H. Yang, & M. Fu (Eds.), *Handbook of Asian American psychology* (2nd ed., pp. 29-46). Thousand Oaks, CA: Sage Publications, Inc.

Olson, D. H., Gorall, D. M., & Tiesel, J. W. (2007). *FACES IV and the Circumplex Model: Validation Study.* Retrieved from http://www.facesiv. com/pdf/2.development.pdf

Phinney, J. S., & Devich-Navarro, M. (1997). Variations in bicultural identification among African American and Mexican American adolescents. *Journal of Research on Adolescence, 7,* 3-32.

Phinney, J. S., Ong, A., & Madden, T. (2000). Cultural values and intergenerational value discrepancies in immigrant and non-immigrant families. *Child Development, 71,* 528-539.

Pyke, K. (2000). "The normal American family" as an interpretive structure of family life among grown children of Korean and Vietnamese immigrants. *Journal of Marriage and Family, 62,* 240-255.

Redfield, R., Linton, R., & Herskovits, M. (1936). Memorandum on the study of acculturation. *American Anthropologist, 38,* 149–152.

Rohner, R. P., & Pettengill, S. M. (1985). Perceived parental acceptance-rejection and parental control among Korean adolescents. *Child Development, 56,* 524-528.

Shin, M., & Wong, Y. J. (2010, August). *The impact of Asian Americans' perceived parent-child cultural gaps on family conflicts and mental health.* Poster presented at the Annual Meeting of Asian American Psychological Association, San Diego, CA.

Shin, M. (2010). *Therapy and other psychological interventions for Asian American families.* Unpublished manuscript. Department of Counseling and Educational Psychology, Indiana University, Bloomington, IN.

Spiegel, J. (1983). An ecological model of ethnic families. In M. McGoldrick, J. Pearce, & J. Giordano (Eds.), *Ethnicity and family therapy* (pp.31-51). New York: Guildford.

Steinberg, L., Dornbusch, S. M., & Brown, B. B. (1992). Ethnic differences in adolescent achievement: An ecological perspective. *American Psychologist, 47,* 723-729.

Steinberg, L., Lamborn, S., Darling, N., Mounts, N., & Dornbusch, S. M. (1994). Over-time changes in adjustment and competence among adolescents from authoritative, authoritarian, indulgent, and neglectful families. *Child Development, 65,* 754-770.

Steinberg, L., Mounts, N. S., Lamborn, S. D., & Dornbusch, S. M. (1991). Authoritative parenting and adolescent adjustment across varied ecological niches. *Journal of Research on Adolescence, 1,* 19-36.

Stewart, S. M., Bond, M. H., Kennard, B. D., Ho, L. M., & Zaman, R. M. (2002). Does the Chinese construct of guan export to the West? *International Journal of Psychology, 37,* 74-82.

Stewart, S. M., Rao, N., Bond, M. H., McBride-Chang, C., Fielding, R., & Kennard, B. (1998). Chinese dimensions of parenting: Broadening western predictors and outcomes. *International Journal of Psychology, 33,* 345–358.

Szapocznik, J., & Kurtines, W. (1993). Family psychology and cultural diversity: Opportunities for theory, research, and application. *American Psychologist, 48,* 400-407.

Szapocznik, J., Santisteban, D., Kurtines, W., Perez-Vidal, A., & Hervis, O. (1984). Bicultural effectiveness treatment for enhancing intercultural adjustment in Cuban American families. *Hispanic Journal of Behavioral Sciences, 6*, 317-344.

Tang, N. (1992). Some implications of Chinese philosophy and child-rearing practices. *Psychoanalytic Study of the Child, 47*, 371-390.

Tardif, C. Y., & Geva, E. (2006). The link between acculturation disparity and conflict among Chinese Canadian immigrant mother-adolescent dyads. *Journal of Cross-Cultural Psychology, 37*, 191-211.

Tsai-Chae, A. H., & Nagata, D. K. (2008). Asian values and perceptions of intergenerational family conflict among Asian American students. *Cultural Diversity and Ethnic Minority Psychology, 14*, 205-214.

Tseng, V., & Fuligni, A. J. (2000). Parent-adolescent language use and relationships among immigrant families with East Asian, Filipino, and Latin American backgrounds. *Journal of Marriage and the Family, 62*, 465-476.

Uba, L. (1994). *Asian Americans: Personality patterns, identity, and mental health.* New York: The Guilford Press.

Wong, A., Wong, Y. J., & Obeng, C. (2011). An untold story: A qualitative study of Asian American family strengths. *Asian American Journal of Psychology*. Advance online publication. doi: 10.1037/a0025553

Wong, S. K. (1997). Delinquency of Chinese-Canadian youth: A test of opportunity, control, and intergeneration conflict theories. *Youth and Society, 29*, 112-133.

Wong, Y. J., Tran, K. K., Schwing, A. E., Cao, L. H., Ho, P. P. -H., & Nguyen, Q.-T. (2011). Vietnamese American immigrant parents: A pilot parenting intervention. *The Family Journal, 19*, 314-321.

Wu, C., & Chao, R. K. (2005). Intergenerational cultural conflicts for Chinese American youth with immigrant parents: Norms of parental warmth and the consequences. *International Journal of Behavioral Development, 29*, 516–523.

Wu, C., & Chao, R. K. (2011). Intergenerational cultural dissonance in parent-adolescent relationships among Chinese and European Americans. *Developmental Psychology, 47*, 493-508.

Xiong, Z. B., Detzner, D. F., & Cleveland, M. J. (2004). Southeast Asian adolescents' perceptions of immigrant parenting practices. *Hmong Studies Journal, 5*, 1-20.

Xiong, Z. B., Eliason, P. A., Detzner, D. F., & Cleveland, M. J. (2005). Southeast Asian immigrants' perceptions of good adolescents and good parents. *The Journal of Psychology, 139*, 159-175.

Ying, Y. (1999). Strengthening intergenerational/intercultural ties in migrant families: A new intervention for parents. *Journal of Community Psychology, 27*, 89-96.

Ying, Y., Coombs, M., & Lee, P. A. (1999). Family intergenerational relationship of Asian American adolescents. *Cultural Diversity and Ethnic Minority Psychology, 5*, 350–363.

Ying, Y., & Han, M. (2007). The longitudinal effect of intergenerational gap in acculturation on conflict and mental health in Southeast Asian American adolescents. *American Journal of Orthopsychiatry, 77*, 61–66.

Ying, Y., & Han, M. (2008). Parental contributions to Southeast Asian American adolescents' well-being. *Youth Society, 40*, 289-306.

Yu, K. H. (1982). *The growth and development of Korean-American children: The psychosocial development of minority group children.* New York: Brunner/Mazel Press.

Zane, N., & Mak, W. (2003). Major approaches to the measurement of acculturation among ethnic minority populations: A content analysis and an alternative empirical strategy. In K. M. Chun, P. B. Organista, & G. Marín (Eds.), *Acculturation: Advances in theory, measurement, and applied research* (pp. 39-60). Washington, DC: American Psychological Association.

Zhou, M. (1997). Growing up American: The challenge confronting immigrant children and children of immigrants. *Annual Review of Sociology, 23*, 63-95.

In: Parenting
Editors: Peter Barberis and Stelios Petrakis
ISBN: 978-1-62257-881-8
© 2013 Nova Science Publishers, Inc.

Chapter 6

CULTURE AND PARENTING: A REVIEW

*Isabelle Roskam**

University of Louvain, Psychological Sciences Research Institute, Belgium

ABSTRACT

The study of the parenthood has generated a large number of works on the intercultural plan. The main reason of this craze is doubtless that the parenthood is considered as an important vector of the transmission of cultural models, values and practices across human beings within societies. The parents indeed have for universal mission the education of their children. And what is the purpose of the education if it is not to bring the children to become socially competent adults integrated into the cultural group in which they are brought to live? This way, the study of the parenthood in cross-cultural psychology participates in this idea according to which the behavior of both the parents and the children can only be understood in relation to the environment they belong to (Friedlmeier, Chakkarath, and Schwarz, 2005; Kagitçbasi, 2007).

The first objective of the intercultural studies is to highlight what is common to all the human beings regardless of their cultural membership. The common elements are labeled "universals" (Laungani, 2007). Universals relative to parenthood are considered in the current paper from several scientific works among which those of LeVine (1977) as a major reference describing the universal purposes of the parental function. Also the works of Keller (2007) have been considered as particularly relevant since they focus on the existence of universal behavioral patterns in parents.

The second objective of the intercultural studies consists in gauging the magnitude of the influence arising from the culture (Laungani, 2007). The present contribution approaches the question of the parenthood in the light of the cultural peculiarities through two important concepts: "developmental niche" (Harkness and Super, 1986) and "parental ethnotheories" (Rubin and Chung, 2007). These theoretical underpinnings of these two concepts are explained and illustrated through recent empirical studies (e.g. Cho, Sandel, Miller, and Wang, 2005).

Beyond their main theoretical contribution, these cross-cultural studies on parenting have evident implications in our multicultural societies and in particular for immigrant families, for example in the way they adjust to their host culture, build their social

---

* E-mail: isabelle.roskam@uclouvain.be.

network or find psychosocial support in their surroundings. Moreover, cross-cultural studies on parenting offer to social workers working with immigrant population an excellent means to take distance with regard to their own models or values and to protect themselves of an evident risk of ethnocentrism (Baubet and Moro, 2009).

The study of parenthood has generated a large number of works on the intercultural level. The main reason for this trend is doubtless that parenthood is considered to be an important vector for the transmission of cultural models, values and practices between human beings within societies. After all, raising their children is parents' universal mission, and what is the purpose of that parenting activity if not to turn children into socially competent adults integrated into the cultural group in which they live? Parents thus want their children to acquire what they perceive as important in society (Tam and Lee, 2010). In this way, the study of parenthood in cross-cultural psychology buys into this idea that the behavior of both parents and children can only be understood in relation to the environment to which they belong (Friedlmeier, Chakkarath, and Schwarz, 2005; Kagitçbasi, 2007).

1. UNIVERSAL PARENTHOOD

The first objective of intercultural studies is to highlight what is common to all human beings regardless of their cultural membership (Lonner, 2011). The common elements are labeled "universals" (Laungani, 2007; Berry, Poortinga, Breugelman, Chasiotis, and Sam, 2011). Elements common to multiple cultures are considered to be "universals" until we are able to identify at least one culture within which these elements differ. The search for "universals" offers a means of approaching human nature. The term "nature" suggests that human beings share certain physical and psychological characteristics. This concept of "nature" fascinated the philosophers in their centuries-long search for the "general laws" of human nature. Plato, for example, referred to the essence of humanity. Later, the idea of a universal human nature was questioned. Locke was among the philosophers who criticized this idea by proposing the notion of *tabula rasa*. From this opposition was born the debate about heredity *versus* environment. However, the quest for universals was never abandoned, and numerous authors have adopted an intermediate position recognizing the existence of universals while admitting the importance of the environment in particular cultural settings. Thus the human being is considered to be a "cultural animal", to the extent that it is capable of modifying its behavior according to its learning. It is also capable of transmitting this learning to future generations without any genetic contribution (Laungani, 2007; Berry et al., 2011).

The work of LeVine (LeVine, 1977) constitutes one of the main references in the field of universal parenthood. The author tried to highlight the common denominator between parents, regardless of the culture to which they belong. His work focused on the universal purposes of parenthood. Every parent all over the world, he claimed, has the universal objectives of 1/ensuring their children's survival and health, 2/ stimulating their children in order to ensure their social and cognitive development, 3/ transmitting culturally adapted values by giving guidelines to their children which will allow them to fit into their society. These assumptions received recent empirical support. Cultural models of parenting were studied by Suizzo (2002) among 455 Parisian parents, who were asked to assess the level of importance of practices of daily care. Three major factors were extracted from the analyses: awakening and exposing their children to a range of stimuli, ensuring their children's proper presentation according to socially accepted daily rules, and responding to and bonding with their children in response to their need for intense proximity and protection. The first factor specifically refers to LeVine's second objective of stimulation, while the second refers to his third objective of transmission of cultural values and the third to his first objective of health. The same factorial structure was recently replicated among Brazilian mothers (Vieira et al., 2010).

Cultural variations were observed not in the content of these three universal objectives but in their ranking. Their hierarchy depends on the cultural context in which the parents and their children are living. If a child is reared in a context where there are obvious risks to his/her health, such as infections or a high level of violence, the primary parental purpose is going to be ensuring the survival and health of the child rather than his/her intellectual or social development, which will be relegated to a position of less importance. On the other hand, in a context where the survival and health of the child do not generally give cause for concern, behavioral objectives and the transmission of values are going to prevail in terms of parental priorities. In the recent study of Vieira et al. (2010), less importance was attributed by Brazilian mothers to proximity and protection in comparison with the two other universal goals. Such a ranking can partly be explained by the moderate infant mortality rate, i.e. 2%[1].

While the work of LeVine focuses on universal goals in parenting, that of Keller (2007) is more centered on the existence of a directory of universal parental behaviors. Given that human beings come into the world in a state of great dependence (altriciality), it has been hypothesized that nature must have equipped the caregivers with a behavioral directory predisposing them to parenting. The hypothesis posits a universal propensity to parenthood. Keller went in search of this universal behavioral directory with mother-baby (0-2 years of age) dyads. Her empirical work conducted in Germany, Greece, India, Cameroon and Costa Rica brought to light six sub-systems which make up the directory. The first sub-system is that of primary care, including nurturing, hygiene and shelter. Other sub-systems concern physical contact (such as carrying babies or cosleeping), physical stimulation (such as touch games or massage), stimulation by means of objects (such as the use of toys or the exploration of the physical environment), eye contact (as the peek-a-boo game), and the narrative envelope, stressing the importance of language in the construction of the self. The empirical results indicated that this behavioral directory is present in all the cultures that were considered, in other words, that all the mothers, irrespective of their culture, adopt behavior stemming from these various sub-systems. These results thus support the hypothesis of universality put forward by Keller. Such a behavioral directory would have a universal function of ensuring the survival of the altricial baby, but also of transmitting from birth relevant information about the construction of the image of self and others. However, as was the case for the hierarchical organization of the universal parental goals described by LeVine, Keller argues that cultures differ in the way in which they combine the sub-systems and the proportions in which they adopt them. For example, cultures based on independent values would be characterized by a frequent combination of eye contact and stimulation by means of objects. Eye contact allows the parent to interact with the child while remaining at a distance.

---

[1] http://www.indexmundi.com

It gives each of the protagonists a personal space and an independent role. Stimulation by means of objects allows the parent to promote cognitive development through the exploration of the physical world as well as encouraging the child to play independently of his/her caregiver. Cultures based on interdependent values would be characterized by a frequent combination of physical contact and physical stimulation, ensuring the durability of the physical bond in the service of social cohesion. Through these early interactive contexts, it is argued, caregivers favor the development of an image of an independent / autonomous self *versus* an interdependent / collectivist self. Parents hence have ideas about what is normatively important in society, corresponding to perceived normative values that they want their children to acquire so as to maximize their chance of future social adaptation to this society. The influence of norms on human behavior has been extensively studied by social psychologists. This work has led to an understanding of how and to what extent parents transmit values that they do not personally endorse, but regard as normatively important (Schwartz, 2011; Tam and Lee, 2010).

2. CULTURAL PARENTHOOD

2.1. The Developmental Niche and Parental Ethnotheories

The second objective of the intercultural studies is to gauge the magnitude of the influence that the culture has (Laungani, 2007). Two concepts are particularly important for approaching the question of parenthood in the light of cultural characteristics. The first is that of the "developmental niche". The concept of niche was borrowed from ecological biology, and refers to the place occupied by a body or a function in the bio-system. It was introduced to anthropological and psychological contexts by Harkness and Super (1986). It is used to describe and analyze the developmental settings of children in various cultures. This approach examines the cultural regulation of the child's micro-environment in order to understand the processes by which children acquire culture. The concept of niche is characterized by three components: the physical and social environment (physical layout, toys or objects given to the child, caregivers and peers present), the psychology of those who take care of the child (their cultural values, their implicit theories about development and childrearing) and the childrearing behaviors of those who take care of the child.

In all cultures, the environment of the child is organized to favor the acquisition of certain skills and the transmission of certain values. To this end, multiple developmental niches both coexist and follow one another throughout a person's life. These niches are largely determined by the culture on the grounds of what it considers to be appropriate for the optimal development of children. In this view, the culture influences the development of the child by providing him/her with a sequence of niches. In our Western cultures, for example, children have at their disposal objects specially designed for them, i.e. thanks to the production of toys, children's books and so on, and also spend time in settings explicitly designed for them, such as day-care centers or nursery schools. The example of the school context and the way in which education is dispensed in nursery school, then in primary school, then in secondary school and finally in colleges and universities, is an interesting illustration of the succession of these developmental niches in our Western cultures. Children are subject to increasing expectations of autonomy and instructions emanating from caregivers other than their parents. They are gradually led to make personal choices and to think about their life plans independently from those of their parents. In other cultures, children stay in physical contact with their relatives for longer. They are free to handle adults' daily objects and they develop in settings shared with adults, e.g. in traditional agriculture and in the small business sector. This sort of niche is suitable for the transmission of know-how and the renewal of the models concerned in order to ensure the continuity and cohesion of the social group.

Within every culture, an important role exercised by the parents is to determine which setting is suitable for a child according to his/her age, the skills he/she displays or still needs to acquire, and the values which must be transmitted. In our Western societies, the parents' choice to enroll their child in a particular kind of school for example, or to encourage them to engage in leisure activities such as scouting or sports such as golf is an example of the role they play in the selection of the niches in which their child develops. The description of developmental niches in intercultural research is crucial to the interpretation of the differences observed in behavioral and developmental outcomes in children.

The second concept is that of "parental ethnotheories". These are based on ideas about the upbringing and development of the child. They can be related to the second component of the concept of developmental niche, in that they relate to the values and beliefs of those who take care of the child. They correspond to implicit ideas, mostly unconscious and widely shared by the members of the same culture, about what is and is not good for the child, about what is and is not fair, and about appropriate and inappropriate ways of reacting to the behavior of the child. They can be thought of as models that the parents have concerning their child, their role as a parent, and their family.

These ethnotheories can be seen as truisms, in that they act as strongly interiorized principles against which the parents have few arguments. They largely determine the childrearing behaviors adopted by the caregivers, in particular the parents, and the organization of the everyday life of the children and their family. Encouraging children's autonomy in our Western societies appears self-evident to most parents. The empowerment of the child through the encouragement of autonomy is widely supported in all the niches in which Western children develop, e.g. in the family circle, in daycare centers, at school from a young age, and in sport. The encouragement of autonomy prepares children to become socially competent adults in our Western cultures, which are characterized by a high degree of individualism and competitiveness. In this way, the developmental niches are effective in fulfilling their role of ensuring the acquisition of the culture and the transmission of dominant values. Conversely, the parental ethnotheories of societies more based on collectivist values would lead to practices encouraging interdependence, with the aim of ensuring the cohesion of the social group rather than the empowerment of individuals.

2.2. Cultural Variations in the Encouragement of Autonomy

Numerous studies using both quantitative and qualitative methods have given empirical support to and illustrated the influence of these ethnotheories on childrearing behaviors. Some studies have focused on cross-cultural comparisons between cultures living apart, while others have focused on comparisons between ethnic groups sharing a common territory. As an example of a cross-cultural comparison, differences were found in maternal parenting behaviors and conversational styles between 38 German and 35 Hindu mothers (Keller, Borke, Chaudhary, Lamm, and Kleis, 2010). The German mothers' cultural model focused on independence, while that of the Hindus focused on relatedness. These models were seen to be expressed both in mothers' conversational behaviors with their three-month-old babies and in play behaviors with their 15-month-olds. Conversational behaviors were conceptualized in terms of relational *versus* autonomy-based styles, while play behaviors were conceptualized in terms of didactic *versus* autonomy-based styles. The Hindu mothers were characterized by a more relational and less autonomy-based conversational style and by a style of play that was more didactic than autonomy-based. The German mothers on the contrary were characterized by an autonomy-based style in both conversation and play situations. Since conversational behaviors were good predictors of play behaviors, it was suggested that parenting style forms consistent and continuous socialization settings in which dominant cultural values are transmitted to children. Another piece of recent research compared 220 Argentinian, Italian and American mothers with five-month-old infants (Bornstein, Putnick, Suwalsky, Venuti, de Falco, Zingman de Galperin, Gini, and Heslington Tichovolsky, 2012). The emotional relationship was analyzed across all samples. Cross-cultural differences were displayed, with the Italian mothers being more sensitive and their infant more responsive than in the Argentinian and American dyads. Although the three countries are comparable in terms of general sociodemographics, they differ in their cultural background. Argentina is characterized by collectivist values, in particular familism. Respect and obedience are among the most important socialization goals. Italian mothers encouraged emotional expression and social competence.

Withdrawal and inhibition were regarded as poor social skills and attributed to difficult temperament (Super, Axia, Harkness, Welles-Nyström, Olaf Zylicz, Parmar, Bonichini, Rios Bermudez, Moscardino, Kola, Palacios, Eliasez, and McGurk, 2008). American mothers' childrearing behavior was characterized by individualism, with frequent encouragement of autonomy and self-reliance. These contrasting ethnotheories explained why, for example, Italian mothers, with their expectation of mutual socio-emotional expressiveness, were more sensitive than Americans, with their pervasive individualistic orientation (Bornstein et al., 2012).

The case of different cultures living side-by-side is also interesting, since it makes it possible to highlight contrasts between groups sharing a common territory but developing within distinct cultural boundaries. In one study, 69 Italian and 69 German-Italian mothers of two-to-five-year-old children from a region of South Tyrol were compared (Taverna, Bornstein, Putnick, and Axia, 2011).

The authors hypothesized differences in cultural niches and therefore ethnic differences in childrearing. The results showed that German-Italian mothers reported that they encouraged greater autonomy in their children than Italians, and children's autonomy was associated with their well-adjusted behavior. The United States also offers good opportunities for cultural comparisons, since different ethnic groups cohabit there. Childrearing beliefs in independent thinking *versus* obedience and physical discipline practices were compared among 155 Vietnamese and 153 Cambodian immigrants in the US (Tajima and Harachi, 2010). The results showed that childrearing was highly influenced by ethnic culture, but also by migration. Parents developed parenting goals intended to help their children to adapt to the new social environment. Their ethnotheories resulted in a mix of Westernized parenting beliefs and those enduring from their culture of origin.

2.3. Cultural Variations in Socialization Goals

Cultural variations in parental ethnotheories have also been appraised in empirical studies demonstrating that the importance given to children's self-esteem as a socialization goal differs between cultures. A study conducted with interviews among 16 American and 16 Taiwanese mothers and grandmothers showed differences in this respect between the American and Taiwanese samples (Cho, Sandel, Miller, and Wang, 2005). While self-esteem was an evident priority purpose of socialization for the American mothers and grandmothers, it was not for the Taiwanese respondents. Whereas the American mothers and grandmothers related many of their childrearing behaviors to the goal of giving the child positive self-esteem, the Taiwanese respondents considered child's self-esteem to be a peripheral element without any specific relation to their childrearing behavior and their socialization goals. These results showed that within the developmental niche, i.e. the family setting, the caregivers displayed childrearing practices guided by their ethnotheories. In the American families, the parent-child interactions aimed to ensure that the child developed positive self-esteem, as a contributing factor to social adaptation in Western societies based on values such as independence, individualism and competition. In their interviews, the American mothers and grandmothers associated self-esteem with the concepts of strengths and skills. In the Taiwanese families on the other hand, the meaning of self-esteem was less valuable. It was associated with psychological vulnerability such as frustration, stubbornness or disobedience. As these notions were seen as antithetical to social adaptation and not valued highly in the social reference group, parent-child interactions aimed at developing positive self-esteem were naturally absent or even regarded as undesirable among the mothers and grandmothers. This study demonstrates that self-esteem is not a universal need. Such an assumption was further supported by a recent study conducted with 98 American and 120 Japanese adult participants, who were asked to assess hypothetical subjects of unspecified age and gender. The participants received information about each subject's self-esteem with five positive and five negative items from the Rosenberg Self-Esteem scale. They had to assess each target on 13 characteristics, such as likeability, capability, psychological health, adjustment, probability of successful life outcomes, need for psychological counseling, arrogance and depression. The results first showed that American participants believed high self-esteem to be more important than Japanese participants. The subjects with high self-esteem were also regarded as better adjusted and more successful by the American than by the Japanese participants. Finally, in a study using Harter's scales (Child Dev 53(1):87–97, 1982) of self-esteem evaluation among 258 Belgian and Portuguese 5th graders, more Portuguese than Belgian children thought their scholastic, social and physical competence had increased in the last year (Vandenplas-Holper, Roskam, and Fontaine, 2010). This positive change was also attributed to internal agency beliefs by Portuguese children more than by Belgian children. These cross-cultural differences were interpreted as related to Portuguese educational discourse, whose developmental model places far more emphasis than is found in Belgian educational discourse on positive change and internal agency beliefs about such change. Although this discourse was located at the level of the macro-system, it may nevertheless be supposed that the macro-systemic emphasis on positive change and agency beliefs has been translated at the micro-system level of the classroom and the family into educational discourse and childrearing practices adjusted to the children's level of development. The school and family micro-systems can thus be considered as 'developmental niches' (Harkness and Super, 1986) playing the role of interfaces between children and culture. They are conceptualized as the nexus through which elements of the larger culture are filtered (Harkness and Super, 2006).

The cultural variations in the emphasis given to the development of the self have been supposed to lead to variations in child development (Chiu and Kim, 2011). In other words, the socialization experiences that the child has in his/her developmental niche have consequences for self-representation, in line with cultural conceptions that differ with respect to the attention paid the self. The classical task of mirror self-recognition with a mark test was administered to 215 18-to-24-month-old infants from Kenya, Fiji, Saint Lucia, Grenada, Peru, Canada and the United States. American and Canadian infants displayed spontaneous self-oriented behaviors towards the mark, while significantly fewer infants from the non-Western locations did so. Rübeling, Keller, Yovsi, Lenk, Schwarzer, and Kühne (2011) hypothesized that the figure size of young children's drawings of themselves was mediated by cultural conceptions of the self. The drawings of 76 Cameroonian rural children were compared with those of 72 German urban children. The two subgroups were matched for age, drawing competence, developmental stage and structural level of human drawing. The familial niche of Cameroonian children is characterized by extended families with three or more generations living together, with the father as head of the household. The Cameroonian child is a gift of God, initiated into its ancestral home and assigned to a symbolic gender identity and sex role. Childcare is considered to be a communal responsibility. By contrast, the German family context is characterized by individualistic values of responsibility, in which children's wishes and preferences are acknowledged by the parents. As expected by the authors, both the figure size and the head size of Cameroonian children's drawings were significantly smaller than those of German children. These differences were interpreted according to the cultural values and emphasis on the self.

2.4. Cultural Variations in Cosleeping Practices

Cosleeping is another good example of the role played by parents' ethnotheories in their childrearing behavior. In Western societies, sleeping with one's children is usually considered inappropriate. Children are encouraged to sleep in their own bed and in their personal bedroom from the first weeks or the first months of their life. Cosleeping is considered to be potentially deleterious with regard to the development of the child's autonomy and inconsistent with the respect for each individual's space to which Western people aspire. Cosleeping is also considered to lower the quality of sleep and even to be dangerous because of the risks of suffocation of the child by the adult. Furthermore, it undermines the needs for intimacy of the parental couple. The practice of cosleeping is nevertheless naturally present in many cultures. In the more collectivist societies, it protects children and helps transmit the dominant values of social cohesion by imparting the sense of membership of a community. In the traditional villages of Cameroon for example, the mothers sleep with all their children to the age of two or three years (Keller, 2007). They are positioned according to their birth order, with the youngest close to the mother. Sleeping under the protection of somebody older than them is supposed to protect the children. When the space becomes insufficient for the sibship or when the children have become older (four years old on average), they sleep with siblings or with the grandmother. Mostly, the fathers sleep in their own room somewhere else in the house. The reasons, based on their ethnotheories, given by the mothers for these sleeping arrangements are both the ease of feeding the child and the fact that the child sleeps well and safely. In this study of Keller (2007) with German and Cameroonian mothers, Cameroonian mothers who had been informed about the sleeping arrangements made by German mothers for their children described them as maltreatment. The Cameroonian mothers judged the adequacy of the German arrangements with reference to their own ethnotheories, leading them to reject and even condemn practices conflicting with their cultural assumptions and beliefs! It is interesting to note that, in agreement with the universal goals proposed by LeVine (1977), the mothers' purposes are the same in the two cultures: to make sure that the child sleeps and develops safely. But the mothers differ in how they plan to reach such a goal: the rejection of cosleeping *versus* its systematic practice, in line with their ethnotheories.

Other empirical findings about ethnic or racial differences support the assumption that children's sleeping arrangements reflect culturally distinct parental values and practices. Milan, Snow, and Belay (2007) found that in the Unites States, ethnic differences exist in where children sleep, how they are put to bed, and the level of concern mothers have about their child's sleep. This was the finding from a survey of 3,068 white, Latino and Afro-American families, and the differences could not be accounted for solely by socio-demographic, environmental and pragmatic variables. Most of the children in white families slept alone (47% alone, 30% with siblings and 23% with parents), while most of the children from Latino families slept with the parents (57% with parents, 23% with siblings and 20% alone), and Afro-American children slept mostly with parents (37%) or siblings (41%), but rarely alone (22%). One of the dominant values in Latino families is familism, stressing the importance of parent-child relationship. Cosleeping is viewed as a way in which the transmission of the value system is ensured across generations. In white families, the emphasis was placed on individuation and individual achievement. Afro-American families were characterized by collectivist and traditional values, leading the sleeping arrangements to be organized with the siblings or the parents. Practices such as bedtime routines were also seen to differ across ethnic groups, e.g. whites gave a comfort object to enhance the child's ability to tolerate separation from parents, but did not give a bottle because of negative connotations with concepts such as dependency. These practices were in line with a widely shared parental goal of helping children to establish independence because this is viewed as a positive adult characteristic. Recent findings are consistent with these results of Milan et al. (2007). Parents of infants and toddlers from Australia, Canada, China, Hong Kong, India, Indonesia, Korea, Japan, Malaysia, New Zealand, the Philippines, Singapore, Taiwan, Thailand, the United Kingdom, the United States and Vietnam were asked to complete an Internet-based version of the Brief Infant Sleep Questionnaire. The most common sleeping arrangement in Caucasian families (N=9,218) was that the child fell asleep independently in his/her own bed (57%), compared with only 4% of children living in Asian regions (N=20,069). Furthermore, sleep routines were characterized by bottle-feeding, nursing and cosleeping in Asian families and by waking up again and being left to cry themselves back to sleep in bed alone in another room in Caucasian families. In Egyptian families, reports of sleeping arrangements from 78 participants from 16 families were studied by Worthman and Brown (2007). About 69% of the sleep events (both naps and nights) involved cosleeping, with 24% of these including more than one co-sleeper. The influence of parental sleep-related cognitions on children's sleep behavior was also shown by Sadeh, Flint-Ofir, Tirosh, and Tikotzky (2007) in Tel Aviv. Two subsamples were enrolled in the study, a clinical sample of 48 infants referred because of night-waking problems and a control sample of 48 infants with no sleep difficulties. The parents completed questionnaires about their views on children's sleep, and the infants' sleep was monitored by actigraph for one week. Group differences were found as expected with regard to both infant sleep quality and parents' cognitions. In particular, parental cognitions about difficulties in limit setting were associated with poorer sleep quality.

Differences also exist among Western societies with regard to parental ethnotheories about infants' sleep. A recent study aiming to highlight cultural models in child development compared in particular the ethnotheories of 60 Dutch and 60 American families (Harkness and Super, 2006). The results showed that Dutch parents believed that children needed to sleep to develop well. They therefore reported that they established regular patterns of sleep. On the other hand, the American parents asserted that needs related to infants' sleep were determined by the infant's temperament and by his/her age. In this cultural model, the parents had no role to play in this domain. These ethnotheories were related both to the parents' childrearing behaviors in these two Western cultures and to children's behavioral outcomes. The results showed that Dutch parents had a regular bedtime for their children, adopted routines based around their children's level of tiredness and encouraged the children to have naps during the day according to regular schedules. The American parents by contrast put the children in the bed at irregular times without established routines and considered the nap as optional, according to the needs expressed by the child. The results indicated that the Dutch children slept for longer on average and behaved in a less agitated way than the American children.

2.5. From Parental Ethnotheories to Prototypical Personality Traits

The studies that have been reviewed illustrate how parental ethnotheories lead to certain skills, certain behavior and certain features being reinforced, e.g. autonomy in the individualistic societies or interdependence in the collectivist ones. Children from the same culture should consequently be more alike than children from different cultures. To confirm this statistically would involve demonstrating that the intra-cultural variance of children's behavior and personality is lower than the inter-cultural variance. In other words, a prototypical child could be defined in every culture, which that culture tends to promote through the way it conceives of the child's development and upbringing, and through the childrearing behaviors which ensue. Cultural practices may actually lead to differences in children's temperament and personality traits. Such an assumption has been supported in empirical research concerning six Western cultures, i.e. Australia, Italy, the Netherlands, Spain, Sweden and the United States (Harkness and Super, 2006). The parents from 60 families in each cultural subgroup were invited to describe their child freely. An analysis of the contents of all the parental descriptions showed that a number of characteristic features of Western societies, including sociability, activity and willingness, were collectively reported and valued in these six cultures. Other features were reported more frequently and valued more highly in some cultures than in others. For example, the American parents were more focused on children's intelligence, while the Italian parents were more concerned about how pleasant their children were. The Swedish parents valued the happy character of the child; the Spanish parents advanced the fact that their child were of good character.

A similar procedure involving free description by mothers of their children was used by Raghavan, Harkness, and Super (2010) in the United States in order to study parents' cultural belief systems, i.e. ethnotheories, and to what extent they influence children's settings and activities. The authors studied cultural variations between ten Asian Indian immigrant mothers and ten matched Euro-American mothers. Each mother was asked to freely describe their five-to-fifteen-year-old daughter, and the mothers' discourse was analyzed in depth. Several core descriptors were highlighted, and the preferred descriptors in each group referred to culturally important and desirable qualities. Among the descriptors that were exclusively used by the American mothers were independent, well-rounded, athletic, assertive and outspoken. They referred to the prototypical independent, self-confident, self-actualizing woman in a competitive setting. Among the most frequent descriptors employed by the Indian mothers were responsible, respectful, hospitable, modest and argumentative. They referred to collectivist values of being able to fit into a group. So the words used most frequently by American and Indian mothers to describe their daughter were considered as indicators of their implicit cultural model of what a girl should be like at a particular age (Raghavan et al., 2010).

Other empirical findings gave support to this conclusion. Super et al. (2008) studied parental ethnotheories of children's temperament in Australia, Italy, the Netherlands, Poland, Spain, Sweden and the United States. The 299 mothers were asked to assess their three-to-eight-year-old child's temperament with a standardized questionnaire, but also to rate how difficult they considered their child to be in overall terms. The results showed as a general trend that low adaptability and negative mood were associated with difficulty in all cultures. Specific patterns were also revealed such as difficulty being associated with high intensity in the Netherlands and the United States, with negative approach in Italy and with high distractibility in the Netherlands. These results suggest that the mothers have both shared and culturally distinctive conceptualizations of what makes a child difficult. For example, the Italian pattern of association between negative approach and difficult temperament was consistent with a cultural model of parenting where the child has to be introduced to various social situations and encouraged to have emotionally close relationships with others. In this developmental niche, rearing a shy or withdrawn child is actually a challenge for the parents.

CONCLUSION

Cross-cultural research in psychology gives us an understanding of parenthood in its universal and culturally specific aspects. Cross-cultural studies provide empirical comparative data between cultures, but these studies also propose a powerful framework. The concepts of "developmental niche" and of "ethnotheories " that have been reviewed here are important to the understanding of cultural variations in parenting and child development. Furthermore, beyond their main theoretical contribution, cross-cultural studies of parenting have evident implications in our multicultural societies and in particular for immigrant families, e.g. in the way they adjust to their host culture, build their social network or find psychosocial support in their surroundings. Moreover, cross-cultural studies of parenting offer social workers working with immigrant populations an excellent means of gaining perspective on their own cultural models or values and of protecting themselves against the obvious risk of ethnocentrism (Berry et al., 2011; Keith, 2011).

REFERENCES

Bornstein, M.H., Putnick, D.L., Suwalsky, J.T.D., Venuti, P., de Falco, S., Zingman de Galperin, C., Gini, M., and Heslington Tichovolsky, M. (2012). Emotional Relationships in mothers and infants: culture-common and community-specific characteristics of dyads from rural and metropolitan settings in Argentina, Italy and the United States. *Journal of Cross-Cultural Psychology, 43* (2), 171-197.

Broesch, T., Callaghan, T., Henrich, J., Murphy, C., and Rochat, P. (2011). Cultural variations in children's mirror self-recognition. *Journal of Cross-Cultural Psychology, 42* (6), 1018-1029.

Brown, R.A. (2010). Perceptions of psychological adjustment, achievement, outcomes, and self-esteem in Japan and America. *Journal of Cross-Cultural Psychology, 41* (1), 51-61.

Cho, G.E., Sandel, T.L., Miller, P.J., and Wang, S. (2005). What do grandmothers think about self-esteem? American and Taiwanese folk theories revisited. *Social Development*, 14 (4), 701-721.

Friedlmeier, W., Chakkarath, P., and Schwarz, B. (2005). *Culture and human development.* New York: Psychology Press.

Harkness, S., and Super, C. (1986). The developmental niche: A conceptualisation at the interface of child and culture. *International Journal of Behavioural Development*, 9, 545–569.

Harkness, S., and Super, C. (2006). Themes and variations: Parental ethnotheories in Western cultures. In K.H. Rubin and O. B. Chunk (Eds.), *Parenting beliefs, behaviors, and parent-child relations. A crosscultural perspective* (pp. 61–79). New York: Psychology.

Hofstede, G. (2001). *Culture's consequences: Comparing values, behaviors, institutions, and organizations across nations* (2nd ed.). Thousand Oaks, CA: Sage.

Kagitçibasi, C. (2007). *Family, self, and human development across cultures. Theory and applications*. Mahwah: Lawrence Erlbaum Associates.

Keller, H. (2007). *Cultures of infancy*. Mahwah: Lawrence Erlbaum Associates.

Keller, H., Borke, J., Chaudhary, N., Lamm, B., and Kleis, A. (2010). Continuity in parenting strategies: a cross cultural comparison. *Journal of Cross-Cultural Psychology, 41* (3), 391-409.

Laungani, P.D. (2007). *Understanding cross-cultural psychology*. London: Sage.

LeVine, R.A. (1977). Childrearing as cultural adaptation. In Leiderman, P.H., Tulkin, S.R. and Rosenfeld, A.H. (Eds.), *Culture and Infancy*. London, Academic Press (pp. 15-27).

Milan, S., Snow, S., Belay, S. (2007). The context of preschool children's sleep: racial/ethnic differences in sleep locations, routines, and concerns. *Journal of Family Psychology, 21* (1), 20-28.

Mindell, J.A., Sadeh, A., Kohyama, J., and How, T.H. (2010). Parental behaviors and sleep outcomes in infants and toddlers: a cross-cultural comparison. *Sleep Medicine, 11*, 393-399.

Raghavan, C.S., Harkness, S., and Super, C.M. (2010). Parental ethnotheories in the context of immigration: Asian Indian immigrant and Euro-American mothers and daughters in an American town. *Journal of Cross-Cultural Psychology, 41* (4), 617-632.

Rübeling, H., Keller, H., Yovsi, R.D., Lenk, M., Schwarzer, S., and Kühne, N. (2011). Children's drawings of the self as an expression of cultural conceptions of the self. *Journal of Cross-Cultural Psychology, 42* (3), 406-424.

Rubin, K.H., and Chung, O.B. (2007). *Parenting beliefs, behaviors and parent-child relations. New York*: Psychology Press.

Sadeh, A., Flint-Ofir, E., Tirosh, T., and Titotzky, L. (2007). Infant sleep and parental sleep-related cognitions. *Journal of Family Psychology, 21*(1), 74-87.

Suizzo, M-A. (2002). French parents' cultural models and childrearing beliefs. *International Journal of Behavioral Development, 26* (4), 297-307.

Super, C.M., Axia, G., Harkness, S., Welles-Nyström, B., Olaf Zylic, P., Parmar, P., Bonichini, S., Rios Bermudez, M., Moscardino, U., Kolar, V., Palacios, J., Eliasz, A., and McGurk, H. (2008). Culture, temperament, and the "difficult child": a study in seven Western cultures. *European Journal of Developmental Science, 2* (1/2), 136-157.

Tajima, E.A., and Harachi, T.W. (2010). Parenting beliefs and physical discipline practices among southeast Asian immigrants: parenting in the context of cultural adaptation to the United States. *Journal of Cross-Cultural Psychology, 41* (2), 212-235.

Tam, K-P., and Lee S-L. (2010). What values do parents want to socialize in their children? The role of perceived normative values. *Journal of Cross-Cultural Psychology, 41* (2), 175-181.

Taveerna, L., Bornstein, M.H., Putnick, D.L., and Axia, G. (2011). Adaptive behaviors in young children: a unique cultural comparison in Italy. *Journal of Cross-Cultural Psychology, 42* (3), 445-465.

Vandenplas-Holper, C., Roskam, I., and Fontaine, A-M. (2010). Self-perceived stability and change in children's competence. *European Journal of Psychology of Education*, 25 (1), 1-17.

Vieira, M.L., Seidl-de-Moura, M.L., Lordelo, E., Piccinini, C.A., Dal Forno Martins, G., Mafioletti Macarini, S., Ribeiro Moncorvo, M.C., Ramos Pontes, F.A., Colino Magalhaes, C.M., Ribeiro Salomao, N.M., and Rimoli, A.O. (2010). Brazilian mothers' beliefs about childrearing practices. *Journal of Cross-Cultural Psychology, 41* (2), 195-211.

Wothman, C.M., and Brown, R.A. (2007). Companionable sleep: social regulation of sleep and cosleeping in Egyptian families. *Journal of Family Psychology, 21* (1), 124-135.

In: Parenting
ISBN: 978-1-62257-881-8
Editors: Peter Barberis and Stelios Petrakis
© 2013 Nova Science Publishers, Inc.

Chapter 7

PARENTAL INFLUENCE THROUGH SOCIAL STRUCTURES: HOW SOCIAL INSTITUTIONS ARE USED TO PROMOTE PARENTAL CONTROL OVER MATE CHOICE

Menelaos Apostolou[1,*]
[1]University of Nicosia, University of Nicosia, Nicosia, Cyprus

ABSTRACT

Parents and children are not genetically identical and this leads to conflict between the two. One area of disagreement is mate choice, with children choosing spouses who do not comply with the preferences of their parents. In turn, this gives the incentive to the latter to control the mating decisions of their daughters and sons. To facilitate this control, parents employ social institutions that have originally evolved to serve different functions. This chapter attempts to explore how two of these social structures namely, inheritance rights and marriage transactions such as the bridewealth, are used by parents to promote control over mating. In addition, the cross-cultural variability of these institutions is further explored. Finally, the implications of the use of these social structures on mate choice and on the workings of sexual selection under parental choice are also examined.

INTRODUCTION

Parents and children are not genetically identical and as a consequence their genetic interests do not overlap. Disagreement between the two parties is reflected in several dimensions one being mate choice (Apostolou, 2007a). More specifically, the mating decisions of children do not always find the agreement of their parents, which in turn

---

[*] E-mail: m.apostolou@gmail.com.

motivates the latter to control the mate choices of the former (Apostolou, 2010c). In this chapter I will argue that in order to achieve this goal, parents employ social structures present in a given society, and by doing so they become more effective manipulators of their children's mating behavior.

I will start my discussion by demonstrating that the fact that parents and their children are not genetically identical results into in-law and mate preferences diverging. That is, what children prefer in a husband or in a wife is not the same with what their parents prefer in a son– or in a daughter-in-law. Consequently, parents have the incentive to influence the mate choices of their children in order to get in-laws that best satisfy their preferences. To achieve this end parents employ social institutions such as inheritance rights and marriage transactions such as the bridewealth. In the first case, in order to impose their will, parents manipulate the wealth that passes to their sons in the form of inheritance, while in the second case they manipulate the monetary assistance their sons require in order to arrange a desirable marriage.

IN-LAW PREFERENCES VS. MATE PREFERENCES

In-law Preferences

A good in-law choice can bring considerable survival and reproductive advantages to the parents and their family (Apostolou, 2007a). For instance, an industrious and capable in-law will become a reliable source of resources which are needed for survival and reproduction. However, prospective in-laws differ in all dimensions which are of interest to the parents: some are hardworking while others are lazy, some are wealthy while others are poor and so on.

In consequence, considerable evolutionary pressure is exercised on parents to evolve preferences that enable them to choose the best possible in-laws. To put it differently, parents with a predisposition to prefer sons- and daughters-in-law with beneficial qualities (e.g., industriousness), have an advantage over other parents who do not share these preferences. Eventually, the former will replace the latter leaving us with a population of parents with well-defined preferences (Apostolou, 2007a).

In order to explore in-law preferences, Apostolou (2007a) asked a group of British parents to rate the desirability of a number of traits in a prospective son- and in a daughter-in-law. It was found that parents have a hierarchy of preferences in which certain traits were considered more important than others. In particular, traits such as kind and understanding, good health, and good earning capacity were found at the top of the parental hierarchy, followed by traits such as education/intelligence, good cook/housekeeper, and good family background in the middle of the parental hierarchy. Finally, traits such as physically attractive and chastity were found at the bottom of the parental preferences' hierarchy.

Another study employed anthropological evidence from 67 pre-industrial societies and identified 13 qualities that parents desire in an in-law (Apostolou, 2010b). Among the most frequently reported traits were good character, good family background, industry and be a good worker, followed by favourable social status, wealth, and similar family social status. The least frequently reported traits were good looks and chastity.

Other studies, not specifically designed to identify in-law preferences, provide information on what parents desire in an in-law. In particular, Hynie et al. (2006) investigated the in-law preferences of Chinese immigrants in North America and found good social status and understanding to be among the most preferred traits. Borgerhoff Mulder (1988) reported that, among the pastoral Kipsigies in Kenya, parents prefer as sons-in-law individuals who enjoy high social status, are wealthy, educated, have a good character and are industrious. Yu, Proulx, and Shepard (2007) found that Matsigenka women in Peru prefer men with masculine faces for sons-in-law and interpreted this finding as a preference for good providers, as masculine men are, on average, perceived as better resource providers. Finally, Apostolou (2007b) found that among hunters and gatherers, parents prefer sons-in-law who are good hunters and have a good family background, while they prefer daughters-in-law who are industrious and come from good families.

Mate Preferences

The choice of a long-term mate is also associated with considerable fitness benefits, which in turn has resulted in the evolution of mate preferences. For instance, individuals with no particular preference for the health status of their partners would be as likely to mate with a healthy individual as with an individual of poor health. However, individuals with a predisposition to prefer as mates those who enjoy a good health would be more likely to have a healthy partner.

Consequently, individuals endowed with this preference will be better-off than the rest as they will have healthy spouses who will be around for longer and who are also more likely to give them healthy children. Therefore, individuals with beneficial mate preferences will eventually replace those who lack such preferences (or who have less beneficial preferences) leaving behind a population of mate-seekers with well-defined mate preferences.

In order to study mate preferences, Buss et al. (1990) asked participants in 37 countries to rate a set of traits in a potential mate. They found that people placed high in their hierarchy of preferences traits such as mutual attraction/love, good health, and dependable character. In the middle of their preferences hierarchy, traits such as sociability, ambition/industriousness, and good looks were found. Finally, at the bottom of the hierarchy of mate preferences, traits such as chastity and similar religious background were found. Substantial work has been completed on exploring mate preferences, and these findings have been replicated in many instances (for a review see Buss, 2003).

PARENT-OFFSPRING CONFLICT OVER MATING

Parents have evolved preferences that enable them to choose the best possible in-laws while their children have evolved preferences which enable them to choose the best spouses. Nevertheless, parents and children are not genetically identical, and for this reason they do not share the same interests with respect to mate choice as specific traits in a mating candidate give unequal benefits to each party. The result of this is that in-law and mate preferences diverge, and this combined with the trade-off nature of mating, gives rise to parent-offspring conflict (Apostolou, 2007a; 2008a; Buunk, Park & Dubbs, 2008; Trivers, 1974).

In more detail, starting from the argument that traits give unequal benefits to parents and their children, we can examine how this works with genetic quality: Individuals are more closely related to their children than to their grandchildren. As a consequence, the odds of a particular gene of an individual being passed into the next generation by a spouse or an in-law is 50% or 25% respectively. Therefore, individuals reap more genetic benefits from a spouse than from an in-law of superior genetic quality (Apostolou, 2007a). As beauty is a proxy of good genetic quality (Gangestad et al., 1994), it is expected that it will be preferred more in a spouse than in an in-law.

This hypothesis has been supported by various studies. More specifically, Apostolou (2008b) employed a sample of British parents and found that good looks are preferred more in a spouse than in an in-law. Similarly, Buunk, Park and Dubbs (2008) found that individuals consider an unattractive mating candidate more unacceptable than they think their parents would. Further studies were able to replicate these findings (Apostolou, 2011a; Buunk, & Castro Solano, 2010; Park, Dubbs & Buunk, 2008, Perilloux, Fleischman, & Buss, 2011).

Beauty is not the only area of parent-offspring disagreement over mating. In particular, Apostolou (2008c) found that good family background is preferred significantly more in an in-law than in a spouse. Similarly, Buunk, Park and Dubbs (2008) found that individuals consider a mating candidate who does not come from a good family background more acceptable than they think their parents would. This was also replicated in several more studies (Apostolou, 2011a; Buunk, & Castro Solano, 2010; Park, Dubbs & Buunk, 2008, Perilloux et al., 2011).

Further evidence indicates that parents and children disagree over the religious background of a mating candidate. More specifically, it appears that individuals prefer similar religious background more in an in-law than in a spouse (Apostolou, 2008b; Buunk, et al., 2008; Sprecher & Chandak, 1992). Exciting personality is another trait over which parents and offspring appear to have divergent preferences. In particular, Apostolou (2008c) found that this trait is valued more in a spouse than in an in-law, and Buunk et al. (2008) found that mate seekers consider the lack of this trait and other related qualities (i.e., sense of humor, artistic ability, creativity) in a spouse much more unacceptable than their parents.

Non-overlapping in-law and mate preferences along with the tradeoffs nature of mate choice mandate that the mate choices of children will be costly to their parents. In particular, individuals of high mate value will not be willing to engage in long-term mating with individuals of low mate value (Apostolou, 2011c; Gangestad & Simpson, 2000): if you are a '10' it is unlikely that you will agree to marry a '5'. This means that if you are a '5' you will probably want to marry a '10', but you will need to settle for someone closer to '5'. Consequently, when you exercise mate choice, you have to make compromises because you are constrained by your own mate value. Similarly, if your parents exercise mate choice for you, they also need to make compromises as they are also constrained by your mate value: they want to get a '10', but they have to settle for someone around '5'. The crucial point is that since traits give unequal benefits to parents and offspring, the compromises that each party is willing to make differ, which, in turn, results in conflict between the two (Apostolou, 2008a; Buunk et al., 2008).

For instance, when they exercise mate choice, individuals will be willing to exchange more 'units' of other traits (say wealth) in order to get more of beauty which is a proxy of genetic quality (Gangestad et al., 1994). This imposes a cost on their parents as their loss in social status is not compensated by the gain in beauty, as this trait gives them fewer benefits than it gives to their children. Conversely, if parents were to exercise choice for their children, they would be willing to give up more 'units' of beauty to get more of other traits such as social status. This imposes a cost on children as the gain in social status does not justify their loss in genetic quality because the latter is more valuable to them than it is to their parents.

This hypothesis was tested with the use of a budget allocation method (Apostolou, 2011c). In particular, parents were given a budget of mate points and they were asked to allocate them in traits for a prospective son-in-law and a daughter-in-law. Similarly, their children were given the same budget to be allocated to the same traits, but this time in a prospective husband and in a prospective wife. It was found that children compromised on qualities such as good family background in order to get more beauty in a spouse, while their parents compromised on beauty to get more of good family background. It seems then, that the differences between in-law and mate preference guide children to make compromised which do not satisfy their parents.

SOCIAL INSTITUTIONS AND PARENTAL CONTROL OVER MATING

If parents leave their children to exercise mate choice on their own, the latter are likely to choose mates who do not satisfy parental preferences. Accordingly, parents have the incentive to influence their daughters' and sons' mate choices in a way that best promotes their interests. Parental attempts to control mating are likely to give rise to social structures that uphold this control. For instance, across human cultures we find social institutions such as the foot-binding, arranged marriage, female circumcision, the purdah and so on, that have evolved specifically for the purpose of regulating mating.

For instance, in the custom of female circumcision the clitoris is removed handicapping in effect a woman's ability to experience sexual pleasure. It is estimated that there are more than 100 million women, mainly in Africa, whose bodies have been altered by some form of female circumcision (Gruenbaum, 2001; Toubia, 1993). It is further estimated that an additional two million girls undergo some form of female genital cutting each year (Gruenbaum, 2001). With this custom, parents impair their daughters' ability to exercise mate choice when she is young and more vulnerable to their manipulation.

However, apart from institutions that have evolved specifically for the purpose of regulating mating, parents are also likely to employ social institutions that have evolved to serve a different purpose, for the purpose of controlling mating. In particular, social structures are necessary for the efficient functioning of a given society as they regulate specific aspects of human conduct. Because these institutions have an important role in regulating human behavior, parents employ them also for the purpose of regulating mating.

Inheritance

Parental control over mating is related positively to the amount of investment parents divert to their children (Apostolou, 2007b, 2010c). Given that part of parental investment goes to children in the form of inheritance, inheritance becomes an instrument of parental control over mating. In particular, as survival and reproduction depend on controlled resources, offspring are not indifferent to inheritance rights. In effect, inheritance can be used by parents to manipulate the mating decisions of their children: parents may threaten with partial or even complete disinheritance as a penalty for not accepting a marriage arrangement or finding a spouse who is not acceptable to them.

In more detail, parents maximise their fitness by endowing their offspring with whatever transferable wealth they have accumulated. The fitness-enhancing potential of this wealth is maximised if it is transferred to the descendent whose potential reproductive success is most dependent on these resources. Men have a higher reproductive variance than women, as they can increase their fitness considerably by mating with several partners, while wealth is a decisive factor for securing mates (Hartung, 1976). The transmission of wealth along the male, as opposed to the female line, therefore, maximises parents' fitness by concentrating it on descendants with higher coefficients of relationship and higher reproductive potential (Hartung, 1976). This, along with the fact that wealth is usually controlled by men (Whyte, 1978), results in inheritance passing from father to son (Hartung, 1976; 1982).

Accordingly, a man who controls wealth is influential over the mating decisions of his sons, who have an interest in these resources and risk foregoing their inheritance rights if they disobey their father. Inheritance then becomes an important instrument of parental control over mating in the hand of male parents (Apostolou, 2011b). Accordingly, in a context where male offspring enjoy inheritance rights, male parents are expected to be more influential over marriage arrangements.

More wealth is produced in agropastoral societies than in foraging ones, which takes the form of land and animals. This type of wealth is sustainable in nature (e.g., land), and consequently it can be easier transferred through inheritance. In foraging societies, the little wealth produced is unlikely to increase male's reproductive success substantially. Thus, inheritance rights may not be that important and the small property available may be shared equally between the family members. In consequence, male offspring are more likely to benefit from inheritance rights in agropastoral societies than in foraging ones.

To examine these hypotheses, one study employed anthropological evidence from the Standard Cross Cultural Sample which consists of pre-industrial societies which are relatively independent from each other (Apostolou, 2011b). It was found that when male offspring enjoy inheritance rights, men are more influential over marriage arrangements. It was also found that male offspring are more likely to benefit from inheritance rights in agropastoral societies than in foraging ones. This last finding can partially account for the fact that male parents are more influential over marriage arrangements in agropastoral than in hunting and gathering societies (Apostolou, 2010c).

Marriage Transactions

In most pre-industrial human societies, marriage is associated with some form of transaction which involves the transfer of resources between the parties involved in the marriage. More specifically, out of the 826 societies listed in the Ethnographic Atlas, resources are exchanged in 618 of them (Murdock, 1967). The most common marriage transaction is the bridewealth, which involves the transfer of substantial resources from the groom or his relatives to the family of the bride. In the Atlas of World Cultures bridewealth is reported in 226 societies (N = 563) followed by brideservice in 63 cultures and reciprocal gift exchange in 43 cultures (Murdock, 1981).

Most anthropologists believe that the bridewealth has evolved to be a compensation to the parents of the bride for losing the benefits of her labor. Accordingly, in this model, bridewealth is a compensation for the right to remove the bride from her family (Murdock, 1949; Spiro, 1975). Consistent with this, most of the societies where bridewealth is paid are patrilocal, with the bride moving away from her family after marriage and going to live with the family of her husband (Murdock, 1949). Nevertheless, Schlegel and Eloul (1988) questioned this explanation arguing that most societies in which dowry is given (i.e., the parents of the bride give wealth to the groom) are also patrilocal; thus, if the compensation model was true, it would be as if the bride's family pays to have her removed.

Another explanation is that bridewealth constitutes a guarantee that women will be treated well by their husbands who risk losing their investment if they abuse them (Murdock, 1949). Ogbu (1978) proposed that the primary function of the bridewealth is the legitimization of the marriage: its payment elevates the man to the status of husband and the woman to the status of wife. Kressel (1977) views bridewealth as a symbol which reflects the social status of the parties involved in the marriage.

Other scholars take an economic approach and see bridewealth as a payment for the services of women and the rights in her children with the economic conditions prevailing in each society determining its level (Goldschmidt, 1974; Schneider, 1979). For Ensminger and Knight (1997) bridewealth is an effective mechanism employed by the older men, who control most of the wealth, in order to keep women in their hands.

The arguments above have certainly grains of truth as it is unlikely that there is a monocausal explanation for the evolution of the bridewealth. Still, these theories fail to give a convincing account of why wealth moves from the bride to the groom rather the other way round. This is because most theorists see this institution as a cultural phenomenon which is independent of the human nature. However, marriage transactions can be conceptualized better as cultural epiphenomena associated with phenomena grounded in the interaction of individuals (Murdock, 1971, p. 19) who have a specific nature, a nature shaped by evolution.

On the basis of this reasoning, the female is the scarce reproductive resource which parents are able to control. By doing so, parents can extract immediate resources from men in return for sexual access to their daughter. In many societies, this takes the form of the bridewealth. However, although parents can receive immediate resources from their sons-in-law, bridewealth should not be seen solely as a wealth extraction device and in many societies it is frequently accompanied by a return gift of equal value (Murdock, 1949). Accordingly, it has been proposed that bridewealth has also evolved as an in-law screening device (Apostolou, 2008a): By imposing a heavy cost on their prospective sons-in-law, parents are able to distinguish the ones who have the higher resource capabilities.

Irrespectively of which is the reason primarily responsible for the evolution of the bridewealth, in the societies which is practiced, sons are dependent on the resources of their families so as to be able to afford it. As a family's wealth is usually controlled by its older male members, sons need to rely on their fathers for acquiring the required resources to pay their bridewealth. However, when a son depends on his father to get a wife, the latter has a say over this choice. In consequence, male parents become influential over mating decisions by providing part of the resources necessary for a marriage to proceed.

Accordingly, in societies where bridewealth is practiced, male parents should be more influential over marriage arrangements, while sons would lose some of their freedom to exercise mate choice. More specifically, bridewealth is not found in all societies as certain ecological constraints prevent parents from using it. Thus, in hunting and gathering societies little material wealth is produced which means that parents cannot demand substantial resources from their prospective sons-in-law given that such wealth is not present in this context. Accordingly, it is expected that bridewealth will be more common in agropastoral societies than in foraging ones. This translates into fathers having more influence over their sons' mate choices, and sons having less freedom to exercise mate choice in agropastoral than in foraging societies.

To examine these hypotheses, one study employed anthropological evidence from the Standard Cross Cultural Sample and found that the practice of bridewealth increases the influence of male parents over the mating decisions of their children (Apostolou, 2010a). Moreover, bridewealth is more frequently practiced in agropastoral than in foraging societies, and consequently sons are more dependent upon their fathers and male relatives for shouldering the costs of marriage transactions in agropastoral than in foraging societies.

CROSS-CULTURAL VARIABILITY

The use of social institutions by parents in order to influence the mate choices of their children depends on the prevalence and the relative strength of these institutions in a given society. Accordingly, one needs to ask what determines the cross-cultural variability of institutional presence. I suggest that two of the determinants are the complexity and the size of a given society.

In particular, a complex society is more in need of social structures that will regulate its functioning. For instance, a more complex society has more specialized units of production (e.g., a factory), it has more units that specialize in provide training (e.g., schools), it has more units that specialize in safekeeping the wealth produced (e.g., banks) and so on. The coordination of these units, that make the functioning of a complex society possible, requires the emergence of social institutions such as the law that will regulate their function.

The presence of social institutions is also determined by the size of a given society. More specifically, it has been estimated that the human mind can deal effectively with social relationships that involve around 150 other people (Dunbar, 1992, 1993). This indicates that if a given society exceeds this number, it will require the presence of social structures that will regulate human conduct. Accordingly, the larger a given society is, the more likely it is that social structures that regulate human interaction will be present. This reasoning mandates also that the larger and more complex a given society becomes, the more it needs to rely on its institutions which means that in larger and more complex societies these institutions have more power in regulating human behavior than in smaller and less complex ones.

Based on this reasoning we would expect that social institutions are more prevalent in societies which base their subsistence on agriculture and animal husbandry than in societies which base their subsistence on hunting and gathering. In particular, the latter societies are much less complex and smaller in size than the former, which means that they do not have to evolve social institutions that regulate their functioning. Consistent with this, the bridewealth and inheritance rights are found mainly in agropastoral societies and they are less frequently practiced in hunting and gathering ones.

Furthermore, given the importance of resources for survival and reproduction, it is also reasonable to argue that many of the social structures prevalent in a given society have evolved to regulate the distribution of resources between the society's members. Similarly, given the importance that individuals ascribe to material resources, it is expected that many of these social structures will be employed by parents to influence the mate choices of children. For instance, the bridewealth and the inheritance rights are two institutions that regulate how resources will be distributed in a given society and are also used by parents for the purpose of controlling mate choice.

In this chapter I discussed how bridewealth and inheritance rights can be used by parents to control their children's mating decisions. However, these are not the only social structures that have evolved to serve a different purpose, but are also employed to control mating. Social institutions such as the religion and the secular law constitute other social structures which are employed for this purpose. For instance, both the secular and the divine law have clear mandates that regulate mating behavior, usually in a way that facilitates parental control over mating (e.g., forbidding sexual relationships before marriage).

It can be predicted that in any given society parents would attempt to use the social structures which are present there so as to control mate choice. It can be further predicted that the institutions that parents will be more interested in employing are the ones that have evolved to regulate the transfer of wealth among society's members. The reason why is that resources are scarce and valuable for survival and reproduction, and thus the manipulation the institutions that regulate how resources are distributed is likely to have a more considerable impact on regulating mating than the manipulation of other institutions.

EXPLORING THE IMPLICATIONS OF THE INSTITUTIONAL USE

The prevalence of social structures in a given society makes available means through which parents can exercise control over mating. Parents take this opportunity and employ these social structures to increase their influence over their children's mating decisions. The employment of these institutions in regulating mating is likely to be quite effective. For instance, a son who goes against his father's wishes risks forfeiting his inheritance, which can be substantial. Similarly, a son who decides to marry a woman his parents do not approve will be prevented from doing so as his parents will not provide him with the required resources for paying the bridewealth.

In effect, the use of social structures amplifies the strength of parental influence over mating and in most cases the male parental power over the mate choices of male offspring. This is because in most pre-industrial societies wealth is controlled by men and most social structures have evolved to regulate how wealth is distributed between a society's members. Thus, it is usually the case that social institutions that regulate resources distribution are controlled by men and the manipulation of these institutions affects male offspring. For instance, in inheritance rights, wealth is usually controlled by the father and passes to his son(s).

In evolutionary terms, it has been argued that parental influence over mating affects the course of sexual selection in our species (Apostolou, 2007b, 2010c). More specifically, in a context where parental influence is strong, traits that make individuals more likely to be chosen as in-laws are likely to be selected and increase in frequency in the population. For instance, if a son-in-law has a given trait that makes him more appealing to parents looking for a spouse for their daughters, he will gain reproductive benefits. In consequence, he is likely to have sons who also carry this trait. In this case, this trait will increase in the population through sexual selection under parental choice.

The strength of sexual selection under parental choice is contingent upon the degree of control parents have over their children. Accordingly, in a given society, the practice of social institutions such as the bridewealth, augments parental control over mating and consequently the strength of parental choice as a sexual selection force. Given that social institutions such as the bridewealth have the potential to amplify male parental control over male offspring, and given that these are more frequently found in agropastoral than in foraging societies, it can be predicted that male parental choice will be a stronger sexual selection force in agropastoral than in foraging societies, which appears to be the case (Apostolou, 2010c).

This indicates further that as fathers are able to control the mate choices of their sons, they have a strong say over choosing wives for them. Accordingly, sexual selection forces are exercised on female mate-seekers, as traits that make them more likely to be selected by fathers as daughters-in-law, would increase in frequency in the population under strong positive selection. These selection forces will also operate on women's parents as when arranging a marriage for their sons, fathers are looking to establish beneficial alliances with other families.

A further implication of this is that the agropastoral revolution that took place approximately 10,000 years ago should have given rise to societies which practiced social institution that could be used by parents to control the mate choices of their children. Accordingly, the agropastoral revolution should have resulted in an increase in the strength of parental choice as a sexual selection mechanism. This prediction seems to be corroborated by empirical evidence from historical societies.

In particular, an investigation of the mating patterns of sixteen historical societies (such as Classical Greece and Imperial China), demonstrated that parents had a strong control over their children's mating decisions (Apostolou, in press). That is, in almost all societies in the sample the primary mode of marriage was arranged, with children having little space to exercise mate choice. In addition, most of the decision making power is enjoyed by fathers who dominate marriage arrangements. Although we lack historical evidence from ancestral foraging societies (since these societies had not invented writing), comparisons of the patterns of mating of historical agropastoral societies with the patterns of mating of modern foraging ones demonstrates that parental control over mating had been more prevalent in the former.

This hints that parental control over mating should had been stronger in ancestral agropastoral societies than in ancestral foraging societies.

The evidence from historical societies is important for another reason namely, that it reflects the patterns of mating in the most recent period of human evolution. That is, by virtue of being the most recent, these patterns are likely to have been consequential in human evolution. This is due to the fact that the transition to post-industrialism is a very recent phenomenon so, there has not been enough evolutionary time to reverse any consequences of the agropastoral revolution in shaping the human mind.

To summarize, in this chapter I argued that parents often disagree with the mating decisions of their children. Accordingly, they attempt to control the mate choices of their daughters and sons and for this purpose they use social structures that have evolved to serve different functions. In particular, by manipulating inheritance rights and the resources needed for the payment of the bridewealth, fathers exercise considerable power over the mate choices of their children and primarily over their sons. Social institutions that augment parental power over mating are more prevalent in pre-industrial societies which base their subsistence on agropastoralism than on hunting and gathering, which mandates that parental control over mating is stronger in the former than in the latter societies. Finally, this indicates that the agropastoral revolution 10,000 years ago had increased the influence that parents exercise over their children's mate choices.

REFERENCES

Apostolou, M. (2007a). Elements of parental choice: the evolution of parental preferences in relation to in-law selection. *Evolutionary Psychology, 5,* 70-83.

Apostolou, M. (2007b). Sexual selection under parental choice: the role of parents in the evolution of human mating. *Evolution and Human Behavior, 28,* 403-409.

Apostolou, M. (2008a). Bridewealth and brideservice as instruments of parental choice. *Journal of Social, Evolutionary, and Cultural Psychology, 2,* 89-102.

Apostolou, M. (2008b). Parent-offspring conflict over mating: The case of beauty. *Evolutionary Psychology, 6,* 303-315.

Apostolou, M. (2008b). Parent-offspring conflict over mating: The case of family background. *Evolutionary Psychology, 6,* 456-468.

Apostolou, M. (2010a). Bridewealth as an instrument of male parental control over mating: Evidence from the Standard Cross-Cultural Sample. *Journal of Evolutionary Psychology, 8,* 205-216.

Apostolou, M. (2010b). Parental choice: What parents want in a son-in-law and a daughter-in-law across 67 pre-industrial societies. *British Journal of Psychology, 101,* 695-704.

Apostolou, M. (2010c). Sexual selection under parental choice in agropastoral societies. *Evolution and Human Behavior, 31,* 39-47.

Apostolou, M. (2011a). In-law preferences in a post-industrial society: What parents want in an in-law and how this differs from what their children want in a spouse. *Family Science, 2,* 186-195.

Apostolou, M. (2011b). Inheritance as an instrument of parental control over mating. *Journal of Social and Personal Relationships*, *28*, 374-382.

Apostolou, M. (2011c). Parent-offspring conflict over mating: Testing the tradeoffs hypothesis. *Evolutionary Psychology*, *9*, 470-495.

Apostolou, M. (in press). Sexual selection under parental choice: Evidence from sixteen historical societies. *Evolutionary Psychology*.

Borgerhoff Mulder, M. (1988). The relevance of the polygyny threshold model to humans. In C. Mascie-Taylor & A. Boyce (Eds.), *Human mating patterns* (pp. 209-230). Cambridge: Cambridge University Press.

Buss, D. M. (2003). *The evolution of desire: Strategies of human mating* (2nd ed.). New York: Basic Books.

Buss, D. M., Abbott, M., Angleitner, A., Asherian, A., Biaggio, A., and 45 other co-authors (1990). International preferences in selecting mates: A study of 37 cultures. *Journal of Cross-Cultural Psychology*, *21*, 5-47.

Buunk, A. P., & Castro Solano, A. (2010). Conflicting preferences of parents and offspring over criteria for a mate: A study in Argentina. *Journal of Family Psychology, 24*, 391-399.

Buunk, A. P., Park, J. H. & Dubbs, S. L. (2008). Parent-offspring conflict in mate preferences. *Review of General Psychology*, *12*, 47-62.

Dunbar, R. I. M. (1992). Neocortex size as a constraint on group size in primates. *Journal of Human Evolution, 22,* 469–493.

Dunbar, R. I. M. (1993). Coevolution of neocortical size, group size and language in humans. *Behavioral and Brain Sciences, 16*, 681–735.

Kressel, G. M. (1977). Bride-price reconsidered. *Current Anthropology*, *18*, 441-458.

Gangestad, S. W., & Simpson, J. A. (2000). The evolution of human mating: Trade-offs and strategic pluralism. *Behavioral and Brain Sciences, 23,* 573–644.

Gangestad, S. W., Thornhill, R., & Yeo, R. A. (1994). Facial attractiveness, developmental stability, and fluctuating asymmetry. *Ethology and Sociobiology*, *15*, 73-85.

Goldschmidt, W. (1974). The economics of brideprice among the Sebei and in East Africa. *Ethnology*, *13*, 311-331.

Gruenbaum, E. (2001). *The female circumcision controversy*. Philadelphia: University of Pennsylvania Press.

Hartung, J. (1976). On natural selection and the inheritance of wealth. *Current Anthropology*, *17*, 607–613.

Hartung, J. (1982). Polygyny and inheritance of wealth. *Current Anthropology*, *23*, 1–12.

Hynie, M., Lalonde, R. N., & Lee, N. (2006). Parent–child value transmission among Chinese immigrants to North America: The case of traditional mate preferences. *Cultural Diversity and Ethnic Minority Psychology*, *12*, 230–244.

Murdock, G. P. (1949). *Social structure*. New York: Free Press.

Murdock, G. P. (1967). *Ethnographic Atlas*. Pittsburgh: University of Pittsburgh Press.

Murdock, G. P. (1971). Anthropology's Mythology. *Proceedings of the Royal Anthropological Institute of Great Britain and Ireland, 1971*, 17-24.

Murdock, G. P. (1981). *Atlas of World Cultures*. Pittsburgh: University of Pittsburgh Press.

Ogbu, J. U. (1978). African bridewealth and women's status. *American Ethnologist*, *5*, 241-262.

Perilloux, C., Fleischman, D. S., & Buss, D. M. (2011). Meet the parents: Parent-offspring convergence and divergence in mate preferences. *Personality and Individual Differences, 50*, 253-258.

Schlegel, A. & Eloul, R. (1988). Marriage transactions: labor, property, status. *American Anthropologists*, N.S., 90, 291-309.

Schneider, H. K. (1979). *Livestock and equality in East Africa*. Bloomington: Indiana University Press.

Spiro, M. E. (1975). Marriage payments: a paradigm from the Burmese perspective. *Journal of Anthropological Research*, 31, 89-115.

Sprecher, S., & Chandak, R. (1992). Attitudes about arranged marriages and dating among men and women from India. *Free Inquiry in Creative Sociology, 20*, 1-11.

Toubia, N. (1993). *Female genital mutilation: a call for global action* (2nd ed.).New York: Women, Inc.

Trivers, R. (1974). Parent offspring conflict. *American Zoologist, 24*, 249-264.

Whyte, M. K. (1978). *The status of women in preindustrial societies*. Princeton, NJ: Princeton University Press.

Yu, D., Proulx, S. R., & Shepard, G. H. (2007). Masculinity, culture and the Paradox of the Lek. In V. Swami & A. Furnham (Eds.), *Body beautiful: Evolutionary and sociocultural perspectives* (pp. 88-107). London: Palgrave Macmillan.

In: Parenting
Editors: Peter Barberis and Stelios Petrakis

ISBN: 978-1-62257-881-8
© 2013 Nova Science Publishers, Inc.

Chapter 8

GAY AND LESBIAN PARENTING: THE NOT-SO-UGLY TRUTH

Shea Golding, Joseph Pastuszak and Cliff McKinney
Mississippi State University, MS, US

ABSTRACT

Controversy surrounds lesbian and gay parenting. Some believe gay and lesbian parenting to be detrimental to children's development. A child with gay or lesbian parents may be wrongly believed to have impairments in psychological, social, and gender functioning as a result of their parents' sexual orientation. Specifically, gay and lesbian parents are thought to influence their children's sexual orientation; that is, gay and lesbian parents raise children who also are gay and lesbian. These societal views influence public policy, court rulings, and adoption regulation. Discrimination in these settings acts as a major challenge to gay and lesbian individuals who want to be parents and also as a barrier to their children. Gay fathers are compared with their heterosexual counterparts, just as lesbian mothers are compared with theirs. Similarities and differences also are evaluated between gay and lesbian parent dyads and heterosexual parent dyads. Gay and lesbian parents often parent just as, if not more, effectively than heterosexual parents. Research shows no evidence that gay and lesbian parenting is associated with any additional negative characteristics when compared to heterosexual parenting. Following a discussion of gender differences and barriers, recommendations and future directions related to gay and lesbian parenting are considered.

INTRODUCTION

A growing body of literature surrounds the controversy of lesbian and gay (LG) couples rearing children. LG parenting is a reality that society, as a whole, is straining to understand and accept. The concept of family is ever-evolving, and family structure now includes single parent, step, and blended families, grandparents as legal guardians, and *de facto* same-sex or heterosexual couples (McCann and Delmonte, 2005). Various misconceptions exist about negative results associated with LG parenting which creates challenges for LG individuals that heterosexual men and women do not encounter. For example, LG parents are wrongly thought to be detrimental to the development of children in their care. Specifically, a child with LG parents is wrongly thought to have impairments in psychological, social, and gender functioning as a result of their parents' sexual orientation. Further, some believe these parents may also influence the child's sexual orientation or gender-appropriate characteristics (Tasker, 2005). It also is feared that children of LG parents will be ostracized or teased (Golombok et al., 2003). In part because of these fears, LG parents have been ruled against by courts for the custody of their children on the grounds that they are unfit parents. Reviewing literature on the topic of LG parenting is important to developing a clear and accurate view of the topic. Given the copious amount of misconceptions existing, attributes of LG parents will be discussed, followed by a comparison of LG parents and heterosexual parents and a discussion of barriers LG parents encounter, and, finally, recommendations and future directions will be provided. Overall, research points toward the idea that LG parents are equally likely to produce fit environments for their children.

LG PARENTING

Gay and lesbian parenting has been researched for some time now. However, it initially began to investigate the assumption that lesbian mothers were doing a disservice to their children by taking them away from their heterosexual fathers in divorce cases (Clarke, 2002). This assumption that LG parents are damaging to their children has driven and shaped research as a combative force against heterosexist views. Although there is much research on the parenting characteristics of lesbian mothers, far less is available on gay fathers (McCann and Delmonte, 2005).

It is not abnormal for gay men or lesbian women to desire children. After all, procreation is a strong human motivation, no matter sexual orientation of the would-be or soon-to-be parent. These reasons often include the desire to actively nurture and rear a child and the enjoyment of the presence of children (Bigner and Jacobsen, 1989b). With that in mind, many gay men and lesbian women are parents. According to United States national survey information, 1 in 5 lesbian women and 1 in 10 gay men identified themselves as a parent (Bryant and Demian, 1994). Some of these parents conceived children in the context of a previous or current heterosexual relationship (Patterson, 2006). Children born in a gay or lesbian family are conceived from a variety of methods which require great planning. Lesbian women often utilize self-insemination from private donors or sperm banks. For gay men, it can be more difficult such as arranging surrogacy (Martin, 1993). Both gay men and lesbian women adopt or foster children despite the many limitations (Mallon, 2007).

The stigma against LG parents has very real consequences for same-sex households. According to Bandura (1989), if one perceives themselves to be capable of performing a difficult task, they will put forth great effort to meet difficulties, and thus, will be more skilled in that task. This idea of self-efficacy can be applied to parenting. Stigma against LG parents leads to these parents further preparing for parenthood, and thus becoming more skilled at it (Goldberg and Smith, 2009). Additionally, parents who report greater confidence about their parenting abilities report greater parenting satisfaction (Hudson, Elek and Fleck, 2001). However, this stigma also appears to work against gay and lesbian parents, as there are different stressors on gay and lesbian parents (e.g., social stigma). For example, Tornello, Farr, and Patterson (2011) found that when gay men had less social support and were more sensitive to societal stigma, they reported more parenting stress. Higher levels of parenting stress leads to greater levels of psychological difficulties for both parents and children (Deater-Decker, 2004). In line with this, LG parents feel pressured to be competent in their parenting skills because they feel like they are under harsher scrutiny than other parents (McCann and Delmonte, 2005).

The stigma that gay and lesbian parents face has several incorrect assumptions. First, a child in the household headed by a gay or lesbian parent is more likely to be gay or lesbian him/herself. Second is the assumption that same-sex parents cannot socialize their children with opposite sex features (i.e., masculine or feminine features). Third is that gay fathers are unable to be warm and caring to children as they are not mothers. Lastly, gay and lesbian parents are simply inferior.

To examine whether or not children of same-sex households are more likely to be gay or lesbian, Tasker and Golombok (1997) in the United Kingdom and Bailey and Dawood (1998) in the United States conducted longitudinal studies of children raised in same-sex households. These studies revealed that children from same-sex households are no more likely to be gay or lesbian than children from heterosexual households. In fact, children from same-sex households are more aware and comfortable than others about their own sexual orientation and the sexual orientation of others (McCann and Delmonte, 2005).

A concern has been whether lesbian women can socialize boys with masculine features and whether gay men can socialize girls with feminine features. In contrast, this has been less of a concern with single heterosexual mothers and fathers (McCann and Delmonte, 2005). However, it appears gay men and lesbian women do not diminish the masculine or feminine features of their children. For example, MacCallum and Golombok (2004) note that children from fatherless households have normal levels of masculine features but also more feminine features. According to Golombok et al. (2003), many of those features are related to an individual's sex hormones, and what is not is observed from others outside the family.

Several studies have investigated the parental practices of gay men. According to Lambert (2005), gay fathers are no different from heterosexual fathers in intimacy or involvement with their children. Instead, they exhibit higher levels of warmth and responsiveness, as well as control and set more appropriate limitations in their parenting practices. Further, gay fathers, compared to heterosexual fathers, are more concerned about providing positive parenting than simply financially supporting their families (Scallen, 1981). Gay fathers focus on providing stable homes and positive relationships (Turner, Scadden and Harris, 1990), and household and child-care tasks are shared and not strongly defined by gender roles (McPherson, 1994).

According to Vanfraussen, Ponjaert-Kristoffersen, and Brewaeys (2003), lesbian mothers on the other hand express high levels of warmth, are more involved, and have higher quality of interactions than other mothers. Lesbian mothers often are better at discovering critical issues with their child and provide effective solutions to them. Further, they are more aware of necessary skills for effective parenting than heterosexual parents. Due to the stigma placed on them, lesbian mothers tend to stress tolerance for diversity (Eldridge and Barrett, 2003; Lambert, 2005). Lastly, lesbian mothers report less physical punishment for their children and engage more frequently in imaginative and domestic play with their children than non-lesbian mothers (Golombok et al., 2003).

LG Parenting Compared to Heterosexual Parenting

The stigma and controversy surrounding gay and lesbian parenting has fueled research to investigate whether gay men and lesbians truly are a aversive forces on their children. Initially, research focused on gay and lesbian parents who had children in a previous heterosexual relationship that ended in divorce. The initial data indicated that gay and lesbian parenting was detrimental to the development of their children (Patterson, 2006). However, other research suggests that gay and lesbian parents are similar and often times superior parents compared to heterosexual parents (Negy and McKinney, 2006). Within these contexts, children of gay and lesbian parents have similar outcomes to those of children of divorce (Patterson, 2006). Therefore, it is important to compare gay and lesbian parenting within the context of family structure.

Divorced Parents

The literature strongly supports that divorced lesbian mothers are no different than single divorced heterosexual mothers in their parenting characteristics (Hoeffer, 1981; Kirkpatrick, Smith, and Roy, 1981; Golombok, Spencer, and Rutter, 1983; Green, Mandel, Hotvedt, Gray, and Smith, 1986). The only exception is that they are more likely to maintain contact with their child's father. This relationship dynamic may lead to antagonism, competitiveness, and conflict between parents (Hare and Richards, 1993). However, this period may be more stressful for lesbian mothers, as they are likely transitioning into a new sexual identity as well as undergoing changes in the home (Lynch, 2000). Further, the timing of "coming out" must be handled carefully, as there is a risk of losing custody of the child due to prejudice and discrimination (Fredriksen-Goldsen and Erera, 2003). Golombok and colleagues (1983) interviewed lesbian and heterosexual mothers who had integrated a partner into their household after dissolution of a previous heterosexual relationship. Sons and daughters of lesbian mothers reported more positive relationships with their mothers' new partner compared to children of heterosexual mothers (Tasker and Golombok, 1997). This may be due to the differing roles of the mother's partner. For example, in same-sex couples, the mother's girlfriend may take the role of a second mother, a big sister, or a close family friend. However, children of heterosexual families saw their stepfather attempting to be their "new dad" (Tasker, 2005). Other studies have compared divorced lesbian mothers with divorced heterosexual mothers on the criteria of psychological adjustment (e.g., self-esteem, emotional distress, mental health).

According to several studies, no difference exists between children from divorced lesbian mothers and divorced heterosexual mothers (Golombok, Spencer, and Rutter, 1983; Green et al., 1986; Kirkpatrick et al., 1981). The same can be said when the children's teachers rate their psychological adjustment (Golombok et al., 1983). When examining intelligence levels, as measured by the typical standardized tests, no difference is found between children from divorced lesbian homes and divorced heterosexual mother homes (Green et al., 1986). These children also are no more likely to have a psychological disorder (Kirkpatrick et al., 1981).

A study by Gershon, Tschann, and Jemerin (1999) found that adolescents of divorced lesbian families are more likely to have lower self-esteem only if they perceive higher levels of stigma, lower social support, and have poor coping skills. Otherwise, these children are no different than their peers. According to Golombok et al. (1983), children who were raised in divorced lesbian households have no difference in the quality of their relationships compared to those raised in divorced heterosexual households. They are no more likely to be teased in general (Tasker and Golombok, 1995). The relationship between divorced gay parents and their heterosexual counterparts is much more convoluted. The main reason for this, according to Tasker (2005), is that less research on gay parents exists compared to lesbian parents. In particular, self-esteem and psychological health of children from divorced gay households have not been systematically evaluated. That said, according to Bigner and Jacobson (1989a), divorced gay parents are similar to divorced heterosexual parents in nearly every way, including their level of involvement with their children. However, differences do exist. For example, a study by Crosbie-Burnett and Helbrecht (1993) found that satisfaction of the father, the child, and the father's gay partner often hinges on the family's acceptance of the father's partner.

Planned LG Parents

Lesbian mothers and gay fathers who planned and arranged to be parents within their same sex relationships are examined in comparison to heterosexual parents. Lesbian mothers reported less use of punitive discipline and engaging their children in imaginative play more often than heterosexual mothers (Golombok et al., 2003). Children of planned lesbian parents also report a greater perceived availability and involvement and a closer relationship with their mothers; however, lesbian mothers were more likely to report rigorous disagreements with their children than heterosexual couples (Golombok, Tasker, and Murray, 1997; MacCallum and Golombok, 2004). Lesbian mothers share the responsibilities of parenting more equally than heterosexual couples; that is, the non-biological mother is more likely to be involved in parenting than fathers typically are in heterosexual parent dyads (Chan, Brooks, Raboy, and Patterson, 1998; Vanfraussen, Ponjaert-Kristoffersen, and Brewaeys, 2003).

Some believe that having LG parents will negatively impact children's psychological adjustment. However, parenting stress, relationship dissatisfaction, and parental conflict have been found to be monumental to children's adjustment, rather than parental sexual orientation or family structure (Chan, Raboy, and Patterson, 1998). Although children of single lesbian mothers or lesbian couples reported negative responses to stress more often than children of heterosexual parents, children in lesbian-led families described higher levels of contentment and joy than those of heterosexual parents (Patterson, 1994). No differences have been found regarding self-esteem levels or overall psychological adjustment (Flaks, Ficher, Masterpasqua, and Joseph, 1995; Golombok, Tasker, and Murray, 1997).

Research examining planned gay fathers is very much in its infant stage and is less available than that of lesbian mothers. Planned gay fathers share parenting responsibility more evenly than heterosexual parents (McPherson, 1994). A New Zealand study involving children with gay fathers taking part in kinship arrangements (i.e., the children often did not live with their fathers, and the fathers worked with the children's mother on parenting decisions) found no difference in parental concern and emotional involvement or child wellbeing when compared to heterosexual-led families (Bos, 2010). However, Bos (2010) noted that gay fathers reported feeling less competent in their roles as parents than heterosexual fathers. Research regarding gay fathers is an area that must continue to expand as time goes on.

BARRIERS AND CHALLENGES

Lesbians and gay men, like heterosexual men and women, desire to be parents. Unfortunately, pursuing that desire is not as straightforward for LG individuals as it typically is for heterosexual individuals. Problems that exist in society, such as heterosexism and homophobia, influence the opportunities available to potential LG parents. Social and legal structures are often tailored to the belief that heterosexuality is the established norm for sexuality, an assumption known as hetero-normativity (Perlesz et al., 2006). Marriage and adoption laws were originally made as exclusive rights to certain individuals and are slowly expanding. Contrary to current perceptions, Matthews and Cramer (2006) report that only three states (i.e., Florida, Mississippi, and Utah) prohibit LG adoption, where Mississippi's law explicitly outlaws LG couples from adoption and Utah's law disqualifies all unmarried couples. As gay marriage is not legal in many states, the added challenge of not having a legal marriage or partnership also contributes to barriers to becoming parents. However, the lack of state guidelines banning LG adoptions unfortunately does not translate into challenge-free LG adoptions in the other 47 states. The increased challenges LG individuals face in regard to becoming parents as well as becoming husbands and wives infringes upon the right to pursue happiness—a right guaranteed to *all* citizens. With empirical evidence suggesting no harm in extending these rights to LG individuals and no basis for many stereotypes, it is disconcerting that so many societal labels and legal exclusions remain in place today.

Research suggesting that LG parents do not have the negative influences on children that many wrongly fear is unfortunately ignored by many in favor of moral beliefs and religion. Politicians, likely fearing the loss of more conservative support, fail to fight for the rights of LG individuals. Without equal rights, the LG community faces barriers to pursuing dreams that most people possess and heterosexual individuals are easily able to follow.

Society's views on homosexuality influence the options for those LG individuals who do choose to pursue their desires to be parents. The idea that children of LG parents endure bullying and teasing because of their parents' sexuality is a challenge for LG individuals who wish to be parents. Not only must these individuals consider whether or not it is fair to place a child in the position to suffer extra teasing, some people use this possibility as an argument against LG parenting. In fact, a common objection to granting LG parents custody is the fear that their children will be teased and ostracized by others (Falk, 1989). However, as previously stated, this fear is unfounded; children of LG parents are not more likely to be bullied (Tasker and Golombok, 1995).

The method by which LG couples have children can be a challenge in and of itself. Individuals unable to become pregnant themselves typically have options such as in vitro fertilization, artificial insemination, and adoption. Many adoption agencies, however, have an implicit rule that Caucasian middle to upper class married couples be favored for adopting the preferred children; therefore, children deemed less desirable (e.g., children with special needs or disabilities) go to unmarried couples, single people, and LG parents who are viewed as less favorable themselves (Matthews and Cramer, 2006). The irony must be noted when the unfounded fear that LG parents are unsuitable results in pairing children who need the most skilled parenting with LG individuals (Martin, 1993). The treatment of LG parents as last resorts is not empirically supported, does an injustice to children who deserve parents, and fails to respect the rights of LG individuals as citizens. Because unions and commitments between LG individuals often are not recognized as legal, LG couples experience challenges to their legal rights regarding their children (Oswald, 2002). Same-sex partners lack legal support. Based on a study that surveyed adoption agencies, about 1.6 percent of adoptions for a two-year period involved an LG individual; however, if individuals who did not self-identify sexual orientation but were suspected to be LG were included, this value increases to 2.9 percent (Brodzinsky, Patterson, and Vaziri, 2002). Frequency of LG individuals successfully adopting and fostering children are most likely low estimates because some LG individuals withhold their sexuality to seem more favorable to agencies (Brodzinsky, Patterson, and Vaziri, 2002). Thus, some LG couples encounter problems when the non-legal guardian would like to include the child on his/her insurance or when medical decisions need to be made, as just a couple examples.

RECOMMENDATIONS AND FUTURE DIRECTIONS

Recommendations to LG Parents

LG parents face obstacles that heterosexual parents do not encounter. Taking measures to protect against those obstacles is important for the well-being of both the LG parents and their children.

A strong social support system is very important to LG parents as they work through challenges surrounding biases and stereotypes. While children of LG parents are at no additional risk for teasing than their peers in general (Tasker and Golombok, 1995), the subject matter for bullying (i.e., parents' sexuality) is different for children of LG parents. The truth of the matter is that children will be teased for something, and having LG parents unfortunately can be an "easy target" for bullying. The potential for bullying related to parents' sexuality is a real danger for children of LG parents, but there are factors that can help protect against it. Having parents who are forthcoming about their sexuality, an available support system, and knowing other children with an LG parent act as buffers against homophobic attitudes (Fairtlough, 2008). All parents should view psychological well-being as an important goal, minimizing stress and maladjustment when possible and coping appropriately when stressors cannot be eliminated.

Specifically, LG parents should work through their own distress related to being LG individuals in order to bolster the coping abilities of their children. The ability to cope with homophobia and the fact that the majority of aspects of life center on heterosexuals is a more important factor to assess than sexuality in evaluating LG individuals wishing to adopt children (Mallon, 2007).

Adoption laws call for young people to be integrated into caring and loving families; thus, discouraging or denying LG individuals wishing to become parents directly conflicts with these laws.

Recommendations for Society

To provide sufficient homes for and act in the best interest of children, society needs to join forces to fight for LG rights and protest discrimination against LG individuals (Ryan, Pearlmutter, and Groza, 2004). Many options exist for people interested in being advocates for LG individuals, but it is very important for society to support expanding the rights of this community. Modifications to laws need to be implemented to secure the legal rights of LG parents. Exclusion from rights to marry or form civil unions in some locations not only infringes upon LG individuals' civil liberties, but it also contributes to the challenge of becoming and being effective parents. LG individuals and unmarried individuals can be prejudiced against in regard to adoption policies, a double whammy of discrimination for unmarried LG individuals. Specifically, LG parents deserve legal rights to handle situations requiring legal connections with their children, such as school or insurance. The differential treatment these individuals face in many situations, particularly legal rights, is unsupported, unfounded discrimination. Societal movements (e.g., Straight for Equality; Parents, Family and Friends of Lesbians and Gays) can increase the likelihood of the expansion of rights to LG individuals. Members of society, in general, should strive to understand the truth about LG parenting. The next step should be to improve knowledge about the misconceptions surrounding LG parenting within communities, schools, and families. Advertising campaigns, such as *ThinkB4YouSpeak* which encourages others to consider ramifications before saying things are "so gay," are public statements that work to decrease the amount of derogatory comments and teasing in society over time. Diversity programs in communities and schools can show program members equality and that sexuality does not define a person. Schools are often unprepared to support children from families with LG parents (Ryan and Martin, 2000). This lack of preparation is discouraging and unnecessary. With proper education, teachers and students alike could more appropriately support LG parents and their children. Fears similar to those about children being in environments with peers from LG families exist related to the idea of mainstreaming special education children in classroom settings; however, children of all abilities can learn greater respect from this diversity (Boyle, Scriven, Durning, and Downes, 2011). Increased tolerance and a better understanding of differences in people can be garnered from mainstreamed or inclusive classrooms (Boyle et al., 2011). Similar results will likely be found when research is conducted examining diversity related to sexual orientation in children.

Hetero-normativity, the assumption that heterosexuality is the natural and normal form of sexuality, is a concept that should be minimized; specifically, parents ought not to over-emphasize heterosexuality because it can make the LG community invisible to children (Martin, 2009). All parents should begin talking to their children about the hetero-normativity in society beginning at an early age so that those children can understand the role it plays and begin to accept and comprehend gay and lesbian individuals (Martin, 2009). This practice not only builds the potential for a more accepting generation, but it also could lead to a better environment within the home in the case of children who are LG individuals. The coming out process varies for all LG individuals, particularly between different genders and dyads (Riley, 2010). Coming out is risky because of potential negative responses. A lesbian or gay male must consider each relationship in his/her life and determine whether and how to disclose (Matthews, 2007). LG individuals are twice more likely to disclose their sexuality to their mothers than their fathers (Savin-Williams, 1998). While family and friends can react with shock, denial, or anger as negative reactions or acceptance in positive and ideal cases, the coming out process can result in more social support, more self-acceptance, and also additional distress—potentially related to increased discrimination (Perez and Amadio, 2004).

CONCLUSION

Society should continue to advance and become more accepting of the LG community. After individuals learn to accept things they may not understand, societal acceptance and change can follow. With the policy of separation of church and state, politicians' and voters' religious views should not influence legal decisions as they do currently. However, legal policies and rights can only follow suit when politicians no longer feel the need to appease individuals who oppose LG rights. If individuals opposing LG rights make up a very small minority, policy makers who do believe in and support the rights of the LG community can voice their opinions and push for fair legislation. Activists should insist on political leaders who will speak out for LG rights and vote for legislation and policies, accordingly. Citizens should demand equality and justice *for all* and leaders who will represent those values.

Research challenging the stereotypes and misconceptions about the LG community is necessary to change beliefs. However, greater acceptance will likely lend itself to better research—a circular effect. Once LG individuals begin receiving increased legal rights and acceptance, additional and more informative research can be conducted about LG parenting. Research regarding gay fathers is less prevalent than on lesbian mothers likely because of fear of disclosure (Lambert, 2005). Future research should begin to focus more on gay parenting in addition to lesbian parenting to develop a clearer, more accurate picture of LG parenting. Additional gaps found in the literature that future research should address include investigating differences and similarities in discipline practices between heterosexual and LG parents as well as how LG parenting is viewed internationally and across cultures. Further, parenting research should become more sensitive to situations with LG parents, even if that is not a variable that is being evaluated in a particular study. This practice will increase the availability of data regarding LG parenting. Current LG research focuses on mostly affluent Caucasian LG individuals; thus, future research should endeavor to examine racial, social, and other cultural differences in LG parenting practices. Research regarding interactions between children from heterosexual families and those from LG families can examine the fears some hold and assess the potential benefits from diversity in relationships.

Overall, research clearly demonstrates that LG parenting is at least as good as heterosexual parenting. Given this, methods to overcoming social and political barriers and challenges must be developed so that these individuals are allowed the same civil liberties as others.

REFERENCES

Bailey, J. M., and Dawood, K. (1998). Behavioral genetics, sexual orientation, and family. In C. J. Patterson and A. R. D'Augelli (Eds.) Lesbian, gay, and bisexual identities in families: Psychological perspectives. New York: Oxford University Press.

Bandura, A. (1989). Regulation of cognitive processes through perceived self-efficacy. *Developmental Psychology*, 25(4), 729–735.

Bigner, J. J., and Jacobsen, R. B. (1989a). Parenting behaviors of homosexual and heterosexual fathers. *Journal of Homosexuality*, 18(1-2), 173-186.

Bigner, J. J., and Jacobsen, R. B. (1989b). The value of children to gay and heterosexual fathers. In F. W. Bozett (Ed.), Homosexuality and the family. New York: Harrington Press.

Bos, H. W. (2010). Planned gay father families in kinship arrangements. Australian And New Zealand Journal Of Family Therapy, 31(4), 356-371. doi:10.1 75/anft.31.4.356

Boyle, C., Scriven, B., Durning, S., and Downes, C. (2011). Facilitating the learning of all students: The 'professional positive' of inclusive practice in Australian primary schools. *Support for Learning*, 26(2), 72-78. doi:10.1111/j.1467-9604.2011.01480.x

Brodzinsky, D. M., Patterson, C. J., and Vaziri, M. (2002). Adoption agency perspectives on lesbian and gay prospective parents: A national study.*Adoption Quarterly*, 5(3), 5-23. doi:10.1300/J145v05n03_02

Bryant, A. S., and Demian (1994). Relationship characteristics of American gay and lesbian couples: Findings from a national survey. *Journal of Gay and Lesbian Social Services*, 1(2), 101-117.

Chan, R. W., Brooks, R. C., Raboy, B., and Patterson, C. J. (1998). Division of labor among lesbian and heterosexual parents: Associations with children's adjustment. *Journal of Family Psychology*, 12, 402-419.

Chan, R. W., Raboy, B., and Patterson, C. J. (1998). Psychosocial adjustment among children conceived via donor insemination by lesbian and heterosexual mothers. *Child Development*, 69, 443-457.

Clarke, V. (2002). Sameness and difference in research on lesbian parenting. *Journal of Community and Applied Social Psychology*, 12, 210-222.

Crosbie-Burnett, M., and Helbrecht, L. (1993). A descriptive empirical study of gay male stepfamilies. *Family Relations*, 42(3), 256-262.

Deater-Decker, K. (2004). Parenting stress. New Haven, CT: Yale University Press.

Eldridge, N. S., and Barrett, S. E. (2003). Biracial lesbian-led adoptive families. In L. B. Silverstein and T. J. Goodrich (Eds.), Feminist family therapy: Empowerment in social context (pp. 307-318). Washington, DC: American Psychological Association.

Fairtlough, A. (2008). Growing up with a lesbian or gay parent: Young people's perspectives. *Health and Social Care in the Community*, 16, 521-528.

Falk, P. J. (1989). Lesbian mothers: Psychosocial assumptions in family law. *American Psychologist*, 44, 941-947.

Flaks, D. K., Ficher, I, Masterpasqua, F., and Joseph, G. (1995). Lesbians choosing motherhood: A comparative study of lesbian and heterosexual parents and their children. *Developmental Psychology*, 31, 105-114.

Fredriksen-Goldsen, K. I., and Erera, P. I. (2003). Lesbian-Headed Stepfamilies. *Journal Of Human Behavior In The Social Environment*, 8(2-3), 171-187. doi:10.1300/J137v08n02_11

Gershon, T. D., Tschann, J. M., and Jemerin, J. M. (1999). Stigmatization, self-esteem, and coping among the adolescent children of lesbian mothers. *Journal of Adolescent Health*, 24(6), 437-445.

Goldberg, A. E., and Smith, J. Z. (2009). Perceived parenting skill across the transition to adoptive parenthood among lesbian, gay, and heterosexual couples. *Journal of Family Psychology*, 23(6), 861-870.

Golombok, S., Perry, B., Burston, A., Murray, C., Mooney-somers, J., Stevens, M., and Golding, J. (2003). Children with lesbian parents: A community study. *Developmental Psychology*, 39, 20-33.

Golombok, S., Spencer, A., and Rutter, M. (1983). Children in lesbian and single parent households: Psychosexual and psychiatric appraisal. *Journal of Child Psychology and Psychiatry*, 24(4), 551-572.

Golombok, S., Tasker, F., and Murray, C. (1997). Children raised in fatherless families from infancy: Family relationships and the socioemotional development of children of lesbian and single heterosexual mothers. *Journal of Child Psychology and Psychiatry*, 38, 783-791.

Green, R., Mandel, J. B., Hotvedt, M. E., Gray, J., Smith, L. (1986). Lesbian mothers and their children: A comparison with solo parent heterosexual mothers and their children. *Archives of Sexual Behavior*, 15(2), 167-184.

Hare, J., and Richards, L. (1993). Children raised by lesbian couples: Does context of birth affect father and partner involvement?. Family Relations: *An Interdisciplinary Journal Of Applied Family Studies*, 42(3), 249-255. doi:10.2307/585553

Hoeffer, B. (1981). Children's acquisition of sex-role behavior in lesbian-mother families. *The American Journal of Orthopsychiatry*, 51(3), 536-544.

Hudson, D. B., Elek, S. M., and Fleck, M. O. (2001). First-time mothers' and fathers' transition to parenthood: Infant care, self-efficacy, parenting satisfaction, and infant sex. *Issues in Comprehensive Pediatric Nursing*, 24, 31-43.

Kirkpatrick, M., Smith, C., and Roy, R. (1981). Lesbian mothers and their children: A comparative survey. *The American Journal of Orthopsychiatry*, 51(3), 545-551.

Lambert, S. (2005). Gay and lesbian families: What we know and where to go from here. *The Family Journal: Counseling and Therapy for Couples and Families,* 13, 43-51.

Lynch, J. M. (2000). Considerations of family structure and gender composition: The lesbian and gay stepfamily. *Journal Of Homosexuality*, 40(2), 81-95. doi:10.1300/J082v40n02_06

MacCallum, F., Golombok, S. (2004). Children raised in fatherless families from infancy: A Follow-up of children of lesbian and single heterosexual mothers at early adolescence. *Journal of Child Psychology and Psychiatry*, 45, 1407-1419.

Mallon, G. (2007). Assessing lesbian and gay prospective foster and adoptive families: A focus on the home study process. *Child Welfare Journal*, 86, 67-86.

Martin, A. (1993). The gay and lesbian parenting handbook: Creating and raising our families. New York: Harper Perennial.

Martin, K. A. (2009). Normalizing heterosexuality: Mothers' assumptions, talk, and strategies with young children. *American Sociological Review*, 74, 190-207.

Matthews, C. R. (2007). Affirmative lesbian, gay, and bisexual counseling with all clients. In K. J. Bieschke, R. M. Perez, and K. A. DeBord (Eds.), Handbook of counseling and psychotherapy with lesbian, gay, bisexual, and transgender clients (2nd ed., pp. 201-219). Washington, DC: American Psychological Association.

Matthews, J., and Cramer, E. (2006). Envisaging the adoption process to strengthen gay- and lesbian- headed families: Recommendations for adoption professionals. *Child Welfare Journal*, 85, 317-340.

McCann, D., and Delmonte, H. (2005). Lesbian and gay parenting: Babes in arms or babes in the woods? *Journal of Sexual and Relationship Therapy,* 20(3), 333-347.

McPherson, D. (1994). Gay parenting couples: Parenting arrangements, arrangement satisfaction, and relationship satisfaction. Dissertation Abstracts International, 54.

Negy, C., and McKinney, C. (2006). Application of Feminist Therapy: Promoting Resiliency Among Lesbian and Gay Families. *Journal Of Feminist Family Therapy: An International Forum,* 18(1-2), 67-83. doi:10.1300/J086v18n01_03

Oswald, R. F. (2002). Resilience within family networks of lesbians and gay men: Intentionality and redefinition. *Journal of Marriage and Family*, 64, 374-383.

Patterson, C. J. (1994). Children of the lesbian baby boom: Behavioral adjustment, self-concepts, and sex role identity. In B. Greene, G. M. Herek, B. Greene, G. M. Herek (Eds.), Lesbian and gay psychology: Theory, research, and clinical applications(pp. 156-175). Thousand Oaks, CA US: Sage Publications, Inc.

Patterson, C. J. (2006). Children of lesbian and gay parents. *Current Directions in Psychological Science,* 15(5), 241-244.

Perez, R. M., and Amadio, D. M. (2004). Affirmative counseling and psychotherapy with lesbian, gay, and bisexual clients. In C. Negy (Ed.), Cross-cultural psychotherapy: Toward a critical understanding of diverse clients (pp. 301-325). Reno, NV: Bent Tree Press.

Perlesz, A., Brown, R., Lindsay, J., McNair, R., deVaus, R., and Pitts, M. (2006). Family in transition: Parents, children and grandparents in lesbian families give meaning to doing family. *Journal of Family Therapy*, 28, 175-199.

Riley, B. H. (2010). GLB adolescent's "coming out." *Journal of Child and Adolescent Psychiatric Nursing* 23(1), 3-10.

Ryan, D., and Martin, A. (2000). Lesbian, gay, bisexual, and transgender parents in the school systems. *School Psychology Review*, 29(2), 207-216.

Ryan, S., Pearlmutter, S., and Groza, V. (2004). Coming out of the closet: Opening agencies to gay and lesbian adoptive parents. *Social Work*, 49, 85-95.

Savin-Williams, R. C. (1998). The disclosure to families of same-sex attractions by lesbian, gay, and bisexual youths. *Journal of Research on Adolescence*, 8(1), 49-68.

Scallen, R. M. (1981). An investigation of paternal attitudes and behaviour in homosexual and heterosexual fathers. (Doctoral dissertation, California School of Profession Psychology, Los Angeles).

Tasker, F. (2005). Lesbian mothers, gay fathers, and their children: A review. *Journal of Developmental and Behavioral Pediatrics*, 26, 224-240.

Tasker, F., and Golombok, S. (1995). Adults raised as children in lesbian families. *The American Journal of Orthopsychiatry*,65(2), 203-215.

Tasker F, and Golombok S. (1997). Growing up in a lesbian family: Effects on child development. New York, NY: Guilford.

Tornello, S. L., Farr, R. H., and Patterson, C. J. (2011). Predictors of parenting stress among gay adoptive fathers in the United States. *Journal of Family Psychology,* 25(4), 591-600.

Turner, P. H., Scadden, L., and Harris, M. B. (1990). Parenting in gay and lesbian families. *Journal of Gay and Lesbian Psychotherapy*, 1(3), 55-66.

Vanfraussen, K., and Ponjaert-Kristoffersen, I., and Brewaeys, A. (2003). Family functioning in lesbian families created by donor insemination. *American Journal of Orthopsychiatry*, 73, 78-90.

In: Parenting
Editors: Peter Barberis and Stelios Petrakis

ISBN: 978-1-62257-881-8
© 2013 Nova Science Publishers, Inc.

Chapter 9

PARENTING PRACTICES: THE GOOD, THE BAD, AND WHAT TO DO ABOUT IT

Emily McClelland, Jessie Billups, Shea Golding and Cliff McKinney
Mississippi State University, Mississippi, US

ABSTRACT

Parenting frequently has been defined using a combination of demandingness and responsiveness. The most beneficial parenting style is authoritative parenting, which is high in demandingness and responsiveness. Other aspects of positive parenting that may influence child development include parental involvement, consistency, and non-punitive discipline practices. These effective parenting practices result in more adaptive skills and better adjustment in children. Although research has indicated parenting may have a positive influence on child development, not all types of parenting are beneficial and may result in negative effects such as disruptive behavior, depression, and anxiety in children. Authoritarian (i.e., high demandingness, low responsiveness), permissive (i.e., low demandingness, high responsiveness), and neglectful (i.e., low demandingness, low responsiveness) parenting styles are associated with more maladaptive outcomes in children. Specific maladaptive parenting practices associated with negative outcomes include low warmth, high amounts of control, inconsistent parenting, a lack of parental involvement, and harsh discipline practices. Parents should focus on reducing negative parenting practices and enhancing positive practices. Following a discussion of positive and negative parenting practices, recommendations for improving parenting and parent-child relationships are considered.

INTRODUCTION

Parenting may be defined as a combination of demandingness and responsiveness (Baumrind, 1991a, 1991b). Demandingness may include structure, responsibility, and obedience, and responsiveness may include parental involvement, support, and warmth. Specific parenting styles are associated with these two characteristics. Authoritative parenting (i.e., high demandingness, high responsiveness) is considered to be the most beneficial parenting style and is associated with positive outcomes in children (Baumrind, 1991a, 1991b). Authoritarian (i.e., high demandingness, low responsiveness), permissive (i.e., low demandingness, high responsiveness), and neglectful (i.e., low demandingness, low responsiveness) parenting styles are associated with more maladaptive outcomes in children.

Parenting also may be divided into positive and negative parenting practices. Positive parenting practices are beneficial to child development and include parental involvement, consistency, and non-punitive discipline strategies (McKinney, Milone, and Renk, 2011; McKinney and Renk 2008a, 2008b, 2011). On the other hand, negative parenting practices are harmful to child development and include low warmth, high amounts of control, inconsistent parenting, lack of parental involvement, and the use of harsh or punitive discipline (Middleton, Scott, and Renk, 2009). Parental psychopathology or mental health also may influence parents' abilities to parent as well as the presence of psychopathology in children (McKinney and Milone, 2012). Given the influence of parenting on child development, positive parenting practices will be discussed, followed by a discussion of negative parenting practices, and, finally, suggestions for changing parenting practices will be provided.

THE GOOD

Positive Parenting Practices

Authoritative Parenting. Parenting practices may greatly affect a child's behavior. Specifically, authoritative parenting is associated with more positive parenting practices and positive child outcomes (Baumrind, 1991b). Authoritative parents tend to engage in high levels of demandingness and responsiveness (Baumrind, 1991b), as well as create a sense of mutuality through the use of explanations and reasoning with their children (Paulussen-Hoogeboom, Stams, Hermanns, Peetsma, and van den Wittenboer, 2008). Children raised in authoritative households tend to have higher self-esteem, are less prone to internalizing and externalizing problems, and are more likely to adhere to rules set by parents (McKinney et al., 2011).

Parental Involvement. The presence of positive parenting practices, such as parental involvement, may have a positive impact on children's adjustment and behavior. Parental involvement is an essential component for effective behavior regulation in children (Pettit, Laird, Dodge, Bates, and Criss, 2001). Parental involvement has been defined as the extent to which parents are interested in, knowledgeable about, and willing to take a role in their child's lives (Wong, 2008). Parents who are highly involved in their child's life tend to have a parenting style that is marked by a preventative orientation towards dealing with their child's behavior; it reflects elements of planning, specifically having structured rules and regulations early in the child's development (Pettit et al., 2001). Children raised in environments with high parental involvement, as well as high family involvement, tend to engage in lower levels of disruptive and risky behavior (Fletcher, Steinber, and Williams-Wheeler, 2004) and higher levels of prosocial behavior (Veal and Ross, 2006).

Support and Clear Expectations. Parental support and the use of clear expectations and rules is another important component of positive parenting practices. High rates of parental support and a strong parent-child relationship may act as a protective factor against maladjustment in children and the development of externalizing behaviors (Stadler, Feifel, Rohrmann, Vermeiren, and Poustka, 2010). Children raised in homes with high levels of support tend to be more positively affected and have more well-adjusted behavioral outcomes (Keijsers, Frijns, Branje, and Meeus, 2009). Also, higher levels of perceived parental support are correlated with a more autonomous style of self-regulation in children (Wong, 2008). Parents who set clear expectations and rules for their children tend to have similar positive effects. Children are more likely to adhere to rules set by parents using an authoritative style where lower levels of punitive and inconsistent discipline are used (McKinney et al., 2011). Additionally, setting clear expectations and rules is associated with lower levels of antisocial behavior in children (Kiesner, Dishion, Poulin, and Pastore, 2009).

Consistency and Immediacy. Consistency and immediacy in parenting and discipline also are linked with positive outcomes in children. Consistent behavioral guidelines that are implemented in combination with well-defined schedules promote children's prospects for regularity (Baumrind, 1996). Parents who are taught to be consistent in promoting prosocial behaviors and to punish children's aggression effectively with non-violent discipline yield decreased levels of antisocial behaviors in their children (Stoolmiller, Patterson, and Snyder, 1997). Likewise, maternal consistency may buffer children against detrimental effects on adjustment associated with parental divorce (Wolchik, Wilcox, Tein, and Sandler, 2000). Additionally, children with consistent parents exhibit higher self-esteem, better adaptive skills, and higher achievement in school than their peers with inconsistent parents (Johnson, Shulman, and Collins, 1991).

Inductive Discipline, Time Out, and Praise. Inductive discipline is a discipline strategy where parents supply children with guidelines to follow and utilize logic and reasoning to inform children about the consequences of their behavior (Horton, Ray, and Cohen, 2001). Using induction, parents teach their children standards which lead to internalization and an enhanced ability to empathize with others (Horton et al., 2001). Children's ability to focus on the emotions of others allows them to begin feeling appropriately guilty for misbehavior and indiscretions made toward others (Hoffman, 1970). These discipline practices enable children to rely on their emotions and thoughts to decide whether their actions are wrong and why (Lepper, 1983). Unlike power assertion (i.e., use of physical violence, restricting privileges, or threats) as a disciplinary approach, inductive discipline supports prosocial behavior in children by endorsing empathy development (Krevans and Gibbs, 1996; McKinney et al., 2011).

Time out is defined as the contingent withdrawal of the prospect of gaining reinforcements (MacDonough and Forehand, 1973). Time-out is discouraged as a standalone strategy, but is effective when paired with other practices (Anderson and King, 1974). Combining inductive discipline with time out for bad behavior and praise for good behavior is more effective than any one of these elements alone. The concept of time out is contrasted with an idea that may be considered "time in," which is the environment in which a child participates and of which the child desires to be a part (Everett et al, 2007). Time out is a real consequence for children's misbehavior if implemented in the environment of a supportive and loving family (Morawska and Sanders, 2011).

Positive Parental Mental Health

A parent's mental health may have an impact on their parenting as well as an effect on their child's development. Specifically, the quality of the environment children are raised in based on parental mental health may have immediate and residual effects on a child's development (Lung, Shu, Chiang, and Lin, 2011). Positive parenting practices tend to be associated with adequate support, care, and involvement, which are more likely to be implemented in households with good parental mental health. Children who perceive higher levels of positive and directive parenting styles in their households tend to have fewer psychopathological symptoms (Vostanis et al., 2006). Mothers with good emotional health have been found to act as a protective factor for developmental delays in children (Lung et al., 2011). Additionally, children raised in homes with parents who have mood disorders and have sought therapy and experienced improvement in mental health experience improvements in prosocial behavior and emotion regulation (Solantaus, Paavonen, Toikka, and Punamaki, 2010). Along with psychopathological symptoms, parental stress also may have an effect on parenting and children's outcomes. For example, parents experiencing lower levels of stress tend to use more positive parenting practices (Respler-Herman, Mowder, Yaski, and Shamah, 2012).

THE BAD

Negative Parenting Practices

Negative Parenting Styles. As mentioned previously, the three parenting styles associated with negative parenting practices are authoritarian, permissive, and neglectful. These parenting styles differ from one another with respect to responsiveness or warmth, and demandingness or control (Baumrind, 1991a). Authoritarian parents focus on the use of control with their children and desire obedience (Dwairy, 2008). A specific problem associated with authoritarian parenting is the lack of responsiveness used. As such, parents with an authoritarian parenting style typically fail to use affection or praise with their children; this parenting style may lead to negative psychological consequences in child development and harsh discipline strategies (Dwairy, 2008; McKinney et al., 2011).

A permissive style is associated with a focus on responsiveness or warmth, and the parent lacks an emphasis on controlling the child. Parents with permissive styles of parenting may not like confrontation and may be inconsistent (Dwairy, 2008; McKinney et al., 2011). Finally, neglectful parents fail to be warm or respond to their children and they may not be concerned with demanding anything of their children (Baumrind, 1991a). Neglectful parenting may involve high levels of rejection because the parent does not appear invested in the child's development or adjustment. All of these negative parenting styles are associated with negative outcomes in children such as increased tendencies for developing internalizing and externalizing disorders (McKinney and Milone, 2012).

Control and Rejection. Control and rejection are two specific parenting practices that may have negative impacts on children's adjustment (Dwairy et al., 2010). Excessive parental control may lead to decreased levels of self-esteem and social adaptability and increased rates of depression, anxiety, and behavioral problems (McKinney et al., 2011). Maternal and paternal control and rejection are significantly related to psychological disorders in children (Dwairy et al., 2010). Rejection by parents has similar effects on children across different cultures and has been defined as "an almost universal factor" correlated with psychological problems in children (Dwairy et al., 2010, p. 40).

Inconsistent Parenting. Inconsistent parenting has been defined as a combination of authoritarian and permissive parenting that may result in psychological problems and a lack of connectedness between parent and child (Dwairy, 2008). Parental inconsistency is related to psychological disorders in children much like parental rejection and control (Dwairy et al., 2010). Inconsistent parenting may affect how children learn about and socialize with their environment (Dwairy, 2008). For example, when children are exposed to inconsistent parenting, they have an increased likelihood of developing separation anxiety or a phobia regarding school attendance (Dwairy, 2010). Parental inconsistency is composed of three types: temporal, situational, and mother-father. Temporal inconsistency occurs when parents respond differently to the same circumstance every now and then (Dwairy, 2010). Situational inconsistency develops when parents react differently from one circumstance to another circumstance (Dwairy, 2010). Finally, mother-father inconsistency exists when parents react differently to the same circumstance (Dwairy, 2010). Inconsistent parenting is detrimental for children's development because it may lead to ambivalence that alters a child's psychological progress (Dwairy, 2010). Aspects of inconsistent parenting also may be reflected in discipline strategies, which, when inconsistent, may result in increased depression and other negative adjustment consequences in children (McKinney et al., 2011).

Corporal Punishment. Verbal and physical punishments are considered to be the most ineffective forms of discipline used to reduce problem behaviors (Flaskerud, 2011). Negative outcomes associated with corporal or physical punishment include increased aggression in children due to a modeling of behavior portrayed by their parents (Flaskerud, 2011). Furthermore, use of verbal and physical punishment is correlated with higher rates of externalizing behavior in children (McKee et al., 2007). In addition, the more spanking a child receives, the more anger demonstrated by the child in adulthood (Flaskerud, 2011). Other negative consequences that are exhibited in adulthood are an increased likelihood to spank children, an increased acceptance of hitting a spouse, and an increase in marital discord (Flaskerud, 2011). Outcomes associated with spanking that are found during adolescence are substance use, aggressive behavior, crime, and violence (Flaskerud, 2011). Another outcome linked to corporal punishment is increased suicidal ideation (McKinney et al., 2011). Parenting also is affected by corporal punishment because parents who engage in corporal punishment are more likely to be abusive (Flaskerud, 2011).

Harsh discipline strategies or inconsistent discipline may result in a home environment that the child perceives as hostile, which may lead to symptoms of internalizing disorders in children, such as anxiety and depression. Laskey and Cartwright-Hatton (2009) assessed the relationship between parental anxiety, parental discipline style, and internalizing problems of children. Interestingly, discipline of children may be affected by the level of control parents perceive that they have over their children. When parents feel their control has been reduced by their child, parents are less likely to use positive parenting practices and are more likely to engage in negative parenting practices such as verbal and physical punishment (Laskey and Cartwright-Hatton, 2009).

Additional outcomes related to corporal punishment or spanking are an increased likelihood of hitting a parent, delayed cognitive development, lower educational achievement scores, and higher rates of criminal activity as an adult (Straus, 2005). Overall, spanking is not effective because the child may not understand why he or she is being hit. Using spanking or corporal punishment could reduce the strength of the relationship between parent and child. The relationship may be weakened because a child who is repeatedly disciplined with spanking may begin to feel anger and resentment towards their parent (Straus, 2005). Overall, corporal punishment and other types of harsh or inconsistent discipline are largely ineffective and lead to negative psychological outcomes.

Negative Parental Mental Health

Internalizing and externalizing disorders found in parents may have a negative result on parenting behavior. Psychopathology present in parents may prevent parents from effectively parenting their children (McKinney and Milone, 2012). Parents who have mental disorders may unknowingly demonstrate negative parenting practices associated with their disorder such as not being available for their child, being irritable, not responding to their child, and being controlling (Middleton et al., 2009). In addition, parental symptoms of anxiety, depression, and antisocial behavior are associated with specific negative parenting practices (i.e., low warmth, high control, poor modeling). Specifically, mothers who have anxiety may be more critical of their children, not as warm towards them, and less likely to grant independence (Laskey and Cartwright-Hatton, 2009). Additionally, mothers with depression may demonstrate parenting practices that are inconsistent and lack organization (Laskey and Cartwright-Hatton, 2009). Further, frequency of communication is diminished and is more negative compared to mothers without symptoms of depression (Laskey and Cartwright-Hatton, 2009). Combining aspects of parent and child internalizing problems, Laskey and Cartwright-Hatton (2009) found that the more anxiety parents reported, the greater a reported use of ineffective discipline, specifically discipline that was harsh. In addition, parents who indicated their child had internalizing behavior were more likely to use harsh and coercive discipline practices (Laskey and Cartwright-Hatton, 2009). Further, the presence of psychopathology in both parents increases the chance of psychopathology presenting itself in the child (McKinney and Milone, 2012).

Parental stress also may affect the degree to which parents are able to effectively parent their children and may have negative consequences. For instance, the more stress parents report experiencing in their daily routine, the more they report disruptive behavior in their children (Barry, Dunlap, Cotton, Lochman, and Wells, 2005). Maternal parenting stress has been found to result in a report of more depressive and anxious symptoms in children (Rodriguez, 2011). The relationship between parenting stress and internalizing symptoms of children may be bi-directional; the stress imposed on parents results in maladaptive parenting practices leading to increased internalization of problems in children, and the internalizing symptoms found in children may lead to more parenting stress (Rodriguez, 2011). Additionally, when assessing parenting stress, symptoms of depression endorsed by the parent were associated with similar symptoms of anxiety and depression reportedly portrayed by the child (Rodriguez, 2011).

GENDER DIFFERENCES

Mothers and fathers have been found to implement different parenting practices. Mothers are seen as more involved in their children's lives compared to fathers in the upbringing process (Finley, Mira, and Schwartz, 2008) and tend to be more of the authoritative figure in parenting than fathers (McKinney and Renk, 2008). As previously mentioned, a strong parent-child relationship and authoritative parenting have been associated with more positive outcomes in children. It has been found that fathers that engage in shared activities with their children may improve the quality of the father-adolescent relationship (Goncy and van Dulmen, 2010), which may act as a protective factor in the development of disruptive behavior. Examining cultural differences, paternal parenting behavior appears to be more important in western cultures, and maternal parenting behavior is more important in eastern cultures (Dwairy et al., 2010).

Considering differences in discipline for boys and girls, parents are more likely to use harsher forms of punishment with boys, both verbal and physical (McKee et al., 2007). In particular, fathers use more harsh forms of physical discipline with their sons compared to mothers (McKee et al., 2007). Mothers and fathers use the same amount of negative verbal discipline with their sons and their daughters (McKee et al., 2007). When harsh discipline is used by either parent, an equal likelihood of the child developing externalizing behavior problems occurs for girls and boys (McKee et al., 2007).

PARENTING: WHAT TO DO ABOUT IT

Given the research, positive parenting is associated with more positive developmental outcomes such as higher levels of self-esteem, and lower levels of externalizing and internalizing behaviors (McKinney et al., 2011). As such, it is important for parents to be aware of how to implement effective parenting strategies. For instance, parents should focus on being involved in their child's life, providing clear rules and expectations, and being consistent with regards to discipline and rule implementation. Aside from parenting strategies, it appears to be important to focus on the parent-child relationship. If parents focus on enhancing their parenting abilities, the child may feel more comfortable with disclosing information to their parent about his or her life, which could lead to fewer problems. In support of the benefit of child disclosure and the parent-child relationship, Laird, Marrero, and Sentse (2010) found that younger adolescents who disclose more information to their parents are usually better-behaved.

In addition to using effective parenting practices, it is essential that parents focus on using non-violent discipline strategies. Parents should never spank their children because spanking may lead to more instances of aggressive behavior, lower grades in school, greater social problems, and increased instances of externalizing behavior (Fletcher, Walls, Cook, Madison, and Bridges, 2008; Stormshak, Bierman, McMahon, and Lengua, 2000). As such, it is recommended that children never be spanked (Straus, 2005). The three main reasons children should not be spanked include the following: spanking leads to unseen current negative consequences, but later noticeable effects; spanking is not more effective than any other measure of disciplinary action; and spanking is contradictory in that it promotes violence in the family (Straus, 2005). Instead of engaging in spanking, parents should strive to teach children obedience by explaining what he or she did wrong because a child who is spanked may not learn from the situation and being hit may promote the belief that the parent is dangerous (Straus, 2005).

Other positive discipline strategies that are non-punitive are the use of positive reinforcement, time out, response cost, token economy, and using discipline immediately after a wrong doing. Considering time out, a key part of time out is parental monitoring (Anderson and King, 1974); however, the monitoring should be conducted in a non-reinforcing way. Furthermore, contingent release (i.e., the child may be released from time out once he or she has been quiet for the indicated amount of time) yields better results than other strategies for release (Erford, 1999). To use a time out effectively, the parent should initiate by providing a warning about the problem behavior. If the child does not listen to the warning, the parent should tell the child what he or she did wrong and put the child in an area that will not reinforce negative behavior. Be sure not to talk to the child while he or she is in time out because it could reinforce the behavior. For initial implementation, the time out should be relatively short (e.g., 15 to 30 seconds), and further implementation should build up to one minute in time out for every year of age. If the child does not comply with time out rules (i.e., begins making noses or engaging in disruptive behavior), the first time the rules are violated, the child should be told that the timer will be reset. Make sure the child sees the parent reset the timer. When the child complies with all the rules and the timer is finished, the child should be released from time out and encouraged to complete the task at hand before the time out was implemented.

Having discussed positive parenting and the use of non-punitive discipline, parental mental health is important for good parenting. In fact, it may be particularly difficult for a parent with mental health problems to be an effective parent. Parents should focus on treating any psychological problems and complying to treatment recommendations given that symptoms of parental mental health may influence parenting behaviors. In addition to effectively managing mental health problems, parents should focus on monitoring how their mental health affects their parenting. It may be beneficial for the parent to learn what negative parenting behaviors are associated with the mental disorder the parent faces. Learning positive parenting strategies that can help parents with mental health problems avoid negative parenting may assist parents in engaging in healthy parenting behaviors. Finally, parents should learn how to effectively manage any symptoms of stress they are facing associated with life problems or with parenting. Some ways parents could manage their stress include finding healthy coping strategies such as date nights with a significant other, finding time for the parent to engage in activities he or she enjoys without the child being present, engaging in personal time in isolation from the child, or engaging in exercise for relaxation and stress release.

CONCLUSION

Parenting practices may influence many areas of a child's life, such as academic performance, substance use, and peer relationships. The use of positive parenting practices, specifically authoritative parenting, tend to be associated with more positive outcomes in children (McKinney et al., 2011). Children raised in homes with high rates of parental involvement (Pettit et al., 2001), support (Keijsers et al., 2009), and consistency (Stoolmiller et al., 1997) may effectively reduce problem behavior over time. Also, the use of inductive discipline strategies and lower levels of punitive discipline may be more beneficial in effectively addressing a child's behavior. Positive parenting practices are essential to the development and maintenance of effective behavior regulation in children, as well as throughout the developmental process.

Parenting practices appear to be transmitted from generation to generation (Bailey, Hill, Oesterle, and Hawkins, 2009). Reports of externalizing behavior in adolescence are connected to later substance use in adulthood, which predicted a presence of externalizing behavior in offspring (Bailey et al., 2009). It may be that a combination of externalizing behavior and harsh parenting in one generation predicts externalizing behavior and parenting in the following generation (Bailey et al., 2009). Evidence that parenting affects child adjustment (Dwairy et al., 2010; Rodriguez, 2011) clarifies the need for parent training and suggestions for ways parents may parent their children more successfully.

REFERENCES

Anderson, K. A., and King, H. E. (1974). Time-out reconsidered. *Journal of Instructional Psychology, 1*(2), 11-17.

Bailey, J., Hill, K., Oesterle, S., and Hawkins, J. (2009). Parenting practices and problem behavior across three generations: Monitoring, harsh discipline, and drug use in the intergenerational transmission of externalizing behavior. *Developmental Psychology, 45,* 1214-1226.

Barry, T., Dunlap, S., Cotton, S., Lochman, J., and Wells, K. (2005). The influence of maternal stress and distress on disruptive behavior problems in boys. *Journal of the American Academy of Child and Adolescent Psychiatry, 44,* 265-273.

Baumrind, D. (1991a). Effective parenting during the early adolescent transition. In: Cowan PA (Ed.), *Family transitions* (pp. 111-163). Hillsdale, NJ: Lawrence Erlbaum.

Baumrind, D. (1991b). The influence of parenting style on adolescent competence and substance use. *Journal of Early Adolescence, 11,* 56-95.

Baumrind, D. (1996). The discipline controversy revisited. *Family Relation, 45*(4), 405-414.

Dwairy, M. (2008). Parental inconsistency versus parental authoritarianism: Associations with symptoms of psychological disorders. *Journal of Youth and Adolescence, 37,* 616-626.

Dwairy, M. (2010). Parental inconsistency: A third cross-cultural research on parenting and psychological adjustment of children. *Journal of Child and Family Studies, 19,* 23-29.

Dwairy, M., Achoui, M., Filus, A., Rezvan nia, P., Casullo, M., and Vohra, N. (2010). Parenting, mental health and culture: A fifth cross-cultural research on parenting and psychological adjustment of children. *Journal of Child and Family Studies, 19,* 36-41.

Erford, B. T. (1999). A modified time-out procedure for children with noncompliant or defiant behaviors. *Professional School Counseling, 2*(3), 205-210.

Everett, G. E., Olmi, D. J., Edwards, R. P., Tingstrom, D. H., Sterling-Turner, H. E., and Christ, T. J. (2007). An empirical investigation of time-out with and without escape extinction to treat escape maintained noncompliance. *Behavior Modification, 31*(4), 412-434.

Finley, G.E., Mira, S.D., and Schwartz, S.J. (2008). Perceived paternal and maternal involvement: Factor structures, mean differences, and parental roles. *Fathering, 6,* 68-82.

Flaskerud, J. (2011). Discipline and effective parenting. *Issues in Mental Health, 32,* 82-84.

Fletcher, A.C., Walls, J.K., Cook, E.C., Madison, K.J., and Bridges, T.H. (2008). Parenting styles as a moderator of associations between maternal disciplinary strategies and child well-being. *Journal of Family Issues, 29,* 1724-1744.

Fletcher, A.C., Steinberg, L., and Williams-Wheeler, M. (2004). Parental influences on adolescent problem behavior: Revisiting Stattin and Kerr. *Child Development, 75,* 781-796.

Goncy, E.A., and van Dulmen, M.M. (2010). Fathers do make a difference: Parental involvement and adolescent alcohol use. *Father, 8,* 93-108.

Hoffman, M. L. (1970). Conscience, personality, and socialization techniques. *Human Development, 13,* 90-126.

Horton, N. K., Ray, G. E., and Cohen, R. (2001). Children's evaluations of inductive discipline as a function of transgression type and induction orientation. *Child Study Journal 31*(2), 71-93.

Johnson, B. M., Shulman, S., and Collins, W. A. (1991). Systemic patterns of parenting as reported by adolescents: Developmental differences and implications for psychosocial outcomes. *Journal of Adolescent Research, 6,* 235-252.

Keijsers, L., Frijns, T., Branje, S. T., and Meeus, W. (2009). Developmental links of adolescent disclosure, parental solicitation, and control with delinquency: Moderation by parental support. Developmental Psychology, 45, 1314-1327.

Kiesner, J., Dishion, T.J., Poulin, F., and Pastore, M. (2009). Temporal dynamics linking aspects of parent monitoring with early adolescent antisocial behavior. *Social Development, 18,* 765-784.

Krevans, J., and Gibbs, J. C. (1996). Parents' use of inductive discipline: Relations to children's empathy and prosocial behavior. *Child Development, 67*(6), 3263-3277. doi:10.2307/1131778.

Laird, R.D., Marrero, M.D., and Sentse, M. (2010). Revisiting parental monitoring: Evidence that parental solicitation can be effective when needed most. *Journal of Youth Adolescents, 39,* 1431-1441.

Laskey, B., and Cartwright-Hatton, S. (2009). Parental discipline behaviors and beliefs about their child: Associations with child internalizing and mediation relationships. *Child: care, health and development, 35,* 717-727.

Lepper, M. R. (1983). Social-control processes and the internalization of social values: An attributional perspective. In E. T. Higgins, D. Ruble, and W. W. Hartup (Eds.), *Social cognition and social development* (pp. 294-330). Cambridge University Press.

Lung, F. J., Shu, B.C., Chiang, T.L., and Lin, S.J. (2011). Maternal mental health and childrearing context in the development of children at 6, 18 and 36 months: a Taiwan birth cohort pilot study. *Child: Care, Health and Development*, 37, 211-223.

MacDonough, T. S., and Forehand, R. (1973). Response-contingent time-out: Important parameters in behavior modification with children. *Journal of Behavior Therapy and Experimental Psychiatry, 4,* 231-236.

McKee, L., Roland, E., Coffelt, N., Olson, A., Forehand, R., Massari, C., Jones, D., Gaffney, C., and Zens, M. (2007). *Journal of Family Violence, 22,* 187-196.

McKinney, C., and Milone, M.C. (2012). Parental and late adolescent psychopathology: Mothers may provide support when needed most. *Child Psychiatry and Human Development,* doi: 10.1007/s10578-012-0293-2.

McKinney, C., Milone, M.C., and Renk, K. (2011). Parenting and late adolescent emotional adjustment: Mediating effects of discipline and gender. *Child Psychiatry and Human Development, 42,* 463-481.

McKinney, C., and Renk, K. (2008a). Differential parenting between mothers and fathers: Implications for late adolescents. *Journal of Family Issues, 29,* 806-827.

McKinney, C., and Renk, K. (2008b). Multivariate models of parent-late adolescent gender dyads: The importance of parenting processes in predicting adjustment. *Child Psychiatry and Human Development, 39,* 147-170. doi: 10.1007/s10578-007-0078-1.

McKinney, C., and Renk, K. (2011). A multivariate model of parent-adolescent relationship variables in early adolescence. *Child Psychiatry and Human Development, 42,* 442-462.

Middleton, M., Scott, S., and Renk, K. (2009). Parental depression, parenting behaviors, and behavior problems in young children. *Infant and Child Development, 18,* 323-336.

Morawska, A., and Sanders, M. (2011). Parental use of time out revisited: A useful or harmful parenting strategy?. *Journal of Child and Family Studies, 20*(1), 1-8. doi:10.1007/s10826-010-9371-x.

Paulussen-Hoogeboom, M.C., Stams, G, J., Hermanss, J.M., Peetsma, T.T., and van den Wittenboer, G.L. (2008). Parenting style as a mediator between children's negative emotionality and problematic behavior in early childhood. *The Journal of Genetic Psychology, 169,* 209-226.

Pettit, G.S., Laird, R.D., Dodge, K.A., Bates, J.E., and Criss, M.M. (2001). Antecedents and behavior-problem outcomes of parental monitoring and psychological control in early adolescence. *Child Development, 72,* 583-598.

Respler-Herman, M., Mowder, B.A., Yasik, A.E., and Shamah, R. (2012). Parenting Beliefs, Parental Stress, and Social Support Relationships. *Journal Of Child and Family Studies,* 21, 190-198.

Rodriguez, C. (2011). Association between independent reports of maternal parenting stress and children's internalizing symptomatology. *Journal of Child and Family Studies, 20,* 631-639.

Solantaus, T., Paavonen, E.J., Toikka, S., and Punamaki, R.L. (2010). Preventative interventions in families with parental depression: Children's psychosocial symptoms and prosocial behavior. *European Child and Adolescent Psychiatry, 19,* 883-892.

Stadler, C. (2010). Peer-Victimization and Mental Health Problems in Adolescents: Are Parental and School Support Protective?. *Child Psychiatry and Human Development,* 41, 371-386.

Stoolmiller, M., Patterson, G. R., and Snyder, J. (1997). Parental discipline and child antisocial behavior: A contingency-based theory and some methodological refinements. *Psychological Inquiry, 8,* 223-229.

Stormshak, E.A., Bierman, K.L., McMahon, R.J., and Lengua, L.J. (2000). Parenting practices and child disruptive behavior problems in early elementary school. *Journal of Clinical Child Psychology, 29,* 17-29.

Straus, M. (2005). Children should never, ever, be spanked no matter what the circumstances. In D.R. Loseke, R.J. Gelles and M.M. Cavanaugh (Eds.), *Current Controversies about Family Violence* (2nd ed., pp. 137-157). Thousand Oak, CA: Sage.

Wolchik, S. A., Wilcox, K. L., Tein, J., and Sandler, I. N. (2000). Maternal acceptance and consistency of discipline as buffers of divorce stressors on children's psychological adjustment problems. *Journal of Abnormal Child Psychology, 28*, 87-102.

Wong, M.M. (2008). Perceptions of parental involvement and autonomy support: Their relations with self-regulation, academic performance, substance use and resilience among adolescents. *North American Journal of Psychology, 10*, 497-518.

Veal, M.L., and Ross, L.T. (2006). Gender, alcohol consumption, and parental monitoring. *The Journal of Psychology, 140*, 41-52.

Vostanis, P., Graves, A., Meltzer, H., Goodman, R., Jenkins, R., and Brugha, T. (2006). Relationship between parental psychopathology, parenting strategies and child mental health. *Social Psychiatry and Psychiatric Epidemiology, 4*, 509-514.

In: Parenting
Editors: Peter Barberis and Stelios Petrakis

ISBN: 978-1-62257-881-8
© 2013 Nova Science Publishers, Inc.

Chapter 10

CHALLENGES AND FUTURE DIRECTIONS IN THE EVALUATION OF PARENTING PROGRAMMES

Mairead Furlong[1] and Sinead McGilloway[1]
[1]National University of Ireland Maynooth, Ireland

ABSTRACT

Antisocial behaviour in children is common and has attracted considerable interest in recent years, not least because of the significant negative psychological and economic consequences for affected families and communities. A considerable body of research indicates that parenting programmes, particularly those delivered in group settings and based on behavioural and social learning principles, can produce clinically significant improvements in childhood emotional and behavioural difficulties and in parental mental health. However, despite these encouraging results, several challenges require further exploration. These include: (1) a need for improvements in the overall quality of studies; (2) an analysis of group-based parenting interventions in relation to outcomes about which we know relatively little; (3) a need for improved retention and engagement among socially disadvantaged and culturally distinctive families; and (4) the appropriate and effective translation of evidence into policy and practice. This chapter will discuss these issues and highlight possible avenues for future research which may enhance the evidence-base for, and the wide-scale implementation of, parenting programmes.

INTRODUCTION

Parenting programmes have become popular in recent years in the treatment and/or prevention of childhood conduct problems. Antisocial behaviour in children is common (ranging from 5 per cent to 15 per cent worldwide) and has attracted considerable interest from researchers, practitioners and policymakers alike, not least because of the negative psychological and economic consequences for families, communities and wider society (Cleary, Nixon and Fitzgerald, 2004; Farrington and Welsh, 2007). There are numerous negative long-term outcomes of childhood conduct problems including: an increased risk of future antisocial and criminal behaviour (Fergusson, Horwood and Ridder, 2005); early school leaving and low occupational status (Farrington and Welsh, 2007); mental health and social difficulties (Broidy et al. 2003); as well as greater utilisation of health, education, social and legal services (Scott, Knapp, Henderson and Maughan, 2001; Sainsbury Centre for Mental Health, 2009).

Research evidence from the last 25 to 30 years indicates that parenting programmes, particularly those delivered in group settings and based on behavioural and social learning principles, produce moderate to large statistically significant improvements in child behavioural problems and in parental mental health (e.g. Webster-Stratton, 1984; Sanders and McFarland, 2000; Hutchings et al. 2007a; Furlong et al. 2012). These kinds of group-based parenting programmes typically involve an interactive and collaborative learning format in which programme facilitators teach key behavioural principles and parenting skills (e.g. play, praise, rewards, discipline) to parents and caregivers who then practise the skills that they have learned. It appears that key elements of effective programmes include learning how and when to use positive parenting skills; observation; modelling; behaviour rehearsal; discussion; homework assignments; using peer support, reframing unhelpful cognitive perceptions about their child or about child-management in general; and tackling barriers to attendance (Webster-Stratton and Hammond, 1997; Mihalic and Irwin, 2003; Kling, Forster, Sundell and Melin, 2010). Beneficial outcomes from such parenting programmes have been achieved with both clinical (e.g. Larsson et al. 2008) and non- or sub-clinical preventive populations (e.g. Sanders et al. 2008); in both research (Webster-Stratton and Hammond, 1997) and regular service settings (McGilloway et al. 2012); in different countries across the world (Gardner, Burton and Klimes, 2006; Kim, Cain and Webster-Stratton, 2008; Larsson et al. 2008) and in replications undertaken by independent investigators (e.g. Hutchings et al. 2007a; McGilloway et al. 2012).

However, despite these encouraging results, there are several areas within the parent-training field that are in need of further exploration. The areas discussed in this commentary include: (1) a need for improvements in the overall quality of studies; (2) an analysis of group-based parenting interventions in relation to outcomes about which we know relatively little; (3) improving retention rates and engagement among socially disadvantaged families and for those from different child-rearing traditions; and (4) translating evidence into policy and practice.

1. IMPROVEMENTS IN THE QUALITY OF STUDIES

Although many hundreds of studies have evaluated the effectiveness of group-based parenting programmes, only 13 of these were of sufficient quality to warrant inclusion in a recent Cochrane review of group-based parenting interventions for children with clinically significant conduct problems (Furlong et al. 2012).

Most studies were excluded due to their lack of a randomised control group. All 13 included studies were randomised or quasi-randomised controlled trials (RCTs), but even here, many of the studies failed to address risk of bias around randomisation procedures (e.g. adequate sequence generation and allocation concealment), blinding, high attrition, intention-to-treat analyses, sample size, implementation fidelity and the utilisation of independent, objective measures (rather than self-report measures) (Furlong et al. 2012).

Furthermore, many RCTs in the field do not report on the level of conduct problems of participants using a validated instrument. Such reportage is important as descriptive screening tends to be insufficient for the purposes of methodologically rigorous research (Furlong et al. 2012). Moreover, given that parenting trials generally involve several different parenting groups within the intervention arm, studies might consider analysing their data using hierarchical linear modelling, which is currently considered the optimal analytical strategy for nested data (Duncan, Duncan and Strycker, 2006).

Thus, whilst the results of individual RCTs generally indicate that group-based parenting programmes are a promising intervention for parents of children with behavioural difficulties, further work is required in order to improve the overall quality of studies in this area.

2. EXPLORATION OF FURTHER OUTCOMES

To date, most studies of parenting programmes examine effectiveness in relation to child emotional and behavioural difficulties, parental mental health and parenting competencies (e.g. Hutchings et al. 2007a; McGilloway et al. 2012). However, we know very little about the effectiveness of such interventions in relation to other relevant outcomes, including: child cognitive/educational abilities; parental social support; any potential adverse outcomes (e.g. conflict with partner through the introduction of new parenting techniques into the home [Furlong and McGilloway, 2011]); long-term measurement of outcomes; and evidence of cost-effectiveness.

The lack of long-term outcomes is a particular concern within the parenting field. RCTs typically lose their control group at three to six months post-intervention as it is perceived as unethical to withhold a potentially effective programme from control group participants (e.g. Hutchings et al. 2007a). However, a lack of long-term controlled research undermines our confidence that positive benefits will be maintained in the longer term. Moreover, we may fail to capture effects that may only materialise at a later stage; for instance, research indicates that improvements in educational attainment may only emerge in the longer term (Melhuish, Belsky, Leyland and Barnes, 2008; Griffith, Hutchings and Bywater, 2011). Some long-term research has been conducted on group-based parenting programmes for the intervention group alone, which indicates the maintenance of treatment gains at 18-month follow-up (Bywater et al. 2009) and up to 12 years later (Webster-Stratton, Rinaldi and Reid, 2010). However, it is difficult to draw conclusions, at this stage, in the absence of control groups against which to compare the results. It is also important to consider that a small number of studies have found that a substantial relapse in parenting competencies led to a loss of positive gains at 12-month follow up (e.g. Spaccerelli, Cotler and Henman, 1992; Patterson et al. 2002).

The lack of long-term assessment of outcomes is often attributed to insufficient funding (Fixsen, Naoom, Blase, Friedman and Wallace, 2005), although this is perhaps not completely accurate when outcomes for the intervention group have been measured at eighteen month follow-up in several studies (e.g. Gardner et al. 2006; Bywater et al. 2009); and up to twelve years later in one study (Webster-Stratton et al. 2010). It is more likely that the practice of offering the intervention to the control group, due to its perceived ethicality, has prevented the long-term comparison of treatment and control groups. Arguably, however, we also need to consider whether it is ethical to invest public monies in interventions that produce little or no robust evidence of long-term effectiveness. Possible solutions to this problem may be found within two studies in the parenting field (Hutchings, Lane and Kelly, 2004; Hahlweg, Heinrichs, Kuschel, Bertram and Naumann, 2010) who retained their control group up to four years later. (The former study reported maintenance of positive outcomes at follow up whilst the latter reported a dissipation of positive results.) For instance, Hutchings et al. (2004) provided the control group with standard treatment (e.g. Child and Adolescent Mental Health services [CAMHS]). The other study did not offer the control group any treatment, although this option is less ethically desirable. The results from Hahlweg et al. (2010) suggest that further randomised controlled research is needed on the long-term effectiveness of parenting programmes.

Robust evidence of cost-effectiveness is critical if evidence-based parenting programmes are to be rolled-out to scale (Gardner, 2012) and if policymakers are to make well-informed decisions about the relative cost-effectiveness of different types of parenting programmes. Reassuringly, there has been an increase in recent years in studies that have evaluated the costs of delivering a parenting programme (e.g. Foster, Olchowski, Webster-Stratton, 2007; Mihalopoulos, Sanders, Turner, Murphy-Brennan and Carter, 2007). However, while such preliminary costs studies are useful, the utilisation of high quality costs analyses of parenting interventions is relatively rare (Romeo, Byford and Knapp, 2005).

The most robust cost-effectiveness analyses involve both costs-benefits analyses and/or incremental cost effectiveness ratios, whereby the costs and consequences of delivering a parenting programme are compared with the costs and consequences of standard service provision (Aos, Lieb, Mayfield, Miller and Pennucci, 2004).

Within the parenting field, two rigorous cost-effectiveness analyses have demonstrated that, when compared to usual service utilisation, the Incredible Years parenting programme (a group-based intervention) can reduce clinical levels of conduct problems to non-clinical levels for a modest cost of approximately $2400 per family (GBP £1712; EUR €2217) (Edwards et al. 2007; O' Neill, McGilloway, Donnolly, Bywater and Kelly, 2011). These costs suggest that certain parenting programmes may represent good value for money in terms of public spending, and particularly if positive outcomes can be maintained in the longer term, as potential benefits of the intervention exceed the costs of delivery by several orders of magnitude. For instance, research indicates that the lifetime cost per case of people who have Conduct Disorder from childhood is approximately $355,100 (2008/9 GBP £225,000) and that the lifetime costs per case for those with sub-diagnosis conduct problems from childhood, is approximately $118,350 (2008/9 GBP £75,000) (Sainsbury Centre for Mental Health 2009).

Despite the progress achieved within costs studies in this field, there is still a need for more work in this area and for future costs analyses to adopt, where possible, a more 'complex intervention approach'; this would ensure that the wider costs of delivering the intervention (e.g. adverse reactions to attendance, productivity costs for parents or employment agencies in attending the programme) are examined in more detail, as well as the wider benefits to society, including generalised benefits to other family members, the positive economic effects of improvements in parental mental health and other long-run educational and occupational outcomes (Charles, Bywater and Edwards, 2011). However, we also acknowledge the difficulties involved in adopting such an approach since currently there are relatively little reliable data on the unit costs of individual services within many jurisdictions (O' Neill et al. 2011).

Nevertheless, reportage within economic evaluations could be enhanced across a number of key areas including: the reporting of measures of variance for all parameters; clearly delineating resource use from unit costs; and by carefully selecting outcome measures that can be compared with previous published studies (Furlong et al. 2012).

3. IMPROVING RETENTION AND ENGAGEMENT AMONG SOCIALLY DISADVANTAGED AND CULTURALLY DISTINCTIVE FAMILIES

Although parenting programmes generally report positive outcomes for families, approximately one third of parents fail to derive any clinical benefit (Drugli, Fossum, Larsson and Morch, 2009; McGilloway et al. 2012). The failure to benefit from the intervention is primarily attributed to the often high rates of attrition/drop out from parenting programmes, which sometimes can be as high as 50 per cent (Forehand and Kotchick, 1996; McMahon and Kotler, 2004; Liabo and Richardson, 2007). A number of other factors including socioeconomic disadvantage, disrupted family life, and parental psychopathology have all been associated with high attrition and poorer treatment outcomes in parent training (Reyno and McGrath, 2006). Some parenting programmes have improved retention rates with high-risk families by addressing access and childcare barriers (e.g. Webster-Stratton and Hancock, 1998).

Others have evaluated adjunctive treatments to parent training, including marital skills training (Dadds, Schwartz and Sanders, 1987) and problem-solving skills training (e.g. Kazdin, 2003), and reported increased engagement of high-risk clients, as well as enhanced outcomes for families. Multi-component or 'wrap-around' interventions may also be necessary to support the most vulnerable families (e.g. Hutchings et al. 2007b).

Parenting programmes have been delivered across many different countries in the US, Europe, Australia and Asia and to various ethnic groups, although the vast majority of studies involve Caucasian participants (e.g. Sanders and McFarland, 2000; Webster-Stratton, Reid and Hammond, 2004; Kim et al. 2008; Hahlweg et al. 2010). Despite generally positive findings, there is a growing awareness that cultural factors (e.g. distinctive child rearing traditions and values) may impinge upon the recruitment and retention of families who receive parenting interventions (Weissberg et al. 2003). For instance, one study in Ireland (Furlong and McGilloway, 2011) found that many parents (52%) were not convinced that building a positive relationship with the child through play and praise would be an effective method of dealing with behavioural problems.

They also expressed some discomfort that the praise and rewards, which are such an intrinsic part of most parenting programmes, might cause their children to become overbearing and arrogant. Such resistance to the tenets of the parenting programme might be best understood against a historical and cultural backdrop of common parenting practices in Ireland, which has traditionally valued obedience, compliance and modesty, punishment of misdemeanours, coupled with a lack of positive reinforcement for desirable behaviours

(Greene, 1994; Littleton, 2009). However, resistance to positive attention is not exclusively a localised issue as there is evidence that other cultures (e.g. South East Asia) demonstrate similar opposition to praise (e.g. Paiva, 2008).

Thus, there is a growing awareness that providers of parenting programmes should attempt to become more culturally sensitive so that parents are encouraged in early sessions, to share their family and cultural traditions and experiences of being parented as children (Webster-Stratton, 2009). This approach, whilst not without its challenges, shows respect for different cultures and parenting styles, and encourages parents to talk about any resistances to the new parenting skills which might, in turn, enhance retention rates.

4. TRANSLATING EVIDENCE INTO PRACTICE

The implementation of evidence-based parenting programmes into practice is unlikely to affect the incidence of conduct problems in young children unless careful attention is given to the quality of implementation. Many evidence-based programmes have been adopted in different settings with widely varying outcomes and, in general, research indicates that high quality implementation fidelity produces superior treatment outcomes (Fixsen et al. 2005; Eames et al. 2009). The importance of implementation fidelity (i.e. the degree to which the delivery of a programme adheres to the original protocol) is further highlighted in a recent Cochrane review (Furlong et al. 2012) that demonstrated that evidence-based parenting programmes can be successfully transported to 'real world' service settings, but only if the intervention is implemented with fidelity.

Nevertheless, it would appear that the importance of implementation fidelity is not yet sufficiently widely acknowledged and many tend to believe that implementation of at least some components of an effective parenting programme is better than doing nothing at all (Webster-Stratton, 2011). However, this view is problematic since research has demonstrated that the removal of programme components or the addition of non-curricular elements may undermine any beneficial effects of the programme, and, in some cases, may actually cause harm to participants (Aber, Jones, Brown, Chaudry, and Samples, 1998; Petrosino, Turpin-Petrosino, and Finckenauer, 2000).

Thus, knowledge on 'best practice' implementation strategies is key to the widespread replication and dissemination of evidence-based parenting programmes (Mihalic and Irwin, 2003; Hutchings et al. 2007b). Research indicates that high quality skills-based training and supervision are critical in augmenting adherence to programme protocols (e.g. Fixsen et al. 2005; Forgatch and Degarmo, 2011). However, less is understood about how a complex ecology of organisational, policy and funding structures may also impact upon the 'real world' implementation of parenting programmes (Fixsen et al. 2005). Preliminary research in this area suggests that some of the more important organisational factors may include: (1) a high degree of 'fit' between the value system of the parenting programme and the existing agency, such that the intervention is perceived as suitable for the client group (Sanders and Turner, 2005); (2) the provision of adequate time and resources to allow staff to balance the delivery of the parenting programme with other work responsibilities (Sanders and Turner, 2005); and (3) a high degree of practitioner 'buy-in', such that they are convinced of the relative advantages of the new programme over previous/current approaches (Breitkrenz et al. 2011).

Other relevant components involve intra-agency development and/or inter-agency co-operation that facilitate the ongoing funding and referral streams needed to implement and support the high quality implementation of parenting programmes (Fixsen et al. 2005). Quality implementation includes the provision of adequate staff training and supervision and childcare support for parents who attend the parenting programme (Webster-Stratton, 2011). However, several barriers to effective inter-agency collaboration amongst children's services have been reported across various countries. These typically include: poor leadership; lack of consensus on goals; territorialism; poorly defined roles and responsibilities; lack of commitment from staff and funding constraints (Dowling, 2004; Sloper, 2004; Statham, 2011). Arguably therefore, it takes considerable vision and perseverance to reach the stage where running a parenting programme becomes part of 'normal practice' within an organisation (Fixsen et al. 2005).

Currently, the absence of a policy framework within many countries means that the provision of parenting programmes within mainstream services remains sporadic and intermittent (Shulruf, O' Loughlin and Tolley, 2009). Thus, it is necessary to establish a national policy initiative which would create local and national funding avenues for the wide scale implementation of evidence-based parenting programmes, as in Norway (Ogden, Amlund Hagen, Askeland and Christensen, 2009). In addition, the roll out of parenting programmes depends on identifying inhibiting and facilitating factors regarding research utilisation (e.g. Bostrom, Kajermo, Nordström and Wallin, 2008) and preferred methods of knowledge transfer/exchange among child care researchers, policy makers and professionals (e.g. as undertaken by the Australian Institute of Family Studies [Bromfield and Arney, 2008]). Moreover, in order to influence policy development in this area, it may also be important to utilise a number of 'entry points' in the health and social care system and to liaise with a variety of key players, including researchers, clinicians, service providers, managers, policy-makers/civil servants and service-users.

CONCLUSION

Behavioural, group-based parenting programmes have enriched the lives of many families through clinically significant improvements in both parental mental health and in childhood emotional and behavioural difficulties. Nevertheless, there are a number of areas that offer significant potential in terms of enhancing the evidence-base for parenting programmes.

We acknowledge that there are several challenges for researchers and service providers in (i) improving the quality of studies, (ii) reporting on rarely-assessed outcomes, (iii) developing the programme so as to support vulnerable families and (iv) in translating evidence into practice. Such difficulties may include, for example: labour-intensive collaboration with children's services in order to promote evidence-based practice; increased statistical and economic expertise among researchers; and the difficulty of conducting long-term, controlled, assessments. However, it is hoped that addressing these challenges will enhance the effectiveness, and wide-scale implementation of evidence-based parenting programmes throughout the world.

REFERENCES

Aber, J. L., Jones S. M., Brown, J. L. Chaudry, N., and Samples, F. (1998). Resolving conflict creatively: Evaluating the developmental effects of school-based violence prevention program in neighborhood and classroom context. Development and Psychopathology, 10, 187-213.

Aos, A. R., Lieb, J., Mayfield, M., and Pennucci, P. (2004). Benefits and costs of prevention and early intervention programs for youth. Available at http://www.wsipp .wa.gov/rptfiles/04-7-3901.pdf.

Boström, A., Kajermo, K. N., Nordström, G., and Wallin, L. (2008). Registered nurses' use of research findings in the care of older people. Journal of Clinical Nursing, 18, 1430-1441.

Breitkreuz, R., McConnell, D., Savage, A., and Hamilton, A. (2011). Integrating Triple P into Existing Family Support Services: A Case Study on Program Implementation. Prevention Science, 12, 411–422.

Broidy, L. M., Nagin, D. S., Tremblay, R. E., Bates, J. E., Brame, B., and Dodge, K. A. (2003). Developmental trajectories of childhood disruptive behaviours and adolescent delinquency: a six site, cross-national study. Developmental Psychology, 39(2), 222–45.

Bromfield, L. and Arney, F. (2008). Integrating strategies for delivering evidence-informed practice. Melbourne: Australian Institute of Family Studies.

Bywater, T., Hutchings, J., Daley, D., Whitaker, C., Yeo, S. T., and Jones, K. (2009). Long-term effectiveness of a parenting intervention for children at risk of developing conduct disorder. The British Journal of Psychiatry 195(4), 318–24.

Charles, J. M., Bywater, T. and Edwards, R. T. (2011). Parenting interventions: a systematic review of the economic evidence. Child: Care, Health and Development. DOI: 10.1111/j.1365-2214.2011.01217.x:1–13

Cleary, A., Nixon, E. and Fitzgerald, M. (2004). From child to adult: A longitudinal study of children and their families. Dublin, Ireland: Department of Social and Family Affairs.

Dadds, M. R., Schwartz, S. and Sanders, M. R. (1987). Marital discord and treatment outcome in the treatment of childhood conduct disorders. Journal of Consulting and ClinicalPsychology, 55, 396–403.

Dowling, B., Powell, M. and Glendinning, C. (2004). Conceptualising successful partnerships. Health and Social Care in the Community, 12 (4): 309-17.

Drugli, M. B., Larsson, B., Fossum, S., and Mörch, W. (2009). Five- to Six-Year Outcome and its Prediction for Children with ODD/CD Treated with Parent Training. Journal of Child Psychology and Psychiatry. Doi:10.1111/j.1469-7610.2009.02178.x.

Duncan, T. E., Duncan, S. C. and Strycker, L. A. (2006). An introduction to latent variable growth curve modelling: Concepts, issues and applications (2nd Ed). Mahwah, NJ: Lawrence Erlbaum Associates.

Eames, C., Daley, D., Hutchings, J., Whitaker, C. J., Jones, K., Hughes, J. C., and Bywater, T. (2009). Treatment fidelity as a predictor of behaviour change in parents attending group-based parent training *Child: Care, Health and Development*. doi:10.1111/j.1365-2214.2009.00975.x

Edwards, R. T., O'Ceilleachair, A., Bywater, T., Hughes, D. A., and Hutchings, J. (2007). Parenting programme for parents of children at risk of developing conduct disorder: cost effectiveness analysis. *BMJ*, 334(7595), 683–8.

Farrington, D. and Welsh, B. C. (2007). *Saving children from a life of crime: Early risk factors and effective interventions*. New York: Oxford University Press.

Fergusson, D., Horwood, L. and Ridder, E. (2005). Show me the child at seven: the consequences of conduct problems in childhood for psychosocial learning in adulthood. *Journal of Child Psychology and Psychiatry*, 46(8), 837–49.

Fixsen, D. L., Naoom, S. F., Blase, K. A., Friedman, R. M., and Wallace, F. (2005). Implementation Research: A Synthesis of the Literature. Tampa, FL: University of South Florida, Louis de la Parte Florida Mental Health Institute, The National Implementation Research Network.

Forehand, R. and Kotchick, B. (1996). Cultural diversity: A wake-up call for parent training. *Behavior Therapy*, 27, 187-206.

Forgatch, M.S. and Degarmo, D. S. (2011). Sustaining Fidelity Following the Nationwide PMTO Implementation in Norway. *Prevention Science*, 12, 235–246.

Foster, M. E., Olchowski, A. E. and Webster-Stratton, C. H. (2007). Is stacking intervention components cost-effective? An analysis of the Incredible Years program. *Journal of the American Academy of Child and Adolescent Psychiatry*, 46(11), 1414–24.

Furlong, M. and McGilloway, S. (2011). The Incredible Years Parenting Program in Ireland: A qualitative analysis of the experience of disadvantaged parents. *Clinical Child Psychology and Psychiatry*. In press. DOI: 10.1177/1359104511426406

Furlong, M., McGilloway, S., Bywater, T., Hutchings, J., Smith, S. M., and Donnelly, M. (2012). Behavioral and cognitive-behavioral group-based parenting interventions for early-onset conduct problems in children age 3-12 years. *Cochrane Database of Systematic Reviews*, Issue 2. Art. No.: CD008225. DOI: 10.1002/14651858 .CD008225.pub2. http://onlinelibrary. wiley.com/doi/10.1002 /14651858.CD008225. pub2/abstract

Gardner, F., Burton, J. and Klimes, I. (2006). Randomised controlled trial of a parenting intervention in the voluntary sector for reducing child conduct problems: outcomes and mechanisms of change. *Journal of Child Psychology and Psychiatry*, 47, 1123-32.

Gardner, F. (2012). Review: group-based behavioural and cognitive-behavioural parenting interventions are effective and cost-effective for reducing early-onset child conduct problems. *Evidence-based Mental Health*, Apr 25, 2012. [Epub. ahead of print].

Greene, S. (1994). Growing up Irish: Development in context. *The Irish Journal of Psychology*, 15, 354-71.

Griffith, N., Hutchings, J. and Bywater, T. (2011). Evaluating the Incredible Years Toddler parenting programme with parents of high-risk children living in disadvantaged areas of Wales. *Paper presented at the Society for prevention research 19th Annual Meeting*, Washington D.C.

Hahlweg, K., Heinrichs, N., Kuschel, A., Bertram, H., and Naumann, S. (2010). Long-term outcome of a randomised controlled universal prevention trial through a positive parenting program: is it worth the effort?. *Child and Adolescent Psychiatry and Mental Health*, 4(14), 1–14.

Hutchings, J., Lane, E. and Kelly, J. (2004). Comparison of two treatments of children with severely disruptive behaviours: Four-year follow up. *Behavioural and Cognitive Psychotherapy*, 32, 15–30.

Hutchings, J., Bywater, T., Daley, D., Gardner, F., Whitaker, C., Jones, K., Eames, C., and Edwards, R. T. (2007a). Parenting intervention in Sure Start services for children at risk of developing conduct disorder: pragmatic randomised controlled trial. *BMJ*, 334, 678.

Hutchings, J., Bywater, T. and Daley, D. (2007b). A pragmatic randomised controlled trial of a parenting intervention in Sure Start services for preschool children at risk of developing conduct disorder: How and why did it work? *Journal of Children's Services*, 2 (2), 4-14.

Kazdin, A. E. (2003). Problem-solving skills training and parent management training for Conduct Disorder. In: A. E. Kazdin and J. R. Weisz (Eds.), *Evidence-Based Psychotherapies for Children and Adolescents* (pp. 241-263). NY: The Guilford Press.

Kim, E., Cain, K. C. and Webster-Stratton, C. (2008). The preliminary effect of a parenting program for Korean American mothers: a randomised controlled experimental study. *International Journal of Nursing Studies,* 45(9), 1261–73.

Kling, A., Forster, M., Sundell, K., and Melin, L. (2010). A randomised controlle effectiveness trial of parent management training with varying degrees of therapist support. *Behavior Therapy,* 41(4), 530–42.

Larsson, B., Fossum, S., Clifford, G., Drugli, M., Handegard, B., and Morch, W. (2008). Treatment of oppositional defiant and conduct problems in young Norwegian children. *European Child and Adolescent Psychiatry*, 18, 42-52.

Liabo, K. and Richardson, J. (2007). Conduct Disorder and offending behaviour in young people. London: Jessica Kingsley Publishers.

Littleton, J. (2009). Putting children first. In: T. Flannery. (Ed.). *Responding to the Ryan Report*. Dublin: Columba Press.

McGilloway, S., Ni Mhaille, G., Bywater, T., Furlong, M., Leckey, Y., Kelly, P., Comiskey, C., and Donnelly, M. (2011). A Parenting Intervention for Childhood Behavioral Problems: A Randomised Controlled Trial in Disadvantaged Community-based Settings. *Journal of Consulting and Clinical Psychology*, 80(1), 116-127. DOI: 10.1037/a0026304.

Melhuish, E., Belsky, J., Leyland, A. H., and Barnes, J. (2008). Effects of fully-established Sure Start local programmes on 3-year old children and their families living in England: a quasi- experimental observational study. *Lancet,* 372(9650), 1641–47.

Mihalic, S. and Irwin, K. (2003). Blueprints for Violence Prevention: From Research to Real-World Settings-Factors Influencing the Successful Replication of Model Programs. *Youth Violence and Juvenile Justice,* 1(4), 307-329.

Mihalopoulos, C., Sanders, M. R., Turner, K. M. T., Murphy-Brennan, M., and Carter, R. (2007). Does the Triple P-Positive Parenting Program provide value for money? *Australian and New Zealand Journal of Psychiatry*, 41(3), 239–46.

Ogden, T., Amlund Hagen, K., Askeland, E., and Christensen, B. (2009). Implementing and Evaluating Evidence-Based Treatments of Conduct Problems in Children and Youth in Norway. *Research on Social Work Practice,* 19, 582. DOI: 10.1177/1049731509335530

O' Neill, D., McGilloway, S., Donnolly, M., Bywater, T., and Kelly, P. (2011). A cost effectiveness analysis of the Incredible Years Parenting Programme in reducing childhood health Inequalities. *European Journal of Health Economics*, available "Online First" at http://www.springerlink. com/openurl.asp. doi:10.1007/s10198-011-0342-y 2011.

Paiva, N. D. (2008). South Asian parents' constructions of praising their children. *Clinical Child Psychology and Psychiatry*, 13 (2), 191-207.

Patterson, J., Barlow, J., Mockford, C., Klimes, I., Pyper, C., and Stewart-Brown, S. (2002). Improving mental health through parenting programmes: block randomised controlled trial. *Archives of Disease in Childhood*, 86, 472–7.

Petrosino, A., Turpin-Petrosino, C. and Finckenauer, J. O. (2000). Well-meaning programs can have harmful effects! Lessons from experiments of programs such as Scared Straight. *Crime and Delinquency*, 46, 354-379.

Reyno, S. M. and McGrath, P. J. (2006). Predictors of parent training efficacy for child externalizing behaviour problems – a meta-analytic review. *Journal of Child Psychology and Psychiatry*, 47 (1), 99-111.

Romeo, R., Byford, S. and Knapp, M. (2005). Annotation: Economic evaluations of child and adolescent mental health interventions: a systematic review. *Journal of Child Psychology and Psychiatry*, 46, 919–930. doi: 10.1111/j.1469-7610.2005.00407.x

Sainsbury Centre for Mental Health. (2009). *The chance of a lifetime: preventing early conduct problems and reducing crime*. Available at: www.scmh.org.uk

Sanders, M. R. and McFarland, M. (2003). Treatment of depressed mothers with disruptive children: a controlled evaluation of cognitive behavioral family intervention. *Behavior Therapy*, 31(1), 89–112.

Sanders, M. R. and Turner, K. M. (2005). Reflections on the Challenges of Effective Dissemination of Behavioural Family Intervention: Our Experience with the Triple P – Positive Parenting Program. *Child and Adolescent Mental Health*, 10, 158–169.

Sanders, M. R., Ralph, A., Sofronoff, K., Gardiner, P., Thompson, R., and Dwyer, S. (2008). Every family: a population approach to reducing behavioral and emotional problems in children making the transition to school. *The Journal of Primary Prevention,* 29(3), 197–222.

Scott, S., Knapp, M., Henderson, J. and Maughan, B. (2001a). *Financial cost of social exclusion: Follow up study of antisocial children into adulthood*. BMJ, 323, 191.

Shulruf, B., O' Loughlin, C. and Tolley, H. (2009). Parenting education and support policies and their consequences in selected OECD countries. *Children and Youth Services Review*, 31, 526-532.

Sloper, P. (2004). Facilitators and barriers for co-ordinated multi-agency services. *Child: Care, Health and Development*, 30, 571-80.

Spaccarelli, S., Cotler, S. and Penman, D. (1992). Problem-solving skills training as a supplement to behavioral parent training. *Cognitive Therapy and Research,* 16(1), 1–17.

Statham, J. (2011). *Working together for children: a review of international evidence on interagency working, to inform the development of Children's Services Committees in Ireland*. Dublin: Department of Children and Youth Affairs.

Webster-Stratton, C. (1984). Randomised trial of two parent training programs for families with conduct-disordered children. *Journal of Consulting and Clinical Psychology,* 52(4), 666–78.

Webster-Stratton, C. and Hammond, M. (1997). Treating children with early-onset conduct problems: a comparison of child and parent training interventions. *Journal of Consulting and Clinical Psychology,* 65(1), 93–109.

Webster-Stratton, C. and Hancock, L. (1998). Parent training: Content, methods and processes. In: E. Shafer. (Ed.). *Handbook of Parent Training* (2nd Ed, pp. 98-152*).* New York: Wiley and Sons.

Webster-Stratton, C., Reid, M. J. and Hammond, M. (2004). Treating children with early-onset conduct problems: Intervention outcomes for parent, child, and teacher training. *Journal of Clinical Child and Adolescent Psychology*, 33 (1), 105-24.

Webster-Stratton, C. (2009). Affirming diversity: Multi-cultural collaboration to deliver the incredible years parent programs. *International Journal of Child Health and Human Development*, 2 (1), 17-32.

Webster-Stratton, C., Rinaldi, J. and Reid, J. M. (2010). Long-term outcomes of Incredible Years Parenting Program: predictors of adolescent adjustment. *Child and Adolescent Mental Health* Sep. 14 [Epub. ahead of print]. Doi: 10.1111/j.1475 3588.2010.00.00576.x

Webster-Stratton, C., Reinke, W. M. and Herman, K. C. (2011). The Incredible Years Teacher Training: The Methods and Principles that Support Adaptation and Dissemination with High Fidelity. *School Psychology Review*, 40, 509-529.

Weissberg, R. P., Kumpfer, K. L. and Seligman, M. E. P. (2003). Prevention that works for children and youth: An introduction. *American Psychologist*, 59, 425-32.

In: Parenting

ISBN: 978-1-62257-881-8

Editors: Peter Barberis and Stelios Petrakis

© 2013 Nova Science Publishers, Inc.

Chapter 11

A CULTURAL MELTING POT: PARENTING PRACTICES IN A GLOBAL WORLD

Melanie Morse and Cliff McKinney
Mississippi State University, Mississippi, US

ABSTRACT

An individual's culture plays an important role throughout life; culture's influence on parenting is no exception. It is clear that parents play a valuable role in transmitting the values, rules, and standards of society to children. Globally, a range of parenting practices has emerged. What is considered to be normative parenting for a child varies across cultures. Differing parenting styles may be found between individualist and collectivist cultures, with the latter showing a stronger preference for authoritarian parenting. Cultural norms for family roles may be thought to influence parenting practices. Individualist cultures tend to emphasize an individual's independence from others, while collectivist cultures emphasize an individual's interdependence with his or her family, community, and country. As individualist cultures encourage autonomy, assertiveness, and a need for privacy, parenting practices may be more relaxed than in a collectivist culture. Specific examples across cultures will be discussed. Given the sometimes conflicting viewpoints of individualist and collectivist parenting, researchers and clinicians working with parents should ensure that their programs are culturally sensitive and appropriate. Suggestions for working with culturally diverse groups are discussed.

A CULTURAL MELTING POT: PARENTING PRACTICES IN A GLOBAL WORLD

It is clear that parents play a valuable role in transmitting the values, rules, and standards of society to children. Cauce (2008) wrote that children become members of a culture through the modeling of parental and other behaviors. During a baby's first years, he or she is immersed in a largely one-sided conversation with the parent or caregiver, thus facilitating the development of language. Infants gain exposure to people through reciprocal vocalizations and such infants show preference for learning and categorizing their native language. Exposure to language primes the brain's circuitry for learning the native language (Kuhl, 2007). Indeed, humans learn from socialization and exposure to language is an important step in understanding social norms as well as their own family's unique rules.

PARENTING IN COLLECTIVIST VERSUS INDIVIDUALIST CULTURES

From their parents, children learn what is expected of them in various situations. Values are passed down across generations and, within a culture, every family certainly has their own traditions and rules outlining a situation's prescribed behavior. It also is important to keep in mind that what is acceptable and considered commonplace in one culture (or family) may be a viewed as a complete violation of cultural norms elsewhere. Cultural differences are primarily studied between collectivist (i.e., Guatemala, Ecuador, Panama, Columbia, Pakistan, Taiwan, South Korea) and individualist cultures (i.e., United States, Australia, Great Britain, Canada, Netherlands, New Zealand, Italy). The main differences between the two cultures are often thought to focus on the importance of the group rather than the individual, respectively. For instance, a family from a collectivist culture (i.e., typically emphasizing the interdependence of its members as a part of society as a whole) may be more apt to provide advice encouraging a child's development of group identities through mutual cooperation. A family from an individualist culture (i.e., typically emphasizing personal achievement in which each member is distinguishable from the other) would be more likely to encourage their child to think for themselves, allowing for the child to choose his or her own social groups.

Environment may be related to culture and plays an important role in parenting. Depending on one's physical environment, higher or lower levels of parental physical contact may be present. Cauce (2008) pointed out that higher levels of child-parent physical contact are often present among cultures plagued by high infant mortality or harsh living conditions. Evolution has helped to shape parenting across cultures, as higher levels of physical contact in dangerous environments serve to protect a child from potential harm. Staying near an ill infant may help a parent to monitor the infant's condition and provide more appropriate care; providing physical contact serves to soothe both the infant and the parent to some degree.

Environment and parental physical contact. Parental physical contact is clearly influenced by physical environment, but is one's parenting style also influenced by cultural and related environmental factors? It is likely that this is the case. Understanding the cultural context in which parenting occurs is useful in that it may help predict parenting style or differences in parenting. Because collectivist cultures place a greater emphasis on interdependent relationships, it may be the case that parenting is more involved than in individualist cultures, where independence is emphasized. Although parenting styles may be consistent across cultures, one would expect differences to emerge as a result of cultural or social norms. Furthermore, it also is possible that theories and related ideas regarding parenting may be culturally biased towards the culture in which they were developed.

Co-sleeping and culture. Co-sleeping, while present in many cultures, is more popular among collectivist countries. Huang, Wang, Zhang, and Liu (2010) investigated co-sleeping in China. The authors reported that as many as 79% of preschool and 53% of school-aged Chinese children sleep in the same bed as their parents. Co-sleeping may be seen as an extension of collectivism, as it emphasizes family bonds. Furthermore, the authors noted that Chinese parents view this practice as a means of both monitoring the child throughout the night and providing reassurance to the child through the mother's presence.

Conversely, prevailing research among Western nations has labeled co-sleeping as unsafe, and the practice is generally discouraged. Huang and colleagues (2010) noted that co-sleeping often results in reports of increased daytime drowsiness for children. The authors also noted that co-sleeping has been associated with Sudden Infant Death Syndrome (SIDS), although some argue that co-sleeping actually prevents the disease, as many co-sleeping mothers are lighter sleepers. Hunsley and Thoman (2002) investigated differences between co-sleeping and non-co-sleeping infants. The researchers found that co-sleeping has major developmental implications for children and that, in a Western context, co-sleeping may be stressful for children, as it is associated with non-optimal neurobehavioral functioning. One's cultural perspective clearly plays a role in his or her opinion regarding co-sleeping.

PARENTING STYLES AND CULTURE

Are Parenting Styles Universal?

Sorkhabi (2005) studied the applicability of Baumrind's parenting styles (i.e., authoritarian, authoritative, permissive, neglecting) to collectivist cultures. According to Baumrind (1991), authoritative parents are high in demandingness and high in responsiveness, authoritarian parents are high in demandingness and low in responsiveness, permissive parents are low in demandingness and high in responsiveness, and neglecting parents are neither demanding nor responsive. Sorkhabi noted that Baumrind's parenting typology was developed in the United States and has primarily been applied to individualist cultures, so it was important to determine whether this typology applied to collectivist cultures as well. Sorkhabi reported that Baumrind's parenting styles, as related to child outcomes (i.e., achievement, maladjustment), have been found to be present in both collectivist and individualist cultures. The main difference across cultures appeared to be between authoritative and authoritarian parenting, in that collectivist cultures have not shown a difference between authoritative and authoritarian parenting on adolescents' grades. Because individualist cultures tend to value self-chosen goals, collectivists' emphasis on the family and greater community could play a role in academic success.

In other words, Sorkhabi's (2005) finding regarding authoritative and authoritarian parenting and academic performance among collectivist cultures could be due to pressure from the collectivist whole to succeed academically. The author clarified that parental warmth has been associated with positive child outcomes across cultures, regardless of parenting style. Sorkhabi also noted that parenting factors such as lack of positive affect are interpreted similarly by children across cultures. Regardless of culture, children are able to identify neglecting parenting styles, for example, as being marked by lack of parental warmth. Although collectivist and individualist cultures have differing emphases on relationships (i.e., collectivism emphasizes fewer, but more stable, interpersonal relationships, whereas individualism emphasizes many loosely-linked social relationships), a warm, loving parental relationship appears to be important in both cultures.

It is important to keep in mind that, within cultures, a variety of parenting styles are present. Sorkhabi's (2005) research identified the presence of authoritative, authoritarian, permissive, and neglecting parenting styles across both collectivist and individualist cultures. Although specific parenting attitudes and ideas regarding best practices certainly vary by culture, Baumrind's parenting styles remain constant.

Parenting in Collectivist Cultures

Keshavarz and Baharudin (2009) investigated parenting styles present in Malaysia, a collectivist culture. Previous research indicated that Malaysian youth tend to be high in agreeableness, low in extraversion, and low in openness as compared to sampled American youth (Mastor, Jin, and Cooper, 2000). In their investigation of parenting in Malaysia, the authors found that unity, sharing, and caring for the family and community were important cultural values transmitted from parents to children (Keshavarz and Baharudin, 2009). As is the norm for collectivist cultures, Malaysian parents tend to employ an authoritarian parenting style. The authors noted that Malaysian children are expected to obey their parents without question and that special attention is given to spiritual growth as a child matures. Another important factor that the authors presented was acculturation and the growing exposure of Western culture to Malaysia through the media. Keshavarz and Baharudin (2009) reported that Western media challenges Malay cultural norms, as Western parenting practices including authoritative parenting style are unacceptable to many Malaysian parents. It is likely that some Malaysians have, at least partially, embraced Western norms, but a collectivist authoritarian parenting style appears to be the prevailing choice for Malaysian parents at the present time.

Why is collectivist parenting different? Keshavarz and Baharudin (2009) posed arguments based on the assumption that the differences between parenting styles in collectivist and individualist cultures are likely due to the different family relationships and self-conceptualization across cultures. The authors noted that, while individualist cultures tend to view an authoritative parenting style as the best choice for positive youth outcome, collectivist cultures such as Malaysia may view authoritarian parenting style as being more suitable for positive youth outcome. One must keep in mind that a collectivist implementation of authoritarian parenting may appear more appropriate given the dominant collectivist values. Keshavarz and Baharudin reiterated that authoritarian parents are usually less affectionate and provide fewer rewards for their children. Authoritarian parents have high expectations for their children to follow explicit rules and may use more severe punishment than what is typical of other parenting styles.

Because collectivist cultures value group cohesion, Keshavarz and Baharudin (2009) explained that an authoritarian family in a collectivist culture may be more likely to implement strict punishment when a child violates group rules or works against conformity with the larger community. In a collectivist culture, strict punishment for violation of such group norms may be viewed as appropriate because interdependence is so important. Collectivist parents may appear to be authoritarian because one-on-one relationships, such as those within a family, are secondary to a child's overall role in the family or community. Therefore, fewer direct rewards from the parent would be necessary, as the child gains reward from interdependence with others. Keeping in mind that Malaysian youth are high in agreeableness, it makes sense that individuals in a collectivist culture may suppress their own needs in favor of addressing the needs of others in the group. Because the needs of others are often placed before one's own needs, Keshavarz and Baharudin wrote that authoritarian parenting styles may be more appropriate given collectivist values.

Collectivist parenting and academic outcomes. Chao (1994) explored the effects of parenting behaviors of parents from collectivist culture on academic performance. Chao noted that Chinese parenting has typically been labeled as restrictive, controlling, or authoritarian. Chao's results indicated that the sampled Chinese-American parents were more authoritarian in their parenting styles than their European-American counterparts. The author added that a major flaw in simply labeling Chinese parents as "authoritarian" is that this label purports that Chinese parents aim to dominate the child, when these parents are actually working to ensure that their children develop harmonious relationships with the collectivist whole. Consistent with collectivist values, peer influences have been found to have a greater effect on Asians' academic success than parental influences (Steinberg, Dornbusch, and Brown, 1992). Chao stated that control and governance in the Chinese classroom separate this academic environment from others, especially those in individualist cultures.

Regarding academic performance, Chao's (1994) findings indicated that Chinese-American parents may encourage strong academic performance through "training." Chao explained that training encompasses high parental control in parent-child interactions, as well as support and concern. Training outlines a reciprocal relationship in which children are loyal and respectful to parents and authority figures (i.e., teachers, community members) and these authority figures have a responsibility to teach, discipline, and generally govern the child. Training may make authoritarian parenting seem less harsh because it provides a positive influence on children's overall outcome through improved academic performance. Chao noted that the concept of training is unique to collectivist cultures and may explain why some Asian cultures report stronger academic performance than Western cultures. Chinese parents, for instance, may come across as intensely concerned and controlling towards their children, but these parenting behaviors may have a positive effect the child's overall outcome, especially academically.

Parenting as a Function of Cultural Values

Another important difference between the appropriateness of authoritarian parenting across cultures is a child's interpretation of the parent-child relationship. Baumrind (1972) noted that, when parental behavior is consistent with cultural values, children are more accepting of the specific parenting behaviors in question. For instance, a verbal reprimand may be well-received by a child who understands that the purpose of the reprimand is to help instill positive societal values. Specifically, Baumrind purported that variables such as ethnicity and socioeconomic status are part of one's cultural background and influence parenting behaviors. Baumrind investigated parenting styles of 16 African American families in the United States and found that the predominately authoritarian parenting style utilized by these families was perceived somewhat negatively by others, especially those of the prevailing liberal, middle class viewpoint.

Baumrind's (1972) results indicated that few differences in parenting style emerged between boys of African American and Caucasian ethnicities. However, African American girls, as compared to Caucasian girls, more often had parents classified as authoritarian-rejecting. For instance, Baumrind noted that African American girls' independence and individuality was encouraged less frequently. However, while these African American girls were less achievement oriented, the difference was not significant; these girls, as compared to their Caucasian peers, were well-adjusted and independent. Baumrind explained that African American girls may be independent and at ease even in novel settings because they often take on the role of caregiver to younger siblings. In other words, authoritarian parenting does not necessarily lead to poor child outcomes. Authoritarian parenting may be more appropriate in a larger family in which children must care for younger siblings because these children must learn to be self-sufficient and fulfill prescribed household roles independently.

PARENTING IN A DIVERSE WORLD: PRACTICES, EVALUATION, AND RECOMMENDATIONS

One confounding factor in parenting research is the constant immigration and emigration of families to and from various cultures. Anyone with the resources could quickly and easily be on the other side of the world within a relatively short amount of time (i.e., a day or so via air travel). Given the increased accessibility and subsequent globalization, one might expect to find a blend of collectivist and individualist ideals among some families. It is certainly becoming more difficult to tease apart the differences between different cultures as families are increasingly exposed to an array of global ideals and environments.

Parenting among Immigrant Families

When a family moves to a new environment, they may adopt some or all of that culture's parenting practices. Abad and Sheldon (2008) investigated parental support and ethnic identification among second-generation immigrant young adult college students. Results indicated that paternal (and not maternal) autonomy and support is associated with higher endorsement of the natal culture (i.e., the culture from which the family comes). It may be the case that identification with the natal culture, especially during a period of transition such as college, serves to bolster a person's sense of identity. Furthermore, the authors identified fathers as being instrumental in helping children understand their societal roles across cultures.

Yaman, Mesman, van IJzendoorn, Bakermans-Kranenburg, and Linting (2010) focused on parenting differences between Turkish immigrant and Dutch families with 2-year-old children displaying externalizing behaviors. The researchers recruited second-generation Turkish immigrant mothers so that any possible effects of acculturation could be assessed; acculturation was assessed by measuring the mothers' frequency with which and with whom both Dutch and Turkish are spoken. Mothers were given measures assessing their child's externalizing behaviors and maternal sensitivity was measured during participation in a set of three problem-solving tasks with her child. The researchers observed maternal discipline as mother-child dyads participated in a four-minute clean-up task following problem-solving tasks.

Results indicated that one difference between Turkish and Dutch mothers was age: Turkish mothers were significantly younger and less educated than Dutch mothers (Yaman, Mesman, van IJzendoorn, Bakermans-Kranenburg, and Linting, 2010). Furthermore, the researchers found that Turkish mothers were less sensitive during the problem-solving tasks, giving less clear instructions and less support to their child. Turkish mothers were also found to be more intrusive than Dutch mothers throughout the tasks, an expected finding given that individualist cultures such as the Netherlands value autonomy in parenting so that the child is given independence of choice in many situations. Dutch mothers were generally found to be more authoritative than their Turkish counterparts. The authors noted that, while Turkish mothers employed some principles of authoritarian parenting, they had a more progressive interpretation of this parenting style than what might be expected of mothers living in Turkey, a collectivist culture. The authors explained this finding by suggesting that these Turkish immigrants may have shifted from traditionally strict authoritarian parenting practices to elements of authoritarian parenting including inductive reasoning and explaining.

Overall, results indicated that more maternal support means less maternal intrusiveness, more clear instructions, and a tendency to discipline in an authoritative manner. Yaman et al. (2010) found that second-generation Turkish immigrant mothers did employ some authoritative parenting behaviors and, more notably, tended to employ less strict authoritarian parenting behaviors, likely due to acculturation. When parents embrace a new culture, they are more likely to incorporate its values (including parenting values) in their own daily practices. Yaman and colleagues' research suggests that second-generation immigrants may be more readily adopting the parenting practices of their new cultures than first-generation immigrants. Indeed, the patterns of parenting behavior between second-generation immigrant mothers from a collectivist culture and individualist mothers in their host culture were comparable.

The Role of Environment on the Parent-Child Relationship

Just as a child's environment influences his or her development, the environment is influenced by an array of factors including maternal mental health, family background, and the prevailing social structure. Burns and Radford (2008) investigated parent-child interactions among Nigerian families. The authors explained that Nigerian culture places an emphasis on obedience without question from the child, and that a child is expected to be responsible. The authors further reported that parent-child interactions among Nigerian families may be different than in Western cultures, as West African mothers are rarely the sole caregivers of their children. As in some collectivist cultures, child-rearing in Nigeria is marked by a community contribution – children are frequently attended to by siblings and older women of the community.

Burns and Radford (2008) hypothesized that Nigerian parents will expose correction as a means of teaching correct behaviors in response to children's errors. The authors analyzed parent-child interactions of three Nigerian mother-child dyads living in London. The mothers in the sample were born in Nigeria, whereas the children were born in England. Mother-child dyads were videotaped for approximately 15-20 minutes in their home environment. Analysis of parent-child interactions indicated that all three dyads engaged in tuitional modeling, meaning that the mother attempted to get her child to respond by providing explicit instructions. For instance, one mother directly elicited the response of clapping by modeling the behavior for her child. Direct modeling of behaviors is certainly not unique to Nigerian culture and reveals that some behaviors involved in Nigerian parent-child interactions are universal.

In their evaluation of the mother-child interactions, the authors also found that initiation-response-evaluation (IRE), initiation-evaluation (IE), and initiation-confirmation-topic pursuit (ICT) patterns were evident in the Nigerian mothers' interactions with their children (Burns and Radford, 2008). IRE patterns are characteristic of classroom-type interactions, in which the mother asks a question, the child responds, and the mother responds appropriately with praise, if appropriate. IE patterns are different in that the child initiates the interaction. ICT patterns are also initiated by children and are more involved a continued pursuit of the child's topic. If these patterns of interaction seem familiar, it is likely because they are utilized by many parents across cultures.

Recommendations for Clinicians

Burns and Radford (2008) concluded that Nigerian mother-child dyads are different in that their interactions do include strong elements of classroom talk, in that interactions are often quite directive and correction is frequently utilized. The authors suggest that, as when working with any culturally diverse family, therapists must take into account both the context of the interaction as well as cultural beliefs driving the behavior of the interaction. For example, a Nigerian mother may come off as somewhat controlling because of the emphasis on correction and directing of child behaviors. Clinicians must keep in mind that this directiveness is driven by the mother's desire to build her child's skill set. It is essential that clinicians encourage all positive aspects of parent-child interactions and work individually with the child to help him or her understand the meaning behind parental behavior. Similarly, parents should be encouraged to explore the meanings of their own interactions with their children.

The findings of Yaman et al. (2010) also have implications for clinicians working with immigrant parents. In their study, second-generation Turkish immigrant mothers living in a collectivist culture were found to utilize some aspects of authoritarian parenting (i.e., intrusiveness, less sensitivity, fewer clear instructions), but also displayed elements of authoritative parenting comparable to Dutch mothers. Given that second-generation immigrants may be more open and accepting of parenting practices in their host country, clinicians should identify whether or not this acculturation and acceptance is present upon first meeting with first or second-generation immigrants. If the clinician is working with second or later-generation immigrants, they may be more open to implementing the clinician's recommendations, especially if those recommendations are consistent with the prevailing parenting practices in the host culture.

Keeping in mind the various cultural values and parenting practices presented, the importance of factoring in the client's cultural values in providing treatment and recommendations cannot be understated. Clinicians who are not culturally sensitive will likely encounter difficulties throughout treatment. For instance, a family from a collectivist culture may have a difficult time giving their child opportunities for autonomy; the therapist must be careful to consider whether it is even appropriate to give the child complete autonomy as would be expected in an individualist culture and, if so, to work gradually towards that goal. Clients who feel that the therapist is pushing his or her own cultural values may feel alienated and choose to terminate treatment early.

As has been discussed previously, one must keep in mind that, even within a culture, a variety of practices emerge. For instance, a clinician may find him or herself working with a family who does not allow their child to engage any chosen activities outside of school. It could be the case that the child is required to study from the moment that he returns home from school. While this may seem like a very strict approach from a Western culture, the clinician must work to try to understand the parents' intentions rather than generalizing and labeling the family as oppressive. In order to understand the full picture of the child's experience, the clinician must understand the motivation behind the parents' rule. These particular parents may come from a culture in which high academic performance is considered an essential goal for children. The parents may feel that they are appropriately encouraging academic success by making their child study constantly when not in school; the child may actually appreciate this pressure from his parents if he views the behavior as being consistent with the cultural values (Baumrind, 1972).

Conversely, a client may present complaining that his parents gave him too much autonomy and that any behavior was praised in excess by his parents; perhaps the client now has trouble making decisions and identifying the difference between right and wrong. The client reports that he has had to relocate to China for work, and that he is having a hard time adjusting. An unwise clinician might blow the case off, labeling the client as a "spoiled brat." Another clinician might approach the case from a collectivist perspective, asking the client to try to reconnect with his family and incorporate himself in the community. The successful therapist will work with the client to understand how cultural issues may be affecting his outlook. The therapist should work with this client to better understand how both his and his parents' individualist values have played a role in current behaviors. Regardless, the clinician must approach the situation from a global standpoint in order to best address the presenting issues.

It is also important to remember that rare, outlying behaviors emerge across cultures as well. For instance, an annual Vegetarian Festival is held in Thailand. The festivities, held primarily in Phuket, are a colorful display. Festival participants wear white and abstain from eating meat for nine days. A few religious devotees pierce their cheeks with swords and other sharp objects, believing that the Chinese gods will protect them from pain and suffering. Remarkably, few of these devotees have any scars from the piercings. It is easy to see how a clinician who is not culturally aware may react strongly to hearing such a story. A strong, adverse reaction could, as mentioned, serve only to drive away the client. In working with culturally diverse clients, therapists must strive to be open-minded and, as with any case, consider the motivation driving the behavior in order to fully understand the client.

CONCLUSION

A variety of parenting approaches are present, and many parenting practices vary by culture. Individualist cultures tend to value autonomy, while collectivist cultures value the interdependence of the individual with one's family and greater community. While Baumrind's parenting styles (i.e., authoritarian, authoritative, permissive, neglecting) have been found to be present across individualist and collectivist cultures, the latter shows a strong preference for authoritarian parenting (Sorkhabi, 2005; Keshavarz and Baharudin, 2009). Research suggests that parenting differences between these cultures could be due to the values underlying each culture (Keshavarz and Baharudin, 2009). It is also important to remember that certain parenting behaviors may be well-received by children when such behaviors are consistent with cultural values (Baumrind, 1972). Given the diverse parenting practices that are present across cultures, clinicians should work to be open-minded and share the advantages and disadvantages associated with certain parenting practices. For instance, Huang, Wang, Zhang, and Liu (2010) reported that clinicians play a valuable role in parents' decisions regarding co-sleeping, as parents look to clinicians and healthcare professionals to determine whether or not they should share a bed with their child. The authors noted that clinicians may point out that nighttime separation may become a problem for children ages three to four accustomed to co-sleeping, leading a child to have a fear of certain objects or the dark and requesting to re-initiate co-sleeping. Others may argue that a practice other than co-sleeping is unkind and would fail to instill values of interdependence in a child. Regardless of the situation, the clinician should attempt to educate him or herself so that he or she is culturally competent. Clinicians who treat the client as a member of a diverse, global community will likely see a more positive treatment outcome.

REFERENCES

Abad, N. S., Sheldon, K. M. (2008). Parental autonomy support and ethnic culture identification among second-generation immigrants. *Journal of Family Psychology*, *22*, 652-657.

Baumrind, D. (1972). An exploratory study of socialization effects on black children: Some black-white comparisons. *Child Development*, *43*, 261-267.

Baumrind, D. (1991). The influence of parenting style on adolescent competence and substance use. *Journal of Early Adolescence*, *11*, 56-95.

Burns, A., and Radford, J. (2008). Parent-child interaction in Nigerian families: Conversation analysis, context and culture. *Child Language Teaching and Therapy*, *24*, 193-209.

Cauce, A. M. (2008). Parenting, culture, and context: Reflections on excavating culture. *Applied Developmental Science*, *12*, 227-229.

Chao, R. K. (1994). Beyond parental control and authoritarian parenting style: Understanding Chinese parenting through the cultural notion of training. *Child Development*, *65*, 1111-1119.

Huang, X., Wang, H., Zhang, L., and Liu, X. (2010). Co-sleeping and children's sleep in China. *Biological Rhythm Research*, *41*, 169-181.

Hunsley, M., and Thoman, E. B. (2002). The sleep of co-sleeping infants when they are not co-sleeping: Evidence that co-sleeping is stressful. *Developmental Psychobiology, 40,* 14-22.

Keshavarz, S., and Baharudin, R. (2009). Parenting style in a collectivist culture of Malaysia. *European Journal of Social Sciences, 10,* 66-73.

Kuhl, P. K. (2007). Is speech learning 'gated" by the social brain? *Developmental Science, 10,* 110-120.

Mastor, K. A., Jin, P., and Cooper, M. (2000). Malay culture and personality: A big five perspective. *American Behavioral Scientist, 44,* 95-111.

Sorkhabi, N. (2005). Applicability of Baumrind's parent typology to collective cultures: Analysis of cultural explanations of parent socialization effects. *International Journal of Behavioral Development, 6,* 552-563.

Steinberg, L., Dornbusch, S., and Brown, B. B. (1992). Ethnic differences in adolescent achievement: An ecological perspective. *American Psychologist, 47,* 723-729.

Yaman, A., Mesman, J., van Ijzendoorn, M. H., Bakermans-Kranenburg, M. J., and Linting, M. (2010). Parenting in an individualistic culture with a collectivistic cultural background: The case of Turkish immigrant families with toddlers in the Netherlands. *Journal of Child and Family Studies, 19,* 617-628.

In: Parenting
Editors: Peter Barberis and Stelios Petrakis

ISBN: 978-1-62257-881-8
© 2013 Nova Science Publishers, Inc.

Chapter 12

FAMILY OF ORIGIN HERITAGE, INDIVIDUAL WELL-BEING, AND RELATIONSHIP SATISFACTION IN YOUNG COUPLES

Raffaella Iafrate, Silvia Donato and Anna Bertoni
Catholic University of Milan, Italy

ABSTRACT

Parenting experiences children have lived within their families can play an important role for adult children's couple relationship, not only in terms of the actual behaviors and practices parents have engaged in during childhood and adolescence, but also in terms of the heritage of values, norms, and models adult children perceive that have settled from those experiences. The present study was designed to investigate the interplay among perceived family heritage, partners' individual well-being, and their relationship satisfaction. Two hundred and twenty premarital couples completed self-report measures of family heritage, personal well-being and relationship satisfaction. Structural equation modeling was used to test the connections among these variables. Results indicated that perceiving a positive family heritage promoted partners' psychological well-being, which in turn sustained a satisfying couple relationship. Results were discuss also in terms of their implication for family prevention programs.

Keywords: Family of origin; couple; relationship satisfaction; individual well-being

INTRODUCTION

Parenting experiences children have lived within their families can play an important role for adult children's couple relationship, not only in terms of the actual behaviors and practices parents have engaged in during childhood and adolescence, but also in terms of the heritage of values, norms, and models adult children perceive that have settled from those experiences.

Psychosocial research has devoted great attention to the variables linked to couple satisfaction not only to understand the factors that can define the quality of couple relationship, but also to design effective interventions to prevent marital distress and separation. The quality of couple relationship is influenced both by partners' behavioral exchanges, like communication or conflict resolution, and the relationships the couple has with its familial and social context (Cigoli & Scabini, 2006; Fincham & Beach, 2010; Scabini & Cigoli, 2000; Scabini & Iafrate, 2003). A crucial role, within the familial context of couples, is played by the quality of the parenting experiences partners have lived within their families of origin, not only in terms of the actual parenting practices parents have engaged in during their children's development, but also in terms of the heritage that adult children have obtained from those experiences.

The present study was designed to analyze the interplay among this latter and so far neglected aspect of the family of origin, that is perceived family heritage, partners' individual well-being, and relationship satisfaction.

FAMILY OF ORIGIN IMPACT ON ADULT CHILDREN

Partners' experiences in their families of origin and their impact on their couple relationship are still little explored in the literature and generally considered by different theoretical perspectives (see Topham, Larson, & Holman, 2005). Multigenerational family theory suggests that individuals acquire the bases of their interpersonal relationships within their families (Framo, 1981; Hoopes, 1987). Along with this perspective the influence of partners' families of origin remains strong even when individuals do not have continuous contacts with their families (Bartle-Haring & Sabatelli, 1998). According to Social-learning theory (Bandura, 1977), moreover, most of the behavioral repertoires the individual manifests within his/her couple relationship are learned during childhood through the observation of parents interacting with each other and with children. On the other hand, Attachment theory posits a connection between parent-child attachment styles and children's cognitive models and behavioral patterns (Ainsworth et al., 1978; Bowlby,1969, 1973, 1980), which tend to extend to all the other relationship partners, determining the behaviors the individual will manifest in his/her future relationships (Main, Hesse, & Kaplan, 2005).

Inspired by these theoretical perspectives research on family of origin influences, yet not numerous, can be divided into (a) studies that investigate the effects of family of origin variables on adult children's individual adjustment, and (b) studies that explore the influence of relationships lived in the family of origin on children's couple relationship.

Within the first line of research studies explore, on the one hand, how parents' couple relationship may influence children's adjustment and, on the other hand, how parent-child relationships and parenting practices may have an impact on children's psychological well-being and social competences.

As for parent's couple relationship, numerous studies have targeted the effects of parents' divorce on children (see Amato & James, 2010) and in particular a relatively recent line of research investigates these effects on children's outcomes in young adulthood (Cigoli, Iafrate, & Giuliani, 2002; Darlington, 2001; Wallerstein, 2005). Research on marital violence as well extended its focus on the effects of interparental violence on children's well-being beyond childhood and adolescence to the long-term effects it may have once children become adults (e.g., McNeal & Amato, 1998).

With regard to the parent-child relationship and parenting practices research has studied how an inadequate definition of boundaries in parent-child relationship (in terms of parentification, triangulation, psychological control, etc.) had an adverse influence on adolescent and young adult children's individuation processes, especially on female children (Mayseless & Scharf, 2009). Particularly relevant, moreover, it appeared the negative influence of intrusive parenting (Barber, 1996) on children's self-perception (self-esteem, self-image) as well as internalizing and externalizing behaviors (Luyckx et al., 2007).

Moreover, research has investigated how not only parenting styles but also parent-child interpersonal relationships have an impact on children's adjustment. In particular, numerous studies have shown the effects of attachment styles developed within the family of origin on adult children's psychological wellbeing (e.g., Mallinckrodt & Wei, 2005) and the adverse effects of negative parent-child relationship patterns on adult children's social relationships (e.g., Kim et al., 2001).

With regard to the second line of research, several studies showed a link between some family of origin characteristics and the quality of young adult children's romantic relationships, in particular their marital satisfaction. Similar to the first line of research some of these studies were focused on the effects on children's couple relationship of their parents' marital relationship and other studies on the influence of the relationships partners had with their parents when they were children or, more rarely, of the relationships they currently have with their parents.

As for the quality of parents' couple relationship studies have highlighted a sort of intergenerational transmission of marital functioning -especially for dysfunctional patterns (Caspi & Elder, 1988) and divorce (Amato & Booth, 1997; Bumpass, Martin, & Sweet, 1991). Research has also explored the intergenerational transmission of marital satisfaction (Amato & Booth, 1997; Booth & Edwards, 1989) and, more recently, of partners' relational competences, such as couple problem-solving, conflict strategies, forgiveness and dyadic coping (Bryant & Conger, 2002; Donato, Iafrate, Bradbury, & Scabini, 2012; Paleari et al., 2009; Story et al., 2004; Whitton et al., 2008).

Other studies considered that a crucial role in these intergenerational effects is played by parent-child relationships and parenting practices (e.g., Amato 1996; Simons, Lin, & Gordon, 1998). A few studies (Bertoni, 2003; Bertoni & Bodenmann, 2010) have investigated current relationships and exchanges that partners maintain with their families of origin (in terms of quantity and quality of contacts, considered as forms of potential family support) and shown that such relationships discriminate between satisfied and dissatisfied partners.

Family Heritage and Children's Personal and Couple Well-being

The literature reviewed so far presents two areas that need to be further explored. The first area refers to the type of family of origin variables considered. As remarked above, within the two abovementioned lines of research different family of origin predictors have been considered, from parents' couple relationship (in terms of divorce, conflict, satisfaction, etc.), to parent-child early relationship (in terms of parenting practices, differentiation levels, attachment styles, etc.) and (fewer studies) to parent-adult child current relationships. Within this range of predictors research has generally posed more emphasis on how negative family of origin experiences increase children's psychological distress and lower their marital quality, while little attention has been devoted to the influence of positive family experiences on adult children's positive adjustment.

Moreover, even though relationship scholars have called for the importance of adult children's perceptions of their family of origin experiences on their future relationship adjustment (e.g., Busby, Gardner, & Taniguchi, 2005), almost no research has focused on the impact that partners' perception of the heritage received within their families of origin (in term of values, principles, relational models) may have on their couple relationship (for an exception see Wamboldt & Reiss, 1989). Studying this family heritage means to investigate what partners perceive to have "inherited" by their parents or families of origin in terms of behavioral models, value transmission, and promotion of responsibility. In line with the work of Wamboldt and Reiss (1989) family heritage can be defined as something partners bring with them from their families of origin and as a sort of judgement of the experience lived in them. According to the authors couples can either fully accept this family heritage and decide to continue it, or they can partly accept it and refuse what they believe is in contrast with their new family, or even reject it completely. Exploring the role of partners' recognition of a family heritage allows to deepen and enrich the idea of intergenerational continuities with a transformative component, that is children may, or may not, recognize and accept what has been transmitted to them by their families.

The second area that has been less explored in the literature refers to the study of the interplay among family of origin variables, partners' individual adjustment, and relational outcomes. Only a few empirical models, in fact, have focused on how adult children's romantic relationships may be influenced by the interplay among family of origin features, individual characteristics, and couple processes (e.g., Bryant & Conger, 2002; Busby, Gardner, & Taniguchi, 2005; Tallman et al. , 1999).

Objective and Hypotheses

The present study investigated children's perception of their family heritage and its effects on partners' individual and relational well-being. We hypothesized that partners' individual well-being and relationship satisfaction were promoted by a positive perception of the heritage received within the family of origin, and more specifically, that perceiving a positive family heritage promoted a positive perception of oneself and fulfillment in one's life, which in turn sustained a satisfying couple relationship. Several studies, in fact, have demonstrated the link between partners' psychological well-being (mostly in terms of psychological distress) and their couple relationship outcomes (Davila et al., 2003; Papp, Goeke-Morey, & Cummings, 2007; Whisman, Uebelacker, & Weinstock, 2004). Moreover, other models of the impact of family of origin variables on the couple relationship (Bryant & Conger, 2002; Busby, Holman, & Taniguchi, 2001; Tallman et al., 1999) proposed that family of origin variables influence the quality of the couple relationship both directly and indirectly through partners' individual characteristics and well-being.

METHOD

Participants and Procedure

Two hundred and twenty premarital heterosexual couples living in the North of Italy participated in the study. The average duration of the relationship was 6 years ($SD = 4$). Women's mean age was 30 ($SD = 4$) and men's mean age was 32 ($SD = 5$). Thirty-six percent of couples were cohabiting; among non-cohabiting partners 62% of women and 59% of men were living with their parents. The form of household was not significantly related to any of the investigated variables. Some partners ended their formal education after the first 8 years (8% of women and 15% of men), while most reached a terminal high school degree (49% of women, 61% of men), a college or university degree (36% of women, 21% of men) or a post-graduate qualification (7% of women and 3% of men). Twenty-seven percent of women and 19% of men reported a household income up to 1.500 € per month, 56% of women and 58% of men between 1.500 and 3.000 €, 17% of women and 18% of men between 3.000 € and 5.000 €, 4% of women and 5% of men over 5.000 €.

Couples were recruited through advertising in premarital courses and were given a packet of questionnaires that included two separate and distinct versions (one for each partner), together with instructions to complete the questionnaires independently. All participants signed an informed consent form. Subjects were not paid for their completion of questionnaires.

Measures

In addition to providing demographic information, all participants completed the following scales.

Family heritage (items adapted from Donati & Colozzi, 1997). Children's perceptions of family heritage was evaluated using four items adapted from a set designed by Donati and Colozzi (1997) to assess children's "sense of being generated" by the adult generation (i.e., parents, grandparents, teachers, and adults in general). The items used here were referring to parents only (item examples: "Parents generally convey positive as well as negative things to children. Do you think your mother/father has conveyed positive things to you?"; "Do you think your mother/father has been a positive model for your life?"). Items referring to mothers and fathers were averaged. Respondents expressed their opinions on each item using a 4-point scale (1 = not at all, 2 = a little, 3 = somewhat, 4 = very much). Higher scores indicated a more positive view of the heritage received from parents (Cronbach's Alpha = .80 for women and = .80 for men).

Satisfaction With Life Scale (Diener, Emmons, Larsen, & Griffin, 1985). This scale of personal well-being measures the individual's satisfaction in several areas of his/her life. The scale comprises 5 items administered on a 7-point scale (1 = completely agree; 7 = completely disagree). Item example: "In most aspects may life corresponds to my ideal." (Cronbach's Alpha = .81 for women and = .81 for men).

Quality of Marriage Index (Norton, 1983). It is a 6-item measure of couple satisfaction. Five items are administered on a 7-point scale whereas the last item, measuring a global perception of couple satisfaction, is administered on a 10-point scale (Item example: "The relationship with my partner makes me happy"). To estimate the structural equation model we used the first five items: Cronbach's Alpha for these five items = .87 for women and = .88 for men.

Analytical Strategy

Structural equation modeling. In order to assess the influence of the family heritage on personal and couple well-being we used structural equation modeling to test our theoretical model (see Figure 1), separately for women and men, using the software AMOS 7.0.

Structural equation models can be evaluated from two points of view: The overall goodness-of-fit of the model and the value and significance of each parameter in the model (Byrne, 1998; Jöreskog & Sörbom, 1988).

As for the overall goodness-of-fit four statistics were used: 1) the chi-square test ($\chi2$) [an acceptable χ^2/df ratio is usually considered to be not more than 1:3 (Marsh, Balla, & MacDonald, 1988)]; 2) the Root Mean Square Error of Approximation (RMSEA, Steiger & Lind, 1980) [values $\leq$ .05 are regarded as optimal and values ranging between .05 and .08 are considered acceptable (Hu & Bentler, 1999)]; 3) the Composite Fit Index (CFI, Hu & Bentler, 1998) [values of .90 or higher are considered satisfactory (Bentler, 1990), while > .95 are regarded as optimal (Hu & Bentler, 1999)]; and 4) the Goodness of Fit Index (GFI, (Jöreskog & Sörbom, 1988) [values of .90 or higher are generally considered acceptable (Hu & Bentler, 1999)].

As for the significance of the parameters it was tested in structural equation modeling using t-values. T-values for each parameters provide a test of the hypothesis that a parameter equals 0.

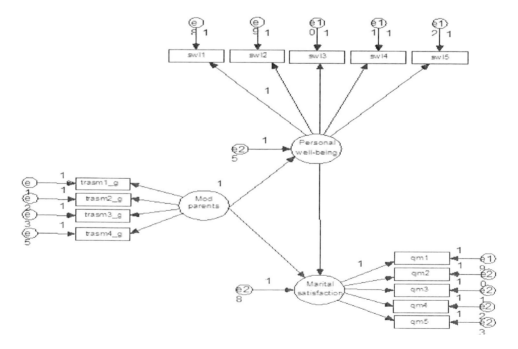

Figure 1. Theoretical model tested.

RESULTS

Preliminary Analyses

Preliminarily, GLM analyses with repeated measures were performed on each study variable by entering Gender (women vs. men) as within-subject factor. As for family heritage we did not find a significant main effect of Gender [F (1, 219) = 0.867, p = ns]. Men and women did not differ in terms of the perceptions of the heritage received from parents.

Moreover, also in terms of personal and relationship well-being no main effect of Gender was found [F (1, 219) = 1.088, p = ns for personal well-being and F (1, 219) = 0.123, p = ns for relationship satisfaction]. Men and women reported similar levels of personal and relational satisfaction.

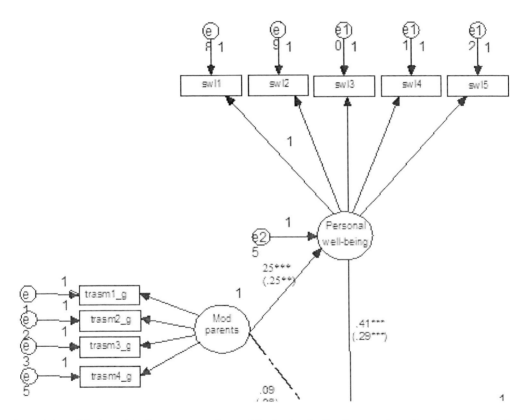

Figure 2. Empirical models for women and men. Men's standardized parameter estimates are reported within parentheses (** $p < .01$; *** $p \leq .001$).

Family Heritage Effect on Relationship Satisfaction through Partners' Personal Well-being

The association between family heritage, partners' personal wellbeing, and relationship satisfaction was tested through the estimation of the model presented in Figure 2.

We found satisfactory fit indices for both women and men (see Table 1). As shown in Figure 2, for both women and men the association between family heritage and relationship satisfaction was no more significant once controlled for their personal well-being, thereby showing a full mediation of this latter variable. As revealed by bootstrapping estimates the true indirect effect (point estimate = .10 for women; point estimate = .07 for men) was estimated to lie, with 95% confidence, between 0.04 and 0.20 for women and between 0.02 and 0.15 for men. Because zero was not in the 95% confidence intervals, we could conclude that, for both partners, the indirect effect was indeed significantly different from zero at $p = .05$ (two tailed). For both women and men partners' perception of the heritage received within their family of origin positively predicted relationship satisfaction through its positive impact on partners' personal well-being.

Table 1. Fit indices of the models tested

Models	χ2 (p)	df	RMSEA	GFI	CFI
Women					
Mediational model	113.4 (p=.002)	74	.05	.93	.97
Men					
Mediational model	170.1 (p=.000)	74	.08	.90	.93

CONCLUSION

The present study was aimed at analyzing the link among perceived family heritage, partners' well-being and couple satisfaction. Extending past research on intergenerational influences on partners' individual and relational outcomes, we decided to focus on partners' perception of the heritage they received from their parents rather than on partners' early or current experiences in the family of origin (e.g., parent-child relationship, parental marital relationship, parent-adult child contacts). According to Busby and colleagues (2001) any family of origin experience is filtered by the individual's evaluation of the influence that such experiences had on his/her adult relationships. In particular, we hypothesized that partners' individual well-being and relationship satisfaction were promoted by a positive perception of the heritage they received from their parents and, more specifically, that perceiving a positive family heritage promoted partners' fulfillment with their lives, which in turn could promote a satisfying couple relationship.

Results showed that partners' perception of the heritage received within their family of origin positively predicts partner's personal well-being, in terms of their satisfaction with their lives. This findings extends previous research on the influence of the family of origin on adult children's well-being by highlighting not only how negative experiences in the family of origin (e.g., parents' divorce, violence, an inadequate definition of boundaries, intrusive parenting, etc.) can undermine children's adjustment, but also how a positive perception of what children have received from their parents can support their psychological well-being.

This datum, moreover, acquires a more complex meaning in light of the mediational role that children's psychological well-being has revealed in the present findings, which showed that, thanks to its positive impact on partners' well-being, perceiving a positive family heritage also promotes partner's relationship satisfaction. Being more satisfied as individuals as well as partners thanks to the acknowledgment that a positive heritage has been received testifies not only the importance of family of origin for adult children as well, but also the interconnection between the individual's personal life and the familial context he/she belongs to.

In general, findings that positive family of origin characteristics, and not only negative ones, may support partner's well-being and relationship success argue for the value of family prevention, especially when incorporates a focus on family of origin experiences.

More specifically, the present results show how promoting a positive re-elaboration of partner's family of origin experiences contributes to their psychological adjustment and, in turn, to their couple relationship success. In addition these findings also suggest that assessing couples' family of origin histories and partners' personal perception of what they received from their parents can be useful to detect risk for psychological distress and couple dissatisfaction and therefore make prevention programs more effective.

These findings must be considered in light of the limitations of the present study. First, the use of a convenience sample limits generalizability of results to a broader population. Second, the correlational nature of the present work does not allow to verify the direction of effects. Moreover, longitudinal research could help to identify how children's perception of their family heritage may change over time.

Despite these limitations the present study argues for the relevance of analyzing children perceptions of their family heritage, which taps a more symbolic aspect of intergenerational relationships and suggests that an important part of what is transmitted between generations may be not only behaviors *per se,* but also a set of values and principles that can promote children's well-being in a variety of contexts, as individuals and as partners.

REFERENCES

Ainsworth, M. S., Blehar, M. C., Waters, E., & Wall, S. (1978). *Patterns of attachment: A psychological study of the Strange Situation.* Hillsdale: Lawrence Erlbaum Associates.

Amato, P. R. (1996). Explaining the intergenerational transmission of divorce. *Journal of Marriage and the Family, 58,* 628-640.

Amato, P. R., & Booth, A. (1997). *A generation at risk: Growing up in an era of family upheaval.* Cambridge: Harvard University Press.

Amato, P. R., & James, S. (2010). Divorce in Europe and the United States: Commonalities and Differences across Nations. *Family Science, 1,* 2-13.

Bandura, A. (1977). *Social learning theory.* Englewood Cliffs: Prentice-Hall.

Barber, B. K. (1996). Parental psychological control: Revisiting a neglected construct. *Child Development, 67,* 3296-3319.

Baron, R. M., & Kenny, D. A. (1986). The moderator-mediator variable distinction in social psychological research: Conceptual, strategic and statistical considerations. *Journal of Personality and Social Psychology, 51,* 1173-1182.

Bartle-Haring, S., & Sabatelli, R. (1998). An intergenerational examination of patterns of individual and family adjustment. *Journal of Marriage and the Family, 60,* 903-911.

Bentler, P. M. (1990). Comparative Fit Indexes in Structural Models. *Psychological Bulletin, 107*, 238-246.

Bertoni, A. (2003). La qualité conjugale: Relations des couples satisfaits et des couples insatisfaits. In C. Rodet (Ed.), *La transmission dans la famille: secrets, fictions et idéaux* (pp. 231-237). Paris: Ed. L'Harmattan.

Bertoni, A., & Bodenmann, G. (2010). Satisfied and dissatisfied couples: Positive and negative dimensions, conflict styles, and relationships with family of origin. *European Psychologist*. Advance online publication. doi: 10.1027/1016-9040/a0000151.

Bowlby, J. (1969), *Attachment and loss, Vol. 1: Attachment.* New York: Basic Books.

Bowlby, J. (1973). *Attachment and loss, Vol. 2: Separation.* New York: Basic Books.

Bowlby, J. (1980). *Attachment and loss, Vol. 3: Loss, sadness and depression.* New York: Basic Books.

Bryant, C. M., & Conger, R. D. (2002). An intergenerational model of romantic relationship development. In A. L. Vangelisti, H. T. Reiss, & M. A. Fitzpatrick (Eds.), *Stability and Change in Relationships* (pp. 57-82). New York: Cambridge University Press.

Bumpass, L. L., Martin, T. C., & Sweet, J. A. (1991). The impact of family background and early marital factors on marital disruption. *Journal of Family Issues, 12*, 22-42.

Busby, D. M., Gardner, B. C., & Taniguchi, N. (2005). The family of origin parachute model: Landing safely in adult romantic relationships. *Family Relations, 54*, 254-264.

Busby, D. M., Holman, T. B., Taniguchi, N. (2001). Relationship evaluation of the individual, cultural and couple contexts. *Family Relations, 50*, 308-316.

Byrne, B. M. (1998). *Structural equation modeling with LISREL, PRELIS, and SIMPLIS: Basic concepts, applications, and programming*. Mahwah: Lawrence Erlbaum Associates.

Caspi, A., & Elder, G. H. (1988). Emergent family patterns: The intergenerational construction of problem behaviour and relationships. In R. A. Hinde, & J. Stevenson-Hinde (Eds.), *Relationships within families* (pp. 334-353). Oxford: Clarendon Press.

Cigoli, V., Giuliani, C., & Iafrate, R. (2002). Il dolore del divorzio: adolescenti e giovani adulti tra ravvicinamento e distacco alla storia familiare. *Psicologia Clinica dello Sviluppo, 7*, 473-492.

Darlington, Y. (2001). When all is said and done: The impact of parental divorce and contested custody in childhood on young adults relationships with their parents and their attitudes to Relationships and Marriage. *Journal of Divorce and Remarriage, 35*, 23-42.

Davila, J., Karney, B. R., Hall, T. W., & Bradbury, T. N. (2003). Depressive symptoms and marital satisfaction: Dynamic associations and the moderating effects of gender and neuroticism. *Journal of Family Psychology, 17*, 557-570.

Diener, E., Emmons, R. A., Larsen, R. J., & Griffin, S. (1985). The satisfaction with life scale. *Journal of Personality Assessment, 49,* 71-75.

Donati, P., & Colozzi, I. (1997). *Giovani e generazioni. Quando si cresce in una società eticamente neutra*. Bologna: Il Mulino.

Fincham, F. D., & Beach, S. R. H. (2010). Marriage in the new millennium: A decade in review. *Journal of Marriage and Family, 72*, 630-649

Framo, J. L. (1981). The integration of marital therapy with sessions with family of origin. In A. S. Gurman & D. P. Kniskern (Eds.), *Handbook of family therapy* (pp. 133-158). New York: Brunner/Mazel Press.

Hoopes, M. H. (1987). Multigenerational systems: Basic assumptions. *American Journal of Family Therapy, 15*, 195-205.

Hu, L., & Bentler, P. M. (1998). Fit Indices in Covariance Structure Modeling: Sensitivity to Underparameterized Model Misspecification. *Psychological Methods, 3*, 424-453.

Hu, L., & Bentler, P. M. (1999). Cutoff Criteria for Fit Indexes in Covariance Structure Analysis: Conventional Criteria Versus New Alternatives. *Structural Equation Modeling, 6*, 1-55.

Jöreskog, K. G., & Sörbom, D. (1988). *Lisrel 7. A guide to the Program and Applications.III.* Chicago: Spss Inc.

Kim, K. J., Conger, R. D., Lorenz, F. O., & Elder, G. H. Jr. (2001). Parent-adolescent reciprocity in negative affect and its relation to early adult social development. *Developmental Psychology, 37*, 775-790.

Luyckx, K., Soenens, B., Vansteenkiste, M., Goossens, L., & Berzonsky, M. D. (2007). Parental psychological control and dimensions of identity formation in emerging adulthood. *Journal of Family Psychology, 21*, 546-50.

Main, M., Hesse, E., & Kaplan, N. (2005). Predictability of behavior and representational processes related to attachment in the Berkeley Longitudinal Study: Attachment at 1, 6, and 19 years of age. In K. E. Grossmann, K. Grossmann, & E. Waters (Eds.), *The power of longitudinal studies in attachment.* New York: Guilford Press.

Mallinckrodt, B., & Wei, M. (2005). Attachment, social competencies, interpersonal problems, and psychological distress. *Journal of Counseling Psychology, 52*, 358-367.

Marsh, H. W., Balla, J. R., & McDonald, R. P. (1988). Goodness-of-fit indices in confirmatory factor analysis: The effect of sample size. *Psychological Bulletin, 102*, 391-410.

Mayseless, O., & Scharf, M. (2009). Too Close for Comfort: Inadequate Boundaries With Parents and Individuation in Late Adolescent Girls. *American Journal of Orthopsychiatry, 79,* 191-202.

McNeal, C., & Amato, P. R. (1998). Parents' Marital Violence Long-Term Consequences for Children. *Journal of Family Issues, 19*, 123-139.

Norton, R. (1983). Measuring marital quality. A critical look at the dependent variable. *Journal of Marriage and Family, 45*, 141-151.

Paleari, F. G., Donato, S., Iafrate, R., & Regalia, C. (2009). The tendency to forgive in premarital couples: Reciprocating the partner or reproducing parental dispositions? In E. Cuyler & M. Ackhart (Eds.) *Psychology of Relationships,* (pp. 191-212). Hauppauge: Nova Science Publishers.

Papp, L. M., Goeke-Morey, M. C., & Cummings, E. M. (2007). Linkages between spouses' psychological distress and marital conflict in the home. *Journal of Family Psychology, 21*, 533-537.

Scabini, E., & Cigoli, V. (2000). *Il Famigliare.* Milano: Ed. Cortina.

Scabini, E., & Iafrate, R. (2003). *Psicologia dei legami familiari.* Bologna: Il Mulino.

Simons, R. L., Lin, K., & Gordon, L. C. (1998). Socialization in the family of origin and male dating violence: A prospective study. *Journal of Marriage and the Family, 60*, 467-478.

Steiger, J. H., & Lind, J. C. (1980). *Statistically based tests for the number of common factors.* Paper presented at the annual meeting of the Psychometric Society, May, Iowa, City, IA.

Story, L. B., Karney, B. R., Lawrence, E., & Bradbury, T. N. (2004). Interpersonal mediators in the intergenerational transmission of marital dysfunction. *Journal of Family Psychology, 18*, 519-529.

Tallman, I., Gray, L. N., Kullberg, V., & Henderson, D. (1999). The intergenerational transmission of marital conflict: Testing a process model. *Social Psychology Quarterly, 62*, 219-239.

Topham, G. L., Larson, J. H., & Holman, T. B. (2005). Family-of-origin predictors of hostile conflict in early marriage, *Contemporary Family Therapy*, 27, 101-121.

Wallerstein, J. S. (2005). Growing up in the divorced family. *Clinical Social Work Journal, 33*, 401-418.

Wallerstein, J. S., Lewis, J. M., & Blakeslee, S. (2000). *The Unexpected Legacy of Divorce: The 25 Year Landmark Study*. New York: Hyperion.

Wamboldt, F. S, & Reiss, D. (1989). Defining a family heritage and a new relationship identity: Two central tasks in the making of a marriage, *Family Process*, 28, 317-325.

Whitton, S. W., Waldinger, R. J., Schulz, M. S., Allen, J. P., Crowell, J. A. & Hauser, S. T. (2008). Prospective associations from family-of-origin interactions to adult marital interactions and relationship adjustment. *Journal of Family Psychology*, 22, 274-286.

In: Parenting
Editors: Peter Barberis and Stelios Petrakis

ISBN: 978-1-62257-881-8
© 2013 Nova Science Publishers, Inc.

Chapter 13

INFLUENCES ON THE UTILIZATION OF PROACTIVE COPING DURING PREGNANCY AND EARLY PARENTHOOD

Susanne N. Biehle[*]

DePauw University, Greencastle, IN, US

ABSTRACT

Much has been written about the challenges of pregnancy and parenthood; however, few studies exist that examine how mothers prepare to cope with the potential challenges they will face during this major life transition. While pregnancy is filled with excitement in anticipation of the baby's arrival, it is also a period of time marked with an increased risk of stress and worry (e.g. Biehle & Mickelson, 2011; Melender, 2002). One way that expectant parents can minimize this stress is through the utilization of effective coping strategies. A plethora of literature examines the impact of stress, but prior literature has focused almost exclusively on how individuals deal reactively with taxing situations (Schwarzer & Knoll, 2003). More recently, the stress and coping literature has begun to include coping for events before they occur, referred to as proactive coping (e.g. Aspinwall & Taylor, 1997; Greenglass, 2002; Schwarzer & Knoll, 2003). The literature on proactive coping is relatively new and has never been examined during the transition to parenthood. Due to this void in the literature, the current study utilized a sample of 118 first-time expectant mothers to examine the potential correlates and predictors of utilizing proactive coping during the transition to parenthood. The current study found a mother's internal locus of control and optimism were concurrently related to more proactive coping during pregnancy and at 1-month postpartum, while rumination was not. These results suggest the importance of examining predictors of coping during the transition to parenthood.

[*] Correspondence concerning this article should be addressed to Susanne N. Biehle, Ph.D., DePauw University, Department of Psychology, 118 Harrison Hall, Greencastle, IN 46135; E-mail: susannebiehle@depauw.edu.

INTRODUCTION

Although many life events are often unplanned or unexpected, there are many instances when individuals know that a life event is impending. For these events, research on traditional coping strategies fails to explain how individuals plan for upcoming events. While everyone encounters stressors they consider demanding, individuals must work to alleviate the distress that results from these events and, if possible, attempt to modify these stressors. Coping resources have the potential to help to minimize potentially harmful consequences of stressful experiences (Pearlin, Menaghan, Lieberman, & Mullan, 1981). For example, by having financial resources to help them care for the baby or by having a social network to rely upon for support, expectant parents may feel more at ease for the potentially stressful life event of becoming a parent. Therefore, rather than only occurring after a stressor has been encountered, coping can help us deal with events of the present and future (Greenglass, 2002). Thus, coping can also be conceptualized as something that can take place in anticipation of a stressor occurring. Schwarzer and Knoll (2003) have identified three types of future-oriented coping: anticipatory, preventative, and proactive coping. Anticipatory coping refers to coping that occurs in response to a critical event that is likely to occur in the near future. Preventative coping is coping with an uncertain threat that may potentially occur in the distant future. In contrast, proactive coping involves accumulating resources for an upcoming challenge that may potentially provide self-growth, where the individual can learn more about themselves. While these three methods of future-oriented coping may be useful in coping with an anticipated stressor, the current study focuses on proactive coping in expectant mothers, as the transition to parenthood is both a period of potential stress and a life transition that provides the opportunity for individuals to learn more about themselves.

PROACTIVE COPING

Schwarzer and Knoll (2003) have identified proactive coping as involving the accumulation of resources for an upcoming stressor; however, proactive coping is also a mix of coping and self-regulation. Specifically, individuals are attempting to both reduce and minimize demands viewed as posing a potential threat, harm, or loss to them, while also modifying their behavior to move toward personal goals and create more balance in their life (Carver & Scheier, 1990; Lazarus & Folkman, 1984). In proactive coping, individuals see the potential risks, demands, and opportunities in the future but do not appraise them as being specifically threatening or harmful. For example, an individual may be close to losing their job, but rather than being upset about the loss of their current job they may view their situation as an opportunity for growth in a new career. Therefore, this individual realizes not only the potential demands of the situation, but also the opportunities to make a negative circumstance work for them through providing growth.

Proactive coping has also been conceptualized as a method of assessing personal goals for the future and working to protect them (Schwarzer & Taubert, 2002). This proactive coping model includes five components: 1) building a reserve of resources, 2) recognition of potential stressors, 3) appraisal of potential stressors, 4) preliminary coping, and 5) eliciting feedback about their efforts to cope with potential stressors (see Folkman & Moskowitz,

2004, for a review). This model of proactive coping can be applied to many situations, including expectant parents preparing for the arrival of their child. Before the baby is born, parents build a reserve of tangible goods, such as money and baby items, to prepare for the baby. Expectant parents also recognize potential stressors that may occur and appraise them, such as the balance they will need to find between their work and home life. Parents can begin coping by preparing the nursery and buying items that will help meet the baby's needs. Expectant parents may seek feedback about their efforts from their parents or friends with children, who may help them identify things they still need to do.

Despite the fact that reactive and proactive coping are similar in that they are both attempting to reduce the negative implications of a stressor, Aspinwall and Taylor (1997) discuss three specific ways in which proactive coping is different than other types of coping. First, proactive coping is used prior to traditional coping as a means to accumulate resources to prepare for the stressor, rather than after a stressor occurs when specific needs are addressed through reactive coping strategies. For example, when a couple is expecting a baby, the expectant parents may be able to save money during pregnancy for added expenses or medical bills that will arise when the baby comes. If parents do not anticipate the additional financial responsibilities a baby brings, they could easily get behind on bills, which would create additional stress for the parents.

Second, different skills are required to cope with an imminent stressor as opposed to one that has already occurred. In the example of expecting a baby, during pregnancy the expectant parents begin to gather information about how to care for the baby. Parents who proactively cope by gathering information during pregnancy need the skills to gather information from many sources and synthesize it so that they are prepared when stressful situations arise in the postpartum period. However, parents who reactively cope by seeking information only as situations arise in the postpartum period need to know where the best resources are so that they can get needed information as quickly as possible to handle a specific situation. Therefore, the temporal nature of the coping may require different skills.

Third, various coping strategies are differentially effective with proactive coping than with coping reactively to an event. If a parent proactively copes for parenthood by taking baby preparation classes and learns what to do in an emergency, they are more prepared if an emergency arises with the baby. However, if a parent waits to reactively cope with a dangerous situation, they may not have the knowledge to perform CPR or to help a baby that is choking, and may not be able to seek out the needed information in time to help the baby. Therefore, while the parents in both situations are coping with the emergency, the time at which they learn strategies, such as CPR, can alter the outcome of the situation. Therefore, there are some potentially stressful situations, such as the transition to parenthood, where coping prior to the event may help to reduce some of the individual's stress and even potentially make the situation less stressful overall.

INDIVIDUAL DIFFERENCES IN PROACTIVE COPING

While the prior literature has demonstrated some of the potential advantages of utilizing proactive coping, all individual do not always engage in this type of coping prior to a stressful event occurring. The next step in understanding the proactive process is to determine which individuals are more likely to utilize proactive coping. Individual differences have been identified as impacting the ability to effectively utilize proactive coping strategies (Ouwehand, de Ridder, & Bensing, 2006). For example, prior research has suggested that it may be easier for individuals of the middle or upper social classes to utilize proactive coping because they have a surplus of resources and use these assets to prepare for future events (e.g. Aspinwall & Taylor, 1997; Ouwehand, de Ridder, & Bensing, 2009). In addition, individuals who are cognitively overloaded because they are ruminating on this or other current events in their lives may not have the ability to accurately recognize an imminent stressor, and therefore may not be able to proactively cope for it (Kruglandski & Webster, 1996).

Another characteristic found to be related to proactive coping is that of perceived control. Whether or not an individual feels they are capable of influencing their environment has been linked with more active problem-solving (Greenglass & Fiskenbaum, 2009). Typically, if an individual feels they can control their situation and reduce threats and challenges they encounter, they are more likely to try to actively engage in attempts to reduce the impact of an anticipated stressor (Schwarzer, 1993). Therefore, the more internal an individual's locus of control is the more proactive coping they should engage in. However, to my knowledge, no studies have specifically looked at locus of control with proactive coping.

In addition, optimism has been found to be helpful in facilitating proactive coping (Aspinwall & Taylor, 1997; Sohl & Moyer, 2009), as optimism may be useful in believing that one's efforts today can have a positive impact on events in the future. While optimism appears to be related to individual differences in proactive coping, it has not been examined with the transitional stressor of parenthood. While the literature is beginning to examine proactive coping and potential individual differences, the current study will expand on this literature by systematically examining whether locus of control, rumination, or optimism impacts expectant mothers' proactive coping.

METHODS

Sample

The participants in the current study were composed of 118 heterosexual married or cohabitating mothers that were expecting their first child and in their third trimester of pregnancy. Mothers were also required to be fluent in English and needed access to a computer to complete the online questionnaire to be eligible to participate. The sample was primarily composed of married mothers (91%). Mothers on average had been married/cohabitating for 3 years (See Table 1 for demographic information). The mean participant age was 29 years, ranging from 20 to 42 years. The majority of the sample was White (92%), with a college education or an advanced degree, and approximately 70% of the sample reported a household income of $60,000 or more. Of the 118 mothers who completed the baseline interview, 105 mothers completed the interview at 1-month postpartum (89% retention). Mothers who attrited were unable to be reached after numerous attempts. Descriptive analyses were conducted and no differences where found between those who attrited and those who remained in the study on any demographic or baseline study measures.

Table 1. Descriptive Statistics of Demographic Variables

		M	*(SD)*	Range
Age		29.28	3.83	20-42
Years Married		3.00	3.00	0.1 - 14
Education				
	High School	1.7%		
	Some College	12.7%		
	College	54.2%		
	Advanced Degree	31.4%		
Income				
	$0-$19,999	2.5%		
	$20,000-$40,000	9.30%		
	$40,000-$60,000	13.60%		
	$60,000-$80,000	28.00%		
	$100,000-$120,000	14.40%		
	$120,000 +	17.80%		

Methods

Participants were recruited from local birthing classes and online message boards. Additionally, the snowballing technique was used to recruit participants. IRB approval was obtained before conducting the study and all participants gave their informed consent before participating. Mothers who agreed to take part in the study completed interviews in their third trimester (between 24-32 weeks of pregnancy) and at approximately 1-month postpartum (between 4-6 weeks postpartum). Participants completed questionnaires online through a website created for the study. The online interview took each participant less than 30 minutes to complete at each wave of the study. Mothers who completed each wave were entered into a raffle for $200 in gift cards.

Materials

Sociodemographics. The following demographic information was collected from mothers and considered as potential control variables: age (range from 20 to 42 years); time living with partner (range from 1 month to 14 years); and relationship status (married or cohabiting). Education level was categorized as some high school, high school, some college, college education, or advanced degree. Household income represented total family income at the time of the interview and was categorized in seven categories from as less than $20,000 to more than $120,000. See Table 1 for sample descriptive.

Table 2. Descriptive Statistics of Major Study Variables

	M	*(SD)*	Range
Proactive Coping			
Pregnancy	31.50	(4.48)	18 - 39
1-Month	32.76	(4.40)	20 - 40
Locus of Control			
Pregnancy	33.97	(3.10)	23 - 40
1-Month	34.79	(2.93)	25 - 40
Optimism			
Pregnancy	16.42	(3.84)	7 - 24
1-Month	17.49	(3.99)	4 - 24
Rumination			
Pregnancy	22.35	(5.36)	10 - 34
1-Month	22.44	(5.35)	10 - 35

Proactive Coping. Proactive coping was assessed using the *preventative* subscale of the Proactive Coping Inventory (PCI; Greenglass, Schwarzer, & Taubert, 1999). This subscale most accurately assesses proactive coping in the way that Aspinwall and Taylor (1997) discussed the construct and has also been used by other authors to assess proactive coping (e.g. Sohl & Moyer, 2009). A sample item is "I plan my strategies to change a situation before I act" which is answered on a scale from 1 = not at all true to 4 = completely true. A sum score of the items was created with higher numbers indicating more proactive coping (Pregnancy: α =.83; 1-Month: α =.82).

Locus of control. To measure locus of control, the Locus of Control (LOC, Kessler et al., 1994) was used. The LOC is an 11-item questionnaire that measures the degree to which individuals feel in control of their lives. A sample item is "My life is determined by my own actions," which is answered on a scale from not at all true = 1 to very true = 4. A sum score of the items was created with higher numbers indicating feeling more internal locus of control (Pregnancy: α = .60; 1-Month: α = .64).

Rumination. A modified version of the Rumination Responses Scale (RRS; Treynor, Gonzalez, & Nolen-Hoeksema, 2003) was used to measure rumination. A sample item is "How often do you think about "What am I doing to deserve this?" when feeling down, sad or depressed?," which is answered on a scale from 1 = almost never to 4 = almost always. A sum score of the items was created with higher numbers indicating that participants engage in more rumination (Pregnancy: α = .78; 1-Month: α = .75).

Optimism. The Revised Life Orientation Test (LOT-R; Scheier, Carver, & Bridges, 1994) is a brief, 6-item measure of optimism. Sample items include "At uncertain times, I usually expect the best" and "I rarely count on good things happening to me" which was answered on a scale from 0 = strongly disagree to 4 = strongly agree. A sum score of the items was created with higher numbers indicating that participants are more optimistic (Pregnancy: $\alpha = .79$; 1-Month: $\alpha = .84$).

Statistical Analyses

Prior to testing the main hypotheses, frequency distributions on all variables were examined. Basic regressions were performed on the major demographic study variables (e.g., age, income, education) to determine which variables were significantly related to predictor and outcome variables and thus needed to be controlled for in the analyses. In the current analyses, only income was found to be a significant covariate and was therefore controlled for in all analyses. Potential personal and situational predictors of proactive coping were examined to determine which variables were related to increases in proactive coping. To determine if locus of control, rumination, or optimism had a main effect on proactive coping, multiple linear regression analyses were used. I hypothesized that mothers who are high in internal locus of control, who engage in less rumination, and who report more optimism will engage in more proactive coping during pregnancy.

Descriptive Statistics

With respect to the major study variables, mothers reported significantly more proactive coping at 1-month postpartum than during pregnancy (t(105) = -.10; $p < .01$). Additionally, mothers reported having more optimism at 1-month postpartum than during pregnancy (t(105) = -4.00; $p < .001$) and stronger internal locus of control at 1-month postpartum than during pregnancy (t(105) = -3.72; $p < .001$). There was not a significant different between pregnancy and 1-month postpartum in regards to reported rumination (t(105) = .00; $p > .05$).

Predictors and Correlates of Proactive Coping

The literature on proactive coping is relatively new and little is known about predictors of proactive coping, especially during the transition to parenthood. In light of this, for the current analyses, I conducted multiple regressions (controlling for the mother's level of income) to examine the cross-sectional association of optimism, rumination, and locus of control with proactive coping at the same time point during pregnancy and at 1-month postpartum, as well as longitudinally from pregnancy to 1-month postpartum. Results of the analyses are discussed below.

Cross-sectional Analyses

Pregnancy

During pregnancy, mothers who reported more internal locus of control also reported engaging in significantly more proactive coping during pregnancy ($\beta = .24$; $p < .01$). Additionally, mothers who reported being more optimistic reported engaging in marginally more proactive coping during pregnancy ($\beta = .16$; $p = .07$). However, mother's reported level of rumination was not found to be significantly related to how much they engaged in proactive coping during pregnancy ($p = .44$).

1-Month

Similar to results obtained for mothers during pregnancy, at 1-month postpartum mothers who reported more internal locus of control reported engaging in significantly more proactive coping at 1-month postpartum ($\beta = .29$; $p < .01$), and mothers who reported being more optimistic reported engaging in marginally more proactive coping at 1-month postpartum ($\beta = .17$; $p < .08$). Also, as during pregnancy, mother's reported level of rumination was not found to be significantly related to proactive coping at 1-month postpartum ($p = .47$).

Longitudinal Analyses

In addition to examining the relationship between optimism, rumination, and locus of control with proactive coping concurrently, longitudinal analyses were also conducted using multiple regression analyses controlling for proactive coping during pregnancy and income. I anticipated that certain individual characteristics may have a more significant impact on proactive coping across time rather than at the same time point. However, no significant effects were found for mother's reported level of internal locus of control ($p = .21$), rumination ($p = .57$), or optimism ($p = .27$) during pregnancy on levels of proactive coping at 1-month postpartum.

CONCLUSION

The literature on proactive coping is relatively new and therefore, to my knowledge, no prior studies have examined this aspect of the coping process during the transition to parenthood. The transition to parenthood is a period of disequilibrium, with first-time parents experiencing novel situations and expectations (Levy-Shiff, 1999). Many first-time expectant parents report feeling stressed and unprepared for becoming a parent and its accompanying adjustments and changes (e.g. Vanzetti & Duck, 1996). Therefore, it is anticipated that new parents begin coping before these changes occur by using proactive coping strategies. The primary goal of the current study was to examine potential individual difference factors that may predict engagement in proactive coping. From the prior literature, I hypothesized that a mother's level of optimism, rumination, and locus of control would influence the degree to which she engaged in proactive coping both during pregnancy and at 1-month postpartum. The current study found an internal locus of control and optimism were concurrently related to more proactive coping, while rumination was not. The implications and future directions of the study findings are discussed below.

In the current study, three potential individual difference variables were examined as predictors of proactive coping during pregnancy and at 1-month postpartum: locus of control, optimism, and rumination. Locus of control was consistently shown to be related to proactive coping during both pregnancy and 1-month postpartum - with mothers who reported having more internal locus of control reporting more proactive coping. These findings support prior literature on proactive coping, which suggests that individuals who feel they are more capable of influencing their environment should engage in more active types of problem-solving, such as proactive coping (Greenglass & Fuskenbaum, 2009). Individuals who have a higher internal locus of control may feel they have more control over influencing future stressors in their environment - thus, it is understandable why they would engage in more proactive coping to prepare for the anticipated stressors that accompany parenthood. In addition to locus of control, marginal results were also found for optimism with mothers who reported being more optimistic reporting marginally more proactive coping both during pregnancy and at 1-month postpartum. Because proactive coping could be viewed as a more positive type of future-oriented coping, where individuals are able to do something in the present to help events in the future (e.g. Schwarzer and Knoll, 2003), it makes sense that individuals who are more optimistic would also engage in more of this style of coping. However, the results for optimism in the current study were only marginal. Future studies need to replicate these findings with a larger sample size and over a longer duration of the transition to parenthood to determine if optimism has a stronger role in later proactive coping.

One surprising finding was the lack of results for mother's reported level of rumination and proactive coping. I expected that individuals who engaged in more rumination would be less likely to proactively cope with events because they were focused on past events rather than looking towards events in the future. However, this hypothesis was not supported with the current data. One possible explanation for the lack of results may be that the items measuring rumination tapped into the trait of how much a person ruminates in general, rather than rumination specifically related to the transition to parenthood. Future studies using a more state-based measure specific to the transition to parenthood may yield different results.

Limitations and Applied Implications

There are several caveats to consider with respect to the current findings. One limitation is the homogenous nature of the current sample. Because the sample consisted primarily of White, middle-class mothers transitioning to parenthood, it is unclear how these results will generalize to other parents, including multiparous parents. It may be that middle-class mothers have more resources to deal with the transition than those with lower incomes or education and therefore, may experience fewer stressors or stressors of a different nature than other demographics. Therefore, additional studies are needed to examine the impact of social context on proactive coping during pregnancy. Additionally, the current study only examined proactive coping in mothers; thus, these results cannot be generalized to fathers. Because fathers are not physically experiencing the pregnancy, they may prepare for parenthood differently than mothers. Fathers may be able to focus on coping with different potential stressors of parenthood. For example, fathers may be able to proactively cope with the added cost of having a baby by working more hours. Also, it may be that fathers are less likely to proactively cope during pregnancy than mothers – as the reality of the transition does not "hit home" until the baby is born.

Additionally, future studies may wish to examine additional potential predictors of proactive coping. One such variable could be the amount of stressors and uplifts an individual is encountering related to preparing for a stressful event. The transition to parenthood is typically filled with many new situations that can create both stressors and uplifts for parents; however, little is known about the relationship between stressors and uplifts on the proactive coping process. For example, does someone who is experiencing more stressors (or uplifts) engage in more proactive coping? Individuals who are experiencing more pregnancy uplifts may engage in more proactive coping because they are focusing on the positives of the pregnancy and may be more optimistic about the impact of their present coping to minimize future stressors. However, a mother who reports experiencing many pregnancy stressors may be taxed from coping with present stressors and may not have the resources or fortitude to worry about future situations. To conclude, while the current study does have some limitations, it is novel in that it examined proactive coping in first-time mothers, which has previously been neglected; this study lays the foundation for future research to expand on the coping literature during this dynamic life transition.

REFERENCES

Aspinwall, L.G., & Taylor, S.E. (1997). A stitch in time: Self-regulation and proactive coping. *Psychological Bulletin, 121*, 417-436. Retrieved from http://psycnet. apa.org/journals/bul/121/3/417.pdf.

Biehle, S. N., & Mickelson, K. D. (2011). Role of worries in expectant parents on perinatal mental health and relationship satisfaction. *Personal Relationships, 18,* 697-71. doi:10.1111/j.1475-6811.2010.01335.x.

Carver, C. S., & Scheier, M. F. (1990). Origins and functions of positive and negative affect: A control-process view. *Psychological Review, 97,* 19-35. doi: 10.1037/0033-295X.97.1.19.

Folkman, S., & Moskowitz, J.T. (2004). Coping: Pitfalls and promise. *Annual Reviews of Psychology, 55,* 745-747. doi: 10.1146/annurev.psych.55. 090902.141456.

Greenglass, E. (2002). Proactive coping. In E. Frydenberg (Ed.), *Beyond coping: Meeting goals, vision, and challenges* (pp. 37-62). London: Oxford University Press. Retrieved from http://www.psych.yorku.ca/ greenglass/pcinven.php.

Greenglass, E.R., & Fiksenbaum, L. (2009). Proactive coping, positive affect, and well-being: Testing for mediation using path analysis considerations. *European Psychologist, 14,* 29-39. doi:10.1027/1016-9040.14.1.29.

Greenglass, E. R., Schwarzer, R., & Taubert, S. (1999). The Proactive Coping Inventory (PCI): A multidimensional research instrument. [On-line publication]. Available at: http://userpage.fu-berlin.de/~health/ greenpci.htm.

Kessler, R. C., McGonagle, K. A., Zhao, S., Nelson, C. B., Hughes, M., Eshleman, S., et al. (1994). Lifetime and 12-month prevalence of *DSM–III–R* psychiatric disorders in the United States: Results from the National Comorbidity Survey. *Archives of General Psychiatry, 51,* 8–19. Retrieved from http://ajp.psychiatryonline.org/article.aspx? articleID=170440.

Lazarus, R. S., & Folkman, S. (1984). *Stress, Appraisal, and Coping.* New York: Springer.

Levy-Shiff, R. (1999). Fathers' cognitive appraisals, coping strategies and support resources as correlates of adjustment to parenthood. *Journal of Family Psychology, 13,* 554-567. doi: 10.1037/0893-3200.13.4.554.

Melender, H.L. (2002). Fears and coping strategies associated with pregnancy and childbirth in Finland. *Journal of Midwifery and Women's Health, 47*, 256–263. doi: 10.1016/S1526-9523(02)00263-5.

Ouwehand, C., de Ridder, D. T. D., & Bensing, J. M. (2006). Situational aspects are more important in shaping proactive coping behavior than individual characteristics: A vignette study among adults preparing for ageing. *Psychology and Health, 21*, 809-825. doi: 10.1080 /14768320500537639.

Ouwehand, C., de Ridder, D. T. D., & Bensing, J. M. (2009). Who can afford to look to the future? The relationships between socio-economic status and proactive coping. *European Journal of Public Health*, 1-6. doi: 10.1093/eurpub/ckp047.

Pearlin, L.I., Menaghan, E.G., Lieberman, M.A., & Mullan, J.T. (1981). The stress process. *Journal of Health and Social Behavior, 22*, 337-357.

Scheier, M. F., Carver, C. S., & Bridges, M. W. (1994). Distinguishing optimism from neuroticism (and trait anxiety, self-mastery, and self-esteem): A re-evaluation of the Life Orientation Test. *Journal of Personality and Social Psychology*, 67, 1063-1078.

Schwarzer, R. (1993). *Stress, Anxiety and Action Regulation* (3rd Edition). Stuttgart, Germany: Kohlhammer.

Schwarzer, R., & Knoll, N. (2003). Positive coping: Mastering demands and searching for meaning (Chapter. 25). In S. J. Lopez & C. R. Snyder, *Positive psychological assessment: A handbook of models and measures* (pp. 393-409). Washington, DC: American Psychological Association.

Schwarzer, R., & Taubert, S. (2002). Coping with stress. In E. Frydenberg (Ed.), *Beyond coping: meeting goals, visions and challenges*. Oxford, UK: Oxford University Press.

Sohl, S.J. and Moyer, A. (2009). Refining the conceptualization of a future-oriented self-regulatory behavior: Proactive coping. *Personality and Individual Differences*, 47, 139-144. doi: http://dx.doi.org/10.1016/ j.paid.2009.02.013

Treynor, W., Gonzalez, R., & Nolen-Hoeksema, S. (2003). Rumination reconsidered: a psychometric analysis. *Cognitive Therapy and Research, 27*, 247–259. doi: 10.1023/A:1023910315561

Vanzetti, N., & Duck, S. (1996). *A Lifetime of Relationships.* Detroit: Brook/Cole.

In: Parenting
Editors: Peter Barberis and Stelios Petrakis

ISBN: 978-1-62257-881-8
© 2013 Nova Science Publishers, Inc.

Chapter 14

Parenting: Challenges, Practices and Cultural Influences from Japanese Cohort Study

Tokie Anme
University of Tsukuba, Japan

Abstract

As economic development has swept across the globe, cultural values and the role of the parenting in various societies have become casualties of the drive towards social change and progress. As many industrialized nations face the economic strains of changing dependency ratios, societies will have to create social programs to meet the needs of their new demographic and child rearing environment. The long-discussed notion of empowerment is a useful concept or goal in this new world, but one which requires a concrete framework for implementation – a framework which can cross national and cultural boundaries to be utilized in many different situations. This chapter examines Japanese experiences as one of the model for future.

1. Introduction

Investigating the culture influences in parenting challenges and practice is indispensable to understand human development as clearly as we can in all its complexity so that we can improve the real lives of our children. Longitudinal research studies are essential methods to identify the dynamic interaction between "Parenting" and "Culture" over time.

Many longitudinal research studies have been conducted all over the world, and have been producing important results that have shown the inextricable relationship between the child care environment and child development. Discussions about the implications of parenting, its quality and its quantity, on children in middle childhood and adolescence abound, and in recent years several have explored the implications with mixed findings (Jaffee, Hulle & Rogers, 2011, Vandel, 2010).

Japanese parenting are shifting according to social change, such as decline fertility and increase child abuse. Three bills formulated in response to declining fertility have passed in 2003, which are (1) the Law for Measures to Support the Development of the Next-Generation, (2) Amendments to the Child Welfare Law, and (3) The Law for Basic Measures to Cope with Declining Fertility Society. The Law for Measures to Support the Development of the Next-Generation states that the government formulates a basic direction for local governments, firms and public organizations to map out a concrete plan to reconcile work and childcare. Following the basic direction, local governments, firms and public organizations are to make a plan that includes objectives, and specific action plans to attain the stated objectives. The Law also stipulates that business federations to assume a role of the Center for Promoting Measures to Support the Development of the Next-Generation to help firms to formulate action plans. Local governments, firms and public organizations that are working to promote Measures to Support the Development of the Next-Generation are also allowed to organize Local Commission for Measures to Support the Development of the Next-Generation.

Ahead of above Laws, the Child Abuse Prevention Law was enforced in 2000. Child abuse is defined as physical, sexual and mental harm inflicted upon children as well as parental neglect to take care of children. The number of cases brought to child guidance centers for consultation has dramatically increased since 1990, and currently reaching over 55,000 cases in 2010. Other than caregiver's mental pathology and worsening household financial situation, it is argued that overburden of mothers who are taking care of children without any help from family members or neighbors lie behind the recent rise in the number of cases. The recent survey conducted by child abuse prevention centers indicates that the share of abusive caregivers is higher for those without any help for childcare than caregivers who are able to get some kind of help. The Child Abuse Prevention Law also stipulates the government to establish comprehensive measures to detect abused children at the earliest stage as possible as well as to provide appropriate care for these children.

On the other hand, early socialization in Japan has received much attention from cross-cultural researchers. Japan is attractive to researchers because it is comparable to Western countries in the level of industrialization, education, employment, and per capita income, but it appears to have some traditional childrearing values distinct from those of Western cultures (Azuma, 1986). Researchers also contend that early childhood is a crucial period for later educational success, during this period, children are exposed to fundamental aspects of society and learn social and intellectual skills needed to become successful members of each society. Japanese culture and parental beliefs and actions have often been characterized by global cultural orientations such as collectivism and interdependence as opposed to individualism and independence (Oyserman, Coon, & Kemmelmeier, 2002).

2. PARENTING CHALLENGES AND PRACTICE

Our research team is conducting three longitudinal investigations:

1) The "Japan Children's Study (JCS)" has been conducted for five years to develop valid measures of child development and environmental factors, as well as elaborate

planning for future a larger-scale cohort study. Four hundred children in a birth cohort and one hundred five-year-olds in a cohort have participated in this study, sponsored by Research Institute of Science and Technology for Society, Japan Science and Technology Agency (RISTEX-JST) (2010ab).

2) The "Japan Child Care Cohort Study (JCCCS)" have been conducted for twelve years with thirty thousand children in child care (2012, 2010cd).

3) The "Tobishima Cohort Study (TCS)" has followed five thousand community-dwelling residents for twenty years (Anme & McCall, 2008).

These kinds of field studies which include children, caregivers, and communities are imperative to secure valid outcomes in understanding the parenting with culture influences.

In these studies, we developed questionnaire measures for rating the home environment (Index of Child Care Environment, ICCE) by conducting hundreds of home visits initially utilizing the Home Observation for Measurement of Environment (HOME), which is used in more than 100 countries now.

Also a measure for social competency and interaction feature of children (Interaction Rating Scale, IRS) was developed with internationally comparative frameworks so it is easy-to-use in practice. So both of these measures are now considered culturally valid.

The IRS consists of 10 subscales that fall into two categories: child-related items and caregiver items. The former assesses child 1) Autonomy, 2) Responsiveness to caregiver, 3) Empathy, 4) Motor self-regulation, and 5) Emotional self-regulation. The latter assesses caregiver, 6) Sensitivity to child, 7) Responsiveness to child, 8) Respect for child's autonomy, 9) Social-emotional growth fostering, and 10) Cognitive growth fostering.

Each child-related subscale includes five items. These items are rated in two different ways. First the item is identified as having occurred or not (coded as a "yes" or "no"). Following this, it is also coded for level of occurrence on a five-point scale (1=frequently evident, 2=evident, 3=sometimes evident, 4=rarely evident, 5=never evident).

The child-related 25-item survey specifies behaviors that children typically emit as they interact with their caregivers (e.g., Child looks at caregiver's face for social referencing). Each of the five subscales is identified with a general observation (i.e. Autonomy: Child initiates interaction with caregiver) and this is scored as having occurred or not as well as for level of occurrence. In addition, particular behaviors associated with this subscale are also scored in a similar manner. Thus, within the scale of Autonomy, one of the five behaviors specified is "Child vocalizes while looking at the task materials." In this manner, observations yield five sub-scores for the five items in each subscale as well as a total score for that subscale. The IRS has been shown to have good reliability and construct validity (Anme, 2007).

Using these scales in cohort studies, several useful evidences came out for practice.

Figure 1 shows the relation between parenting and child social competence development by longitudinal study. High social competence child get more high quality parenting during their toddler age.

Table 1 reports the results of the Chi-square test between factors at the toddler age and the child's health at school age. The delay of fine motor at the toddler age was significantly related to anxiety at school age. Interestingly, being the only child was related being easily fatigued at school age. It also presents the relationship between the care-giver's factors expressed when the child was a toddler and the child's health at school age. Not singing songs together in the early years was significantly related to poor physical strength at school age. Not going to the park with parents was related to headaches at school age.

Utilize ICCE and IRS, we found positive effects of parent's attitudes of "Praise" at both children's 4 and 9 months of age, on the level of children's social competence at 18 months, after controlling for the genetic and environmental factors (Shinohara, 2010).

These findings indicate that individualistic and collectivistic values coexist in the context of socialization. Although considerable permissiveness characterizes early childrearing in Japan, caregivers carefully train their children in proper expressions, bodily movements, and acceptable behavior (Lanham & Garrick, 1996). Caregivers also recognize the importance of the child's being able to distinguish self from others and to know the limits of self-interest that are imposed by others' needs, and they believe that the child's awareness and knowledge of self are essential for understanding others and achieving cooperation (Hendry, 1986). This coexistence indicates that the dichotomy between two global cultural orientations does not sufficiently capture within-culture diversity (Gjerde & Onishi, 2000a, 2000b).

The compensatory-process, and lost-resource perspectives (Vandell et al, 2010) suggest that the effects of parental characteristics, including poor mental health and lower socioeconomic status, may be compensated for by quality nonmaternal care. Thus, if the home environment is lacking, high quality professional child care can help mitigate difficulties in the former.

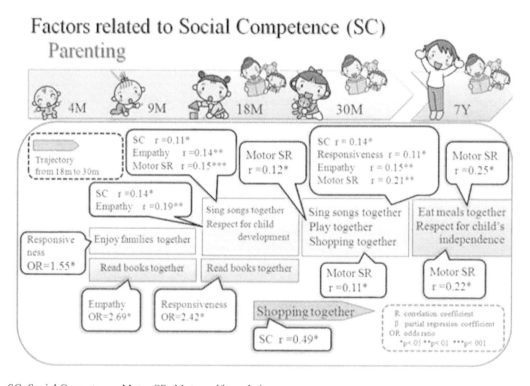

SC: Social Competence, Motor SR: Motor self-regulation.

Figure 1. Parenting and Social Competence Development.

Table 1. Parenting at toddler age and the health at school age

	Category	Anxious	Easy to fatigue	Poor physical strength	Headaches
		%	%	%	%
Child factors at toddler age					
Fine motor	delayed	42.9*	0.0	14.3	14.3
	normal	10.6	17.4	13.6	10.6
Siblings	no	14.7	26.3**	14.7	13.7
	yes	9.7	11.9	13.1	9.1
Caregiver factors when child was at the toddler age					
Singing songs together	no	16.7	16.7	33.3*	16.7
	yes	11.1	17.0	12.3	10.3
Going to park with parents	no	9.5	15.9	15.9	17.5*
	yes	12.0	17.3	13.0	8.7

** p<0.01; * p<0.05.

3. PARENTING AND CULTURE INFLUENCES

Research on early socialization has demonstrated that Japanese caregivers emphasize the maintenance of social harmony and encourage young children to be empathetic to and to avoid bothering others (Rothbaum, Pott, Azuma, Miyake, & Weisz, 2000). Harmonious relationships have been valued since the middle of the 17th century (Kojima, 1996).

The concept of amae, the dependence on another's benevolence or indulgence, characterizes harmonious interpersonal relationships, and sound amae relationships are said to build on mutual trust between two individuals (Doi, 2001), which may makes heterogeneity in the social orientations of individuals within cultures.

In light of previous findings (Ujiie, 1997), Japanese parents expect children to conform to parental directives in a cooperative manner. Also, it is conceivable that Japanese caregivers would consider their child's resistance and assertions in conflict situations not merely as selfish but also as the child's attempt to establish personal boundaries. As a disciplinary strategy, Japanese mothers prefer to use explanation and reasoning to persuade young children to change their behavior rather than simply to accept their behavior or to use power-assertive methods such as commands and coercion.

Also, it has been found that Japanese childrearing involves individualistic values such as respect for autonomy, competence, and self-development of young children. Empirical studies on maternal expectations concerning child development showed that Japanese caregivers expected preschool-aged children to be instrumentally independent at an earlier age than English mothers (Joshi & MacLean, 1997). Along with instrumental independence, mothers encouraged young children to formulate and express opinions and to develop autonomy and self-reliance, and they believed that these actions helped them to develop a sense of identity (Hendry, 1986). In addition that, Japanese caregivers showed preferences for young children's autonomous resolution of interpersonal conflicts in preschool settings (Killen & Sueyoshi, 1995) and perceived establishing friendships with other children as forms of desirable independence (Osterweil & Nagano, 1991). Doi (2001) demonstrated that by having opportunities to exhibit amae behavior and to receive indulgence from caregivers in early childhood, children will learn to exert their independence.

CONCLUSION

The principal conclusion of these multisite research projects is that child rearing behaviors by the caregiver may be important in explaining children's future social, vocational, motor and intelligence development, adaptation and health. Items strongly related to child development, such as "going to the park together with child," may serve as a proxy items for a number of factors at home, because they indicate the opportunity to engage in activities outside the home, with other children, and in proximity of their caregivers.

Literature does suggest that center-based care exerts some influence upon children. Studies report that the quality of care is the most consistent child-care predictor, with higher quality of care relating to greater social competence and cooperation and less problem behavior at both two and three years of age (NICHD, 1998). These kinds of current studies have shown us the types of measures and strategies that we can effectively use to achieve truly understanding human development.

Further research to bridge between parenting and culture over longer periods of time will enhance our knowledge and skills to realize better understanding and education for children.

REFERENCES

Anme T. et al. (2012) Health of school-aged children in 11+ hours of center-based care, *Creative Education*, 3(2).

Anme T. et al. (2010a) Gender differences of children's social skills and parenting using Interaction Rating Scale (IRS), *Procedia Social and Behavioural Sciences*, 2, 260-268.

Anme T. et al. (2010b) Trajectories of social competence by using Interaction Rating Scale (IRS) as an evidence-based practical index of children's social skills and parenting, *Journal of Epidemiology*, 20, 419-426.

Anme T. et al. (2010c) Child development and childcare in Japan, *Journal of Early Childhood Research*, 8(2), 193-210.

Anme T. et al. (2010d) Effectiveness of Japan's extended/night child care: A five-year follow up, *Procedia Social and Behavioural Sciences*, 2, 5573-5580.

Anme T, McCall M. (2008) Care, *Culture and Community Empowerment: Theories and Methods for an International Approach*, Kawashima Press. 1-124.

Anme T, Yato Y, Shinohara R & Sugisawa Y. (2007) "The reliability and validity of the assessment method for children's social competence: Parent-child Interaction Rating Scale". *Japanese Journal of Health Care and Welfare*, 14, 23-31.

Azuma, H. (1986). Why study child development in Japan? In H. Stevenson, H. Azuma, & K. Hakuta (Eds.), *Child development and education in Japan* (pp. 3 – 12). New York: Freeman.

Doi, T. (2001). *Zoku amae no kozo* ([The structure of amae Part II]. Tokyo: Kobundo.

Gjerde, P. F., & Onishi, M. (2000a). In search of theory: The study of "ethnic groups" in developmental psychology. *Journal of Research on Adolescence,* 10, 289 – 298.

Gjerde, P. F., & Onishi, M. (2000b). Selves, cultures, and nations: The psychological imagination of "the Japanese" in the era of globalization. *Human Development,* 43, 216-226.

Hendry, J. (1986). *Becoming Japanese: The world of the preschool child.* Manchester, England: Manchester University Press.

Jaffee, SR., Hulle, CV., Rodgers, JL.(2011). Effects of Nonmaternal Care in the First 3 Years on Children's Academic Skills and Behavioral Functioning in Childhood and Early Adolescence: A Sibling Comparison Study, *Child Development,* 82, 1076-1091.

Joshi, M. S., & MacLean, M. (1997). Maternal expectations of child development in India, Japan, and England. *Journal of Cross-Cultural Psychology,* 28, 219 – 234.

Killen, M., & Sueyoshi, L. (1995). Conflict resolution in Japanese social interactions. *Early Education and Development,* 6, 317 – 334.

Kojima, H. (1996). Japanese childrearing advice in its cultural, social, and economic contexts. *International Journal of Behavioral Development,* 19, 373 – 391.

Lanham, B. B., & Garrick, R. J. (1996). Adult to child in Japan: Interaction and relations. In D. W. Shwalb & B. J. Shwalb (Eds.), *Japanese childrearing: Two generations of scholarship* (pp. 97 – 124). New York: Guilford.

NICHD Early Child Care Research Network.(1998). "Early child care and self-control, Compliance and problem behavior at twenty-four and thirty-six months". *Child Development,* 69(3), 1145-1170.

Osterweil, Z., & Nagano, K. N. (1991). Maternal views on autonomy: Japan and Israel. *Journal of Cross-Cultural Psychology,* 22, 362 – 375.

Oyserman, D., Coon, H. M., & Kemmelmeier, M. (2002). Rethinking individualism and collectivism: Evaluation of theoretical assumptions and meta-analyses. *Psychological Bulletin,* 128, 3 – 72.

Rothbaum, F., Pott, M., Azuma, H., Miyake, K., & Weisz, J. (2000). The development of close relationships in Japan and the United States: Paths of symbiotic harmony and generative tension. *Child Development,* 71, 1121 – 1142.

Shinohara R, Anme T, et al. (2010) Trajectories of children's social competence and the caregiver's attitude of "praise": longitudinal perspective, *Journal of Epidemiology,* 20, 143-149.

Ujiie, T. (1997). How do Japanese mothers treat children's negativism? *Journal of Applied Developmental Psychology,* 18, 467 – 483.

Vandell, DL., Belsky, J., Burchinal, M., et.al.(2010). Do Effects of Early Child Care Extend to Age 15 Years? *Results From the NICHD Study of Early Child Care and Youth Development, Child Development,* 81, 737-756.

INDEX

T